THE EUROPEAN DREAM

CONTENTS

For Carol

*And for
the Erasmus generation
of college students in Europe*

ABOUT THE AUTHOR

JEREMY RIFKIN is an internationally renowned social critic and the best-selling author of *The End of Work*, *The Biotech Century*, *The Age of Access*, and *The Hydrogen Economy*, each of which has been translated into more than fifteen languages. He is president of the Foundation on Economic Trends in Washington, D.C. Since 1994, Mr. Rifkin has been a fellow at the Wharton School's Executive Education Program, where he lectures to CEOs and senior corporate management from around the world on new trends in science and technology and their impacts on the global economy, society, and the environment. He is also an adviser to heads of state and government officials in a number of countries. Rifkin currently serves as an adviser to Romano Prodi, president of the European Commission, the governing body of the European Union. His monthly column on global issues appears in many of Europe's leading newspapers and magazines. He lives with his wife, Carol Grunewald, in Washington, D.C.

ACKNOWLEDGMENTS

I WOULD LIKE to thank Sarah E. Mann for a masterful job in directing the research for the book. Coordinating the sheer volume of material that went into the preparation of the book was a daunting challenge. Nevertheless, under Sarah's stewardship, the process was always keenly focused and discerning. I have great admiration for Sarah's organizational skills and her ability, under fire, to keep the research mission in hand, on track, and up to date.

I would also like to thank the following people for their help at various stages of the project: Clara Mack, Alexia Robinson, Michelle Baker, Loring Katawala, Jennifer Brostek, Sima Habash, Peter Kossakowski, Ryan Levinson, Vanessa Mambrino, Alex Merati, Jay Parekh, Jiehae Park, Boris Schwartz, Alex Taylor, and Audren Zmirou.

I would also like to thank my father-in-law, Ted Grunewald, for valuable research-related contributions along the way. I'd also like to thank Ted and my mother-in-law, Dorothy Grunewald, for the many lively and provocative conversations that helped provide perspective for the book.

I'd also like to thank my longtime literary agent Jim Stein for his encouragement and support.

I'd like to thank the Tarcher group for ten years of collaboration on five different books. Special thanks to my old friend Jeremy Tarcher, for making a place for me in his publishing fold. I would also like to thank Joel Fotinos, my publisher, for his unwavering support over the years with regard to our various publishing ventures. My thanks also to Ken Siman, my publicist, for always going the extra mile, Lance Fitzgerald for his help in securing our foreign markets, and Mark Birkey for his excellent copyediting of the book.

I'd like to thank my editor Mitch Horowitz for the many long and fruitful discussions that helped shape so much of the thinking and direction of the book. Every author hopes to work with an editor who is collaborator and friend, prod and enthusiast. I consider myself fortunate to have such an editor.

Finally, I'd like to thank my wife, Carol Grunewald, for her inspiration. Doing this book was her idea. We have both spent a great deal of time shuttling back and forth to Europe over the years, meeting diverse people and experiencing the depth and richness of what Europe has to offer. In the process, we have come to know Europe together. Her insights are woven throughout the book.

PREFACE TO THE U.K. EDITION

THE U.K. HAS always been ambivalent about the European Union and its role in it. The English Channel, though it only separates the British Isles from the European continent by less then 150 miles at its widest point, has proved to be a significant force in the development of the U.K. sense of identity as well as its sense of destiny. The U.K.'s close transatlantic ties with America, dating back to its colonial occupation, has been the other external force that has figured so prominently in forging its consciousness.

Island nations play a unique role in history. Their mastery of the sea makes them the world's traders. They bring distant peoples into contact with one another. But island nations live a kind of schizophrenic existence. While they reach out to the world, they also tend to be fiercely independent and self-reliant.

It's, perhaps, understandable then, given their independent nature, that the English became the first to champion the rights of the individual, to establish a private property regime, to create a modern market economy and nation-state regime. Great Britain was also the wellspring of some of the great theological and ideological struggles of the early modern era. England was a refuge for Protestant reformers and it was English philosophers who were at the forefront of the European Enlightenment. The U.K.'s contribution to European and American history is, indeed, formidable.

But, if the British were the architects of so many of the conventions and institutions that constitute the modern age, they now find themselves betwixt and between a fading American Dream and a newly emerging European Dream in the coming global era, not sure where their own philosophical allegiances lie. The reason is that Britain is of two states of mind. Having contributed significantly to the social philosophies that underlie both dreams, they are torn between which course to take into the future.

The American Dream, with its emphasis on the work ethic and advancing individual material self-interest in the marketplace, has deep roots in British capitalist tradition. The European Dream, with its attention to sustainable development and promoting the social welfare of the larger community, also grows out of the U.K.'s long socialist and labor reform traditions.

The U.K., then, is uniquely positioned to play a bridge role between the older American Dream and the newly emerging European Dream. Were it to cast its fate with the European Union, while maintaining its special relationship with America, the U.K. could potentially help create an ideological synergy between the two great super powers of the 21st century. The U.K. could champion the risk-taking, entrepreneurial sensibilities and sense of individualism that is so characteristic of the American way of life, within the corridors of Europe. At the same time, the U.K. could help Americans better understand the need to expand their dream beyond individual self-interests to include the general welfare of the larger community and a global consciousness more befitting a globalizing world.

Of one thing we can be assured. In the 21st century, no country will be able to go-it-alone in an increasingly global economy. Either the U.K. becomes the 51st American state—de facto—or it takes its place at the European table. I say this because the U.K. will never fully enjoy the advantages that come with being part of a seamless market and shared political space if it continues to straddle the fence, being neither a true American state nor a full partner in the new Europe. How, for example, does the U.K. expect to maintain its own currency ten years from now when most of the rest of the world is doing business in Euros and dollars?

The U.K. needs to understand that the United States and the European Union are going to increasingly realize that their own prosperity and security depends on their cooperation with one another, if for no other reason than the fact that they each represent the two largest markets in the world. What does the U.K. have to offer to either of these mega-powers that they can't better secure by dealing directly with each other? In other words, I can see why the U.K. needs either the U.S. or Europe, but not why either of the other two ultimately need the U.K. So where does this leave the U.K.?

If Great Britain chooses to attach its destiny to that of America, it will ultimately have to accept an American agenda and an American frame of mind as its own. If, however, the U.K. chooses to become an integral part of continental Europe, it will have to accept the duties and obligations that go along with surrendering some measure of sovereignty to become part of a transnational political space. But, instead of seeing full membership in the European Union in purely negative terms, as something being forced on them by the flow of global events, the U.K. ought to consider Europeanization as a historic opportunity, with vast potential benefits for the British people. By being a critical part of a larger European agenda, the U.K. can play a leadership role in helping shape the European Dream and laying the groundwork for a truly global consciousness in the coming century.

Equally important, the U.K.'s ability to draw America and Europe closer together depends on it being squarely in the EU fold. Otherwise, what is the potential strategic value—either economic or political—it brings to the game? Britain's ultimate influence and power lies in helping to lead Europe, not trail behind it.

The human race is becoming connected. Nation-state boundaries, once a source of security in an unpredictable world, are increasingly seen as too restrictive to accommodate the many new identities, affiliations and loyalties that make up a network way of life. The question for the British people, and peoples everywhere, is whether to be constrained inside old political containers, or to reach out and establish new political arrangements more suitable to an era of ever greater interdependence.

The real lesson in a globally connected world is that no people can any longer exist as an island unto themselves. The U.K. too, will have to choose to be part of a larger political affiliation. The only question is whether it will make its home with America or Europe.

INTRODUCTION

I WAS A YOUNG ACTIVIST in the 1960s. Like many of my contemporaries, I found myself caught up in "The Great Social Upheaval." African Americans were demanding their right to sit at the front of the bus in Montgomery, Alabama, and marching on the streets of Chicago with raised clenched fists, chanting "Black Power." American boys were coming home from Vietnam in body bags, first in dribbles, then in waves. College students were demanding an end to an unjust American war in Southeast Asia and barricading themselves in university administration offices in protest against an undemocratic educational system that denied them a voice and vote in academic decisions that affected their lives.

Liberation was in the air. You could smell it. Tired of nuclear air-raid drills, cold wars, men in gray flannel suits, and the stultifying sameness of American suburban life, young people everywhere were in revolt. Free speech, open sex, rock and roll, drugs, and flower power made their way across the country and into every American town and city. The rebellion kept metamorphosing: at times, it was difficult staying abreast or even holding on. Class politics gave way to cultural politics, then sexual politics, and, finally, ecological politics. Che Guevara and Huey Newton posters were put up on walls and then taken down to make room for posters of the

Beatles and Rolling Stones, and then they, in turn, were taken down to make room for posters showing the Earth's photo taken from outer space.

The Old Left gave way to the New Left. Historical consciousness and abstract talk of dialectics, materialism, and imperialism began to lose resonance to therapeutic consciousness. Instead of quoting from Karl Marx's *Communist Manifesto* or Mao's *Little Red Book*, young people were more likely to share their own innermost feelings and talk about the dynamics of their interpersonal relationships as politics became group therapy. Talk of political revolution gave way to the quest for more personal spiritual transformation. By the early 1970s, process had all but trumped ideology. In the wings, however, were new movements ready to make their mark. The women's movement, the environmental movement, the human rights and animal rights movements, the gay movement, all broke through and began to command the public's attention.

Everyone, it seemed, was demanding the right to be recognized. People were coming out of closets, opening doors, beating down on fences and barricades, pushing before microphones and cameras, in a mass adrenaline rush whose only apparent purpose, at times, was to eliminate boundaries and borders of every conceivable kind. It was madness of a particular ilk. At the eye of the storm were two crosscutting currents: the first, a restless yearning for some kind of higher personal calling in what was perceived to be an increasingly materialistically oriented world; the second, the need to find some sense of shared community in a society grown remote and uncaring. We all dreamed of a new age where each person's rights were respected, no one was left behind, cultural differences were welcomed, everyone could enjoy a good quality of life and still live sustainably with the Earth, and people could live together in peace and harmony.

Most of us railed against the American empire, which was blamed for just about every ill besetting society. Some even reverted to terrorist activity in the vain hope of bringing the system down. A similar social upheaval was taking place at the same time in Europe and elsewhere around the world.

But through it all, virtually every young American activist I knew believed, deep down, that if fundamental changes were to occur, they would start here in America and spread to the rest of the world. That's because even in the darkest days of our disbelief, we kept the belief in the American Spirit—that unflagging conviction that America is a special place with a special calling. Although not one of my friends in the "movement" would dare admit it, we all retained the unique American sense that here in this country anything and everything is possible to achieve if only we feel strongly enough and are determined enough to make a difference. European youth were far less convinced that anything they did would really ever make a difference. Their politics were motivated more by defiance than by reform.

Now, more than thirty years later, the tables have turned. Much of the feelings we once had about what's wrong with the world and what needs to be done to remedy it failed to take root and mature here in America. Yes, we have our fair share of public interest groups advancing any one of a number of ideas and causes whose lineage can be traced back to the restless yearnings bubbling up from the ghetto streets and college campuses more than a generation ago. But, curiously, it is in Europe where the feelings of the sixties generation has given rise to a bold new experiment in living—one whose shadowy outline was just barely perceptible to us back then in the days of our youth.

One could point to many reasons why Europeans seem to be leading the way into the new era. But among all the possible explanations, one stands out. It is the cherished American Dream itself, once the ideal and envy of the world, that has led America to its current impasse. That dream emphasizes the unbridled opportunity of each individual to pursue success, which, in the American vernacular, has generally meant financial success. The American Dream is far too centered on personal material advancement and too little concerned with the broader human welfare to be relevant in a world of increasing risk, diversity, and interdependence. It is an old dream, immersed in a frontier mentality, that has long since become passé. While the American Spirit is tiring and languishing in the past, a new European Dream is being born. It is a dream far better suited to the next stage in the human journey—one that promises to bring humanity to a global consciousness befitting an increasingly interconnected and globalizing society.

The European Dream emphasizes community relationships over individual autonomy, cultural diversity over assimilation, quality of life over the accumulation of wealth, sustainable development over unlimited material growth, deep play over unrelenting toil, universal human rights and the rights of nature over property rights, and global cooperation over the unilateral exercise of power.

The European Dream exists at the crossroads between post-modernity and the emerging global age and provides the suspension to bridge the divide between the two eras. Post-modernity was never meant to be a new age but, rather, was more of a twilight period of modernity—a time to sit in judgment about the many shortfalls of the modern era. If the sixties generation of protests and experimentation was aimed at both knocking down old boundaries that constrained the human spirit and testing new realities, it came with an intellectual companion in the form of post-modern thought.

The post-modernists asked how the world came to be locked into a death chant. What were the reasons that led to the dropping of the atomic bombs over the Japanese cities of Nagasaki and Hiroshima, and the establishment of Nazi death camps in Europe, detention camps in the Gulag, and Maoist re-education camps in the Chinese countryside? How did we end up in a world more divided than ever between rich and poor? Why were women, people of color, and ethnic minorities around the world discriminated against or, worse yet, held in conditions of bondage? Why were we destroying the environment and poisoning our biosphere? Why were some nations continually bullying other nations and seeking hegemony through war, conquest, and subjugation? How did the human race come to lose its innate sense of deep play and become machinelike drones, even to the point of making ceaseless work the very definition of a person's existence? When and why did materialism become a substitute for idealism and consumption metamorphose from a negative to a positive term?

The post-modernists looked to modernity itself as the culprit. They placed the blame for much of the world's ills on what they regarded as the rigid assumptions underlying modern thought. The European Enlightenment, with its vision of unlimited material progress, came in for particular rebuke, as did market capitalism, state socialism, and nation-state ideology. Modernity, argued the post-modernist thinkers, was at its core deeply flawed. The very ideas of a knowable objective reality, irreversible linear progress, and human perfectibility were too rigidly conceived and historically biased, and failed to take into consideration other perspectives and points of view of the human condition and the ends of history.

The new generation of scholars was leery of overarching grand narratives and single-minded utopian visions that attempted to create a unified vision of human behavior. By locking humanity into the "one right way" of thinking about the world, post-modernists contend, modern thought became dismissive of any other points of view and ultimately intolerant of opposing ideas of any kind. Those in power—be they capitalists or socialists, conservatives or liberals—continue to use these meta-narratives to keep people contained and controlled, argue the post-modernists. Modern thought, according to the critics, has been used to justify colonial ventures around the world and keep people divided from one another and in conditions of subservience to the powers that be.

It was the stifling nature of these all-encompassing grand visions and single-minded utopian ideas about how people were expected to behave and act in the world that the sixties generation rebelled against. The post-modernists provided the rationalization for the revolt, arguing that there is no one single perspective but, rather, as many perspectives of the world as there are individual stories to tell. Post-modern sociology emphasizes pluralism and tolerance of the different points of view that make up the totality of the human experience. For the post-modernists, there is no one ideal regime to which to aspire but, rather, a potpourri of cultural experiments, each of value.

The post-modernists engaged in an all-out assault on the ideological foundations of modernity, even denying the idea of history as a redemptive saga. What we end up with at the end of the post-modern deconstruction process are modernity reduced to intellectual rubble and an anarchic world where everyone's story is equally compelling and valid and worthy of recognition.

If the post-modernists razed the ideological walls of modernity and freed the prisoners, they left them with no particular place to go. We became existential nomads, wandering through a boundaryless world full of inchoate longings in a desperate search for something to be attached to and believe in. While the human spirit was freed up from old categories of thought, we are each forced to find our own paths in a chaotic and fragmented world that is even more dangerous than the all-encompassing one we left behind.

Post-modern thought didn't make significant inroads into what we call middle America. It has always been more influential in Europe. Over half of all Americans are devoutly religious—more so than any other industrialized people—and they just don't buy the idea of a relativist world. Religious Americans still believe in a grand scheme of things and live their beliefs intimately each day. More secular Americans, while not wedded to an overarching religious frame of reference, are generally committed to another all-encompassing social vision—the Enlightenment idea of history as the steady and irreversible advance of material progress. There is, however, a third, smaller grouping in America, which is made up largely of the activist and counterculture generation of the 1960s, and their now grown children, who are far more comfortable with post-modernity. They tend to view the world less in terms of absolute values and ironclad truths and more in terms of relative values and changing preferences and are generally more tolerant of other points of view and multicultural perspectives.

Political analysts divide America into two cultural camps, the reds and the blues, and argue that the former reflect America's strongly held conservative religious values while the latter are far more liberal and cosmopolitan in their orientation. The red population, according to pollsters, is geographically concentrated in the Southeast, Middle-west, prairie states, Rocky Mountain states, and the southwest region of the country. The blue part of the population is clustered more in the Northeast, upper Middle-west, and the West Coast.

Although a convenient shorthand for analyzing voting trends, what the pollsters miss is that a majority of Americans, red and blue, ascribe to an American way of life that is steeped in modernist ideology. Even the blues, with their greater tolerance for other perspectives and points of view, are inclined to believe that there is an overriding purpose to the human journey and a right way to live in the world.

Europeans, in comparison, have been much more eager to critique the basic assumptions of modernity and embrace a post-modern orientation. Their willingness has much to do with the devastation wrought by two world wars and the specter of a continent lying in near ruins in 1945 as a result of blind adherence to utopian visions and ideologies.

European intellectuals, understandably, led the charge against the modernity project. They were anxious to make sure that the old dogmas would never again take them down the road to destruction. Their across-the-bow attack on meta-narratives led them to champion multiculturalism and eventually universal human rights and the rights of nature. Multiculturalism was viewed by the post-modernists as an antidote, of sorts, to modern thought, a way of countering a doctrinaire single frame of reference with multiple perspectives. The rights agenda broadened the assault on a single perspective even more. Universal human rights and the rights of nature were a way of recognizing that every person's story is of equal worth and that the Earth itself matters. But here is where the logic of post-modernity began to run up against its own internal contradiction. The very recognition of universal human rights and the rights of nature suggests a meta-narrative. "Universal" means something everyone recognizes and accepts as fundamental and indivisible. Rather unintentionally, post-modernists dug their own grave by acknowledging that there exists at least one universal idea to which everyone can potentially agree—that is, that every human life has equal value and that nature is worthy of respect and consideration.

The European Dream takes over where post-modernity trails off. Stripped to its bare essentials, the European Dream is an effort at creating a new historical frame that can both free the individual from the old yoke of Western ideology and, at the same time, connect the human race to a new shared story, clothed in the garb of universal human rights and the intrinsic rights of nature—what we call a global consciousness. It is a dream that takes us beyond modernity and post-modernity and into a global age. The European Dream, in short, creates a new history.

It has been fashionable of late, within American conservative intellectual circles, to discuss the question of the end of history. Some, like Francis Fukuyama, argue that with the fall of Soviet Communism, liberal market-oriented democracies have triumphed and will likely not be replaced by any alternative models in the future. Although somewhat sophomoric, the debate over the end of history illustrates the bias of many contemporary historians, who assume that history is no more than the unfolding struggle between competing economic and political ideologies over how resources are to be expropriated and made productive, how capital and property are to be controlled and distributed, and how people are to be governed. For some, the American Dream, with its emphasis on unfettered individual accumulation of wealth in a democratically governed society, represents the ultimate expression of the end of history.

The new European Dream is powerful because it dares to suggest a new history, with an attention to quality of life, sustainability, and peace and harmony. In a sustainable civilization, based on quality of life rather than unlimited individual accumulation of wealth, the very material basis of modern progress would be a thing of the past. A steady-state global economy is a radical proposition, not only because it challenges the conventional way we have come to use nature's resources but also because it does away with the very idea of history as an ever-rising curve of material advances. The objective of a sustainable global economy is to continually reproduce a high-quality present state by aligning human production and consumption with nature's ability to recycle waste and replenish resources. A sustainable, steady-state economy is truly the end of history defined by unlimited material progress.

If the European Dream represents the end of one history, it also suggests the beginning of another. What becomes important in the new European vision of the future is personal transformation rather than individual material accumulation. The new dream is focused not on amassing wealth but, rather, on elevating the human spirit. The European Dream seeks to expand human empathy, not territory. It takes humanity out of the materialist prison in which it has been bound since the early days of the eighteenth-century Enlightenment and into the light of a new future motivated by idealism.

This book is about the older American Dream and the newly emerging European Dream. In a sense, it represents a first rough cut, with all the shortcomings that accompany an effort of this kind.

While I remain viscerally attached to the American Dream, especially to its unswerving belief in the pre-eminence of the individual and personal responsibility and accountability, my hope for the future pulls me to the European Dream, with its emphasis on collective responsibility and global consciousness. I have attempted, in the pages that follow, to find some synergism between both visions, with the hope of reaching a synthesis that combines the best of each dream.

Of this much I'm relatively sure. The fledgling European Dream represents humanity's best aspirations for a better tomorrow. A new generation of Europeans carries the world's hopes with it. This places a very special responsibility on the European people, the kind our own founding fathers and mothers must have felt more than two hundred years ago, when the rest of the world looked to America as a beacon of hope. I hope our trust is not trifled away.

New Lessons

from the

Old World

1

The Slow Death of the American Dream

M Y FATHER, Milton, was born in Denver, Colorado, in 1908. My mother, Vivette, was born three years later in El Paso, Texas, just this side of the Mexican border. They were among the last generation to grow up during a time when cowboys still roamed the range, although in greatly diminished numbers, and the frontier was still fresh in people's minds. My parents were Westerners. They were weaned on that very special catechism that we have come to know as the American Spirit. My parents' worldview was uncomplicated and very much the product of the frontier mentality. My mother would tuck me in at night, and instead of reading me childhood stories about goblins and fairies, she would recount the day's activities, of what had been accomplished and what was left to be done, always leaving me with a sense of anticipation of what exciting things lay ahead the next day. I could hardly wait. My mother believed that each person had a destiny. We are each chosen to make something out of ourselves, to contribute something to the world. But for her, destiny was not fate, but rather opportunity waiting to be seized and acted upon. Whether one lived out one's destiny depended on how strongly one believed in his or her ability to affect the world.

My mother used every situation as a pretext to push home the principle that guided her life and the lives of so many Americans of her era. She would say to me, "Jeremy, in America, you can do anything you choose to do and be anyone you choose to be, if you want to do it or be it badly enough." Personal willpower, for my mom, was the force that opened up the door to all the possibilities of the future. "Believe in yourself," she would say, "and you will be able to move mountains." Of course, for my mom's generation, still close to America's frontier past, all of this just seemed to make common sense. A half century later, when such exhortations began to fade from the collective memory, educators, psychiatrists, and parents began to re-introduce them in a more structured if not artificial way, in the form of "self-esteem" seminars and instruction. But, in the new contrived context, the exercise seems a bit too desperate, perhaps because it lacks any kind of historical context or mission. Self-esteem has come to mean "feeling good about oneself," often without any specific end in mind.

While my mom provided the inspiration to allow my imagination to take flight, it was my dad who provided the measure of American realism and practicality to make my dreams come true. He would say, "Son, a lot of people dream of doing great things, but what separates the dreamers from the doers is discipline and hard work." Then he would invariably attach his own sense of statistical probability to the chances of success. "My boy, always remember that success in life is the result of ninety-nine percent hard work and one percent talent . . . and don't ever forget, no one is ever going to hand you success in life or give you something for nothing. You are on your own."

A Nation of Dreamers

There you have it. The American Credo. These are the aphorisms that most little boys—fewer girls—grew up on, at least until very recently. I have asked many of my European friends if their parents passed on similar teachings, only to be greeted with puzzled expressions. So, I suspect that this particular legacy is uniquely American.

It's interesting to note that although people have been living the American Dream for two centuries, the term didn't become part of the popular lexicon until 1931. Historian James Truslow Adams published a book entitled *The Epic of America*, in which the term "American Dream" was used for the very first time.[1] Adams originally wanted to use the term in the title of the book, but his editor, Ellery Sedgwick, refused, saying that "no red-blooded American would pay $3.50 for a dream."[2] Adams's retort at the time was that "red-blooded Americans have always been willing to gamble their last peso on a dream."[3] In hindsight, Adams's intuition about the American psyche proved far closer to the mark. Today, around the world, people know about the American Dream and can articulate its meaning. The term has become so well known that in most languages, people simply refer to it in the English vernacular.

For an American, it's peculiar to think that people of other cultures and lands have no counterpart to the American Dream. When I ask people from around the world what their dream is, they are taken aback. How strange it must be for them to know so much about our American Dream without having one of their own. That's beginning to change. My sense is that a European Dream is now beginning to take shape and form. It's still in its birthing stage, but its contours are already becoming clear. In many respects, the European Dream is the mirror opposite of the American Dream, making it easier to understand by holding it up to the American image and noting the many dissimilarities.

The American and European dreams are, at their core, about two diametrically opposed ideas of freedom and security. Americans hold a negative definition of what it means to be free and, thus, secure. For us, freedom has long been associated with autonomy. If one is autonomous, he or she is not dependent on others or vulnerable to circumstances outside of his or her control. To be autonomous, one needs to be propertied. The more wealth one amasses, the more independent one is in the world. One is free by becoming self-reliant and an island unto oneself. With wealth comes exclusivity, and with exclusivity comes security.

The new European Dream, however, is based on a different set of assumptions about what constitutes freedom and security. For Europeans, freedom is not found in autonomy but in embeddedness. To be free is to have access to a myriad of interdependent relationships with others. The more communities one has access to, the more options and choices one has for living a full and meaningful life. With relationships comes inclusivity, and with inclusivity comes security.

The American Dream puts an emphasis on economic growth, personal wealth, and independence. The new European Dream focuses more on sustainable development, quality of life, and interdependence. The American Dream pays homage to the work ethic. The European Dream is more attuned to leisure and deep play. The American Dream is insepara-ble from the country's religious heritage and deep spiritual faith. The European Dream is secular to the core. The American Dream is assimila-tionist. We associate success with shedding our former cultural ties and becoming free agents in the great American melting pot. The European Dream, by contrast, is based on preserving one's cultural identity and liv-ing in a multicultural world. The American Dream is wedded to love of country and patriotism. The European Dream is more cosmopolitan and less territorial. Americans are more willing to employ military force in the world, if necessary, to protect what we perceive to be our vital self-interests. Europeans are more reluctant to use military force and, instead, favor diplomacy, economic assistance, and aid to avert conflict and prefer peace-keeping operations to maintain order. Americans tend to think locally, while European's loyalties are more divided and stretch from the local to the global. The American Dream is deeply personal and little concerned with the rest of humanity. The European Dream is more expansive and systemic in nature and, therefore, more bound to the welfare of the planet.

That isn't to say that Europe has suddenly become Shangri-la. For all of its talk about inclusivity, diversity, and preserving cultural identity, Eu-ropeans have become increasingly hostile toward newly arrived immi-grants and asylum seekers. Ethnic strife and religious intolerance continue to flare up in various pockets across Europe. Anti-Semitism is on the rise again, as is discrimination against Muslims and other religious minorities. While European nations and the European public berate American mili-tary hegemony and what they regard as a trigger-happy foreign policy, they are more than willing, on occasion, to let the U.S. armed forces safe-guard European security interests.

Meanwhile, the Brussels' governing machinery, say European Union (EU) supporters and critics alike, is a labyrinthine maze of bureaucratic red tape that frustrates even the most optimistic Europhiles. EU govern-ment officials are often accused of being aloof and unresponsive to the needs of the European citizens they are supposed to serve. European Union staff have been caught up in financial scandal. Special interests—and especially the farm lobby—are accused of exerting undue influence over the allocation of EU funds. The small member states accuse Ger-many and France of bullying and bulldozing through protocols and

treaties favorable to their interests and, worse yet, of not obeying the existing EU directives when inconvenient, and thus creating a double standard within the Union. Most recently, both countries announced they
would refuse to adhere to the EU requirement that their budget deficit be
restricted to 3 percent of their Gross Domestic Product (GDP). (The
GDP is a measure of the value of total output of goods and services produced each year.) Germany and France accuse the smaller and poorer
states of not being grateful for all the economic assistance they have extended to them over the years. Everyone accuses the United Kingdom of
periodically sabotaging efforts to create a stronger union of European
peoples. For their part, the Brits waffle back and forth, not sure whether
their own best long-term interests rest with being part of a greater Europe
or going it alone. On top of all this, economic reforms inside the Union
have slowed of late, raising serious doubts about Europe's hope of becoming the world's most competitive economy by the end of the decade. The
list of grievances, frustrations, slights, and mishaps is tediously long but
probably no more so than one might expect of charges aimed at other
government entities in the world today.

The point, however, is not whether the Europeans are living up to the
dream they have for themselves. We Americans have never fully lived up
to our own dream. Rather, what's important is that Europe has articulated
a new vision for the future that's different in many of its most fundamental aspects from America's. It is this basic difference in how Europeans and
Americans envision their future that is so important to understanding the
dynamic that is unfolding between these two great superpowers of the
twenty-first century.

But I'm getting slightly ahead of the story. We will delve into these
two very different dreams throughout the remainder of the book, with an
idea to understanding why the European Dream might be better positioned to accommodate the many forces that are leading us to a more connected and interdependent globalized society.

To appreciate the new European Dream, however, we need to better
understand what made the American Dream so compelling for so many
people, both here and around the world, for more than two centuries.
That dream, so powerful and seductive that it captured the imagination
and heart of much of humanity, is now losing its luster—aging if you
will—as new global realities force a rethinking of the human vision in the
coming era. What were once considered the prime virtues of the Ameri-

can Dream are increasingly viewed as drawbacks and even impediments to the fulfillment of human aspirations, a reality few would have imagined just a short while ago. The fall of the American Dream is, in many ways, inseparably linked to the rise of the new European Dream. That is because it is the very shortcomings of the older vision that are making the new vision appear so attractive.

Before we begin this exploration of changing dreams, a confession is in order. I have a deep attachment to the American Dream. It has been my spiritual and philosophical guide for all of my life. Whatever I have done with my life, I owe much of it to following the American Dream that my parents passed down to me when I was a child. But, I also have to admit that the misgivings I now have about how I've lived my own life are also deeply entwined with the myth of the American Dream, something that I hope will become more clear in the pages and passages that follow as we explore the end of one great human journey and the beginning of another.

If I were to be given the choice of living my life over, I would likely choose to be an American again. There is so much to admire about this country. Its beauty and its majesty are what come to the minds of newcomers when they first visit our shores. It has long been a beacon in a troubled world; a place where a human being could become what he or she chose to be.

What really separates America from all of the political experiments that preceded it is the unbounded hope and enthusiasm, the optimism that is so thick at times that it can bowl you over. This is a land dedicated to possibilities, a place where constant improvement is the only meaningful compass and progress is regarded to be as certain as the rising sun. We are a people who threw off the yoke of tyranny and vowed never to be ruled by arbitrary elites of any kind. We eschew hereditary transmission and class distinctions, embrace the democratic spirit, and believe that everyone should be judged solely on his or her merits.

Americans have long been aware of our special circumstance. We think of America as a refuge for every human being who has ever dreamed of a better life and been willing to risk his or her own to come here and start over. Cynicism, skepticism, and pessimism are completely alien to the American way and find little support among the American people. ⌐ he same be said of Europe?

at's why it saddens me to say that America is no longer a great

Yes, it's still the most powerful economy in the world, with a military presence unmatched in all of history. But to be a great country, it is necessary to be a good country. It is true that people everywhere enjoy American cultural forms and consumer goods. Rap music, action movies, and other forms of entertainment, as well as our brand-name clothes, are eagerly snapped up around the world. America is even envied, but it is no longer admired as it once was. The American Dream, once so coveted, has increasingly become an object of derision. Our way of life no longer inspires but, rather, is looked on as outmoded and, worse yet, as something to fear, or abhor.

Even most Americans, if we took the time to really think about it, would have to say that we have somehow gotten off track, lost our way. We are not as sure about who we are and what we stand for, about what motivates and inspires us on both a personal and a collective basis. To some extent, it's the American Dream itself that has led us to our present sense of malaise. Its central tenets are less applicable in a globally connected world, something we will explore at great length throughout the book. Just as important is the fact that the American Dream has been truncated, with part of its essence being left by the wayside, leaving the core hollow. We'll come back to the second point shortly.

A Chosen People

The first thing to understand about the American Dream is that from the very beginning it was meant to be exclusive to America. It was never meant to be a dream shared with or exported to the rest of the world. Its power rested in its particularism, not in its universalism. One can only pursue the American Dream on American soil. The dream's uniqueness to the American context is what made it so attractive and America so successful. Its exclusivity is now what makes it increasingly suspect and inappropriate in a world that is beginning to forge a global consciousness.

When the Pilgrims landed at Plymouth Rock in 1620, they truly believed that they had been delivered by God from the yoke of their European oppressors. The last of the Protestant reformers, these refugees saw themselves as the new Israelites and likened their perilous journey to that of the Jews of old who fled their Egyptian taskmasters and, after having wandered aimlessly in the desert for forty years, were delivered by Yahweh to Canaan, the promised land. Their spiritual leader, John Winthrop, told his small flock just before disembarkation that they were "the chosen people," called upon by God, to be an example and light to the world. "For we must Consider that we shall be as a City upon a Hill, the eyes of all people are upon us . . ."[4] If we fail in our service to the Lord, Winthrop warned, "We shall shame the faces of many of God's worthy servants, and cause their prayers to be turned into curses upon us till we be consumed out of the good land whither we are agoing."[5] If, on the other hand, they served their Lord by improving their lot, God would look over them and reward them.

While schoolchildren today learn about the great daring and sacrifices of these brave and humble servants of the Lord, they were not always so well received by their own contemporaries. Some, like Archbishop Richard Hooker, saw in their "puritan" ways a certain holier-than-thou attitude that made them less fit to walk among common men and more disposed to live "in some wilderness by themselves."[6]

The Pilgrims, and other oppressed religious orders and sects that came after them, saw the great American wilderness as a fallen nature ready to be subdued and reclaimed for God's glory. They saw themselves, in turn, as God's emissaries, his stewards, who by dint of faith and perseverance would tame a wilderness and create a new Eden—a promised land that would flow with milk and honey.

The notion of a "chosen people" continued to resonate down through American history, becoming the leitmotif of the American Dream. Herman Melville's book *White-Jacket: or, the World in a Man-of-War* speaks to the exuberance and zeal Americans felt, being a chosen people, destined for greatness. He writes,

> We Americans are the peculiar, chosen people—the Israel of our time, we bear the ark of the Liberties of the world. Seventy years ago, we escaped from thrall, and besides our first birth-right— embracing one continent of Earth—God has given to us, for a future inheritance, the broad domains of the political pagans, that shall yet come and lie down under the shade of our ark, without bloody hands being lifted. God has predestinated, mankind expects, great things from our race; and great things we feel in our souls.[7]

Many Americans continue to see themselves as a chosen people and America as the promised land. They believe that America is destined for greatness and that the American way is God's way. Our very success seems proof positive that we were in fact chosen. God has indeed rewarded us for our faith and service with the most prosperous and powerful nation on Earth. Most Europeans find this aspect of the American Dream odd, even a little scary. The very notion that God has made of us a chosen people and our nation a promised land often elicits chuckles of disbelief, especially among a more secular European population who long ago left a personal God behind. But what our European friends seem to miss is that it is this very element of the American Dream that has been the driving engine behind the American sense of confidence—many Europeans might say arrogance—that each of us can "move mountains" as long as God is on our side.

Every school day, our children pledge their allegiance to "one nation under God." Our currency is inscribed with the motto "In God we trust." While we try to make sure to separate church and state, the private life of the vast majority of Americans is taken up with God. We are the most devoutly religious people of any advanced industrial nation in the world.

Americans' religious beliefs often spill over into the political arena. Nearly half of all Americans (48 percent), for example, believe that the United States has special protection from God.[8] Some prominent Evangelical Protestant leaders even suggested that the reason the World Trade Center towers and the Pentagon were attacked and nearly three thousand people sent to their deaths was because God was displeased with America's errant ways and no longer afforded special protection to his chosen people.

A strong majority (58 percent) of the American public say that the strength of American society is "predicated on the religious faith of its people."[9] Nearly half of the American people say that it is necessary to believe in God to have good values.[10] Six in ten Americans say that their faith is involved in every aspect of their lives,[11] and 40 percent say that they have had a profound religious experience that has changed the direction of their lives.[12]

Americans live their faith each day. Thirty-six percent of the public pray several times a day, while an additional 22 percent pray once a day, 16 percent pray several times a week, and 8 percent pray once a week.[13] Sixty-one percent attend religious services at least once or twice a month, while nearly half (45 percent) attend services at least once a week.[14] Given America's deep religiosity, it's understandable that 71 percent of the public favor starting each school day with a prayer.[15]

What's even more surprising to Europeans is how literal Americans view the scriptures. Sixty-eight percent of the public believe in the devil.[16] Even among college graduates and those with post-graduate degrees, 68 percent and 55 percent, respectively, believe in the devil.[17] More than one-third of all Americans are biblical literalists, who believe that every line of the Bible is the actual word of God and not simply inspired interpretation or made-up stories.[18] (By the way, 93 percent of Americans own a Bible.)[19]

America's deep religious convictions have butted up against American secular education almost from the very beginning of the public-school movement. Nowhere has the struggle between the two been more fiercely waged than over the question of whether to teach evolution or creationism in the nation's schools. Forty-five percent of Americans believe that "God created human beings pretty much in their present form at one time within the last 10,000 years or so."[20] It's no wonder that 25 percent of Americans believe that creationism should be required teaching in the public schools, while another 56 percent say creationism should at least be offered in the curriculum.[21]

Even more disturbing to many nonbelievers in the United States and Europe is the fact that 40 percent of the American people believe that the world will end with an Armageddon battle between Jesus and the Antichrist. Forty-seven percent of those who believe in Armageddon also believe that the Antichrist is on Earth now, and 45 percent believe that Jesus will return in their lifetime. The majority of those who believe that Armageddon is coming point to natural disasters and epidemics, like AIDS, as signs of disruption and chaos prophesied in the Bible.[22] If there is a silver lining to the Armageddon story, it is that 82 percent of Americans believe in Heaven, and 63 percent say they're likely to go there. Only 1 percent believe they're going to Hell.[23]

I've heard it said by more than a few commentators that while Americans and Europeans squabble over big and small matters, they are still far more alike than different in their basic attitudes and outlooks. The religious statistics suggest otherwise. While six out of ten Americans say their religion is "very" important in their lives,[24] in European countries religion is barely a factor in people's day-to-day lives. Even in Catholic Italy and Poland, only a third of the public say that religion is very important to them.[25] In Germany, only 21 percent say that religion is very important to them, while the percentage in Great Britain drops to 16 percent and in France to 14 percent, and in the Czech Republic, it's 11 percent.[26] In Sweden, the numbers are even lower, 10 percent, and in Denmark, 9 percent.[27] Nor is Europe alone. In Korea, only 25 percent of the population considers religion to be very important in their lives, and in Japan only 12 percent consider themselves very religious.[28] While half of all Americans attend church every week, by comparison, less then 10 percent of the population of the Netherlands, Great Britain, Germany, Sweden, and Denmark attend religious services even once a month.[29] Across Western Europe nearly half the population almost never goes to church, and in Eastern Europe the number is even lower.[30]

Many Europeans no longer believe in God. While 82 percent of Americans say that God is very important to them, approximately half of all Danes, Norwegians, and Swedes say that God does not matter to them.[31] When it comes to religious beliefs, American views are much closer to the views of people in developing countries and very much at odds with the rest of the industrialized world.

Does any of this really make much of a difference? Nothing is more fundamental to how people think and behave in the world than their personal values. In the case of the majority of Americans, religious values color how we act, not only at home but also abroad. For example, American attitudes on the nature of good and evil differ substantially from those of our European friends. The World Values Survey asked respondents in various countries to choose which of two different views of morality best reflected their own attitudes: "There are absolutely clear guidelines about what is good and evil. These apply to everyone, whatever the circumstances"; or, "There can never be absolutely clear guidelines about what is good and evil. What is good and evil depends entirely upon the circumstances of our time. . . ."[32] Most Europeans, and even Canadians and Japanese chose the second response, while Americans were more likely to favor the first response.[33]

Because of our deep religious conviction that there are absolute and knowable guidelines about what constitutes good and evil and these guidelines never waver, regardless of the circumstances, we tend to see the world itself as a battleground where good and evil forces are continually at play. For that reason, our foreign policy has always been conducted, at least in part, as an unfolding moral saga pitting the forces of good against the forces of evil. Other countries might see our military intervention in more material terms, believing that for Americans, like others, self-interests and utilitarian gain are the prime movers. That may be. But, at least as far as justifying war, it has always been sold to the American public as a struggle of good against evil. During the Cold War, our efforts to curtail Communist expansion were viewed as a moral crusade against "Godless Communism." In the waning years of the Cold War, President Reagan referred to the Soviet Union as the "evil empire." After the fall of Communism, we turned our moral compass on the threats posed by rogue regimes and terrorist groups. In the wake of the attacks of September 11, President George W. Bush rallied the American people by referring to our efforts to ferret out terrorists as a great crusade. Later, the president would refer to Iraq, Iran, and North Korea as the "axis of evil." Although Europeans cringe at America's use of religious language to define the global struggle, the White House rhetoric finds a willing audience in the American heartland.

The belief that we are a chosen people has made Americans the most patriotic people in the whole world. In a study conducted by the National Opinion Research Center, the U.S. ranked first of twenty-three countries in its citizens' sense of national pride.[34] Seventy-two percent of Americans say they are very proud of their country.[35] No other industrial country in the world boasts that kind of pride. Less than half of the people in the Western democracies—including Great Britain, France, Italy, the Netherlands, and Denmark—"felt 'very proud' of their nationalities."[36] It's not surprising, given America's patriotic ardor, that American men and women are far more willing to fight for their country than citizens of thirty other nations, according to a poll conducted by the Gallup Organization.[37]

Europeans view with alarm America's patriotic fervor and feeling of national pride, and especially America's sense of cultural superiority. Six out of ten Americans believe that "our people are not perfect, but our culture is superior to others."[38] By contrast, only 37 percent of the people in Great Britain and 40 percent of Germans feel that their culture is superior to others.[39] And here's the kicker: only one out of every three Frenchmen believe that their culture is superior to others.[40]

What most concerns many Europeans is America's belief that everyone else should conform to the American way of life. According to the Pew Global Attitudes Projects, 79 percent of Americans believe that "it's good that American ideas and customs are spreading around the world," while less than 40 percent of Europeans endorse the spread of American ideas and customs.[41]

What's particularly interesting in all of these surveys about patriotism, nationalism, and ideas about cultural superiority is that among Europeans and people of other regions around the world, national pride is declining with each successive generation. America is the exception. A whopping 98 percent of American youth report being proud of their nationality, compared with only 58 percent of British youth and 65 percent of German youth.[42] Most Americans see these numbers as a positive sign of the vitality of the republic. Many Europeans wonder if America is lost in the past. In a globalizing era where allegiance to country is becoming less important in defining individual and collective identity, the fact that Americans remain so passionately committed to the conventional nation-state political model puts us squarely on the side of traditional geopolitics, but hardly in the vanguard of a new global consciousness.

As long as the majority of Americans find their solace in religious faith and continue to believe that we are a chosen people, looked over and protected by God's grace, there is little likelihood that our sense of nationalism and patriotism will wane. I don't mean to suggest that a sense of nationalism has disappeared from the world stage. But, what is clear is that for virtually all of the industrialized nations, and for many developing countries, the nation-state is no longer the only platform for expressing one's beliefs and convictions and for fulfilling one's aspirations. The European Dream, as we will see later on in the book, is the first transnational dream to emerge in a global era. If national pride is shrinking in Europe, it's not for the reason that Europeans are less enamored of their countries but, rather, because their identities and loyalties now reach below and beyond nation-state borders to encompass a richer and more deeply layered sense of embeddedness in the world.

It's going to be very difficult for Americans to adjust to a borderless world of relationships and flows where everyone is increasingly connected in webs and networks, and dependent on one another for one's individual and collective well-being. What happens to the American sense of being special, of being a chosen people, in a world where exclusivity is steadily giving way to inclusivity? Does God really care less about the whole of his earthly creation than he does about the North American part? Europeans might find such a conjecture funny, but, believe me, many Americans remain wedded to the notion of our special status as God's chosen ones. If we were to give up that belief, or even entertain doubt about its veracity, our sense of confidence in ourselves and the American Dream might experience irreparable harm. Frequently, American athletes and celebrities, political leaders and businesspersons say, when interviewed on television, that whatever adversities they have overcome or accomplishments they've achieved or successes they've enjoyed they owe to their religious faith and God's grace. I have yet to hear a single European sports figure, celebrity, or political leader make a similar claim.

It should be pointed out that not every immigrant who came to America was inspired to do so because of religious convictions—most did not. While some found religion once they were here, many others never did but were still able to live out the American Dream. Even today, a very sizable minority of Americans are not very religious at all, but they still identify with the American Dream. That's because the notion of a chosen people has become so pervasive in American culture over the course of the past two centuries that it has shed some of its earlier religious roots and become ingrained in the American psyche.

Religious or not, most Americans believe that we enjoy a special status among nations and peoples. Why is this belief so important? Europeans don't feel they are a chosen people, and yet they seem able to make their way in the world. But here's the difference. Europeans often ask me how it is that Americans are always so upbeat about their future. In large part, it's the idea of being a chosen people that makes us Americans such eternal optimists. We have no doubt that we are destined for greatness, both individually and as a people. It makes us willing to take more risks than other people because we believe that we are being watched over and taken care of and fated to succeed.

The Withering of the American Work Ethic

Although the idea of being a chosen people has afforded Americans a sense of confidence in our ability to make something of our lives, there is another key element to the American Dream, without which it would never have become so powerful a vision. If John Winthrop represented the spiritual side of the American Dream, it was Benjamin Franklin who provided the practical guidance. Franklin's vision of America drew its inspiration from the European Enlightenment with its emphasis on materialism, utilitarianism, and individual self-interest in the marketplace. Franklin looked out over the pristine American wilderness and saw vast untapped resources that could be harnessed and made productive. He envisioned America as a kind of grand laboratory for the exploration of science and technology. His idea of the American Dream was a nation of inventive genius, continually engaged in creating wealth and expanding the reach of the marketplace. Franklin favored the utilitarian to the sacred and aspired to create a material cornucopia rather than be delivered up to eternal salvation. His America would be made up of an industrious people grounded in the practical arts.

If Winthrop offered salvation, Franklin offered self-improvement. For every act of revelation, the pioneers were administered a dose of utilitarian rationality, making Americans, at one and the same time, the most fervently religious and aggressively pragmatic of any people on Earth—a status we retain to this very day. Franklin took seriously Thomas Jefferson's radical claim in the American Declaration of Independence that every human being has an inalienable right not only to life and liberty but also to the pursuit of happiness. No government before that had ever suggested that people might have a right to pursue their own happiness. How does one strive to be happy? Franklin believed that happiness was obtained by ceaseless personal improvement—that is, making something out of oneself.

The American Dream, then, brought together two great European traditions into a sort of grand alliance that, while contradictory on the surface, ignited a vision of human agency more powerful than anything that had previously existed in the annals of human history. While part of the American Dream was to remain focused on Heaven and eternal redemption, the other part of the dream was to remain focused on the forces of nature and the pull of the marketplace. This unique melding of religious fervor and down-home utilitarianism proved a powerful force on the American frontier and later in the building of a highly advanced industrial, urban, and suburban society.

The reason the American Dream has remained so durable is that it speaks to the two most basic human desires—for happiness in this world and for salvation in the next world. The former required perseverance, self-improvement, and self-reliance, and the latter unswerving faith in God. No previous dream offered the prospect of the best of both worlds—the here and now, and the world to come.

While America's religious commitment remains strong, there is growing evidence that the second component of the American Dream is beginning to weaken. In recent years, a younger generation of Americans seems to have all but eliminated the part of the Declaration of Independence where Jefferson says that everyone has the right "to pursue" happiness, and has, instead, shortened the clause to read that everyone has the right to happiness. Franklin, recall, was forever admonishing the readers of his *Poor Richard's Almanack* to keep their noses to the grindstone. Franklin-esque aphorisms, all of which exhort the virtues of discipline and hard work, have all but been forgotten: "Idle hands are the Devil's workshop," "Never put off till tomorrow what can be done today," "A stitch in time saves nine." The American Dream was built on the idea that success comes from applying oneself, being resourceful, and becoming self-reliant. Franklin's proverbs were the last thin threads of what was once a single weave uniting a secular utilitarianism of the Enlightenment with the older Calvinist religious tradition, what Max Weber later referred to as "the Protestant work ethic." (We will discuss the Reformation theology in more detail in chapters 4 and 5.) Today, a growing number of younger Americans have broken with the work ethic. For them, the American Dream has less to do with faith and perseverance and more to do with luck and chutzpah.

One of the most intriguing public opinion polls I've come across, in all of the years of looking at such surveys, asked young people under the age of thirty whether they believe they will become rich. Fifty-five percent of all young people answered affirmatively, believing that they would become rich.[43] One might suspect that of young Americans. Don't forget, the Horatio Alger stories—that it's possible for every American to go from "rags to riches"—is what the American Dream is all about. But what was really fascinating about the survey was the follow-up question. When asked how they would acquire such riches, 71 percent of those who were employed believed that there was no chance that they would get rich by their current employment.[44] Well, what about future employment prospects? It turns out that an overwhelming 76 percent of young people between the ages of eighteen and twenty-nine believe that, regardless of the job one has, Americans are not "as willing to work hard at their jobs to get ahead as they were in the past."[45] I assume they are including themselves among the lot.

When *Newsweek* conducted this survey, it asked whether it was likely the respondents would become rich, if not by their work, then by investments, inheritance, or good luck. As to investments, the poll was done in 1999, when the bull market was supercharged and investors were recording record gains on their stocks. No longer. Inheritance is a possibility, but most of the baby-boom generation is awash in debt and not likely to be able to pass on a fortune—at least not enough to cover the 55 percent of young people who believe they are going to be rich.[46] That leaves us with luck. All of these categories—investment, inheritance, and luck—require little in the way of hard work and perseverance, the kind of qualities Franklin had in mind as the quintessential virtues for getting ahead in America. My own suspicion is that a lot of kids think they are just going to be lucky. It will somehow come to them without having to work hard for it.

I'm reminded of a book written by the late social critic Christopher Lasch—which he entitled *The Culture of Narcissism*. It was Lasch's contention that the consumer ethos had gained such a deep hold on the American psyche that most Americans, and especially the young, are drowning in momentary pleasures and trivial pursuits. He writes: "The pursuit of self-interest, formerly identified with the rational pursuit of gain and the accumulation of wealth, has become a search for pleasure and psychic survival. . . . To live for the moment is the prevailing passion—to live for yourself, not for your predecessor or posterity."[47]

Shortly after Lasch's analysis, the late New York University educator Neil Postman published his own account of America's wayward narcissism in a book entitled *Amusing Ourselves to Death*. Both of these keen observers of American culture worried that younger Americans were increasingly caught up in a media culture that sold the idea of instant gratification of one's desires. The result was that each successive generation of Americans was less willing or even less able to work hard and postpone gratification for future rewards. The narcissist's temporal frame is immediate and self-centered. Past commitments and future obligations are considered unnecessary restraints and impediments to instant gratification. In this new culture of narcissism, everyone feels entitled, and far less willing to put off happiness until tomorrow. America's $330 billion advertising industry is relentless in its pursuit of the idea that you and I can have everything that we desire now. Why wait? To ensure that end, America has sported a consumer credit-card culture that allows us to enjoy now and pay later. Many Americans are living well beyond their means and awash in consumer debt—all of which perpetuates the narcissistic behavior that Lasch and Postman noticed was sweeping fast into American life.

Has the American Dream descended from its once lofty peak where it combined Christian eschatology with Enlightenment utility and rational behavior, and just become a dream of having good luck? Apparently, for a growing number of Americans, the answer is yes.

Getting Something for Nothing

Americans have always been risk-takers. That's part of what the American Dream is all about. We used to associate American risk-taking with the willingness to start over in a new land, tame a wilderness, invest in an idea, or start a new business. Today, for a growing number of Americans, risk-taking has been reduced to little more than gambling.

In 2002, seven out of ten Americans engaged in some form of legal gambling. Fifty-seven percent of Americans purchased a lottery ticket in the past year, and 31 percent of Americans gambled in casinos.[48] The annual growth rate of American gambling has been a steamy 9 percent in the past decade, which means that gambling has been growing significantly faster than the U.S. economy as a whole.[49] Americans are now spending more money on gambling than on movies, videos, DVDs, music, and books combined.[50] In 2002, Americans spent $68 billion on legal gambling at racetracks, at casinos, and on lotteries, compared to $27 billion in 1991.[51] When I was a child, in the 1950s, only the state of Nevada allowed gambling. Today, forty-seven states have legalized gambling. The states raise more than $20 billion from lotteries and casinos, or more than 4 percent of their total revenue.[52]

Gambling has fast become the national pastime and, for many Americans, a near obsession. Powerball jackpots can exceed $300 million. It's not unusual for people to wait in lines that are sometimes five hundred people deep, spending most of their day queued up to purchase a single ticket.[53]

More than $400 million a year is given over to advertising state lottos and other games.[54] Much of the advertising is spent on exploiting the American Dream theme of rags to riches. The New York Lottery lures customers with the slogan "A Buck and a Dream." The Chicago Lottery exclaims, "This could be your ticket out."[55]

Gambling, like drugs, has become a dangerous addiction for millions of Americans. Both cater to the need for instant gratification—happiness now. The National Research Council (NRC) estimates that upwards of 3 million Americans are "lifetime" pathological gamblers, an additional

1.8 million Americans are "past year" pathological gamblers, 7.8 million people are "lifetime" problem gamblers, and 4 million are "past year" problem gamblers.[56] More troubling is the rising number of adolescent gamblers who fall in the "past year" pathological or problem category— approximately 20 percent of American youth.[57]

The desire for instant success has become pervasive across American culture. Legal gambling is only one of the many venues Americans increasingly pursue in hopes of realizing the American Dream. For a while, in the late 1990s, the stock market was all the rage. Millions of Americans gambled away their life savings in hopes of becoming instant millionaires. High-tech stocks became the new ticket to success. The smart investor became the new Horatio Alger protagonist—except, unlike the original American hero who had to work hard and overcome adversity to succeed, his modern sequels merely had to listen to tips on the street, pick would-be winners, and place a call to their brokers. In the end, the market came tumbling down, leaving millions of baby boomers and Gen Xers without adequate savings for their retirement years and having to face the prospect of working well into their seventies to make ends meet.

For many younger Americans, the new genre of TV reality shows has become the latest vehicle to hitch their star to. Thousands of young people line up to audition for shows like *All American Girl, American Idol, American Juniors, America's Next Top Model, Average Joe, The Apprentice, The Bachelor* and *Bachelorette, Big Brother, Meet My Folks, Mr. Personality, Next Action Star, Fame, The Family, Joe Millionaire, Star Chamber, Survivor, 30 Seconds to Fame,* and *Who Wants to Marry a Millionaire?* In 2004, there were more than 170 reality shows on American television.[58]

All of the participants in these shows hope to be discovered, to become famous, to be a celebrity. While some of the shows require a certain amount of talent and expertise, most just require the participants to show up and be themselves. Andy Warhol's prescient prediction, more than thirty years ago, that in America everyone would have their fifteen minutes of fame, is now being played out nightly on American TV, as ordinary people put themselves in front of the cameras so that millions of other Americans can watch them live out their lives.

For the lucky few who make it on to these reality shows, fame is indeed short-lived. Most quickly shrink back into the anonymity of day-to-day life after their appearance on the shows. But, for millions of American viewers, seeing someone just like themselves on TV becoming famous, even for an instant, keeps alive the idea that it could happen to them as well . . . all it takes is a little luck. In the meantime, millions of viewers can live out the American Dream vicariously by watching the fortunate few who beat the odds, convinced that the dream is still alive and that their turn is coming.

Many social critics would argue that what millions of Americans are really embracing is not the American Dream so much as the American daydream. The authentic American Dream combines faith in God with the belief in hard work and sacrifice for the future. The new substitutes—legal gambling, celebrity television shows, and the like—are grounded in fantasy and delusion. We have become, say the critics, a people who have grown fat, lazy, and sedentary, who spend much of our time wishing for success but are unwilling to "pay our dues" with the kind of personal commitment required to make something out of our lives.

This is a harsh judgment, but probably increasingly true for a number of young middle-class Americans who grew up coddled and spoiled by doting parents who showered them with every conceivable pleasure and experience money could buy, often before they were even old enough to appreciate it. Overindulged, these sons and daughters of baby-boomer parents are unlikely candidates for the kind of personal commitment required to keep the authentic American Dream alive. Faith, discipline, hard work, self-reliance, and self-sacrifice are hardly the terms one would normally use to describe today's American middle-class youngsters. Ennui is a more accurate description of the emotional and mental state of growing numbers of American young people. "Been there, done that" is a phrase one often hears from kids. By the time these youngsters have reached early adulthood, they have been everywhere, done everything, seen everything, and had everything. They have little or nothing to look forward to or to aspire to. Their dreams have been answered even before they had a chance to dream them. For these young Americans, the most difficult life task is motivation itself. It's no wonder that alcohol, drugs, and gambling are all on the rise. When the future is no longer something to work toward and fill in but is something already experienced and left behind, then only momentary pleasures are left to ward off the boredom and make it through another day.

Some observers of the American scene have argued that one of the reasons that the American Dream is losing currency is that we have over-empowered our kids, giving them an inflated sense of ego and, with it, a belief that they are entitled to success because of their many special attributes. One educator once put it this way: "Today kids get an A just for showing up." I was recently teaching a class of young business leaders, half of whom were from Europe, the other half from America. The Europeans said they were perplexed that whenever they attended a business meeting where a presentation was given by an American businessperson, the Americans in attendance would shower the speaker with congratulations for doing a brilliant job even if he or she was merely delivering a rather standard talk about not very interesting things. The Europeans complained that because Americans are constantly over-empowering one another, the bar for performance continues to be lowered and standards of excellence compromised. After all, if you are always being told that everything you do is insightful, well conceived and thought out, and effectively executed, then why try harder?

A sense of entitlement goes hand in hand with over-empowerment. If one is continually told how great he or she is, he or she eventually begins to believe it and comes to expect that all good things should come to him or her. For these young people, the American Dream is no longer thought of as a quest but is regarded more as a right.

The desire for instant gratification, when combined with a sense of over-empowerment and entitlement, can create a volatile emotional mix. The narcissistic personality type is generally less able to handle life's many frustrations, and more prone to antisocial behavior, even including using violence to get what they feel they deserve and are entitled to.

Is the once noble quest of the American Dream turning dark and foreboding at the hands of a new generation? A tracking poll of the views and values of Canadian and U.S. citizens over an eight-year period from 1992 to 2000 offers some insight into the matter. Canadians and Americans were asked to "agree or disagree" that when one is extremely tense or frustrated, a little violence can offer relief, and that "it's no big deal." In 1992, 14 percent of Americans and Canadians agreed that a little violence is okay.[59] By 1996, the proportion of Canadians believing that a little violence was justified had fallen to 10 percent, while the proportion of Americans had leaped to 27 percent.[60] In 2000, the proportion of Canadians went back up slightly to 14 percent, but the Americans who thought a little violence was okay shot up to 31 percent, nearly one-third of the American public.[61]

Even more disquieting, Canadians and Americans were asked if "it is acceptable to use violence to get what you want." In 1992, 9 percent of

Canadians and only 10 percent of Americans said using violence to get what you want was acceptable.[62] By 1996, however, 18 percent of Americans felt that it was all right to use violence to get what you want, while still only 9 percent of Canadians thought the same way.[63] In 2000, the gap between Canadians and Americans had widened even more. Twelve percent of Canadians thought violence was justified to get what they wanted, while 24 percent of Americans felt the same way.[64] That's nearly one out of four Americans believing that using violence to get what they want is acceptable. Michael Adams, who heads up the polling organization Environomics, concluded that "Americans are prepared to put a lot more on the line than Canadians to achieve their version of the American Dream," including committing acts of violence, if necessary.[65]

American Civic-Mindedness

Wait a minute! Can it really be that bad? True, Americans are more focused on becoming rich than any other people. And yes, we are probably more self-involved and overindulged than many other people in the world. But what about the other side of the American character, the civic side that the French philosopher Alexis de Tocqueville found so appealing about the young America when he visited the country in 1831? Tocqueville took notice of the American penchant to create voluntary associations to advance civic welfare, a phenomenon largely absent in Europe at the time. He wrote,

> Americans of all ages, all stations in life, and all types of disposition are forever forming associations. There are not only commercial and industrial associations in which all take part, but others of a thousand different types—religious, moral, serious, futile, very general and very limited, immensely large and very minute. Americans combine to give fetes, found seminaries, build churches, distribute books and send missionaries to the antipodes. Hospitals, prisons, and schools take shape that way. Nothing, in my view, more deserves attention than the intellectual and moral associations in America.[66]

While Americans are far and away the most individualistic people in the world, we also give an enormous amount of our time to serving the communities in which we dwell. Fraternal organizations, youth clubs, neighborhood and civic associations, arts and educational groups, sports and recreational activities, and numerous other efforts of a like kind have long been a staple of American life. We have always prided ourselves on being a nation of civic-minded volunteers. Could we be both self-centered and community-minded at the same time?

Although seemingly paradoxical, the American proclivity to civic-mindedness has come to reflect our deeply held notions about individual freedom. Americans have always had misgivings about ceding too much power to the state. For us, freedom has meant the ability to amass personal wealth and become independent. We have long viewed the government's role as a guarantor of individual property rights and have eschewed the notion that it ought to play an activist role in helping to provide for the general welfare or redistribute wealth to the less fortunate among us. (More on this in chapter 2.) So, from the very beginning, Americans preferred to keep taxes low and limit government involvement in the community in order to optimize individual accumulation of wealth and ensure greater personal control over the disposition of one's property. Helping the needy, in turn, became a matter of individual choice.

Lester Salamon, the director of the Johns Hopkins Center for Civil Society Studies, notes that America's unique civil society tradition grew out of our history of individualism. He points out that "a strongly individualistic cultural ethos . . . has produced deep-seated antagonism to concentrated power." The result is that Americans are "reluctant to rely too heavily on government to cope with social and economic problems, thus leaving such significant problems to be tackled through private voluntary effort."[67] That's why, for example, in America, unlike Europe, half of all U.S. colleges and hospitals, and two-thirds of the social service organizations, are in the not-for-profit sector rather than the public sector.[68]

America's strong religious roots also account for the proliferation of civil society institutions. Many of the nation's nonprofit health, education, and social service institutions were created as extensions of religious institutions. For example, Americans opted, early on, to establish hospitals in the not-for-profit sector, rather than rely on government to provide health care for the citizenry. Today, 46 percent of the employment in the not-for-profit sector resides in the health-care arena.[69]

Anxious to ensure against a single official state religion, as was the case throughout most of Europe, Americans made the decision to separate church and state, allowing diverse religious sects to flourish. They did and, among other things, created their own colleges and universities to provide religious instruction along with a general education.

When we peel off all the many layers of the American not-for-profit sector, what becomes obvious is the looming presence of the religious community in the civil society as compared to European nations. American religious organizations make up 11 percent of the nonprofit employment and nearly one-third of all the volunteering, whereas in Western Europe, religious employment is only 3.5 percent of all nonprofit paid employment, and religious volunteering is only 11 percent of all volunteer work.[70]

Granted, a substantial amount of volunteer activity in the religious community is geared toward social services like feeding the poor, providing shelter for the homeless, and making available health-care services to the needy. Still, the overwhelming number of volunteer hours are spent on pastoral and other activity related to the religious institutions' own perpetuation.

Many proponents of nonprofit engagement argue that civil society organizations are better equipped than government agencies to administer social services to those in need because they are in the communities they serve and are better informed and more motivated to serve their neighbors. All true. The problem is that the volunteer not-for-profit sector in the United States has not been able to provide anywhere near the same level of assistance to the needy and poor that government could were it to play a more activist role—as it does in Europe. And, even with all of the praise heaped on Americans' civic efforts to provide social services, the fact remains that, in the United States, paid employment in the not-for-profit social services sector still ranks below the average in a comparative study of twenty-two nations. While, on average, one out of four paid jobs in the nonprofit sector in the twenty-two nations studied are in social services, in the United States, only 13.5 percent of all paid nonprofit jobs are in social services.[71]

None of this is to suggest that America's civil society is not a formidable force. But much of the motivation behind American civic-mindedness can be traced back to the individualistic and religious roots of the American character. In most of Europe, by contrast, the civil society is far more secular in its orientation and less tied to the Christian notion of individual charity and more to the socialist idea of collective responsibility for the welfare of the community.

Moreover, many of America's not-for-profit organizations have traditionally served as social supports for the business sector. Adult organizations like Kiwanis Club and Ruritan and youth organizations like Junior Achievement and even 4-H are essentially adjuncts to the commercial arena, even though they are, strictly speaking, nonprofit volunteer organizations.

In recent years, a growing number of observers have begun to notice a steady and even precipitous decline in voluntary participation in the not-for-profit sector in America. Harvard's Robert Putnam published controversial findings on the decline of the civil society in his book *Bowling Alone*. He attributes the shrinking of American participation in volunteer activity to a number of factors. Putnam believes that approximately 10 percent of the decline in volunteering is attributable to the pressures of time and money, especially on two-career families. Another 10 percent of the decline, according to Putnam, is traceable to suburbanization and sprawl, and the accompanying increase in commuting time, which leaves less time available for involvement in after-work nonprofit activity. The third reason for the decline, however, says Putnam, is the increasing privatization of leisure-time entertainment, and especially the amount of time spent watching television. He estimates that upwards of 25 percent of the decline in civic participation can be connected to electronic entertainment of all kinds. Finally, Putnam argues that half the decline is simply a generational shift, with younger Americans far less interested in giving their time to others and advancing non-pecuniary social goals.[72] If he is right, it suggests that the American character has hardened, and that time and money pressures and pursuit of personal pleasure has made us even less willing to look out for the social well-being of our neighbors.

If this is indeed the case—there are those who say that our civic-mindedness has not declined quite as much as Putnam and others imply—then the American Dream would seem to be cocooning even further into the promotion of narrow self-interest, with dire consequences for the well-being of society.

There is, however, another side of the story. It's not that all Americans are selfish, are lazy, want something for nothing, and are uncaring toward their fellow human beings. Those Americans exist. There are, nonetheless, millions of other Americans who have worked hard, made good on the American Dream, and shared their good fortune with the less fortunate through personal acts of charity and volunteer activity in the community. But there is also an increasing number of other Americans of good character who have simply given up on the American Dream. They believed. They kept their faith, worked hard, applied themselves, constantly improved their skills, saved and sacrificed for a better future for their children, served their communities, and still came up short. They followed the script, only to find disappointment at the end of the story. While a slim majority of 51 percent of American voters still believe it is possible to live the American Dream, what's shocking is that a third of all Americans (34 percent) no longer think it is possible.[73] For many of them, the price of a lotto ticket has become their only chance of living out the American Dream.

Unfortunately, while the ranks of the overindulged and the undervalued have swollen in recent years, the number of Americans who can still lay legitimate claim to living out the American Dream have dwindled in comparison. The result is that the American Dream has suffered immeasurably, losing much of the power it once enjoyed as the defining story that unites the American people.

2

The New Land of Opportunity

Give me your tired, your poor,
Your huddled masses yearning to breathe free,
The wretched refuse of your teeming shore.
Send these, the homeless, tempest-tossed, to me:
I lift my lamp beside the golden door.[1]

THOSE WORDS were written by a young nineteenth-century American poet, Emma Lazarus, and are inscribed on the plaque at the base of the Statue of Liberty for every émigré to see.

For millions of disheartened Europeans—and later, refugees from other lands—America was the place where they could leave behind their desperate pasts and begin life anew. Here was the great land of opportunity. For most of America's first two hundred or so years, the myth and the reality of American opportunity were close enough to go unquestioned. Life was tough for each new immigrant. There were few social supports to help one along in this new world. On the other hand, for those who were determined to succeed, diligent to the task, and disciplined in the American work ethic, chances were fair to good that they could make a better life, if not for themselves, at least for their children.

Moving on Up

Up until the 1960s, upward mobility was at the core of the American Dream. Then, the dream began to unravel, slowly at first, but picking up momentum in the 1970s, 1980s, and 1990s. Today, the U.S. can no longer claim to be the model of upward mobility for the world. That does not mean that there isn't opportunity for both native-born and newcomers. But the kind of unfettered upward mobility that made America the envy of the world no longer exists.

What's so strange about the current situation is the role reversal that has occurred between the New World and the Old World in less than a quarter of a century. Just one hundred years ago, Europe was hemorrhaging its people—millions of destitute souls risked life and limb to recast their fortunes in a new continent. These new émigrés were full of uncertainty but also of hope. They were escaping, for the most part, from a long history of hereditary entitlements and class divisions that kept the rich in power and the poor in their place. They left a continent where behavior was conditioned by the belief that everyone should know and accept his or her status in life and came to a new continent where each person was expected to make his or her own way and follow his or her dreams.

Now it is America where upward mobility is slowing, and millions of Americans are finding it increasingly difficult to live out their dreams. Yet, the great American myth of upward mobility continues to live on, despite mounting evidence that what was once a great dream has become, for many, a relentless nightmare. And what of that Old World, that caste-bound, class-defined purgatory so many millions of people fled from to start over in the American Eden? It is slowly becoming the new land of opportunity. More and more emigrants are choosing Europe over America than ever before. They sense that a tide of sorts has turned and that the quality of life and the chance of making a better life might be at least as good in Europe as in America. It's here, on the front line of upward mobility, that we first begin to discern some of the many differences that separate the older American Dream from the newer European Dream. The numbers tell the story.

If upward mobility thrives best in a society where there is less of a divide between the very rich and the very poor, then, for sure, Europe is a more promising place for those anxious to move on up. According to the data collected by the Luxembourg Income Study (LIS), the most authoritative database in the world on income distribution, the United States ranks twenty-fourth among the developed nations in income inequality. Only Russia and Mexico rank lower.[2] All eighteen of the most developed European countries have less income inequality between rich and poor. In the U.S., the income of a typical high-income person is 5.6 times the income of a typical low-income person, after adjusting for taxes, transfers, and family size.[3] By contrast, the income of a typical high-income person in Northern Europe is only 3 times the income of a typical low-income person, and in Central Europe, the income of high-end earners is between 3.18 and 3.54 times the income of low-income earners.[4] While inequality is rising even in Europe, the increase is quite modest—with the exception of the U.K.—compared to the sharp increase in the U.S. in income inequality over the past three decades.[5]

Wages and related benefits is the single best indicator of upward mobility in society. Of the twenty most developed countries in the world, the U.S. was dead last in the growth rate of total compensation to its workforce in the 1980s. The average compensation actually fell by 0.3 percent per year during that decade. In the early 1990s, the U.S. average compensation growth rate grew only slightly, at an annual rate of about 0.1 percent. Virtually all of the European countries experienced higher compensation growth. Between 1995 and 2000, the average compensation grew by 1.6 percent in the U.S., still lower than seven other European countries. Much of those gains in the U.S., however, were wiped out with the stock-market plunge in 2000.[6]

Even during the rapid economic recovery of the second half of 2003, the average hourly wage of nonsupervisory jobs in American offices and factories went up only 3 cents, according to the Bureau of Labor Statistics—barely enough to keep even with inflation. This is the slowest wage growth America has experienced in more than forty years.[7] Moreover, the jobs being lost pay around $17.00 per hour, while the new jobs being created pay only $14.50 per hour.[8] At the same time, corporate profits, as a percentage of national income, reached their highest level since the 1960s.[9]

One of the best places to look for signs of upward mobility is the manufacturing sector. Unskilled, semiskilled, and skilled production jobs are often the departure points for moving up the income ladder. In 1979, U.S. manufacturing compensation was the highest of any of the industrialized countries in the world. By 2000, U.S. manufacturing compensation had dropped behind five European countries, and most other European countries had significantly closed the gap.[10]

When it comes to measuring the inequality ratio of the earnings of high-wage earners (those making more than 90 percent of the workforce) and low-wage earners (those making more than only 10 percent of the workforce), the U.S. now enjoys the distinction of having the highest earnings inequality of the top eighteen nations. Looking at all of the numbers together, Lawrence Mishel, Jared Bernstein, and Heather Boushey of the Economic Policy Institute conclude that "income mobility appears to be *lower* in the United States than in other OECD [Organization for Economic Co-operation and Development] countries."[11]

America, it appears, is the land of opportunity for a small segment of high-income earners and a land of misfortune for many others. There are more poor people living in poverty in America than in the sixteen European nations for which data is available. Seventeen percent of all Americans are in poverty, or one out of every six people. By contrast, 5.1 percent of the people of Finland are in poverty, 6.6 percent in Sweden, 7.5 percent in Germany, 8 percent in France, 8.1 percent in the Netherlands, 8.2 percent in Belgium, 10.1 percent in Spain, 11.1 percent in Ireland, and 14.2 percent in Italy.[12]

The Sink-or-Swim Mentality

How did America, the land of opportunity, allow itself to slip to the bottom of the rankings among developed nations—and far below Europe—on income inequality and poverty? The answer to that question may lie in our perception of why some people become rich while others remain poor. We Americans have, by and large, adopted a laissez-faire attitude about business and commerce. If we just provide everyone with the opportunity to go to school, allow the free market to rule, and make sure the government doesn't interfere too much in its workings, the motivated and talented will rise to the top on their own accord. And those that aren't motivated and/or lack talent will not do well—but that's the nature of things. America was always meant to be a land of "equality of opportunity" but not a land of "equality of results." "Sink or swim" goes the old American adage.

In America, we have come to believe that everyone is truly responsible for his or her own destiny. It's the frontier motif, and it is firmly embedded in our national consciousness. Even those Americans who have transformed the authentic American Dream into a pale replica by seeking instant success and fame still feel they are in charge of their fates. All the contrary statistics and figures in the world are not likely to shake the conviction of a majority of our countrymen that America is still the greatest land of opportunity in the world.

The Pew Global Attitudes Project asked people in America, Europe, and elsewhere why some people are rich and others poor. What they found is revealing. Two-thirds of Americans believe that success is not outside of their control. Contrast that figure to Germany, where 68 percent of the people believe the exact opposite. In Europe, a majority in every country—with the exception of the U.K., the Czech Republic, and Slovakia—"believe that forces outside of an individual's personal control determine success."[13] By more than six to one, Americans believe that people who do not succeed in life fail because of their own shortcomings, not because of society.[14] Other surveys support the Pew finding. Asked why people are wealthy, 64 percent of Americans say because of personal drive, willingness to take risks, and hard work and initiative.[15] Why do others fail? Sixty-four percent say because of lack of thrift, 53 percent say lack of effort, and 53 percent say lack of ability.[16] The World Values Survey found that 71 percent of Americans "believe that the poor have a chance to escape from poverty," while only 40 percent of Europeans believe that's the case.[17] Strange indeed, coming from a country that now has the largest percentage of its population in poverty of any major developed nation.

Why the vast disparity between belief and reality? Again, it comes back to the core of the American Dream . . . the tough frontier notion that if left unfettered—especially by government—each man and woman can pursue and achieve his or her dream. No wonder 58 percent of Americans say that "it is more important to have the freedom to pursue personal goals without government interference," while only 34 percent say that "it is more important for government to guarantee that no one is in need."[18]

Undoubtedly, the frontier mythology plays a significant role in understanding American attitudes about inequality and poverty. But there is also likely a more unsavory side to the issue. Racism, note a growing number of commentators, can't entirely be dismissed from the poll results. Dig deeper, and we find that many Americans associate poverty with black America, even though in terms of raw numbers, there are more whites living under the poverty line. But in terms of percentages, a far larger proportion of the black community live below the poverty line. In 2002, the U.S. Census reported that 8 percent of whites and 24.1 percent of blacks, up from 22.7 percent in 2001, are below the poverty line.[19]

Nearly four hundred years after the first slaves arrived in America, the race issue still dominates the American psyche. Any visitor to the U.S. senses, very quickly, the racial tension in the air—it permeates the country. And if the truth were to be told, many white Americans think that black Americans are lazy, at best, or worst, genetically incapable of rising above their circumstances.

Some observers have suggested that one of the reasons Europeans, unlike Americans, are more willing to believe that the poor are poor through no fault of their own but rather because of societal factors is because, until recently, their poor were not racial minorities but, rather, white Caucasians, and therefore the majority was able to identify and even empathize with their plight, believing that "there but for the grace of God go I." Race, especially in America, where the white majority has yet to fully come to grips with more than two hundred years of slavery, becomes the dividing line between "us" and "the other." It's easier to dismiss the disquieting number of people in poverty if they aren't like us, if they are perceived as somehow racially, even biologically, separate. White America can't afford to believe that the American way of life might, in some way, be to blame for the destitute conditions many black Americans find themselves in. The sad reality, however, is that a majority of African Americans come from the legions of the poor, raised on the bleak streets of inner cities, where the opportunities to rise above their dire circumstances are few. The result is that a staggering 12 percent of African American males between the ages of twenty and thirty-four are currently in prison in the United States.[20] Yet most of us continue to turn away from their plight, unwilling to modify the great American belief that, in this country, opportunity abounds.

Given the vast differences in how most Americans and Europeans perceive the notion of equality of opportunity, it's not hard to understand the two very different approaches taken to address the twin issues of income disparity and poverty. While Americans encourage private efforts to alleviate poverty and provide greater mobility, we are, for the most part, unwilling to commit our tax money to the task. If the rich are rich because they are smarter and work harder, and the poor are poor because they are lazy or without ability, then nothing the government does is going to make much of a difference. And besides, it would send the wrong message—namely, that those who worked hard and made something of their lives ought to then sacrifice some of their hard-earned income to compensate those who didn't work hard and lacked the ability to succeed. Redistributing the wealth, say some, would compromise the very soul of the American Dream and make a mockery of the frontier covenant that is at the heart of the American success story. Many Americans believe that the marketplace is still the fairest mechanism for distributing the productive wealth of society.

Europeans, because they have had a long tradition of hereditary status and transmission—some EU countries still have kings and queens—are more used to thinking of society in class terms and are far more willing to entertain the idea of government intervening to redress inequities. On the continent—less so in the U.K.—the market is not held in such unquestioned awe as in America. There is the belief that market forces, if left to their own devices, are often unfair and, therefore, need to be tamed. Government redistribution, in the form of transfers and payments to those less fortunate, is considered an appropriate antidote to unrestrained market capitalism. That is why in Europe the notion of creating social democracies—a mixed system that balances market forces with government assistance—has flourished since World War II.

According to the OECD, while the U.S. devotes only 11 percent of its GDP to redistributing income by way of transfers and other social benefits, the EU countries contribute more than 26 percent of their GDP to social benefits.[21] The U.S. is particularly stingy when it comes to helping the working poor. The legal minimum wage in the U.S. in the 1990s was only 39 percent of the average wage, whereas in the European Union it was 53 percent of the average wage.[22] In the United States, unemployment benefits are also less generous than in the European Union.

Where you really see the difference between the American and European approach to addressing inequities and improving the quality of life of people is in family benefits. The U.S. is only one of three industrialized countries in the world that does not mandate maternity or paternity leave. Even worse, a majority of Americans aren't even eligible for unpaid family leave. In Europe, paid maternity leave extends from three and a half to six months. In Sweden, mothers get sixty-four weeks off and 63 percent of their wages. In Germany, France, Austria, Denmark, the Netherlands, Norway, Portugal, and Spain, paid maternity leave is 100 percent of salary for at least three months.[23] American working fathers and mothers would be shocked to hear how well parents fare across the Atlantic.

American economists and public officials are continually berating European leaders for maintaining such extensive transfer programs, arguing that high taxes to support social-benefit programs leave less money to invest in new market opportunities, undermine entrepreneurial incentive, indulge workers and their families, reward unproductive work, make European workers too expensive to hire, and inevitably make people more dependent on government and less self-reliant and resourceful. They argue that for all of its faults, the U.S. still has a more vibrant economy, its workers are more productive, and fewer people are unemployed, proof that the American economy is still the model for Europe to emulate and not the other way around. How right are they?

Who Is More Productive?

Productivity is the most often cited measure used by economists to explain America's economic success and its superiority over the European Union economy. Productivity is a measure of goods and services produced per hour of labor. Between 1820 and the end of World War II, U.S. output per hour did indeed grow faster in the U.S. than in Europe and, for that matter, every other country in the world, making the U.S. economy the most powerful on the planet. Much of the reason for America's success, in this regard, is attributed to our risk-taking attitude, entrepreneurial acumen, innovative spirit, engineering prowess, and willingness to believe in the goodness of an unhindered capitalist marketplace. Certainly, there is something to be said for all of these arguments. But there were also other advantages America enjoyed over Europe that had more to do with geography than anything else.

To begin with, the sheer expanse of the continent provided the largest single internal geographic market in the world. A common language allowed Americans to carry on commerce with relative ease. Even with new immigrants flooding to America in successive waves—especially after 1890—there was always a labor shortage, which kept wages high compared to Europe. High wages served as a prod to introduce more labor-saving technologies and reduce the cost of output per hour worked. The introduction of a transcontinental rail grid and the laying down of telegraph lines across the country sped up commercial transactions still more.

Equally important to America's growth and productivity were the abundant natural resources that existed in North America. Millions of

acres of woodland meant cheap lumber to construct homes, build factories, and create whole cities. Cheap iron ore from the Mesabi Range
helped make American steel production the cheapest in the world. Large
swaths of fertile and previously unexploited farmland stretching from Indiana to California made American food the cheapest anywhere. And the
discovery of the largest oil reserves on Earth—in the American Southwest—transformed the U.S., making it an undisputed economic colossus
by the early twentieth century. Finally, two great oceans kept America relatively isolated from the kind of warfare that periodically engulfed Europe. Our high tariffs, in turn, encouraged the development of our own
internal market.

Despite all of these natural advantages, the U.S. productivity lead began to erode after World War II. Decimated by two world wars in the
course of half a century, Europe was little more than a shattered shell in
1945. With the help of American financial aid, in the form of the Marshall
Plan, Europe began to rebuild its broken economies.

What is so remarkable is how fast Europe caught up to the United
States. In 1960, the U.S. economy was producing nearly two times more
goods and services per hour than France and the United Kingdom. By
2002, however, Europe had virtually closed the productivity gap with
the U.S., boosting labor productivity per hour worked to 97 percent of the
U.S. level.[24]

European productivity growth outperformed the U.S. during virtually
the entire half century following World War II. Between 1950 and 1973,
European productivity grew by 4.44 percent, compared to 2.68 percent in
the U.S., and from 1973 to 2000, the productivity growth in Europe increased by 2.4 percent, compared to 1.37 percent in the U.S.[25] Between
1990 and 1995, twelve EU countries showed higher productivity growth
than the U.S. While U.S. productivity moved slightly ahead in the last
half decade of the 1990s, showing a 1.9 percent increase in growth, compared to a 1.3 percent growth rate in Europe, seven of the EU countries
still grew faster. In 2002, even with the surge in U.S. productivity, six European nations achieved higher productivity.[26]

Americans have long believed that our workers are the most productive in the world. True, we were somewhat taken aback by reports in the
early 1990s that Japan's workers might be catching up, although the Japanese success turned out to be short-lived. But the very idea that at least
some European countries might outperform American companies and

American workers is unthinkable. Nonetheless, in 2002, the average worker in Norway produced $45.55 of output per hour, compared to $38.83 per hour in the United States. Belgium, Ireland, and the Netherlands also produced more output per hour than the U.S. Still, these are small countries. What about the majors, the countries that count? Well, Germany in 2002 enjoyed higher productivity per hour worked than America. The average worker produced $39.39 of output per hour. And the coup de grâce? French workers produced $41.85 of output per hour, or $3.02 more output per hour than American workers—that's 7 percent greater productivity. France ranked third in the world in productivity per hour at the end of 2002, just behind Norway and Belgium. And five other European countries were running neck and neck with U.S. productivity—Denmark, Austria, Italy, Switzerland, and Finland. (Japan, by the way, ranked a distant seventeenth among industrial nations in productivity.)[27]

Americans are so used to stereotyping the French business community as overly hierarchical and bureaucratic and French workers as somewhat dilettantish and carefree that even when confronted with the evidence, they shake their heads in disbelief. What does it say about American businesses and American workers if the French and five other European nations are actually better at conducting commerce than we are?

I should caution that American productivity has shot up since 2002—experiencing the biggest gains in more than fifty years—raising the very real question of whether European productivity advances will be able to catch up and keep pace or begin to slide in relation to America in the years ahead. Still, Europe's productivity in many sectors continues to compare favorably to or even exceed that of the United States.[28]

Funding basic research has always been the key to advancing productivity. America understands this and has long invested in pure research. Recently, however, European scientists have begun to outpace their American peers in a number of scientific fields. For example, Europe is forging ahead of the United States in particle physics research and is currently building the world's most powerful atom smasher. While it might come as a surprise to most Americans, Europe surpassed the United States in the mid-1990s as the largest producer of scientific literature.[29]

European businesses have been particularly competitive at the cutting edge of the software and communications technology revolutions. Europe went out in front on wireless technology and continues to enjoy a comfortable lead over the U.S. in adoption and market penetration. Industry analysts predict that the increasing integration of wireless technology will help bolster European productivity in the coming decade, keeping the continent competitive with the U.S.

European companies are also jumping ahead of their American counterparts in the next great technology revolution, grid computing, raising the prospect of the kind of qualitative leap in productivity that could leave America behind by the end of the decade.

Grids hook up individual computers, combining their unused power to tackle very complex computing tasks. Scientists envision a not too distant future where millions of computers are connected in multiple regional, national, and global computational grids to create a "universal source of computing power."[30] The grid, says grid specialists Ian Foster and Carl Kesselman, "is an emerging infrastructure that will fundamentally change the way we think about—and use—computing."[31] Researchers in the new field ask us to imagine what the desktop computer will look like "when the power of a supercomputer with capabilities six orders of magnitude greater is just a mouse click away."[32]

When the Swiss pharmaceutical company Novartis needed a new supercomputer for designing drugs, instead of buying one at an enormous cost, the company used software created by United Devices, an American company, to link its 2,700 desktop personal computers together, giving it the same computing power as a single supercomputer. The company has already found a number of new chemical compounds with the aid of its computational grid and is now planning to expand its grid capacity by linking all of its seventy thousand personal computers together, giving it incredible computing power.[33]

According to European scientists and industry observers, Europe is eighteen months ahead of the United States in the introduction of grid technology, and the European Union has announced the launch of two state-of-the-art initiatives in 2004. The first is called Enabling Grids for E-science in Europe and will be the largest international grid infrastructure in the world. The grid will operate in seventy institutions across Europe and will have the computing capability of twenty thousand of today's most powerful personal computers. The second project, coordinated by France's National Center for Scientific Research, will connect seven supercomputers in Europe at optical network speeds. Mário Campolargo, director for the research infrastructure unit at the European Commission, says that "the goal is to establish Europe as one of the most dynamic and creative environments in the world to deploy grid-enabled infrastructures."[34]

The European Union is determined to lead the way in the grid technology revolution, realizing that the potential productivity gains of being first in the field could be enormous and unprecedented for European business. The EU already has in place a five- to ten-year strategic plan and is projected to spend upwards of $428 million between 2002 and 2006 to upgrade the grid infrastructure.[35] Europe's ability to establish unified standards of operation, coordinate activity among competitors, and create public-private partnerships generally gives it a leg up on American companies, where a "go it alone" strategy often results in competing standards, haphazard development of new technologies, and market redundancies. Certainly this has been the case with the wireless technology revolution and now with the new grid technology.

European business is banking on the prospect that increased outlays for pure research and collaborative public-private partnerships to advance new technologies, when combined with the benefits of increasingly seamless internal market operations, will be the winning combination to boost productivity gains to new levels and keep the EU competitive with the U.S.

Live to Work or Work to Live?

Even though Europe's productivity is between 92 and 97 percent of the U.S. level (depending on how the figures are adjusted), per capita income in the EU is just 72 percent of American per capita income. How do we explain the divergence? Some of the difference has to do with the lower employment participation rates in Europe—lower employment in relation to the total population—differences in retirement ages, and unemployment rates. But 75 percent of the difference is attributable to the fewer hours worked in the EU.[36]

It turns out that in France, and virtually every other country in the European Union, workers have opted for more leisure rather than longer work hours and bigger paychecks. The French government instituted a thirty-five-hour workweek in 1999.

The French experiment is particularly interesting because it defies the American logic that hard work and long hours on the job are indispensable to achieving significant gains in productivity and a better quality of life for working people. As already mentioned, French productivity in 2002 was higher than in the U.S., and French workers were enjoying far more leisure time.

The French went to the thirty-five-hour workweek, in part, to create more jobs. If people worked fewer hours, went the reasoning, additional people could be employed, thus reducing the nation's unemployment roles. To make sure there would be no loss in pay, the law mandates the thirty-five-hour workweek at the old thirty-nine-hour pay scale. The government, in turn, is obliged to subsidize the companies by lowering employers' social security contributions so there will be no net loss of revenues to the employers in making the shift to a thirty-five-hour workweek schedule.[37] In addition, the government provides an incentive to companies to create new jobs by agreeing to subsidize the social payments (retirement, health care, workers' compensation, and unemployment insurance) of any newly hired low-wage workers.[38] The annual cost of subsidizing French companies is about $10.6 billion.[39] Much of the funds have come from so-called sin taxes on tobacco and alcohol. The government expects to make up the remainder of the payout by the addition of new workers onto the employment rolls. More people working means fewer people on government assistance. The new workers bring home paychecks, spend money in the marketplace, and pay taxes, all of which accrues to the overall well-being of the French economy. More than 285,000 jobs have been directly created by the thirty-five-hour workweek plan since its inception.[40]

Skeptical at first, most French employers have been won over to the scheme. They're finding that fresh and motivated workers can produce just as much output in seven hours a day as less motivated and more tired workers can in eight hours. And, there has been an ancillary benefit: the thirty-five-hour-workweek law allows employers greater flexibility in assigning work schedules. They can now establish weekend, evening, and holiday shifts, and require employees to spread out their vacation time to accommodate production schedules.[41]

The thirty-five-hour law also built in other accommodations to both management and labor. For example, the thirty-five-hour week may be measured not only by hours worked per week but also by hours per month and days per year. Senior management in companies may be exempted from the working hour restrictions. Overtime, under the new law, must exceed regular pay by at least 10 percent. Moreover, an employee may not

work more than 180 extra hours per year in the absence of a collective bargaining agreement. Overtime that exceeds 180 hours requires a 20 percent pay increase.[42] In a survey of corporate directors conducted in 2001,
60 percent of the respondents polled said that the new law helped improve
productivity by introducing more flexible work arrangements and by creating a new dialogue with workers, which improved morale.[43]

More leisure time has also boosted consumer spending at French
cafés, movie houses, sporting events, and other entertainments. Surveys
show that, for the most part, the French public is enthusiastic about the
shorter workweek. Workers often start their weekends on Thursday and
don't go back to work until Tuesday. Working moms have the option of
staying home on Wednesday, when most French schools are closed.[44]

While the worldwide jobless recovery of the past two years has damp-
ened France's employment prospects, as it has those of the United States
and every other country in the world, had France not introduced the
shorter workweek, there is no doubt that its unemployment rate would be
even higher than it is now.

In a number of other European countries, the average workweek is already thirty-nine hours or less, and most are edging toward the thirty-
five-hour French workweek. Meanwhile, the average vacation time across
Europe is six weeks, and in most countries, vacations are mandated by federal law.[45] In the U.S., employers are not obligated by law to provide any
vacation time. Two weeks' vacation, however, has become a standard in
most industries.

French workers are on the job about 1,562 hours per year, according
to the most recent OECD figures (2000). In contrast, U.S. workers
put in 1,877 hours per year, the most of any of the major industrialized
countries. The average American worker is now working ten weeks more
a year than the average German worker, and four and a half more weeks a
year than the average British worker.[46] Even in Japan, which is known for
its long, grueling workdays, workers clock in for 1,840 hours of work per
year, thirty-seven hours fewer than in the United States.[47]

Europe is far ahead not only in advancing shorter workweeks but also
in creating innovative approaches to human resource management to allow workers greater flexibility in juggling work and lifestyles. Belgium, for
example, has introduced novel legislation called "time credits," which
went into effect in January 2002. The law is designed to create a more

flexible balance between one's work life and home life, and updates an older law called "career breaks."[48]

Under the new "time credits" law, workers can take a maximum of one year off over their entire career or interrupt their work, or reduce it to a half-time job without severing their employment contract and without loss of social security rights. To receive a general career break, the employee has to give a three-month advance notice to the employer but does not have to give any reason for the request. The time credit can be extended up to five years by an agreement with the company. Employees who have worked less than five years receive a monthly government allowance of €379. The allowances rise to €505 for workers who have been employed longer.[49] Workers can also request "thematic leaves" to take care of an ailing family member, to provide medical assistance to a relative, or to take care of a child. Each of these specific career breaks comes with different allowances and allocated times. Each worker can also choose to reduce his or her working hours by 20 percent, which generally works out to be a four-day workweek. Workers over the age of fifty can reduce their work hours by one-fifth to one-half over an unlimited period of time.[50]

American employers would be incredulous at the thought of providing career breaks and time credits and wonder how Belgium's companies could maintain their competitive edge with these kinds of flexible labor schedules. Still, it's interesting to note once again that, like France, the Belgian workforce enjoyed higher productivity in terms of output per hour than the American workforce in 2002.[51]

Europeans like to say that "Americans live to work" while "Europeans work to live." What's the point of making more money, they argue, when you have no leisure time to enjoy it? According to one study, 37 percent of Americans now work more than fifty hours a week, and 80 percent of male workers work more than forty hours a week. And the hours worked by many Americans keep going up while in Europe hours worked keep going down. No wonder 70 percent of American parents complain they lack sufficient time with their children, while 38 percent of Americans say "they always feel rushed," and 61 percent say they rarely have excess time.[52] With so little time available after work, Americans use many of their spare moments just to run errands, pay bills, and fix up the house.

The increase in work hours takes a heavy toll on American health, according to health professionals. Stress-related diseases—heart attacks, strokes, and cancer—are on the rise in America. One recent study by the journal *Psychosomatic Medicine* found that the more often American workers skip their vacations, the higher their health risks are. Men who took an annual vacation were 32 percent less likely to die of coronary artery disease than those who did not take vacations.[53]

The difference in how Europeans and Americans conceive a good economy is reflected in the hours worked on both sides of the Atlantic. If one measures the standard of living in terms of paychecks, Americans are 29 percent wealthier than their European counterparts.[54] But if one measures the good life by the amount of leisure time available, the average European enjoys four to ten weeks more of play each year.[55] The question, then, is, Does that 29 percent of additional wealth buy more joy and happiness—enough at least to justify giving up upwards of two to three months of additional leisure each year? As my wife is fond of reminding me—because I, too, am an American workaholic—"No one has ever regretted on their deathbed that they didn't spend more time at the office."

Ironically, when Americans opt for more work than play, the increase in wages shows up in the GDP figure. But, when Europeans choose more leisure over more work, the GDP is adjusted down to reflect the lost wages and consumption. The way the GDP is set up does not allow it to account for quality-of-life considerations such as increasing leisure time, even though such choices are fundamental economic decisions, just like choosing to work longer hours. (We will delve into the issue of how GDP biases the notion of what constitutes the good economy in greater detail in chapter 3.)

What About Jobs?

There is, however, one place where traditional economic figures still count—that's jobs. And while the American economy can be justifiably taken to task on a number of fronts, admit American economists, the question of jobs is basic to a healthy economy, regardless of the questions one might entertain about fairness or quality-of-life concerns. The American economy can't be that far off the mark, since it has produced far more jobs and put far more people to work over the course of the past decade than almost every other developed country. We found jobs for millions of people after the recession in the late 1980s and early 1990s. We reduced unemployment from a 7.5 percent high in 1992 to 4 percent in 2000, an extraordinary feat by any reckoning. Although unemployment has climbed back up to 5.7 percent (December 2003) in the aftermath of the stock-market crash of 2000, it is undeniable, say the economists, that the American economy has been an engine of job creation and a model for Europe to emulate.[56]

In countless seminars and meetings over the past eight years with business leaders, economists, and politicians on both sides of the Atlantic, my American colleagues have been relentless in their praise of what they call "the American miracle," and have taken advantage of any and every opportunity to lecture their European friends about the superiority of American business know-how that led to the creation of so many new jobs in the 1990s. A closer look suggests that many of the new jobs created had little to do with superior entrepreneurial talent or better managerial skills or the quicker adoption of new technologies, but with other factors that artificially boosted the employment figures for a brief moment only to disappear just as quickly once the stock-market bubble burst.

While U.S. official unemployment was 4 percent at the peak of the late 1990s economic surge, a recent national study found that real unemployment during that period was significantly higher, approaching the unemployment levels in the European Union. That is because more than two million discouraged workers simply gave up and dropped out of the workforce and therefore were no longer counted in the official statistics, and the prison population soared from 500,000 in 1980 to two million people today. Nearly 2 percent of the potential male adult workforce in the United States is now incarcerated.[57] Moreover, many of the workers who did find employment in the boom period between 1995 and 2000 were temporary and part-time, without benefits, and for the most part underemployed. Many of them have now sunk back into the ranks of the unemployed. While the U.S. Labor Department put the official unemployment figure at 6.2 percent in the summer of 2003, real unemployment, when discouraged workers who have given up are counted, is 9 percent of the workforce.[58]

It turns out that the so-called American economic miracle of the late 1990s, which created a temporary bubble of new employment, was illusory. It wasn't so much America's business acumen that fed the commercial expansion but rather the runaway extension of consumer credit, which allowed Americans to go on a wild buying binge. The burst in consumer spending put people back to work for a few years to make all the goods and provide all the services being purchased on credit. The result was that America's family savings rate, which was about 8 percent in the early 1990s, sank to around 2 percent by the year 2001.[59] Many Americans were actually spending more than they earned. With their credit maxed out, millions of Americans took advantage of record low interest rates and refinanced the mortgages on their homes, giving them a quick cash infusion in order to continue buying. Now, in the aftermath of the stock-market bubble burst, Americans have slowed spending, and the temporary decline in unemployment has given way to a steady climb back to the unemployment levels experienced nearly a decade ago.

The U.S. economy is experiencing its worst hiring slump in more than twenty years. Even with a 2.7 percent growth in the economy in 2002, and a steep rise of 4.7 percent in labor productivity—the biggest increase since 1950—more than 1.5 million more workers left the job market altogether.[60] They simply gave up looking for work and are, therefore, no longer counted as unemployed. The old logic that technology gains and advances in productivity destroy old jobs but create as many new ones is no longer true. According to a report prepared by *USA Today* on productivity in America's largest companies, it now takes only nine workers to produce what ten workers did in March 2001. The bottom line, says Richard D. Rippe, chief economist of Prudential Securities, is that "we can produce more output without adding a lot of workers."[61]

The European Union is in the throes of a great debate about the future of work. Saddled with high unemployment, high taxes, burdensome welfare systems, and convoluted regulatory regimes, which some say only perpetuate economic stagnation, critics in government, industry, and civil society are locked in a fierce ideological struggle about whether the rules governing employment, commerce, and trade need to be reformed and, if so, how. Politicians and business and labor leaders squabble over the issues of creating a flexible labor policy, lowering taxes, rewriting the rules governing welfare and pension allotments, and bringing their economic policies in line with the United States.

If the key to creating new jobs, however, was only a matter of making the above reforms, then the United States of America should be experiencing high levels of employment. We have made virtually all of the reforms that the European Union is now attempting to implement. Yet the U.S. workforce is experiencing hard times, and the American economy has still not fully recovered from the last recession. Inventories are not being emptied, most industries are running below capacity, consumer savings are low, personal bankruptcies are at a record high, exports are down, and the stock market has still not regained the ground lost when the bubble burst in 2000–01. Other economies around the world are experiencing similar woes.

All of this bad news begs the question, Does the European Union really believe that its economic future is likely to look up substantially if it merely follows the U.S. lead on labor, welfare, trade, and other reforms? No one would argue that such reforms are unnecessary, although the question of how best to streamline the entrepreneurial spirit without sacrificing the social well-being of the EU workforce is a critical concern.

Myths die hard. Despite the fact that America's job miracle turned out to be short-lived and less robust than the hype would warrant, many European policy leaders and public officials continue to look to the American model for their inspiration and guidance. Their enthusiasm is misdirected. Rather than asking what Americans have done right and what Europeans have done wrong—a favorite pastime of European leaders—Europeans should instead congratulate themselves on creating the most humane approach to capitalism ever attempted, and then ask what kinds of new ideas might be implemented to improve on their existing model. Maintaining the appropriate social benefits and pursuing a high quality of life for its citizens should be viewed by the EU as integral to the task of creating the first truly sustainable superpower economy in the world.

Were the European Union to abandon much of its social net in favor of a more libertarian market approach, its 455 million people might find themselves saddled with the kind of deep social ills that now plague the United States, from greater inequality to increased poverty, lawlessness, and incarceration. That's a high price to pay when we consider the fact that the American model not only has failed to deliver real job growth but also has forced millions of Americans into long-term debt and bankruptcy.

The real challenge facing the EU in the coming years is how to take advantage of its vast natural and human resources and build a powerful continental economy without undermining its longstanding commitment to social and economic justice for all of its citizens. The outcome is anything but certain.

What is not in doubt, however, is that the American Dream and the European Dream differ substantially on the question of how best to ensure every person an opportunity to get ahead and make something of himself or herself in the world. The American Dream has, from the very beginning, put the onus of responsibility on the individual to make of his or her life what he or she can in the marketplace, with few social supports other than the guarantee of a free public education. Europeans, by contrast, believe that society has a responsibility to balance the sometimes ruthless Darwinism of the marketplace by providing social supports to the less fortunate, so that no one falls behind.

Both dreams have their strengths and weaknesses. Europeans are often faulted by Americans for not taking greater personal responsibility for their own destinies. Americans, on the other hand, are often criticized by Europeans for being heartless and not taking proper responsibility for their fellow human beings.

Curiously, Europeans are beginning to heed the American advice by instituting reforms that draw more of a balance between individual initiative and collective responsibility, but there is little evidence that America is altering its dream by incorporating into it a greater sense of shared responsibility for the collective well-being of society. If anything, the American Dream is going the other way, becoming almost a caricature of the rugged individualism so glorified in America's frontier mythology. The result is that some Americans are getting richer while many other Americans are getting poorer. In both instances, the American Dream suffers. The sons and daughters of wealthier Americans grow up in the lap of luxury and come to feel empowered and entitled to happiness and less willing to work hard, sacrifice, and make something of themselves. For them, the American Dream becomes endless momentary pleasure-seeking, devoid of any grand purpose in life. For those Americans who still believe in the American promise, and who have made every effort "to pick themselves up by their bootstraps" and succeed, only to be pulled down over and over again by a market economy and society weighted against them, the American Dream has come to feel like a cruel hoax, a myth without any real substance. For those on the top and for those on the bottom, the American Dream is losing its cachet and, in the process, casting the American people adrift. With only our religious fervor to hold on to, we have become a "chosen people" without a narrative—making America potentially a more dangerous and lonely place to be.

As long as our religious fervor was wed to personal success, the idea of a chosen people helped foster upward mobility and the democratic spirit in America. Now that the American Dream of personal success is taken for granted, trivialized, or, worse yet, become the object of ennui among a growing number of younger well-to-do Americans and become something out of reach for most other poorer Americans, all that's left is the idea of a chosen people. The question then becomes, Chosen for what? Religious fervor in search of a mission, especially when arched with the idea of enjoying a special status in the eyes of God, could metamorphose in threatening ways that we Americans are unaccustomed to thinking about. Already, we've seen in the post–September 11 era a hint of the possibilities, as a growing number of American Evangelical religious leaders, conservative politicians, and intellectuals talk of the coming global showdown between the civilized Christian West and the barbarian Muslim world. To be sure, most Americans of faith don't hold such views, at least not yet. And many other more secular Americans are far removed from any such thoughts. Another 9/11 could change all of that in an instant.

Whether the emerging European Dream can offer an alternative vision more able to accommodate the tumultuous changes occurring in the world today, from globalization of the economy and rising unemployment to the spread of religious terrorism, remains to be seen. We will explore that dream from a number of vantage points and perspectives in the chapters that follow, with the hope of better understanding its potential to open up a new path for the human spirit to travel down.

3

The Quiet Economic Miracle

W E LIKE to vacation there. Around every corner, we experience some token of our past. Many of us still have deep roots in Europe. It's like being in a giant outdoor museum—full of treasures and memories, some horrifying, others noble. It feels good visiting the "Old World." The smells are more intimate; the details of life are more painstakingly cared for. The human nose hasn't come fully alive until it has passed a cheese shop in France and taken in the rush of sumptuous smells emanating from a hundred different cheeses, each with its own particular history, and every one of them better than any cheese we might find in our own supermarkets back home. And then there are the display windows in the shops on Oxford Street in London's fashionable shopping district, the side streets circling the Great Duomo in Milan, and along Paris's Champs Elysees. Every window is its own work of art, suggesting to the Americans passing by that what is inside the store is more than products to sell, they are gifts to share.

For most Americans, Europe is a place to relax, awaken our senses, rejuvenate our spirits, and feed our souls. Nothing is more enjoyable than a stroll along the Rhine River in Basel in the early summer evening, while watching young men and women and whole families floating along the swift current of the water in their inner tubes. Or escaping from the winter frost into a warm and dimly lit sanctuary of a fourteenth-century church in a hill town in Provence. Great memories.

But when it comes to the "real world" of making a living, of income and expenditures, of investments and returns, we Americans don't pay all that much attention to the comings and goings in Europe. We generally prefer to keep our economic sights on the East—to Japan and the Southeast Asian Tiger countries. Of late, American businesspeople have turned an eye toward China, convinced that its vast resources, population, educational skills, and drive make it the next likely great economic power.

While we Americans continue to look to the Pacific and Asian economies for signs of quickening competition and greater commercial opportunities, a quiet economic revolution of a different sort is taking place in the land of our European forebears, of which we know very little and to which we are ill prepared to respond.

Americans are vaguely aware that new economic and political realities are emerging in Europe but, when pressed, are unable to say exactly what they are. We know that there is now a common currency across much of the continent and that we no longer have to make anxious and often misinformed split-second calculations on how much the local currency is worth in dollars as we did before the introduction of the euro. Indeed, because the euro is now virtually on a par with the dollar—actually it's slightly stronger—it is easier for Americans to buy things in Europe, since we no longer have to do a lot of mental math to figure out if we are getting a deal or being cheated. Remember when a dollar was equivalent to 1,700 Italian lire?

And when we go through passport control in London, Frankfurt, Paris, and Milan, we notice that all of the Europeans in the next line over are queuing up under an insignia emblazoned with twelve stars in a circle against a blue backdrop. A single EU passport now suffices for every European traveler. We begin to think of everyone in the other line not as Frenchmen, or Italians, or Germans, or Poles but as Europeans.

We Americans are still conditioned by our memory of the old Europe as a composite of thousands of once walled cities and surrounding countrysides nested inside dozens of rigidly marked-off national boundaries, in a kind of tight mosaic of borders touching up against borders. The old Europe felt tight, even claustrophobic, for Americans used to enjoying what we call "breathing room." I recall a conversation with a teenage son of a close Italian friend of mine more than fifteen years ago. The young man had just returned from his first visit to America, and I asked him what he liked best about his experience. He said, "America is so open."

Now Europe is knocking down the walls, the borders, the boundaries, the endless demarcations that have separated people from their neighbors and strangers for more than two millennia of history. One can rent a car and make a pilgrimage across the continent without ever stopping at a border crossing. How do we know we've left France and entered Spain? Everything suddenly feels more open, more expansive. If it's not exactly the feel of big-sky country and lacks the majesty of America's open spaces, it still no longer feels so small and closed, as it once did traveling the old Europe. There is breathing room now, and no one is quite sure what to do about all of this newly acquired space.

But this much is for sure. There is a new experiment taking place in Europe. The whole of Europe has become a testing ground for rethinking commerce and politics and for re-imagining how people might conduct their lives with one another. The raw figures are daunting and give an idea of the breadth and scope, the sheer magnitude of the experiment. Twenty-five countries—big and small—across Europe have pooled their vast human and natural resources and made at least a partial commitment to share a common destiny. We Americans still think of the European Union as little more than a free-trade zone of sorts, something like the North American Free Trade Agreement (NAFTA) but more advanced. We're mistaken. It's much more.

The people of Europe have a common European Parliament with many powers previously reserved to nation-states, a European Court of Justice that supersedes the laws of the respective countries, and a European Commission to regulate trade, commerce, and a hundred and one other things that used to be handled exclusively by national governments. The Union has established its own military arm, a rapid-reaction force. It has agreed to establish a common foreign policy, and, with the ratification of its new constitution, it will have a Europe-wide foreign minister. In the course of the next two years, the twenty-five governments will ratify a Europe-wide constitution, formalizing their union. While there is still plenty of bickering about how much sovereignty should remain with individual nation-states and how much given over to the Union—the United Kingdom being the most reluctant consort in this new marriage—just as there was in the first one hundred years of the American union, like our own grand experiment, the path taken has the air of destiny.

The Birth of a New Kind of Economic Superpower

Europeans refuse to call their new union the "United States" of Europe for fear of confusing their experiment with our own two hundred years ago, although there are many parallels. Still, the differences are at least as significant as the likenesses, as we will explore in more depth in the pages that follow. What we are witnessing is the birth of a new political entity and a new commercial force on the world scene. The European Union, what some observers call the "reluctant empire," is already a looming giant, although still in its infancy. Four hundred and fifty-five million people are citizens of the European Union. They represent nearly 7 percent of the human race. While still fewer in number than China and India—each with a population exceeding 1 billion—the EU already overwhelms the U.S., whose 293 million people constitute 4.6 percent of the human race, and dwarfs Japan, whose 120 million citizens make up less than 2.1 percent of the human population on Earth.[1]

The European Union is now the largest internal single market as well as the largest trader of goods in the world. The EU is also the world's largest trader in services. In the year 2000, the EU accounted for 590.8 billion euros, or 24 percent of the total world trade in services, compared to the U.S., who ranked second with 550.9 billion euros and a share of 22 percent. Japan was a distant third, with 201.6 billion and an 8 percent share of the global market.[2] Moreover, unlike the United States, which runs on a trade deficit and imports more than it exports, the EU exports more than it imports.[3]

The European Union's Gross Domestic Product of $10.5 trillion in 2003 already exceeds the United States' $10.4 trillion GDP, and as we will see in a later section, even this figure masks additional economic strengths relative to America that are not accounted for in the GDP numbers.[4] The bottom line is that the EU's GDP already comprises nearly 30 percent of the GDP of the world, making the European Union a formidable competitor to America in the global economy.[5] (The EU's GDP is nearly 6.5 times larger than China's.)[6]

Corporeal Europe is still being formed. With the prospect of adding an additional four or five countries to the existing twenty-five countries over the course of the next decade, the Union will grow to fill a landmass stretching from Finland to the Mediterranean and from Ireland to the Black Sea. Much of the European Union's potential depends on its ability to create a streamlined and seamless internal trading market and commercial arena. It is in the early stages of creating a continental-wide transportation network, an integrated electricity and energy network, a common communication grid, a single financial-services market, and a unified regulatory framework for conducting business. The European Union has established what it calls Trans-European Networks (TENs), covering the transport, energy, and telecommunications sectors with the goal of connecting all of Europe under a single state-of-the-art, high-tech grid. The price tag for uniting Europe is expected to reach upwards of $500 billion and will be financed by both government and the private sector.[7]

Europe-wide educational programs are also being pursued. The European Union has initiated three high-profile educational programs: Socrates, Leonardo da Vinci, and the Youth program. Socrates covers general education from nursery school to adult education. The program establishes common educational projects, encourages student and teacher mobility between EU member countries, and is engaged in efforts to harmonize curricula. Its Erasmus project has provided grants to more than one million European students to study in another member country. The Comenius project has brought more than ten thousand schools together in cooperative education efforts across the EU. The Leonardo da Vinci program has helped more than two hundred thousand young people secure job training in another member country. The Youth program provides young people between the ages of fifteen and twenty-five with opportunities to do volunteer service either locally or in one of the other EU member countries.[8]

Perhaps the most challenging task on the road to European integration is accommodating the great disparity in income and job skills between workers in the Western and Northern European countries and workers in the new Central, Southern, and Eastern European economies. The entrance into the Union of seventy-five million new citizens from the Eastern and Southern countries has ignited fear in the West of a possible mass influx of cheap labor—both skilled and unskilled—into already beleaguered old Europe economies. There is also the concern that companies doing business in Western Europe will relocate more and more of their manufacturing and service operations in Eastern Europe, where labor costs are considerably lower. That's already begun to happen.

Gartner, the consulting firm, says that the Czech Republic, Poland, Slovakia, and Hungary are particularly attractive destination sites for Western European companies interested in outsourcing some of their operations to cheaper labor markets. Some companies, like the logistics firm DHL, have built their own operations in Eastern Europe. DHL set up an IT operations center in Prague in 2004.[9] Gillette, an American company, announced plans in 2004 to build a $148 million plant in Poland, shifting manufacturing and distribution from Britain and Germany to take advantage of cheaper labor costs. The new manufacturing facility will eventually employ 1,150 workers. As part of the restructuring, Gillette will close two plants in England and cut production and the size of its workforce in its Berlin factory.[10]

Western Europeans also worry that poor immigrants flocking in from the East will place an additional burden on already overtaxed welfare systems. The fear is so pronounced that most of the fifteen older member nations have already imposed various restrictions to keep Eastern European laborers out of their countries for several years. Eastern Europeans worry that Western European products coming into their economies will undermine domestic producers or raise prices for consumers.

Many other difficulties remain in creating a cohesive internal market across Europe. Still, the positive accomplishments far outnumber the remaining obstacles. Equally important, with English increasingly becoming the lingua franca of Europe—it's already the language used in many university and graduate school courses, especially in the business and science curricula—Europeans will be able to exchange their labor, goods, and services with an ease approaching that of the internal U.S. market. It will not happen overnight, but the process of integrating Europe into a unified internal market is already well along and will continue to gain momentum over the course of the next twenty-five years or so, when it should approach the level of integration we enjoy and even take for granted in the United States.

To the skeptics—and there are many—who doubt whether all of this is even possible, European leaders point out that, just a few years ago, the doubters, including many of America's leading economists and political pundits, were convinced that the introduction of a single common currency across the EU would fail. The euro succeeded beyond even the most enthusiastic projection of its supporters and is now stronger than the dollar—trading at $1.27 as of February 2004—and is becoming a rival in world financial circles.[11] The Russian Central Bank announced in 2003 that it would transfer some of its foreign reserves from dollars to euros, and even China has begun to make a small shift in favor of the euro.[12] Recently, Javad Yarjani, a senior official at the Organization of Petroleum Exporting Countries (OPEC), suggested that its member oil-producing countries might begin selling their oil in euros. After all, Europe is the Middle East's major trading partner and imports far more oil from the Persian Gulf than America. As mentioned, the EU also enjoys a greater share of global trade. Yarjani suggests that if Europe's two key oil producers, Norway and the U.K., were to adopt the euro—which is likely—"this might create a momentum to shift the oil pricing system to euros."[13] If that were to happen, oil-importing nations around the world would no longer need dollar reserves to purchase oil, and the demand for dollars could decline significantly, with serious ramifications for the American economy.

America's growing national debt is largely to blame for a 44 percent rise in the euro and a corresponding 31 percent fall in the dollar between July 2001 and December 2003.[14] The International Monetary Fund (IMF) is so concerned about U.S. debt—the result of a rising budget deficit and trade imbalance—that it issued a report warning that if steps weren't taken to reverse the trend, it could threaten the financial stability of the world economy. IMF economists say that U.S. financial obligations to the rest of the world could be equal to 40 percent of its total economy in just a few years. Economists worry that U.S. borrowing could become so high that it could force up global interest rates, slowing global investment and economic growth.[15]

The U.S. deficit was a staggering $374 billion in 2003 and is expected to exceed $521 billion in 2004.[16] More frightening, the IMF report concluded that the long-term fiscal outlook was even more grim. The IMF economists predict that underfunding for Social Security and Medicare in the U.S. will lead to shortages as high as $47 trillion over the next seven decades.[17] John Vail, senior strategist for Mizuho Securities USA, summed up the feelings of many foreign investors about the value of the dollar, saying, "The currency doesn't have the safe haven status that it has had in recent years."[18] Who would have dared to suggest just five years ago that the euro would be stronger than the dollar by the end of 2003?

So, why are so few Americans paying attention to the dramatic changes taking place on the other side of the pond? To a great extent, it's a question of perception. When we think of Europe, our context is a cultural or historical one. When we think of commerce and politics, however, our frame of reference quickly shifts to the individual countries of Europe—Germany, the U.K., France, and Italy. This older conception that associates commerce and politics with the nation-states of Europe is fast being contradicted by the new reality of a continentally defined superpower whose commercial muscle is beginning to be flexed on a more expansive global playing field.

While making comparisons between the U.S. and particular countries in Europe still makes some sense, at least in the political realm, and especially in foreign-policy matters, it makes less and less sense in the commercial sphere. The companies I am personally familiar with in Europe increasingly think of themselves as European—if not global—companies, just as in the United States, companies long ago stopped thinking of themselves as New York companies or California companies, but rather as American and global companies.

What this all means is that we have to begin to reframe our very concept of European states and begin thinking of them as part of the European Union, just as we think of the fifty American states as part of the United States. This fundamentally changes the way we make comparisons. For example, rather than thinking of Germany in comparison to the U.S., we should think of it in comparison to California—Germany being the largest state in the European economy and California the largest state in the U.S. economy. When we begin to shift the way we make comparisons, everything suddenly changes and we start to grasp the enormity of what's unfolding and the potential consequences for America. If we compare the GDP of Germany—the largest of the twenty-five states of the European Union—to the GDP of California, our largest state, we see that Germany's GDP of $1,866 billion (U.S. dollars) exceeds California's $1,344 billion GDP. The U.K., the European Union's second-largest state, with a GDP of $1.4 trillion, is nearly twice as large as our second-largest state, New York, with a GDP of $799 billion. France, with a GDP of $1.3 trillion, is nearly 50 percent larger than our third most powerful state economy, Texas, with a GDP of $742 billion. Italy, with a GDP of more than $1 trillion, is more than twice as big as our fourth most powerful state economy, Florida, with a GDP of $472 billion. Spain, with a GDP of $560 billion, edges out our fifth biggest state, Illinois, with a $467 billion GDP. The Netherlands boasts an economy larger than New Jersey's. Sweden's economy is bigger than that of Washington State. Belgium's economy eclipses Indiana's. Austria's GDP exceeds Minnesota's. Poland's economy is larger than that of Colorado. Denmark's is bigger than Connecticut's. Finland's GDP exceeds Oregon's. Greece's GDP is dead even with South Carolina's.[19]

When my colleagues and friends—on both sides of the Atlantic—have occasion to applaud or rail against the feats and follies of global companies, it's a sure bet that it's American companies that come to mind. That's not to say that they aren't aware of transnational companies whose headquarters reside somewhere outside U.S. shores. Toyota and Honda in Japan, Samsung in Korea, and BMW, Vivendi, and Nestlé in Europe are familiar names. But they believe that most giant corporations, the ones that dominate world commerce and trade, tend to have American roots. When the German auto giant Daimler-Benz bought out America's third-largest automaker, Chrysler, a few years ago, it was a shock to most working Americans, but treated as something of a fluke. Few Americans realize the power of European transnational companies. Sixty-one of the 140 biggest companies on the Global Fortune 500 rankings are European, while only fifty are U.S. companies, and twenty-nine are based in Asia.[20]

Royal Dutch/Shell and BP are now the fourth and fifth biggest companies in the world. Nokia, the Finnish company, is the number one producer of cell phones, with revenues of $28 billion. The company now controls nearly 40 percent of the worldwide mobile-phone market. Here's a company that was selling toilet paper and rubber boots just thirty years ago. By 1998, its mobile-phone division had surpassed Motorola to become the world's mobile mouthpiece.[21] Vodafone, the British telecom giant, with more than 100 million subscribers in twenty-eight countries, is the number-one or -two wireless operator in a dozen of the biggest markets in the world, including Britain, France, Switzerland, the Netherlands, Italy, and, yes, the United States. It turns out that the largest American wireless operator, Verizon Wireless, is a 45 percent owned joint venture with Vodafone.[22]

Chances are, most Americans aren't familiar with Bertelsmann, the

167-year-old German media company—the world's third largest after Time Warner and Walt Disney—and the largest book publisher in the world. Of course, Americans buy lots of books from the venerable American publisher Random House. What they don't know is that Random House is owned by Bertelsmann. Well, what about other well-known and long-established American book publishers Penguin, Putnam, and Viking? They are all owned by the British publishing giant Pearson.[23]

Americans are proud of Boeing and like to think that no other country surpasses American know-how when it comes to making airplanes. Not so. Airbus, the European consortium, has outperformed Boeing for the past three years and now controls 76 percent of the global airplane market.[24]

It's fair to say that Royal Ahold, the Dutch food retailer, has zero brand-name recognition in America, even though, with nearly $60 billion in revenue in 2002, it's the world's second-largest food retailer. Over the past decade, the Dutch company has quietly bought up virtually every major grocery-store chain east of the Appalachians and now operates more than 1,400 stores still under their original names, like Bi-Lo, Stop & Shop, Giant, and Bruno's. Ahold is currently the biggest food retailer on the East Coast of North America.[25]

Deutsche Post, the recently privatized German post office, is pressing ahead to become the world's leading delivery company and has made more than twenty acquisitions worldwide over the past several years, including the $1 billion purchase of Air Express, the largest U.S. air freight forwarder. It also owns a majority stake in the Brussels-based DHL International, the largest delivery company outside the United States. The American companies, United Parcel Service (UPS) and Federal Express, long bitter rivals, are so worried about the Deutsche Post plan to gain a dominant foothold in the United States that they have joined together, filing protests with the U.S. Department of Transportation, in an attempt to block the German company's expansion efforts in the States. The brouhaha between the American delivery companies and their new German competitor led *The Wall Street Journal* to quip that "American parcel delivery trucks have rumbled across the cobbled streets of Europe for more than two decades. Now European carriers say they want to find out if transparent borders work in both directions."[26]

It's surprising how little regard European companies are given in discussions around globalization. At antiglobalization protests at World Trade Organization (WTO) meetings, World Bank gatherings, and G8

Summits, the attention on the streets is generally on the evil machinations of U.S. transnational companies. Even in world policy forums, the focus is almost exclusively on American companies. Yet in so many of the world's key industries, it's European transnational companies that dominate business and trade.

European financial institutions are the world's bankers. Fourteen of the twenty largest commercial banks in the world today are European, including three of the top four: Deutsche Bank, Credit Suisse, and BNP Paribas.[27] In the chemical industry, the European company BASF is the world's leader, and three of the top six players are European.[28] In engineering and construction, three of the top five companies are European: Bouygues, Vinci, and Skanska; the two others are Japanese. Not a single American engineering and construction company is included among the world's top nine competitors.[29] In food and consumer products, Nestlé and Unilever, two European giants, rank first and second, respectively, in the world.[30] In the food and drugstore retail trade, two European companies, Carrefour and Royal Ahold, are first and second in the rankings, and European companies make up five of the top ten. Only four U.S. companies are on the list: Kroger, Albertsons, Safeway, and Walgreens.[31]

European companies dominate the global insurance industry. Eight of the top ten reinsurance companies are European, including Munich Re and Swiss Re, the first and second rated companies.[32] In the life and health insurance field, the top five are all European companies—ING, AXA, Aviva, Assicurazioni Generali, and Prudential.[33] In the property and casualty field, Allianz, the European company, is number one in the world, and five of the top nine are European companies.[34]

In the telecommunications industry, European companies hold six of the top eleven spots in the rankings.[35] In the pharmaceutical industry, U.S. companies have eclipsed their European rivals in recent years, with Merck, Johnson & Johnson, and Pfizer ranking first, second, and third in the global rankings. Still, GlaxoSmithKline, the British company, is fourth; Novartis, the Swiss company, is fifth; and Aventis, the French company, is sixth. European companies still hold five of the top ten rankings.[36]

In the motor vehicle and parts industry, General Motors and Ford are still on top, but DaimlerChrysler is third, and European automakers Volkswagen, Fiat, Peugeot, BMW, and Renault are all in the top twelve global companies.[37]

In a recent survey of the world's fifty best companies, conducted by *Global Finance*, all but one were European. The only U.S. company to make the list was Hilton. European performers such as Diageo, the giant premium-drink company—it owns Seagram's and Smirnoff;—Anglo American, the London-based mining company; Ryanair, the upstart low-cost Irish air-passenger carrier; SAP, the German business-software company; E.ON, the Düsseldorf-based energy company; the Swedish company Electrolux; L'Oréal, the French cosmetic giant; Diversified Services, the British distribution and outsourcing company; Philips, Europe's largest consumer-electronics company; and Hermes & Mauritz, the Swedish retailer, were among the companies singled out for praise for their innovative leadership and entrepreneurial acumen.[38]

All of this is not to suggest that European companies have suddenly leaped way ahead of their American competitors. In some industries, European businesses are clearly the market leaders, while in others, the U.S. companies still dominate. Rather, the message is that European-based global companies are able to match their American counterparts more often than not. And, in a number of instances, their successes are worth noting and learning from if American business is to stay competitive in global markets.

While Europe more than holds its own with the United States when it comes to its share of global corporate institutions, it also sports more small- and medium-sized enterprises than America. The U.S. business community is forever touting the idea that small businesses are the backbone of the American economy. In truth, the European Union has a far greater number of small- and medium-sized businesses (SMEs) than the U.S. In fact, SMEs currently represent two-thirds of the total employment in the EU, compared to only 46 percent of the total employment in the United States.[39]

Moreover, SMEs have been able to keep pace with the profitability of large companies by pooling their resources and talents in larger networks, including industrial clusters and cooperatives, to gain the advantages of economies of scale and scope without sacrificing the innovativeness and flexibility that often go along with smaller-scale operations.

The European Union has made a point of advancing the interests of SMEs and adopted the European Charter for Small Enterprises in 2000 to help promote their growth and development. Among other things, the

charter calls upon member states and the EU Commission to support education for entrepreneurship, legislation and regulation to help SMEs remain competitive; improved job skills; and the use of successful e-business
models. The EU has even created a "Global Information Network for
SMEs" to help them "exchange information on products, technologies,
and human resources" across borders so they can extend their activities to
the global marketplace.[40]

Measuring Success

On the whole, while the European Union is closing the gap with the U.S.
economy—and is much larger than its nearest rival, the Japanese economy—
it still has a long way to go to reach its goal of becoming the world's most
competitive and dynamic knowledge-based economy by 2010. (That goal
was set out at the European Union Council in Lisbon in March 2000.)
In an effort to benchmark its progress, the EU publishes the European
Innovation Scoreboard (EIS) each year, listing the European Union's
progress in seventeen main economic indicators. The indicators are divided into four categories: human resources for innovation; the creation
of new knowledge; the transmission and application of knowledge; and innovation finance, outputs, and markets. According to the report, the EU
leads the U.S. in three of ten indicators for which data is available: the
number of science and engineering graduates; public research and development (R&D) expenditures; and new capital raised. The EU still lags the
U.S., however, in seven other significant areas, including the share of
manufacturing value-added from high technology, the number of high-
technology patents, and the share of the working-age population with
some form of tertiary education.[41] It is interesting to note, however, that
Europe's leading economies—Denmark, Finland, the Netherlands, Sweden, and the U.K.—outdistanced both the U.S. and Japan in seven of the
ten comparable indicators. Moreover, the EU, overall, has been improving faster than the U.S. in four of the eight comparable indicators: Internet access, the registration of patents in the United States, per capita
information-technology spending, and participation in tertiary education.
The EU has gained on Japan in all seven of the indicators to which there
is comparable data.[42] The report's authors conclude that "the overall pos-

itive trend results suggest that the EU may be catching up with its main competitors."[43]

Most American economists, and even some European economists, are reluctant to acknowledge Europe's dramatic economic strides. Michael Mussa, former chief economist at the International Monetary Fund responsible for putting together the agency's world-growth forecasts, now with the Institute for International Economics in Washington, D.C., predicts that the U.S. growth rate in 2004 will be around 4.5 percent while that of Western Europe will be only 2 percent. Western Europe is expected to fare slightly better in 2005 at 2.25 percent while America's growth rate is expected to drop to 3.5 percent. Europe's less robust growth rate compared to the U.S. is cited as proof that the EU is falling further behind in the race to be the world's most competitive economy.[44]

The reason for Europe's poor performance, argue American economists, lies with the governments' inflexible labor policies, anti-entrepreneurial biases, overtaxation, and burdensome welfare programs—so-called "Euroschlerosis." What they conveniently ignore is that America's recent economic growth has not come without a steep price tag in the form of record consumer and government debt. The cost of stimulating the economy has been steep. The United States had to take on $1.5 trillion of additional debt between 2000 and 2004 and increase its annual government deficit to $500 billion in 2004 alone, while American families saw their savings rate hover at 2 percent. In a sense, America is paying for its improved short-term economic performance, at least in part, by borrowing against the future.[45]

Admittedly, many European companies rival their American counterparts, and the EU economy is nearly as competitive as our own, but doesn't America continue to produce more millionaires? Not so. According to a report compiled by Cap Gemini Ernst & Young along with Merrill Lynch, Europe boasts 2.6 million millionaires—individuals whose financial assets are at least $1 million (U.S. dollars), excluding home real estate—while North America has only 2.2 million millionaires. More telling, Europe added 100,000 millionaires to its roles in 2000, while North America dropped by 88,000 millionaires in the same year.[46] Surprisingly, of the 7.2 million millionaires in the world today, the greatest percentage—32 percent—live in Europe, and their numbers are growing faster than those of any other region.[47]

Although the EU economy is running almost head-to-head with the U.S. economy, the numbers don't tell the whole story. That's because the comparisons between the EU and the U.S. are being made by looking at their respective GDPs. The problem with this approach is that GDP gives a false sense of real economic well-being. For this reason, it has come under increasing criticism in recent years by economic reformers, and even policymakers inside some of the world's leading global economic institutions.

The GDP was created by the U.S. Commerce Department at the height of the Depression in the 1930s and was used first as a gauge for measuring the nation's economic recovery and then to monitor wartime production capacity during World War II. The fault with the GDP is that it doesn't discriminate between economic activity that really improves the standard of living of people and economic activity that does not.

In a scathing critique of GDP in *The Atlantic* magazine several years back, policy analysts Clifford Cobb, Ted Halstead, and Jonathan Rowe likened the tool to "a calculating machine that adds but cannot subtract."[48] In an era where "production"—any kind of production—was considered a sine qua non for measuring well-being, GDP became the standard reference for economists, business leaders, and politicians. GDP counts every economic activity as good. So if crime rises because of unemployment and poverty, requiring an increase in police protection and enforcement, court costs, prison costs, and a beefing up of private surveillance and protection, the economic activity it engenders finds its way into the GDP. If a toxic-waste dump needs to be cleaned up, an oil spill contained, or contaminated groundwater purified, again the economic activity adds to the total GDP. If the use of fossil fuels increases, it is added to the GDP, even though it means a depletion of existing stocks of nonrenewable energy. And if the health of millions of Americans deteriorates because of an increase in obesity, cigarette smoking, alcohol consumption, and drug use, the increased costs of health care are, likewise, added to the GDP. Same with the increased costs associated with protecting the nation against terrorism. The purchase of more missiles, airplanes, tanks, and bombs are all added to the GDP. One would be hard-pressed to say that any of these activities actually result in a net improvement in our quality of life. Here lies the rub. So much of our GDP—and an increasing percentage of it each year—is made up of economic activity that clearly does not improve our well-being.

The late senator Robert Kennedy best summed up the shortcomings of using Gross National Product to define the economic well-being of the country. He wrote,

The Gross National Product includes air pollution and advertising for cigarettes and ambulances to clear our highways of carnage. It counts special locks for our doors and jails for the people who break them. GNP includes the destruction of the redwoods and the death of Lake Superior. It grows with the production of napalm and missiles and nuclear warheads . . . it does not allow for the health of our families, the quality of their education, or the joy of their play. It is indifferent to the decency of our factories and the safety of our streets alike. It does not include the beauty of our poetry or the strength of our marriages, or the intelligence of our public debate or the integrity of our public officials . . . it measures everything, in short, except that which makes life worthwhile.[49]

Even the man who invented the GDP, Simon Kuznets—he later went on to win the Nobel Prize in 1971 for his accomplishment—warned in his first report to the U.S. Congress back in 1934 that "the welfare of a nation" can "scarcely be inferred from a measure of national income."[50] Thirty years later, Kuznets weighed in again on the subject, after having witnessed politicians and economists abusing the tool he invented for more than three decades. He wrote: "Distinctions must be kept in mind between quantity and quality of growth, between costs and returns, and between the short and the long run. Goals for 'more' growth should specify more growth of what and for what."[51]

A number of attempts have been made over the years to come up with a suitable alternative to GDP. The Index of Sustainable Economic Welfare (ISEW), the Genuine Progress Indicator (GPI), the Fordham Index of Social Health (FISH), the UN's Human Development Index (HDI), and the Index of Economic Well-Being (IEWB) are among the more popular indicators. They each attempt to determine "real" economic improvement in human welfare.

The earliest effort at establishing an alternative index was the ISEW, created by then World Bank economist Herman Daly and theologian John Cobb in 1989. Their index begins with personal consumption spending and then adds unpaid domestic labor. Then they subtract activity that is primarily designed to mitigate losses, like money spent on crime, pollution, and accidents. The ISEW also adjusts for income disparity and depletion of natural resources.[52] The GPI includes many of the same criteria but adds the value of voluntary work in the community and subtracts the loss of leisure time.[53] The FISH measures sixteen social-economic indicators, including infant mortality, child abuse, childhood poverty, teen suicide, drug abuse, high school dropout rates, average weekly earnings, unemployment, health insurance coverage, poverty among the elderly, homicides, housing, and income inequality.[54] The IEWB takes into account such things as the family savings rate and the accumulation of tangible capital such as housing stocks, which measure one's sense of future security.[55]

The question of how accurate the GDP is in measuring and monitoring real improvement or deterioration in our quality of life has come home for me over the course of the past twenty years. Beginning in the mid-1980s, I spent upwards of one-third of my time in Europe. I have visited virtually every part of the continent and stayed in small towns, rural communities, and large metropolitan areas. Because I was commuting, sometimes twice a month, back and forth, I was continually bombarded by the differences between America and Europe. The little things often caught my eye. For example, when I walk into men's rooms in Europe, the lights go on automatically and then shut off nine or ten minutes later whether I am done or not. Or when I enter most hotel rooms, I have to insert my card key into a slot for the lights to turn on. When I leave, I retrieve my card key from the slot and the lights automatically turn off. Similarly, when I'm at an airport or approaching an escalator, a light signals my presence and the escalator begins to move. All of these little devices are designed to save energy.

On the streets, I see very few homeless or mentally ill people. Although they certainly exist and their numbers are on the rise, they are not as visible a presence as they are on the streets of New York City, Washington, Chicago, and Los Angeles. People in Europe walk on the streets at night, even in the poor neighborhoods. Women often walk unaccompanied in the parks after dusk. While police are around, they seem fewer and less tense than the ones I'm familiar with on city streets in America.

When I'm in Europe, I rarely come across multitudes of fat and obese people. Sometimes, I can walk an entire day without encountering a single overweight person. In America, by contrast, it seems everyone is grossly overweight and, even more shocking, unaware or unconcerned about their appearance.

In Europe, I see men and women lingering for hours over food and drink in the eateries and outdoor cafés. Although not unusual in itself, what's strange is that I see them at these establishments at all hours, not just at lunch or at the end of the day, as would be the case in America. The first thought that crosses my mind is, Are these people all unemployed or just slow to get back to their desks and their assignments?

And no one seems to be rushing. No one. People still stroll in Europe. The older people often walk with their hands behind their backs, with one hand clasping the opposite wrist. I can't remember the last time I saw large numbers of people stroll on America's big-city streets. And while there is run-down housing and there are very poor neighborhoods all over Europe, they don't, for the most part, compare to the burned-out neighborhoods in the South Side of Chicago where I grew up or the Bushwick/Brownsville section of Brooklyn where I lived and worked as a VISTA volunteer after finishing my graduate studies at the university.

While graffiti on buildings has become epidemic in some parts of Europe—Milan comes readily to mind—I rarely experience the kind of urban blight that characterizes most American towns and cities. There appears to be more symmetry to the way everything is laid out in Europe. Living environments are more in scale. Adjoining neighborhoods, schools, and retail stores are usually within walking distance of one another or just a few minutes away by tram. And, here's a statistic sure to elicit envy: nearly six out of ten Europeans take less than twenty minutes to get to work.[56]

When I visit homes in Europe, people seem to have fewer things and be surrounded by less high-tech gadgetry. But what they do have is generally of very high quality and well taken care of. The same can be said about personal appearance. European men and women I know—mostly in the middle and upper middle class—don't have the extensive wardrobes some of my friends in the States enjoy. But what they do have is very high quality, and so when they go out, they appear to be put together better. The difference, I suspect, is that most mercurial and immeasurable of things called "style." In Europe, it's less about how much one has and more about how to enjoy one's life. Most Europeans are quite clear in this regard.

The point is, there is a very real and demonstrable difference in "the quality of life" one experiences in much of Europe compared with that in most parts of the United States. I have talked to countless Americans and Europeans, from every walk of life, who share similar thoughts on the matter. But, curiously, in my meetings with business leaders, economists, government policy wonks, and elected officials—especially in America—I hear only of how much better off America is, and, in case proof is needed, the GDP is invariably trotted out as a testimonial to the superiority of the American way of life.

But what if we were to really take seriously the criticisms waged against the GDP as a measure of well-being and began to fully take into account alternative criteria for assessing the quality of our lives? I believe it would become clear to any objective observer that, in many ways, the "United States" of Europe—while still in its infancy—has already eclipsed the United States of America and become a new kind of superpower.

Recall that the EU GDP is now approximately $10.5 trillion, while the U.S. GDP weighs in at $10.4 trillion. The $100 billion difference widens, however, if the GDPs are adjusted to reflect the negative activity that does not contribute to the improvement of people's everyday quality of life. Let's begin with the wide disparity in military expenditures. The twenty-five EU nations together devoted $155 billion in 2002 to defense-related spending. The U.S. defense expenditures for this same year totaled $399 billion, or $244 billion more than the total defense outlay for all of the European countries combined.[57] If the $244 billion were to be subtracted from the U.S. GDP, it would bring the U.S. GDP down to $10.16 trillion, broadening the gap between the EU and the U.S. to $344 billion.

Some might argue that subtracting the U.S. military expenditures is a bit unfair since the United States has had to take on the burden of defending Europe since the end of World War II. Were it not for America's superior military machine, and the U.S.'s willingness to act as Europe's protector through the North Atlantic Treaty Organization (NATO), Europe would have long ago had to beef up its own military machine to defend its regional and global interests. Fair enough. On the other hand, many Europeans argue that the U.S. military is far bigger than warranted in a post–Cold War world, and they remind the U.S. that the so-called "peace dividend"—the expected reduction in military expenditures that was supposed to result from the fall of the Berlin Wall and the end of the Cold War—has yet to materialize. While the threat of global terrorism poses new security issues that were not anticipated a decade ago, Europeans argue that these problems are best handled with a combination of police actions, soft diplomacy, and more sophisticated and generous development aid. In any event, say European analysts, if the $155 billion currently spent by all twenty-five European countries for defense was properly reorganized at a European level to establish a single streamlined rapid-reaction force for the continent—that effort is already partially under way—it would more than suffice to meet any potential military contingency.

The U.S.'s exorbitant and wasteful use of energy is another item that, if we adjusted for it, increases the gap even further between the European and U.S. GDPs. In 2000, the then fifteen EU member countries consumed 63.3 quadrillion British Thermal Units (BTUs) of energy. While this amounted to 16 percent of the world's total energy consumption for the year, it was 35.5 quadrillion BTUs less than the U.S. consumed during 2000. In other words, the U.S. consumed 98.8 quadrillion BTUs of energy, or nearly one-third more energy than the fifteen EU countries, even though the combined population of the EU at the time was 375 million people, or 102 million more people than lived at that time in the United States.[58]

The U.S. continues to consume one-third more energy than the European Union, with energy expenditures in excess of $703 billion in 2000 (the most recent figure available). This means that one-third of the total, or $234 billion, is simply a reflection of the wasteful use of energy and, if deducted from GDP, would increase the gap between the EU and U.S. GDP to about $578 billion.[59] If we were also to calculate the increasing expenditures for pollution abatement that result from the burning of one-third more energy than our European friends, the U.S. GDP would need to be adjusted downward again, to reflect the negative economic activity.

The U.S. also spends far more money on fighting crime and administering civil justice than any of the European countries. In 1999, more than $147 billion went into police protection, court administration, and prison maintenance, or 1.58 percent of that year's total GDP.[60] Again, if a portion of the $147 billion were deducted to allow for the gap in expenditures on crime in the U.S. and Europe, the GDP differential between the two superpowers would widen still more.

Other categories could be added to this list. What becomes clear is that the initial gap in GDP—with the United States running slightly behind the European GDP—turns out to be even more when adjustments are made for economic activity that is either destructive or does not contribute in any significant way to improving living standards.

Quality of Life

It's when we turn to very specific benchmarks for measuring economic well-being and quality of life, however, that the European Union begins to shoot ahead of the U.S. When we think about criteria for determining a good quality of life—what an economy should be all about—what comes immediately to mind is access to a decent education, assuring our good health, providing adequate care for our children, and living in safe neighborhoods and communities. In most of these particulars, the European Union has already surpassed the United States of America.

Take, for example, education. Americans are rightfully proud of our public education system. In the seventeenth century, Massachusetts became the first colony in the New World to accord children the right to a free education. (In 1635, Boston Latin School became the first public school in America.) Universal public education is among our most cherished institutions and a signature for a country that has long believed in equality of opportunity. The American Dream is built on the idea that everyone in America, regardless of the station or circumstances to which they were born, ought to be assured an education so that they might make the most of their lives.

No wonder American educators were taken aback by the results of the International Adult Literacy Survey (IALS) conducted in the mid-1990s and designed to compare the cognitive skills of adults in countries around the world. The survey found that Americans with less than nine years of education "score worse than virtually all of the other countries."[61]

In 2000, the OECD reported on a detailed global survey taken to assess reading literacy in various countries. The Program for International Student Assessment (PISA) "focuses on measuring the extent to which individuals are able to construct, expand, and reflect on the meaning of what they have read in a wide range of texts common both within and beyond school."[62] Again, Americans would be surprised to learn that our children rank fifteenth in the world in reading literacy, below eight Western European nations.[63]

Although the U.S. spends about the same proportion of our GDP—3.6 percent—on education as the EU countries, children in twelve European nations rank higher in mathematics literacy, and in eight European countries, the children outscored American kids in scientific literacy. Equally surprising, the average teenager in the EU finishes 17.5 years of education, while American teenagers, on the average, finish only 16.5 years of education. And, in nine European countries, more teenagers enter tertiary education (higher education) than in America.[64]

There is no better index of the well-being of a society than a nation's health. Americans have come to believe that we have the best overall health-care system in the world, and the healthiest population to boot. Although many Americans lament the fact that millions of their fellow citizens cannot afford private health-care insurance and aren't eligible for public assistance, we nonetheless believe that Americans still enjoy a health-care system second to none. Unfortunately, the facts don't support the belief. A comparison of health in the European Union and the United States is enlightening.

In the European Union, there are approximately 322 physicians per 100,000 people, whereas in the U.S., there are only 279 physicians per 100,000 people.[65] Not enough trained physicians is just the beginning of the health story. When it comes to ensuring health at the beginning of one's life, the U.S. ranks a distant twenty-sixth among industrialized nations, at seven deaths per 1,000 births, and scores well below the average in the EU.[66]

The U.S. fairs equally poorly at the other end of the life scale. While the average life expectancy in the European Union—excluding the ten new countries—is 81.4 years for women and 75.1 years for men, for a mean life expectancy of 78.2 years, the U.S. life expectancy for women is now 79.7 years and for men 74.2, for a mean life expectancy of 76.9 years. When the ten new Central and Eastern European countries are added to the EU averages, life expectancy falls to slightly below that of the United States.[67] Still, the fact that life expectancy throughout Western and Northern Europe is higher than in America would no doubt be greeted with incredulity by most Americans. Even worse, according to the World Health Organization (WHO), the U.S. currently ranks a dismal twenty-fourth in disability-adjusted life expectancy, far below our European friends.[68]

The WHO also ranked the countries of the world in terms of overall health performance, and the U.S. fell down even further, into thirty-seventh place. When it came to evaluating the fairness of countries' health care, the U.S. ranked still lower, to fifty-fourth, or last place among the OECD nations.[69]

Sadly, the U.S. and South Africa are the only two developed countries in the world that do not provide health care for all of their citizens.[70] More than forty six million people in America are currently uninsured and unable to pay for their own health care.[71]

The irony is that the United States spends more per capita for health care than any other nation of the world, according to the OECD—$4,900 per person in 2001.[72] Most of the increased cost is attributable to the high administrative costs and margins associated with running a for-profit health-care system. Moreover, because so many millions of Americans are uninsured, they cannot afford preventive care and do not attend to an illness at the outset. Waiting until the illness has advanced to a crisis increases the medical costs significantly.[73] The greater cost of health care is added to the GDP. Currently, more than 10 percent of the U.S. GDP goes to medical care.[74] Again, this is a perfect example of the disconnect between the measure of pure economic activity, reflected in the GDP, and the quality of life a society enjoys. The high cost of medical care in the U.S. boosts the U.S. GDP by more than 10 percent, despite the mediocre quality of the health care and the poor health of the American people.

The GDP and the nation's health intersect in many other interesting ways that are seldom discussed by economists. For example, obesity in the U.S. has now reached epidemic proportions, with more than 30 percent of all Americans now considered chronically obese. Worldwide, more than 300 million people are classified as obese.[75] Much of the growth in girth is attributable to junk food and a snacking culture promoted in the U.S. and now being exported by U.S. companies around the world. Obesity is a major contributing factor in the onset of type 2 diabetes, cardiovascular disease, and cancer.[76]

Although Europe is catching up to America in the increased incidence of obesity—as fast foods become an ever more prevalent part of the European diet—the U.S. obesity rate is still more than twice as high. In the fifteen EU countries for which figures are available, the percentage of obese people is 11.3.[77] Again, the more obese the American population, the bigger the GDP. Fast foods, junk foods, and processed foods account for an ever larger percentage of our total consumption of food. And the margins on these kinds of foods are much higher than for unprepared, unprocessed, raw foods. All of this jacks up the GDP still further. And then there are the medical costs. The World Health Organization estimates that obesity alone increases health-care costs by as much as 7 percent in some countries.[78] So the U.S. GDP continues to expand along with our waistlines, but our quality of life continues to diminish.

The United States has long been considered the land of opportunity. But if opportunity means starting off in life with sufficient financial resources to have a chance to make something out of oneself, then babies born in the European Union are far better positioned to succeed, from the very get-go. Childhood poverty in the United States is among the highest in the developed world. The United Nations Children's Fund (UNICEF) defines poverty this way: people in poverty are those whose "resources (material, cultural, and social) are so limited as to exclude them from the minimum acceptable way of life in the Member States in which they live."[79] The European Union defines poverty more specifically as "those whose incomes fall below half of the average income (as measured by the median) for the nation in which they live."[80] By these standards, 22 percent of all the children in the United States are living in poverty. U.S. childhood poverty now ranks twenty-second, or second to last, among the developed nations. Only Mexico scores lower. All fifteen highly developed European nations have fewer children in poverty than the U.S.[81] Even if we consider absolute poverty, using the U.S. equivalent of what constitutes poverty, U.S. children are still poorer than the children of nine European nations.[82] There are currently 11.7 million American children under the age of eighteen living below the U.S.-defined poverty line. And there are more poor children in America today than there were thirty years ago.[83]

Living in a safe environment is also one of the hallmarks of a good society. We have come to believe that the more affluent a society becomes, the more peaceful it is likely to be. If GDP is the standard, then the United States ought to be one of the safest nations on Earth. Yet Americans can tell you that it's far more dangerous to be out on the streets anywhere in America than to walk virtually everywhere unaccompanied in Europe. The statistics are chilling.

Between 1997 and 1999, the average rate of homicides per 100,000 people in the EU was 1.7. The U.S rate of homicide was nearly four times higher, or nearly 6.26 per 100,000 people.[84] More terrifying still, the U.S. Centers for Disease Control (CDC) reports that the rates of childhood homicides, suicides, and firearm-related deaths exceed those of the other twenty-five wealthiest nations in the world, including the fourteen wealthiest European countries. The homicide rate for children in the U.S. was five times higher than for children in the other twenty-five countries combined. The suicide rate among U.S. children was two times higher than all of the suicides combined in all the other twenty-five countries measured.[85]

It's not surprising that the U.S. incarceration rate is so high compared to that of the European Union. As mentioned earlier, in chapter 2, more than two million Americans are currently in prison—that's nearly one-quarter of the entire prison population in the world.[86] While EU member states average 87 prisoners per 100,000 population, the United States averages an incredible 685 prisoners per 100,000 population.[87]

The European Commission has begun work on developing a "European System of Social Reporting and Welfare Measurement" with an eye toward establishing a more accurate mechanism for measuring the "real" economic progress of its 455 million citizens.[88]

The European Commission study group on the subject has laid out an architectural blueprint of the kinds of things that should go into a social accounting, beginning with the concept of "quality of life," which it defines as the "immaterial aspects of the living situation like health, social relations or the quality of the natural environment."[89] Quality of life also should include "actual living conditions," as well as "the subjective well-being of the individual citizens," says one of the authors of the initial study papers.[90]

In America, while we assume that every person is endowed with "certain inalienable rights, among which are life, liberty, and the pursuit of happiness," we believe that more economic growth will ensure the good life. In Europe, academics, policy people, and the public at large are skeptical. They say that growth, by itself, is no guarantee of a better life for the people. The European Commission is looking at a host of other indicators to measure happiness, including the extent to which social cohesion is deepened, social exclusion is diminished, and social capital is grown. It wants an economy that is sustainable, "that meets the needs of the present without compromising the ability of future generations to meet their own needs."[91]

Europe is not yet ready to abandon the old GDP scale. Yet, the very fact that a world superpower is seriously engaged in the process of re-thinking what the criteria ought to be for measuring economic growth and for determining the basis of a good economy is nothing short of revolutionary. In the United States, at the federal level, except for a single speech on the U.S. Senate floor by Democratic senator Byron Dorgan back in 1995, there has been no discussion of rethinking the way the U.S. defines economic progress.[92] Indeed, it's probably fair to say that were any of the president's council of economic advisers to even introduce the subject, he or she would be met with snickers of disbelief among fellow economists. Yet, in Europe, the powers that be appear willing, even eager, to challenge the old shibboleths and reconstitute some of the most basic assumptions of what economic progress should be about.

What does all of this have to do with the American and European dreams? When people think of the older American Dream, what comes to mind is the idea that anyone can go from rags to riches. By contrast, the new European Dream is more about advancing the quality of life of a people. The first dream emphasizes individual opportunities, the second, the collective well-being of society. When it comes to the question of individual opportunities, however, the evidence suggests that Europe is fast catching up to the United States. As to quality of life, it's clear that Europe has moved ahead of America.

THE TUG BETWEEN EUROPE and America goes even deeper than questions of personal opportunity and quality of life. What really distinguishes the comings and goings in Europe and America today is that Europe is busy preparing for a new era while America is desperately trying to hold on to the old one. There is a sense of excitement across Europe, a feeling of new possibilities. To be sure, the feeling varies somewhat in intensity from country to country and region to region and even between young and old. There are also significant pockets of resistance to a transnational political space. Still, one gets the sense that Europeans know they are creating something new and bold and that the whole world is watching them. If I were to sum it up, I would say that Europe has become a giant freewheeling experimental laboratory for rethinking the human condition and reconfiguring human institutions in the global era.

Many observers—especially Americans—view the developments in Europe with whimsy or disdain or, worse still, indifference. The hard-line cynics are even less charitable, seeing the efforts afoot to create a "United States" of Europe as quixotic, and ultimately futile. European critics voiced similar reservations about our own experiment in forging a United States of America more than two hundred years ago. They proved wrong then, and I suspect we will be proved wrong this time around.

The emerging European Dream isn't just a glib political catchphrase. There are profound changes occurring in Europe at the personal, institutional, and even metaphysical level. Even most Europeans, when pressed, aren't exactly sure what they've gotten themselves into. Our American founders must have felt the same way. But if there are doubts and qualms, a sense of frustration and bewilderment, all that is to be expected of a people in the midst of rewriting the human story.

It is true that Europe is becoming a new land of opportunity for millions of people around the world in search of a better tomorrow. Europe's emphasis on quality of life does indeed distinguish it from the older American model, with its singular attention to growth and the accumulation of personal wealth. But there is much more to the European Dream. In a world growing weary of grand utopian visions and more comfortable with individual story lines, the new European Dream has dared to create a new synthesis: one that combines a post-modern sensitivity to multiple perspectives and multiculturalism with a new universal vision. The new European Dream takes us into a global age.

In order to really understand the depth of the changes that are remaking Europe, it is essential to remember Europe's past. The new European Dream is not so much a repudiation of the past as it is a building off of it. Dreams take us to where we would like to go, but to get there, we first need to know what we are leaving behind. Every journey has a starting point as well as a destination. In the case of the new European Dream, the starting point is not the new millennium or even the post–World War II era but, rather, the twilight period between the late medieval and early modern era, when many of the conventions we have come to know under the heading of "modernity" began to take hold. These conventions include the Enlightenment and the beginning of modern science, the flowering of the individual, the establishment of a private property regime, the formation of market capitalism, and the birth of the nation-state. The shift to a global era is forcing a rethinking of all of these well-worn conventions of the modern age. So, to understand the path that Europe's new dream is forging, we first need to revisit its older byways to gain a reference point and, hopefully, some insights to help guide our journey.

What we are going to find, by retracing European history, are the roots of the American Dream that we discussed in chapter 1. Although historians rarely allude to it, the reality is that the American Dream represents the thinking of a moment of time, frozen in European history and transported whole cloth to American shores in the eighteenth century, where it continued to animate the American experience right up to the present day. The American Revolution took place at the very time that a waning Protestant Reformation was making its final accommodation to the new forces of the Enlightenment. While much of Europe eventually combined elements of the Protestant Reformation theology and Enlightenment ideology into a new synthesis wrapped up in democratic socialism, America did not. Instead, successive generations of Americans chose to live out both the Protestant Reformation and Enlightenment traditions simultaneously and in their purest forms, becoming, at one and the same time, the most devoutly Protestant people on Earth and the most committed to scientific pursuits, a private property regime, market capitalism, and nation-state ideology. The American Dream, in the fullest incarnation, is an amalgam of both these earlier forces that shook Europe from its medieval moorings and propelled it into the modern age. In a very real sense, then, the American Dream is largely a European creation, uprooted and replanted on American soil and bred to fit America's unique environment.

We Americans like to think of ourselves as forward-thinking, with our attention focused on the distant horizon. However, our worldview, strangely enough, is locked into a specific period of time long since passed by in European history. In short, the American Dream is a very old dream and becoming increasingly irrelevant in the new era of globalization.

In the next four chapters, we are going to retrace the philosophical and institutional changes that gave rise to the modern age, in order to better understand Europe's own past and the American Dream that grew out of it. Knowing what Europe is leaving behind is essential to knowing where it's heading as it prepares a new dream for a global era.

THE MAKING

of the

MODERN AGE

Space, Time, and Modernity

THE GREAT TURNING POINTS in human history are often triggered by changing conceptions of space and time. Sometimes, the adoption of a single technology can be transformative in nature, changing the very way our minds filter the world. Consider, for example, the cell phone. Europeans were the first to enthusiastically embrace mobile-communications technology. I remember sitting with my wife in a fashionable upscale eatery in Milan many years ago, when we heard a phone ring from somewhere at a nearby table. The middle-aged man pulled a mobile phone from his jacket pocket and began an animated and lengthy conversation with someone on the other line. My wife turned to me with a quip, "Wait until American teenagers get ahold of this little toy."

Americans Are from Mars, Europeans Are from Venus

Americans subsequently took to cell phones. But the point is that the wireless revolution took off, in a big way, first in Europe. In 2000, the EU boasted 661 cellular mobile subscribers per 1,000 people, compared to only 308 subscribers per 1,000 people in the U.S., putting Europe far ahead of the rest of the world in early adoption of wireless telecommunications technology.[1] After centuries of being surrounded by walls and living in a fortress mentality, suddenly Europeans found a way to break out, to liberate themselves. The cell phone brought with it a new kind of freedom: mobility, to be sure, but different from the kind that drew millions of Americans to buy Henry Ford's cheap Model T car nearly one hundred years earlier.

For Americans, the automobile was a way to grab hold of the vast expanse of the American landscape—to expropriate and colonize it and make it more manageable and manipulable. The very name "auto-mobile" struck a chord. Americans, more than any other people, have come to view security in terms of "autonomy" and "mobility." On the frontier, where human exchange is sparse and the elements threatening, being self-reliant and mobile is a way to ensure one's security. Autonomy, mobility, and freedom have always come as a package in America. To be autonomous is to be independent and not beholden to others. Mobility, in turn, ensures endless new opportunities. The American cowboy and his horse enshrine the myth. Fiercely independent and always on the move, he was a free spirit that captured, so pointedly, the American frame of mind. With the passing of the great American frontier, and the cowboys who tamed it, Henry Ford sold a mechanical surrogate of the horse. The automobile allowed every American to exercise the same sense of freedom that cowboys must have felt atop their steeds, roaming the Western frontier.

In Europe, the sensibilities ran along a different vein. A frontier mentality of sorts existed, but in a more vicarious fashion. The various colonial adventures of the great European powers drew Europeans to the four corners of the Earth. Some came as settlers—to America, Australia, and South Africa—and adopted a frontier psyche. But many others came as colonial administrators, military personnel, and agents representing business and political interests back home. They were extensions of the Old World and never really shed their Europeanness.

For Europeans, the search for security was always more bound up in embeddedness in communities—whether indentured in medieval fiefs or fortressed away in craft guilds in walled towns. One was secure to the extent one was nested in a community that, in turn, was safe from invasion or encroachment from the outside. The drawbridge, the moat, and the lookout tower are the architectural symbols of the European sense of space. The idea of a lone, self-reliant individual freely roaming across an endless frontier even today makes little sense to Europeans.

The early success of mobile-phone technology in Europe speaks volumes. The cell phone keeps individuals connected to their communities. But it also allows individuals to break out from the constraints of geography, to be free of place but still connected to others in time. And this gets to one of the fundamental differences in how Europeans and Americans conceive of space and time. Americans covet exclusive space. Each person strives to be self-contained and autonomous. That's why we put a premium on privacy. Europeans seek inclusive space—being part of extended communities, including family, kin, ethnic, and class affiliation. Privacy is less important than engagement. For Americans, time is future-directed and viewed as a tool to explore new opportunities. For Europeans, time is more past- and present-oriented and used to reaffirm and nurture relationships.

A comprehensive anthropological study of how people use mobile phones in six countries bears out some of the differences in how Europeans and Americans relate to the new wireless technology. In Sweden, for example, "they view someone talking on their mobile as though the person with whom they're speaking is physically in the room."[2] As a result, chatting on a mobile phone while eating lunch alone in a restaurant is perfectly acceptable behavior. Italians believe in constant connectivity and like to be reachable at all times. They have no reservations about using mobile phones in any public setting. Americans are a bit more circumspect in their use of mobile phones. New Yorkers, for example, tend to use their mobile phones more to accomplish tasks but also believe that having wireless conversations in public is often intrusive and a violation of others' private space. While San Franciscans use mobile phones for work- and leisure-related activity and to communicate with friends, some worry about being constantly available all the time, and not having enough alone time.[3]

Some commentators have said that "Americans are from Mars and Europeans are from Venus"—that on a very fundamental level, we think so differently that neither can truly understand the thinking of the other. There's some truth to that argument. While the American consciousness has deep roots in the Old World, the very act of crossing the ocean to recast one's fate and fortunes in new ways marked a psychological breach as deep and wide as the waters that separate the two continents.

Those who came to America were the ones who were forced out of their countries or who no longer found security in their former relationships. Some were adventurers anxious to escape their confinement. Others were poor and destitute, and willing to sacrifice, and even to die, to find a new, more secure existence. The ones who left were in search of a new kind of security. They found it on the American frontier. Those who stayed behind continued to look to tight-knit communities for their solace.

Today, these very different attitudes about security find their expression in a hundred and one different ways in the marketplace, the civil society, and in the halls of government. Europeans tend to favor social democracy and a community commitment to redress the plight of the less fortunate and the poor, whereas Americans preach the virtues of self-reliance and favor a market approach to bettering the lot of their fellow human beings. For Europeans, Karl Marx's words still find resonance: "From each according to his abilities, to each according to his needs." Americans prefer to cast their lot with the Scottish economist Adam Smith, who preached a different kind of catechism. In his celebrated *An Inquiry into the Nature and Causes of the Wealth of Nations*, Smith laid forth the controversial notion that in a perfectly administered capitalist market economy, each individual works to pursue his own interest, and it is his own welfare alone to which he is dedicated. But in the act of securing his own material well-being, he inadvertently increases the general stock and improves the well-being of his fellows and the rest of society.

These two very distinctive and contradictory starting points for defining security lead to two divergent journeys in the age of globalization. The software and computer revolutions, the World Wide Web, the mobile communications revolution, the historic shift from a centralized fossil-fuel-energy era into a decentralized hydrogen-energy future, and the spread of biotechnologies, and soon nanotechnologies, into every nook and cranny of human life are all leading to fundamental changes in the way we human beings conceive of space and time, as well as to a rethinking of the kinds of institutional responses that will be needed to accompany our changing consciousness of the world around us. My hunch is that the newly emerging European Dream is far better suited to addressing the spatial and temporal realities of a globalized world than the older American Dream.

Europe's Obsession with Space and Time

From the great European awakening in the late medieval era till now, successive generations have been steadily extending their spatial reach and quickening the pace, speed, flow, connectivity, and density of human exchange. Human activities extended from village to region, then to territorial nation-states, and now to the globe itself. Europe is, today, at the forefront in the struggle to redefine the human condition and the kind of world we will need to fashion to accommodate our new global reach.

Europe was also the conceptual meeting ground the last time around, at the outset of the modern era, when attention turned to the revolutionary changes in technology and philosophy that, at the time, were beginning to reshape spatial and temporal consciousness. Understanding how Europeans of former generations responded to the challenges of an earlier era, and why they chose the specific philosophical, economic, political, and social paths they did to make the transition to modernity, provides a context and a backdrop for understanding the deep changes occurring today as humanity experiments with new spatial and temporal models for the coming century.

It is the introduction of new technologies that change our consciousness of spatial and temporal relationships. Tools are an extension of our being. They are a way to amplify our senses so that we can expand our reach in order to expropriate space, compress time, and secure ourselves. A gun extends the power of our throwing arm. An automobile is an extension of our legs. Computers amplify our memories.

Between the late medieval age and the early modern era, a spate of dramatic new technologies were introduced into Europe that vastly increased human power over space and time.

The introduction of the heavy wheeled plow into Northern Europe and the substitution of horses for oxen as well as the shift from two-field to three-field rotation brought much more land under cultivation and increased the yield per acre, doubling food production by the thirteenth and early fourteenth centuries.[4] The food surpluses led to a dramatic growth in the human population, which, in turn, led to rapid urbanization. Village hamlets gave way to small towns and then cities. The cities attracted skilled artisans and merchants and stimulated the beginning of sustained domestic commerce and trade, for the first time since the fall of the Roman Empire.[5]

Thousands of water mills and windmills were built across Europe, providing a new source of inanimate power for grinding grain, making beer, sawing wood, producing paper, fulling cloth, and operating the bellows of blast furnaces. By the fourteenth century, Europeans could claim significant strides in substituting mechanical for human power in most of the basic industries.[6]

A German, Johannes Gutenberg, invented the first print press with movable type in 1436, creating a revolution in communications that would become the indispensable command-and-control mechanism for organizing modern commerce and trade and for speeding up transactions and exchanges.

Keeping track of vastly sped-up commercial transactions taking place over much longer distances required the kind of record-keeping that would have simply been impossible in an oral or script culture. Modern bookkeeping, schedules, bills of lading, invoices, checks, and promissory notes, all so critical to the flow of modern commerce, were products of print technology. And print made possible the system of uniform pricing, without which modern notions of market exchange could not have evolved.

Print also changed spatial and temporal relationships in other profound ways. The late Walter J. Ong reminds us that because in oral cultures learning was passed on by word of mouth, storytelling and proverbs were ways to keep knowledge alive. Skills were passed down between parent and child and between master and apprentice by mouth. Very little practical knowledge was ever written down. Because communication was oral, it required close proximity between speakers and listeners. Oral cultures, by their very nature, are more intimate and communal.

Print cultures are very different. The author of an article or book rarely comes into close physical contact with the reader. Writing and reading are both carried out in relative privacy. Print breaks down the communal bond and reinforces the radical new idea of communications between people separated by great distances.

Printed books also brought the world into every home. It was now possible to learn about people in far-off lands. The human imagination was lifted from the parochialism of the immediate environment and allowed to roam the Earth.

The improvements made in the compass and the increasing use of maritime charts and maps allowed European explorers and adventurers to circumnavigate the African continent and cross the Atlantic to America. The colonization of vast new lands had a dramatic effect on Europeans' sense of space.[7] All of a sudden, the world was a much bigger place. Filling it became a European obsession. Millions of Europeans migrated to the far reaches of the Earth in ensuing centuries, spreading their religious, economic, and political beliefs in the firm conviction that they were bringing the light of civilization to the primitive and backward peoples of the Earth. In Britain alone, more than a million people sailed to America, Australia, and New Zealand in just one short twenty-five-year period between 1815 and 1840.[8]

The shift in energy regimes from wood to coal and the introduction of the steam engine in the late eighteenth century greatly accelerated the pace, flow, and density of economic activity. The industrial revolution quickly found its legs. After nearly ten thousand years of society relying on human and animal power and the wind and currents to propel itself, steam power now afforded a qualitative leap in the harnessing of the Earth's energy. The time taken to travel distances was shortened, and human exchanges—of both a social and commercial nature—were sped up. Just a few hundred years ago, the average human being, isolated in rural villages and small walled towns, might come in contact with no more than a few hundred people in a lifetime. By 1863, London—the first city since the fall of Rome to reach a population of more than one million—could boast several mail deliveries a day. A letter posted early in the morning to another London address could not only bring a reply, but do so in time for a further letter from the first writer to be delivered before the day was out.[9]

Faster, cheaper, and safer modes of travel—steamships and trains— broadened people's spatial horizons more profoundly than in any previous period in human history. By 1830, an émigré could set sail from Europe on a steamship to America and pay as little as two pounds for the passage.[10] Journeying over longer distances used to be so dangerous that the root of the word "travel" is "travail." By the nineteenth century, travel had become, of all things, a form of entertainment. An enterprising Englishman, Thomas Cook, began ferrying people by train, and later by ship, to visit places of fascination and interest. He called his adventures "excursions."

The reorganization of space and time in the early modern era wreaked havoc on the institutions of medieval Europe. The Church, the feudal economy, and warrior kingdoms proved too provincial and slow to accommodate the dramatic spatial and temporal changes that were remaking European life, and they eventually gave way to three new institutions— modern science, the market economy, and the nation-state. The new institutions were far better equipped to organize human life in a radically different spatial and temporal setting.

Similarly, today, orthodox science is being shaken to its foundations by new ways of understanding and organizing nature. Likewise, the market economy is being challenged by a new network model for organizing commerce and trade. Meanwhile, the nation-state is steadily making room for regional and global forms of governance that can better assimilate the new technological realities and changes in human consciousness that characterize the era of globalization.

To fully grasp the importance of the current experiment unfolding in Europe, we need to step back and relook at how and why modern science, the market economy, and the nation-state emerged in Europe in the wake of the last great transformation of spatial and temporal consciousness. By doing so, we can begin to appreciate the enormity of the task at hand for the new Europe as it begins to reinvent itself once again for a new era.

Colonizing Nature

A number of important changes occurred in the way Europeans organized their relationship to the natural world in the early modern era. Those changes gave birth to what we know today as modern science.

First, the world of nature was demystified or desacralized, depending on whether you adhere to the rational or romantic school of thought. The very idea of nature as a reality unto itself, a primal kingdom, or fallen Eden, gave way to the more modern utilitarian idea of nature as a storehouse full of raw resources waiting to be made productive by science and put to use in the marketplace.

The artists of the Renaissance, interestingly enough, became the unknowing agents who helped chase God from his earthly kingdom, only to make room for the new overseers, the men of science. Donatello, Uccello, and Piero della Francesca had no idea that the radical new invention called "perspective" would eventually help topple a millennium of church rule.

Our story begins with the great cathedrals of medieval Europe. The first thing American tourists notice when visiting Europe's magnificent places of worship is that there is no way to get a decent photograph of the grand edifices from any distance. Most of the major cathedrals of Europe are ensconced in the center of old cities and surrounded by ring upon ring of buildings extending outward in concentric circles. There is sometimes a plaza in front of the main portico, like the ones at the Cathedral of Nôtre Dame in Paris and the Duomo in Milan. But, for the most part, the cathedrals are buried by their human surroundings. They are meant to be a magnet, drawing everyone from the surroundings to them. They are purposefully in the very center of their communities—a strong reminder that in days of yore, life was lived in a cocoon of embedded relationships and the church was the soul of the community.

We Americans are in love with views, especially from commanding heights. If we can afford it, we'd much prefer to place our home at the very top of a hill, and at a distance from our nearest neighbors, affording us a daily reminder of our autonomy. Our sense of exclusivity makes us feel secure and free. But Europe is laid out differently. Everything is nested up against everything else. The old parts of cities—even the newer sections— are tightly knit together with little space separating neighbors. Partly, this is due to the sheer density of population and the unavailability of land. But mostly, the antecedents stretch back in time to an era where people lived in walled cities or on feudal estates. Outside the city walls and fiefs was a world full of uncertainty and risks. In parts of Northern and Central Europe, until the late medieval era, dense forests lay just beyond the cultivated fields and pastures.

The architecture of old Europe reflects the very different way Europeans of an earlier era perceived space and their own security. In the Middle Ages, one's sense of security was vertically directed. People looked to the heavens in hopes of securing their eternal salvation and looked down to their ancestral grounds beneath them, where security lay in their honored traditions and community associations.

In feudal Europe, people belonged to the land and not vice versa. One was born into a station in life and was expected to fulfill a litany of communal obligations that went hand in hand with one's inherited status. The Christian life was caught up in a larger drama. Space was perceived as a great ladder, a chain of being stretching from the lowliest creatures on Earth to God on high. Each creature was assigned a rung on the ladder of life and expected to serve those higher up as well as to provide for those below. It was a community where rank and membership were determined by heredity.

Examine some of the beautiful paintings and tapestries that line the church walls in Europe, and you notice that all of the living forms—animals and humans—ascend on a flat plane reaching upward like the great ladder of life that they are depicting. Absent is any sense of perspective. It's not that the artists of the time were incapable of showing perspective. Rather, perspective was simply not part of the consciousness of the period. In a world where security is found in a tightly bound vertical plane, perspective is rarely considered.

The introduction of perspective in art during the early Renaissance was a revolution in the human conception of space. For the first time, "man's" gaze turned from the heavens above to the "landscape" beyond. Perspective places the individual, for the first time, at the center of his world. We see the picture through the eyes of the beholder. It is through man's eyes, and not God's grace, that we view the world beyond. And everything in the field of view becomes the object of man's attention. Perspective brings human beings into a new spatial realm of subject-object relationships. It is the beginning point for what the sociologist Max Weber would later describe as the "disenchantment of the world."

The point is, the great cathedrals of Europe were not built with the idea of being seen from a distance. The very act of "placing them in perspective" would be to diminish them and relegate them to a lower status, making them the object of human interpretation. Rather, the great cathedrals were designed with the idea of fixing everyone's gaze upward from the moment they walks inside, which is exactly what every visitor still does when they enter one of these grand temples.

Just imagine the change in consciousness that perspective brought. For early Christians, the world was thought of as just a temporary stage, a place to prepare for one's eternal and everlasting salvation in the world to come. What counted was the community of believers, huddled together—as they are depicted in most medieval paintings—and awaiting the triumphant return of Christ the Lord. Perspective reconfigured human consciousness toward the horizontal world of the here and now and repositioned each human being to eventually become lord over his or her own earthly domain.

Perspective migrated from the canvasses of the Renaissance artists to the writing tables of pre-Enlightenment philosophers, where it became the main conceptual tool for remaking the natural world in "man's image." Francis Bacon, the father of modern science, wrote his two most important works, *The Novum Organum* and *The New Atlantis*, in the early seventeenth century. The idea of perspective figured prominently in his rethinking of spatial relations and man's role on Earth.

Bacon was particularly hard on ancient Greek science, with its emphasis on pondering the why of things. The Greeks, he wrote, had not "adduced a single experiment which tends to relieve and benefit the condition of man."[11] Bacon was far less interested in contemplating nature and far more interested in harnessing it. He preferred the how of things to the why of things. In his master work, *The Novum Organum*, he outlines a radical new schema for organizing the natural world, which he called the scientific method. This new tool borrows critical insights from the artist's conception of perspective. His method was based on the notion of separating the observer from the observed, creating, in effect, a neutral forum for the development of what he called "objective knowledge." The scientific method, like perspective in art, put man at the center of the universe and transformed everything within his field of vision into an object for human expropriation. If the artist appropriated a likeness of nature onto the canvas, the scientist did roughly the same on the laboratory bench. Nature ceased to be a realm of awe and was reduced instead to resources waiting to be remade in man's image. Armed with objective knowledge, Bacon claimed it would be possible to "enlarge the bounds of human empire to the affecting of all things possible."[12]

Whereas the ancients viewed knowledge as a window to the divine, Bacon saw it as a way to exercise power over all of nature. By relying on the scientific method, nature could be "forced out of her natural state and squeezed and molded."[13] Throughout his writings, Bacon emphasized the need to mount an all-out assault against nature. With the scientific method, he boasted that we have "the power to conquer and subdue" nature and "to shake her to her foundations." The goal of the new science, said Bacon, was to "establish and extend the power of dominion of the human race itself over the universe."[14]

While Bacon provided a methodology for organizing nature, it was the great seventeenth-century French philosopher René Descartes who provided the conceptual format for transforming nature into a resource. He found what he regarded as the Rosetta stone for deciphering and manipulating nature's secrets in the universal laws of mathematics. He wrote,

As I considered the matter carefully, it gradually came to light that all those matters only are referred to mathematics in which order and measurement are investigated, and that it makes no difference whether it be in numbers, figures, stars, sounds, or any other object that the question of measurement arises. I saw, consequently, that there must be some general science to explain that element as a whole, which gives rise to problems about order and measurement. This, I perceived, was called universal mathematics. Such a science should contain the primary rudiments of human reason, and its province ought to extend to the eliciting of true results in every subject.[15]

Descartes stripped nature of its subjectivity and aliveness and replaced it with a rational and calculable domain. "To speak freely, I am convinced that it [mathematics] is a more powerful instrument of knowledge than any other that has been bequeathed to us by human agency, as being the source of all things."[16]

The rationalization of nature, in the form of mathematical measurement, brought it a step closer to becoming thought of as a resource. John Locke, the English political philosopher, turned the final screw with his view on the worth of nature. For Locke, any question of the intrinsic value of nature was, to be blunt, bunkum. Locke argued that "land that is left wholly to nature, is called, as indeed it is, waste."[17] Locke contended that pristine nature had no other purpose but to be used by human beings to better their lot. He wrote,

Let anyone consider what the difference is between an acre of land planted with tobacco or sugar, sown with wheat or barley, and an acre of the same land lying in common without any husbandry upon it, and he will find that the improvement of labor makes the far greater part of the value.[18]

Locke, ever the pragmatist, believed that "the negation of nature is the way to happiness."[19] He reasoned that as long as human beings remain vulnerable to the forces of nature, then security could never be assured. True security for Locke, and other Enlightenment thinkers, could be achieved only if "man effectively emancipated [himself] from the bounds of nature."[20] The key to human liberation was the ever greater expropriation, accumulation, and consumption of nature's bounty.

The mathematical rationalization of nature and its conversion to a storehouse of resources marked a turning point of great import in the passage from medieval to modern life. It doesn't mean that medieval man and woman were unmindful of the need to expropriate nature for their survival. In Genesis, God instructs Adam and Eve to be fruitful and multiply and gives them dominion over everything that lives on Earth. As we've already learned, in the late medieval era, Europeans increasingly turned their attention to all sorts of new technologies to secure an ever greater portion of nature's largesse. Nonetheless, their spatial and temporal reference was still, for the most part, focused vertically on the passage to salvation in the next world. There was little thought of remaking God's kingdom into an earthly cornucopia.

The rethinking of all of nature in mathematical terms had another, more subtle effect on European society. From the very beginning of human settlement, space had been synonymous with place. To be somewhere was to be in a unique place with its own history and story. Spaces were about places. By reducing everything in the world—and the universe—to abstract mathematical measurement, Enlightenment philosophers succeeded in effectively eliminating any sense of lived experience. In the new scheme of things, all that really mattered was location and movement. "Give me extension and motion," Descartes exclaimed, and "I will reconstruct the Universe."[21]

Henceforth, the very idea of place slowly diminished and eventually virtually disappeared from intellectual discussions, replaced by the notion of "location," "site," and, later, "point." A place was merely a location or site, or a point of reference between other locations, sites, and points—all measurable. Successive generations were being prepared to rationalize nature, even human nature, as well as the institutions that govern human behavior and activity. The twentieth-century mathematician-philosopher Bertrand Russell once remarked that mathematics has "a beauty cold and austere."[22]

Although Descartes was convinced that mathematics was the key to unlocking the inner workings of the universe, it was the Enlightenment philosopher, Sir Isaac Newton, who provided the mathematical formula for reorganizing the natural world.

Newton discovered the mathematical method for describing mechanical motion. He argued that one law could explain why the planets move the way they do and why an apple falls from the tree in the manner it does.

Newton argued that "all the phenomena of nature may depend upon certain forces by which the particles of bodies, by some causes hitherto unknown, are either mutually impelled toward each other, and cohere in regular figures, or are repelled and recede from each other."[23] According to Newton's three laws: a body at rest remains at rest, and a body in motion remains in uniform motion in a straight line unless acted upon by an external force; the acceleration of a body is directly proportional to the applied force and in the direction of the straight line in which the force acts; and for every force, there is an equal and opposite force in reaction.[24] Newton's three laws of matter and motion were greeted with enthusiasm by scholars almost immediately after they were published, and his mathematical model was soon being taught to students across Europe.

In the new world constituted by Newton and his contemporaries, all of the messy, spontaneous, unpredictable things of life are pushed aside to make room for the neat, orderly, and calculable new world of "matter and motion." In the mathematical universe of the Enlightenment, there was no room for joy, passion, exuberance, empathy, faith, or sorrow. None of these qualities can be reduced to quantities and explained by mathematical formulas. The Enlightenment worldview of empty space and matter in motion was, in the words of the scientist-philosopher Alfred North Whitehead, "a dull affair, soundless, scentless, colorless, merely the bumping of material endlessly, meaninglessly."[25]

The Enlightenment philosophers' concept of nature, with its abstract, rational, mathematical construction, seemed better suited for a world of machines than of human beings. Not surprising. The scholars of the Enlightenment fetishized machine metaphors in their explanations of the workings of nature. Indeed, Enlightenment philosophers were so caught up with the new Promethean power unleashed by machines that they began to construct a cosmology that, in its every detail, bears a striking resemblance to the workings of early modern technology. Descartes, and later Newton, had envisioned all of nature as a giant machine, run by well-ordered mechanical principles. God the benevolent and caring shepherd of Christendom was replaced with God the remote technician who created and set in motion a self-regulating machinelike universe that was orderly, predictable, and autonomous.

Enlightenment thinkers soon extended Descartes's mechanistic worldview to the economy, providing a philosophical rationale for the commercial exploitation of man himself. Borrowing from the Cartesian metaphor,

Adam Smith argued that an invisible hand ruled over the marketplace, assuring the proper functioning of economic life. This invisible hand was likened to the mechanical pendulum of a clock, meticulously regulating supply and demand, labor, energy, and capital, automatically assuring the proper balance between production and consumption of the Earth's resources. If left unencumbered by outside interference or regulation, the invisible hand of capitalism would run like a perpetual-motion machine, securing each individual's autonomy within an autonomous, self-regulating economy. Even today, economists continue to view the economic process in Cartesian terms when they speak of the "market mechanism."

In the new scheme of things, then, the invisible hand becomes the overseer and the marketplace the battleground in man's war against nature and his fellow human beings. Detached, impartial, automatic, and autonomous, the new god governing the marketplace understands only the language of numbers. In its domain, all phenomena are reduced to commodity values: cost per unit, price per pound, dollar per hour, wages per week, rents per month, profits per quarter, and interest compounded semiannually.

Desacralizing Time

The makeover of space, from a sacred realm to a utilitarian plane, and from God's creation to a reservoir of resources, was accompanied by a similar desacralization of time. In the course of just a few short centuries, time was made over to conform with the same scientific criteria used to expropriate space. The medieval sense of time, with its emphasis on the changing cycles and seasons of nature, the unhurried rhythms of daily rounds, and the long periods of prayer time in preparation for eternal salvation, was transformed into a thoroughly modern and scientific tableau, based on objectivity, rationality, mathematical calculation, detachment, and appropriation. Time was denatured and scientized.

The great struggle over the meaning and nature of time began, interestingly enough, with an epic battle between the Church and an incipient merchant class at the end of the medieval era and the beginning of the early modern era. The dispute was over the question of usury. At stake were two different notions of security, one sacred and centered on eternal salvation, the other profane and directed toward a material cornucopia.

The Church prohibited usury. In Matthew 6:24, it is written: "No one can serve two masters, for either he will hate the one and love the other, or he will be devoted to the one and despise the other. We cannot serve God and Money."

Usury was a rare event in the early Middle Ages, as most of Europe was still a subsistence-based economy relying on barter as the dominant form of trade and exchange. As population, cities, and trade began to expand in the twelfth century, money became more important in regulating economic transactions and exchanges. A new class of merchants and bankers began to lend money at interest, reaping tremendous profits in the process.

The Church argued that usury was a mortal sin punishable by eternal damnation. In support of this contention, it cited chapter and verse from both testaments. In Exodus 22:25, God warns his chosen people: "If you lend money to one of my people among you who is needy, do not be like a moneylender; charge him no interest."

The Vatican made it clear that it was not opposed to the "just" price but considered usury an improper gain and, therefore, theft. According to St. Thomas Aquinas:

> Money was invented chiefly for exchange to be made. So the prime and proper use of money is its use in disbursement in the way of ordinary transactions. It follows that it is, in principle, wrong to charge for money lent, which is what usury consists of.[26]

At the heart of the controversy over usury, or profit, was the question of use of time. The merchants argued that "time is money."[27] For merchants, time was critical. Their success depended on their ability to use time to their advantage; knowing when the best time was to buy cheap and sell dear and how long inventory should be allowed to stay on hand; determining the time it would take for goods to arrive, or how long it would take to ship them to their destination; anticipating changes in exchange rates, the rise and fall of prices, changes in labor availability over time, and the time necessary to make a product. The merchant who garnered the most knowledge of how to predict, use, and manipulate these various time frames commanded the best prices and made the most profit.

The Church contended that time belonged exclusively to God, who dispenses it freely in his temporal kingdom. Time is a gift God grants so that human beings may use it to prepare for their future salvation. By usurping time, the merchants, bankers, landlords, and entrepreneurs were usurping God's authority. Summing up the official position of the Vatican, Thomas Chobham argued that in charging interest, "the usurer sells nothing to the borrower that belongs to him. He sells only time which belongs to God. He can therefore not make a profit from selling someone else's property."[28]

If, however, time was reducible to a commodity that could be bought and sold, then the more profit one could amass, the more time one could buy for oneself. By charging greater interest and reaping greater profits, one could buy other people's time as well, thus adding to the amount of time available.

How, then, did human beings ensure their perpetuation and survival? By faith in God or by the accumulation of money? Medieval historian Jacques Le Goff sums up the significance of the great battle to define humanity's future: "The conflict, then, between the Church's time and the merchant's time takes its place as one of the major events in the mental history of these centuries."[29]

The Church eventually capitulated over the question of time, and the merchant's victory cleared the way for the birth of a money economy. "Market price" was substituted for "fair price," and the ground was laid for the ascendance of market capitalism and the slow, steady decline of ecclesiastical power in Europe.

The conception of time changed in another profound way in the period that separated the late medieval era from the early modern. The invention of the schedule and the mechanical clock in the thirteenth century by the Benedictine monks radically altered human beings' conception of time, providing still another critical development on the road to a market economy and nation-state governance.

For much of recorded history, the calendar ruled over human affairs. It served as the primary instrument of social control, regulating the duration, sequence, rhythm, and tempo of life and coordinating and synchronizing the shared group activities of the culture. The calendar is past-oriented. Its legitimacy rests on commemoration. Calendar cultures commemorate archetypical myths, ancient legends, historical events, the heroic deeds of gods, the lives of great historical figures, and the cyclical fluctuations of astronomical and environmental phenomena. In calendar cultures, the future takes its meaning from the past. Humanity organizes the future by continually resurrecting and honoring its past experiences.

The calendar continues to play an important role in contemporary culture. Its political significance has been greatly reduced, however, with the introduction of the schedule. The schedule exerts far greater control over time allocation than the calendar. While the calendar regulates macro time—events spread out over the year—the schedule regulates micro time—events spread out over the seconds, minutes, and hours of the day. The schedule looks to the future, not the past, for its legitimacy. In scheduling cultures, the future is severed from the past and made a separate and independent temporal domain. Scheduling cultures do not commemorate; they plan. They are not interested in resurrecting the past but in manipulating the future. In the new time frame, the past is merely a prologue to the future. What counts is not what was done yesterday, but what can be accomplished tomorrow.

The calendar and the schedule differ in still another important way. While modern calendars have become increasingly secularized, throughout most of history their social content was inseparably linked to their spiritual content. In traditional calendrical cultures, the important times are sacred times and are observed through the commemoration of special holy days. The schedule, in contrast, is associated with productivity. Sacred values and spiritual concerns play little or no role in the formulation of schedules. Time, in the new scheme of things, is an instrument to secure output. Time is stripped of any remaining sacred content and transformed into pure utility.

George Woodcock has observed, "It is a frequent circumstance of history that a culture or civilization develops the device that will later be used for its destruction."[30] The schedule, more than any other single force, is responsible for undermining the idea of spiritual or sacred time and introducing the notion of secular time. Needless to say, the Benedictine monks never for a moment intended the invention of the schedule to be used for any purpose other than to better arrange one's time on Earth in preparation for eternal deliverance. Little did they suspect that it would become the primary tool of modern commerce.

The Benedictine order was founded in the sixth century. It differed, in one important respect, from other Church orders. St. Benedict emphasized activity at all times. His cardinal rule, "Idleness is the enemy of the soul," became the watchword of the order.[31] The Benedictines engaged in continuous activity, both as a form of penitence and a means of securing their eternal salvation. St. Benedict warned the members of his order that "if we could escape the pains of hell and reach eternal life, then must we—whilst there is still time—hasten to do now what may profit us for eternity."[32]

Like the merchant class that would follow in their shadow, the Benedictines viewed time as a scarce resource. But for them, time was of the essence because it belonged to God, and because it was his, they believed they had a sacred duty to utilize it to the fullest in order to serve his glory. Toward this end, the Benedictines organized every moment of the day into formal activity. There was an appointed time to pray, to eat, to bathe, to labor, to read, to reflect, and to sleep. To ensure regularity and group cohesiveness, the Benedictines re-introduced the Roman idea of the hour, a temporal concept little used in the rest of medieval society. Every activity was assigned to an appropriate hour during the day. Consider the following set of instructions from the Rule of St. Benedict:

> The brethren . . . must be occupied at stated hours in manual labor, and again at other hours in sacred reading. To this end we think that the times for each day may be determined in the following manner. . . . The brethren shall start work in the morning and from the first hour until almost the fourth do the tasks that have to be done. From the fourth hour until the sixth let them apply themselves to reading. After the sixth hour, having left the table, let them rest on their beds in perfect silence.[33]

To make sure that everyone began each activity together at the prescribed moment, the Benedictines introduced bells. Bells pealed, jangled, and tinkled throughout the day, hurrying the monks along to their appointed rounds. The most important bells were those that announced the eight canonical hours when the monks celebrated the Divine Offices.

The Benedictines ordered the weeks, and the seasons, with the same temporal regularity as they did the day. Even such mundane activities as head-shaving, bloodletting, and mattress-refilling took place at fixed times during the course of the year.[34]

The Benedictines introduced more than a new temporal orientation when they introduced the "schedule." Eviatar Zerubavel wisely observes that, in appointing prescribed hours for specific activities and in demanding rigid obedience to the performance of these activities at the appropriate time, the Benedictines "helped to give the human enterprise the regular collective beat and rhythms of the machine."[35] Political scientist Reinhard Bendix has described the Benedictine monk as "the first professional of Western Civilization."[36]

To secure proper compliance with the prescribed schedule, the Benedictines developed a tool that could provide them with greater accuracy and precision of time measurement than could be obtained by reliance on bells and bell ringers. They invented the mechanical clock. Lewis Mumford once remarked that "the clock, not the steam engine, is the key machine of the Modern Age."[37] The first automated machine in history ran by a device called an escapement, a mechanism that "regularly interrupted the force of a falling weight," controlling the release of energy and the movement of the gears.[38]

At first, this new invention was used exclusively by the Benedictines as a means of assuring greater conformity with the daily schedule of duties. The clock allowed the clergy to standardize the length of hours. By establishing a uniform unit of duration, the monks were able to schedule the sequence of activities with greater accuracy and synchronize group efforts with greater reliability.

It was not long, however, before word of the new marvel began to spread. By the late fifteenth century, the mechanical clock had stolen its way out of the cloisters and had become a regular feature of the new urban landscape. Giant clocks became the centerpiece of city life. Erected in the middle of the town square, they soon replaced the church bell as the rallying point and reference point for coordinating the complex interactions of urban existence.

Just a century earlier, the grandeur of the Gothic cathedral had marked the status of a community, but now, the erection of the town clock became the symbol of city pride. In 1481, the residents of Lyons petitioned the city magistrate for a town clock, justifying the expenditure of city funds on the grounds that "more people would come to the fairs, the citizens would be very contented, cheerful and happy, and would live a more orderly life."[39]

The first clocks had no dials. They merely sounded a bell on the hour. Indeed, the term "clock" comes from the Middle Dutch word *clocke*, which means "bell." By the sixteenth century, clocks were chiming on the quarter hour, and some were being constructed with dials to demarcate the passing of each hour. In the mid-1600s, the pendulum was invented, providing a much more exacting and reliable timing mechanism. Shortly thereafter, the minute hand was introduced. The second hand did not make its debut until the early 1700s, when it was first used by astronomers, navigators, and doctors to record more accurate measurements.

The idea of organizing time into standardized units of hours, minutes, and seconds would have seemed strange, even macabre, to a peasant serf of medieval times. A day then was roughly divided into three sectors: sunrise, high noon, and sunset. The only other reminders, says Lawrence Wright, were "the seeding and harvest bell that called them to work, the sermon bell and the curfew bell."[40] Occasionally, one might hear the sound of the "gleaning bell, the oven bell when the manor oven was fired to bake the bread, the market bell, and the bells that summoned them to feast, fire, or funeral."[41] Even in these instances, time was not something fixed in advance and divorced from external events. Medieval time was still sporadic, leisurely, unpredictable, and, above all, tied to experiences rather than abstract numbers.

"By its essential nature," observes Lewis Mumford, the clock "dissociated time from human events."[42] It is also true, as historian David Landes, of Harvard University, suggests, that the clock dissociated "human events from Nature."[43] Time, which had always been measured in relation to biotic and physical phenomena, to the rising and setting sun and the changing seasons, was henceforth a function of pure mechanism. The new time substituted quantity for quality and automatism for the rhythmic pulse of the natural world.

The emerging bourgeois class of merchants embraced the mechanical clock with a vengeance. It quickly became apparent that the increasingly complex activities of urban and commercial life required a method of regulation and synchronization that only the clock could provide.

The clock found its first use in the textile industry. While textile production predated the rest of the industrial revolution by two centuries, it embodied many of the essential attributes that were to characterize the coming age. To begin with, textile manufacturing required a large, centralized workforce. It also required the use of complex machinery and great amounts of energy. The new urban proletariat congregated each morning in the dye shops and fulling mills, "where the high consumption of energy for heating the vats and driving the hammers encouraged concentration in large units."[44] This type of complex, highly centralized, energy-consuming production technology made it necessary to establish and maintain fixed hours for the beginning and end of the workday.

Work bells, and later the work clock, became the instrument of the merchants and factory owners to control the work time of their laborers. Historian Jacques Le Goff remarks that here was the introduction of a radical new tool to assert power and control over the masses. He writes, "The communal clock was an instrument of economic, social, and political domination wielded by the merchants who ran the commune."[45]

Whereas in the craft trades and in farming, the workers had set the pace of activity, in the new factory system, the machinery dictated the tempo. That tempo was incessant, unrelenting, and exacting. The industrial production mode was, above all else, methodical. Its rhythm mirrored the rhythm of the clock. The new worker was expected to surrender his time completely to the new factory rhythm. He was to show up on time, work at the pace the machine set, and then leave at the appointed time. Subjective time considerations had no place inside the factory. There, objective time—machine time—ruled supreme.

It was not only in the factory that the clock played an important new role. The bourgeois class found use for it in virtually every aspect of its daily life. This was a new form of temporal regimentation, more exacting and demanding than any other ever conceived. The bourgeoisie introduced the clock into their homes, schools, clubs, and offices. No corner of the culture was spared the reach of this remarkable new socializing tool. Lewis Mumford took stock of this transformation in time consciousness and concluded that

> the new bourgeoisie, in counting house and shop, reduced life to a careful, uninterrupted routine: so long for business; so long for dinner; so long for pleasure—all carefully measured out. . . . Timed payments; timed contracts; timed work; timed meals; from this time on nothing was quite free from the stamp of the calendar or the clock.[46]

To become "regular as clockwork" became the highest values of the new industrial age.[47] Without the clock, industrial life would not have been possible. The clock conditioned the human mind to perceive time as external, autonomous, continuous, exacting, quantitative, and divisible. In so doing, it prepared the way for a production mode that operated by the same set of temporal standards.

The metamorphosis of nature from God's creation to man's resources, the change in the usury laws, the shift from fair price to market price along with the birth of the money economy, and the introduction of the schedule and clock all profoundly transformed Europeans' sense of space and time.

The American Contribution to Space and Time

The new concepts of space and time migrated to America with the early settlers. But, in the New World, the Enlightenment schema took on a somewhat different persona, one more suited to America's frontier spirit. Americans introduced a new tool to harness space and time. Although the idea of efficiency is age old, its modern guise was developed in America in the nineteenth century and soon spread to the rest of the world, changing the way human beings organize the details of daily life. While human beings have used tools for thousands of years, the shift to coal and steam power in the nineteenth century afforded enormous new opportunities to manipulate space and duration. As we mentioned briefly at the beginning of the chapter, for the first time, human beings could break through the upper limits imposed by the rhythms of nature and begin to turn space and time into an ever quickening productive force for material advancement.

Even though Europeans—especially the English and Germans—were quick to use the new steam-driven technologies, it was the Americans who created the intellectual and conceptual mechanism for aligning human performance with the rhythm of the new machines. Efficiency was transformed by American engineers into a set of methodological practices that, in turn, became an all-encompassing tool for organizing space and time. And, it is the modern notion of efficiency that has done more than anything else to shape the contemporary American character and provide the juice to propel the American Dream.

Efficiency meant something quite different in the early eighteenth century. In Samuel Johnson's dictionary of the English language, published in 1755, efficiency still had a theological frame of reference. God is defined as the most efficient first cause. In the biblical account of creation, God commands the heavens and Earth into existence—the perfectly efficient act.

Efficiency metamorphosed into its current form in the late nineteenth century. Scientists and engineers were working in the new field of thermodynamics, measuring energy inputs and outputs and entropy in machines. In the process, they redefined efficiency, transforming it into a purely machine value. Henceforth, efficiency was to be regarded as the maximum output that can be produced in the minimum time, with the minimum input of labor, energy, and capital. The new definition of efficiency migrated quickly from the machine bench to the factory floor, front office, the home, and personal life, to become the measure of human performance and the criteria for determining the value of human activity. More than that, efficiency became the indispensable tool for assuring personal success and the realization of the American Dream. He who is the most efficient, and therefore most productive, goes the reasoning, is the most likely to rise to the top—to make something out of himself. While the new interest in efficiency found its way back to Europe and eventually to Asia, it was taken up more selectively in the work arena, whereas in America it became an all-embracing behavioral norm, conditioning virtually every aspect of life.

Americans are in love with efficiency. It has become our defining attribute and is engrained in our very being as a people. To understand how we came to transform a machine time value into a human behavioral norm, we need to go back to America's Calvinist roots and to our deeply held belief of being a chosen people.

Protestant Reformers of the sixteenth and seventeenth centuries had argued that being self-sacrificing and industrious was a sign that one had been elected for salvation. John Calvin, the French Reformation theologian, denounced the Church doctrine of salvation through good works, confession, and absolution. God can't be lobbied for a place in heaven, said Calvin. The Reformers believed that every human being is elected or damned at birth and that doing good works could not change one's fate. The lingering question, however, for every Christian, was how to know whether, in fact, one had been saved by God's grace. While no one can ever really know, Calvin argued that those who have been saved will fulfill all of God's commandments with zeal, not because it will secure their salvation but rather simply because God wills it. Moreover, everyone has an obligation to believe they have been chosen and to act accordingly. Constant performance serves as a kind of partial proof, or at least a sign, one can look to for hope that he or she has been saved.

Calvin demanded even more from the faithful. He claimed that it wasn't enough just to continue to do whatever one did in the world the best way one knew—that was Martin Luther's concept of calling. Calvin argued that each person is called upon to constantly improve his or her lot in life by increasing their productivity and, in the process, elevating his or her station, if they were to serve the glory of God.

In Calvin's doctrine, each individual was forced to live from moment to moment, continually reassuring himself against his own gnawing doubt, by constantly performing God's will. Even a momentary lapse from a total earthly ascetic commitment could undermine one's personal belief and confidence that he or she is one of the elect.

John Winthrop and the Puritans, and the other Protestant sects that followed on their heels to America, were, in many ways, the most faithful adherents to the Reformation theology. Long after the religious fervor ebbed in Europe, its flame was kept alive in the American colonies by waves of religious asylum seekers anxious to maintain the purity of their beliefs.

Here, the religious zealots faced the sober reality of a wild, untamed continent where physical survival was at least as important as eternal salvation. By combining Calvin's doctrine of relentless productivity with the Enlightenment emphasis on rational behavior, technological prowess, and pragmatic utilitarianism, they were able to eke out an existence and live out their beliefs at the same time.

The new notion of efficiency was ideally suited to the unique American temperament, with its emphasis on Reformation theology and Enlightenment science. Efficiency is a rational, technologically mediated way to continually improve one's productivity. The more efficient one becomes, the more sure one is that he or she is improving his or her lot, all to the glory of God. Being ever more efficient, in turn, becomes a way of convincing oneself that one has been elected to salvation.

Even after the concept of election fell from favor in the Protestant churches by the late nineteenth and early twentieth century, the notion of being ever more efficient and thus more productive had a Salvationist quality to it that was absent when modern efficiency standards were taken up in Europe and elsewhere. We Americans still tend to equate efficiency with good moral values and are often judgmental toward people who are grossly inefficient. Their behavior is seen as slothful—sloth is one of the seven deadly sins. That Salvationist ring is what made Americans not only the first and most willing converts to the modern idea of efficiency but also its greatest champions in the twentieth century.

Europeans often wonder why Americans live to work rather than work to live. The answer lies in our deep metaphysical attachment to efficiency. Being more efficient is being more God-like. God, recall, is the most efficient of all actors. He spoke the world into existence without expending any time, labor, energy, or capital. He created the heavens and Earth de novo. To the extent that human beings can increase production—and create our own earthly Eden—with the exertion of less and less time, labor, energy, and capital, we edge close to the awesome powers of God himself.

With efficiency as the new guide, Americans set out to recondition space and time with an almost evangelical fervor. An American, Frederick W. Taylor, is widely regarded as the father of modern efficiency practices. His principles of "scientific management" were taken up by American industry in the early twentieth century and shortly thereafter by the rest of society and became the foundation for an efficiency ethos that would eventually change the whole world.

If the town clock was the signature of Europe's transition into a new time era, the stopwatch became the American moniker. Using a stopwatch, Taylor divided workers' tasks into small operational components and then measured each activity to ascertain the best time under optimal performance conditions. By studying the minutest details of a worker's movements, Taylor could make recommendations on improving his or her performance to reap ever greater efficiency. Often, time savings would be measured in fractions of a second.

Taylor reduced human behavior to that of a machine and judged performance by the same criteria—that is, how well each worker maximized output in the minimum time, with the minimum input of labor, energy, and capital. Man and machine, for all intents and purposes, became one. By the twentieth century, Americans had so assimilated the new machine value into their lives that they began to describe their own behavior and well-being in machine terms. People were said to be "geared up" or "revved up" when motivated and "stressed," "overloaded," and "burned out" when depleted. We "tune in" to things of interest and "turn off" to things that repel us. Being "connected" or "disconnected" has become a surrogate for engaged or detached.

Soon, efficiency experts were fanning out across America, introducing the newest efficiency methods to the factory floor, front office, and retail establishments. The efficiency craze quickly spilled over into the wider society, where the new value became the litmus test for progress in all areas of life. Progressives brought efficiency into the political arena and began to call for the depoliticization of government and the establishment of scientific management principles in all government agencies and programs. (We will touch on this in more detail in chapter 10.)

The efficiency crusade even reached down into the homes and schools. In 1912, Christine Frederick wrote an article in the influential *Ladies' Home Journal* entitled "The New Housekeeping," urging the nation's housewives to adopt more efficient methods for running the household. She confessed to her readers that she had been needlessly wasting precious time because of inefficient homemaking practices. She wrote, "For years, I never realized that I actually made eighty wrong motions in the washing alone, not counting others in the sorting, wiping and laying away."[48] Frederick asked her readers, "Do we not waste time by working in poorly arranged kitchens? . . . Could not the housework train be dispatched from station to station, from task to task?"[49]

The American educational system was made over by the efficiency movement. The nation's school administrators, principals, and teachers, not to mention students, were criticized for being inefficient and wasteful. *The Saturday Evening Post* charged that "there is inefficiency in the business management of many schools, such as would not be tolerated in the world of offices and shops."[50] In 1912, at the annual meeting of the nation's school superintendents, the delegates were forewarned that "the call for efficiency is felt everywhere throughout the length and breadth of the land, and the demand is becoming more insistent every day." They were told, in no uncertain terms, that "the schools as well as other business institutions must submit to the test of efficiency."[51]

Behavior, post-Taylor, became focused almost exclusively on being efficient every waking moment of the day. Efficiency became the ultimate tool for exploiting both the Earth's resources and human resources in order to advance material wealth and economic progress. Everything in the world became reduced to factors of production to speed output. Successive generations of Americans would come to subject virtually all aspects of human activity to rigorous efficiency standards, reconditioning themselves to behave exactly like machines. The machine was no longer viewed simply as metaphor as it was for Descartes, Newton, Smith, and many of the early modern philosophers. Efficiency experts and, later, human resource managers and management consultants transformed everything in their path to machine criteria. By doing so, Americans went far beyond the mechanistic and instrumental values of the European Enlightenment to become the most thoroughly "modern" people on the face of the Earth.

The efficiency juggernaut so captured the imagination of the American public that some social critics felt compelled to deliver a few well-placed barbs. H. L. Mencken mused that the whole country was suddenly becoming engineers. The mattress manufacturers were becoming "sleep engineers," beauticians had reinvented themselves as "appearance engineers," and garbage men were now referred to as "sanitation engineers."[52]

Not surprisingly, the engineer became the new savior who would lead Americans to the promised land. Author Cecelia Tichi writes, "The engineer renewed the spiritual mission embedded for over two and a half centuries in the national experience. He promised, so it seemed, to lead industrial America directly into the millennium."[53] In 1922, a national survey of six thousand high school seniors reported that nearly one out of every three boys chose engineering as the profession they would most like to enter.[54]

Taylor, and others that followed, brought the efficiency movement over to Europe, where it played moderately well among businesspeople. But it enjoyed a less enthusiastic reception in other quarters of society. Europeans were willing to use the principles of scientific management in the factory and front office to increase productivity, although even there it was greeted with suspicion, especially in family-run business concerns, which still dominated Europe. There, the old-fashioned management practices, which combined benign paternalism, deference to craft tradition, and class antagonism, acted as an anchor to the unbridled enthusiasm that accompanied Taylorism in America. Europeans were even less willing to drag efficiency into the personal, social, and cultural spheres. This again gets to a central difference in the way Europeans approached the manipulation of space and time in the modern era, versus Americans.

If Europeans were more attracted to the town clock, perhaps it's because they viewed it as a means of synchronizing relationships between people. It was a way to orchestrate the collective behavior of the community. If Americans were more drawn to the stopwatch, it's because being constantly productive is afforded such high esteem. That isn't to say that efficiency hasn't been important in Europe. It has been and still is. Yet, while efficiency tends to define American behavior, in Europe, it is considered an important adjunct but not a prime characteristic of human motivation. Europeans have a bit of an aversion to employing efficiency in their personal lives because, at its core, efficiency is an instrumental value. All activities, machine and human alike, become factors to maximize output. Human beings cease to be considered an end, and instead become a means to facilitate production.

Europeans are likely to ask, Would one ever treat someone one really cared for efficiently? Would we say to a loved one, I'm going to show my love by maximizing my output, in the minimum time with the minimum expenditure of labor, energy, and capital? While Americans might say they find such a thought abhorrent, in practice, the concept of "quality time"—the idea of allocating a small, pre-planned segment of time during the day to have a meaningful encounter with one's child—has seeped into the public psyche and become the operational guideline for overly busy parents attending to their children. Among European parents, there is no equivalent to quality time.

Europeans tend to be less expedient and driven in their personal relationships than Americans. They ask, Can one be empathetic or caring in an efficient way? Can one find joy or experience revelation or happiness in an efficient manner?

Americans are more likely to use space and time in a more purposeful manner. We are less laid-back, on the whole, than our European friends. Words like "meander," "muse," and "ponder" are highly regarded in Europe, much less so in America. Americans are happiest being constantly productive. For us, idleness still conjures up a lax morality. Europeans, on the other hand, covet idleness. They take the time to smell the roses. To really enjoy life, my European friends say to me, one must be willing to surrender to the moment and wait to see what might come one's way. Americans are less willing to surrender their fortunes and happiness to fate. Most Americans believe that happiness isn't something that comes to us, but something we must continually work toward. Europeans I know simply don't think and feel the same way.

It all gets back to a basic difference in the American and European dreams. We strive for happiness by doing. Europeans strive for happiness by being. For us, happiness is bound up in personal accomplishments, not the least being our individual material success. For Europeans, happiness is bound up in the strength of their relationships and the bonds of their community. Close relationships and the deep feeling of solidarity, my European friends remind me, take time to nourish. They can't be subject to the dictates of the clock or the requisites of efficiency.

Americans often lament that we are unable to enjoy a quality of life like our European peers. We never will, as long as efficiency remains our most important tool for organizing spatial and temporal relationships. If the promised land is, in fact, a good quality of life, one can't get there if a stopwatch is the only guide.

5

Creating the Individual

MANY AMERICANS BELIEVE that the archetype of the strong, autonomous, self-reliant individual is an American creation. We pride ourselves on not being beholden to others and on being willing to take considerable personal risks to get what we want in the world. It's all bound up with our sense of "rugged individualism." For the most part, our self-perception is warranted. In an eye-opening study on entrepreneurial values, conducted in 2003, the European Commission found that while two out of every three Americans preferred to be self-employed, half of all EU citizens preferred to work as an employee for someone else. Even more interesting is how Americans handle personal risk, versus Europeans. While two out of three Americans say they would start a business even if there was a risk it may fail, nearly one in two Europeans say they would not take the risk, if the business might fail.[1] When Americans, and for that matter, the rest of the world, think of what it means to be an American, the go-it-alone, risk-taking spirit is likely to be the first thing that comes to mind.

Despite the fact that "the individual" is more honored in American society than in any other part of the world, it didn't take root here first. The modern individual is a European transplant whose beginnings date back to the waning years of the medieval age. Spatial and temporal changes, at the time, were effecting deep changes in the day-to-day behavior of European people. A new European man and woman were being born—one less religious and more scientific in outlook. By the nineteenth century, the emerging bourgeois class had all but shed the medieval frame of mind and was thinking and acting in a thoroughly modern way. The radical new idea of the rational "individual" took shape slowly over a period of several hundred years and paralleled the deep changes in the worlds of philosophy, science, commerce, and politics.

The idea of the self was so revolutionary that, for a long time, there were insufficient metaphors to even explain its meaning. In previous times, people had some sense of their own individuality. Still, lives had been lived, for the most part, publicly and communally. In the medieval era, it was unusual to see a person strolling along outside city walls or on a country lane. Historian Georges Duby says that "in the medieval era, solitary wandering was a symptom of insanity. No one would run such a risk who was not deviant or mad."[2]

Life had always been lived in close quarters; understandably so, since beyond the walls, fields, and pastures lay thick and impenetrable forests, wild animals in search of prey, and outlaws. Clustering was a survival strategy whose worth had proven itself time and again. By the nineteenth century, the forests had all been cleared, the wild tamed, and the bandits held at bay. People could now gaze out to the farthest point on the horizon, and what they saw was a world of new possibilities waiting to be exploited. More important, each person approached what Shakespeare called, in *The Tempest*, "this brave new world" alone, his only support being the property he had in his own labor and his worldly belongings.

Contrast the life of a medieval man and woman with their modern heirs. In less than fifteen generations, earth-shattering changes had taken place. Spiritual values had been largely replaced by material values. Theology gave way to ideology, and faith was dethroned and replaced by reason. Salvation became less important than progress. Tasks and daily rounds were replaced by jobs, and generativity became less important than productivity. Place was downgraded to location. Cyclical time, kept track of by the changing seasons, was marginalized, and linear time measured in hours, minutes, and seconds marked off lived experience. Personal relationships were no longer bound by fealty, but rather by contracts. Good works metamorphosed into the work ethic. The sacred lost ground to the utilitarian. Mythology was reduced to entertainment, while historical consciousness gained sway. Market price replaced just price. Deliverance became less important than destiny. Wisdom was narrowed to knowledge. And love of Christ was challenged by love of self. Caste was eclipsed by class, revelation by discovery, and prophesy by the scientific method. And everywhere, people became less servile and more industrious. Europeans remade themselves. In the new Europe, and even more so in the young America, possessing, not belonging, dictated the terms of human intercourse. These were heady changes.

The wrenching away of the person from the collective and the creation of the new self-consciousness came about in some very ordinary, almost banal ways. While Descartes, Newton, and Locke were busy philosophizing about the metaphysics of the new rational world being readied, a much more down-to-earth change in the habits and behavior of everyday people was taking place—one that would prepare successive generations of Europeans to think and act objectively, self-consciously, and autonomously.

Recall the emphasis Enlightenment philosophers put on detaching "man" from nature and transforming reality into a field of objects to be harnessed, exploited, and made into property. Nature, in the Enlightenment scheme, was wild and dangerous, a primal and often evil force that needed to be tamed, domesticated, made productive, and put to the service of man. In many ways, the taming of nature began with the taming of "man" himself. Separating human beings from nature required that they first be separated from their own animal instincts. People, too, had to be made over to make them more rational, calculating, and detached. Creating the self-aware autonomous individual proved to be a challenging task.

Civilizing Human Nature

Today, we think of people as being progressive or conservative. Just a few generations ago, we would have characterized people as modern or old-fashioned. In the late medieval and early modern era, a different kind of categorization was used to differentiate the generations. People were either brutish or civilized. Brutish behavior was associated with a depraved nature. To be brutish was to be animal-like, and animal-like behavior was increasingly described as slothful, lustful, menacing, and soulless.

We have to remember that life in the medieval age was still lived among the animals—domesticated and wild—and close to the soil. Most peasant farmers lived in traditional "long-houses," which combined both house and stable. Farmers and their cattle entered the house from the same entrance and were separated inside only by a lone wall.[3]

The flowering of urban life in the fifteenth century drew distance, for the first time, between city people and their rural surrounds and soon elicited disgust over the close relationship that rural kin still enjoyed with animals and nature. By the late Elizabethan era, the English had banished animals from the house altogether, sequestering them in stables and barns. The English were said to have "despised" the Irish, Welsh, and Scots because they still slept under a common roof with their animals.[4]

The emerging burgher class—which later became the bourgeoisie of the modern era—condemned what it regarded as bestial and brutish behavior that made its fellow human beings behave no better than the "dumb" beasts they cared for. In England, and soon thereafter in France and elsewhere on the continent, civilizing behavior became both mission and obsession of the rising merchant class, aided by the Church and, to a lesser extent, by the nobility. To be civilized was to be well mannered, properly groomed, in control of bodily functions, and, above all, rational and self-possessed. Only when each person could control his own animal nature would he be able to exercise control over the rest of nature. The civilizing process separated man not only from his own animal nature but also from his fellow human beings. He became an autonomous island, a detached free agent, in control of his own body and private space in the world. He became "an individual."

A similar civilizing process occurred in America in the eighteenth and nineteenth centuries on the Western frontier. Mountain men and other loners living in the wilderness, vagrants, and cowboys were singled out and put under the watchful eye of preachers, social reformers, and women in an effort to civilize their behavior and transform them into upright and productive citizens, each personally accountable for his behavior.

The new obsession with civility took a number of different forms in Europe. For example, nakedness, which had not been the subject of consternation in the past, suddenly became a major cause of public concern. The Reformers reminded people that being clothed was what distinguished man from beast. Long hair was also condemned. Bacon noted that "beasts are more hairy than man . . . and savage man more than civil."[5] Working at night was also suspect. The English jurist Sir Edward Coke made the point that night is "the time wherein man is to rest, and wherein beasts run about seeking their prey."[6] Animal epithets were also used with greater frequency to denigrate others. John Milton derided his foes by calling them "cuckoos, asses, apes, and dogs."[7]

The dinner table proved to be the most important classroom for civilizing human behavior and creating a sense of the individual. In 1526, Erasmus published his book on proper table manners and etiquette. It quickly became the bible for civility among the newly emerging bourgeois class.[8]

Eating was a communal affair in medieval Europe. Dinner was often a bawdy event and, at least in the homes of nobles, a spectacle with troubadours, clowns, acrobats, and assorted pets roaming the room. By modern standards, medieval meals were raucous and unpredictable gatherings that had the feel of a Roman bacchanalia. People sat on long, flat benches—others milled around the edges engaging in loud banter. The floors were littered with the garbage from present as well as past meals. Erasmus described the scene as an "ancient collection of beer, grease, fragments, bones, spittle, excrement of dogs and cats, and everything that is nasty."[9]

Food was served in no particular order and came to the table in pretty much the same condition it was in just after being killed. Whole birds, including sparrows, egrets, and herons, were heaped one on top of another in huge dishes and served to the guests. Stews containing whole rabbits and other small animals were mixed together with vegetables and flowers, and served en masse.[10] Custards or fruit tarts might come before, with, or after a stew or game bird, depending on whether they were ready or on the whim of the host.[11]

Utensils were scarce. People ate with their hands or from a trencher, which was a thick slice of stale bread. At the end of the meal, the diners dropped their soaked, stained bread onto the floor for waiting dogs.[12]

Erasmus and others were anxious to elevate the dining experience from a "bestial affair" and place it on a more civilized plane. They introduced a number of innovations designed to separate diners from the animals they killed and later consumed and to create boundaries between the diners themselves.

The practice of bringing an entire animal to the table—a lamb or a pig—to be carved with much solemnity by the host lost favor to the more civilized practice of having servants carve the meat out of sight, in the kitchen.[13] The authors of *The Habits of Good Society*, published in 1859, condemned the "unwieldy barbarism" of carving an entire joint in front of one's guests.[14]

The knife, which had long been the only utensil used by diners, was too close a reminder of the hunt and slaughter of the prey. When the Chinese first saw Europeans eating food with knives, they were aghast. "The Europeans are barbarians," they would say. "They eat with their swords."[15]

The fork was introduced to the table in the late medieval era, first in Venice, then later in Germany, England, and elsewhere.[16] The fork allowed people, in a subtle way, to distance themselves from too close an association with the animals they consumed.

A radical change also took place in the way people ate their food. In the medieval era, people supped from the common bowl, oftentimes spitting back bits of gristle into the cauldron as it made its rounds. A common ladle was introduced in the late medieval era to prevent the guests' mouths from touching the bowl. By the early modern era, the common bowl was done away with altogether. Spoons were added to the utensils, and each person was given his or her own bowl. Similarly, the shared tablecloth, which had customarily served as a common napkin to wipe grease and gravy off hands and mouths, gave way to individual napkins.[17]

By the nineteenth century, a bourgeois dining table might look more like a well-stocked surgical table. Each setting might include several different-sized wineglasses, each tailored to a particular wine, as well as an array of forks, knives, and spoons, each used for a specific part of the meal.[18] And the meal itself was served in a rational, orderly fashion, beginning with an aperitif, followed usually by a soup, a fish dish, meat, salad, dessert, and coffee. The chaotic, slovenly, disorganized medieval table was transformed into an orderly, efficient, rational dining experience. Human hands never touched the animals consumed, and there was little in the way the meal was prepared to suggest any connection between the diners and their prey.

The Birth of Privacy

The changing configuration of living arrangements between the late medieval era and the early modern era also came to play a decisive role in fostering the creation of the autonomous individual. The household, in the medieval era, was a very public place, with few boundaries separating family, kin, and neighbors. By the eighteenth century, the public household had metamorphosed into a private domicile, and family members were often separated from one another by partitions and rooms, each with a designated function. In the new household, each person claimed his or her own private space and possessions, something unheard of in medieval times. The sectioning off of private space made each person that much more aware of his or her own individuality and autonomy. The notion of privacy—a concept without any ontological standing in the late medieval era—was fast becoming the hallmark of the new autonomous individual. Privacy meant the ability to exclude others and was a mark of the new priority given to the individual life as opposed to extended-family relations, which had reigned as the dominant social unit from the very beginning of human experience.

The radical change in living arrangements began inauspiciously with functional and architectural changes in the medieval manor house. The medieval manor house was more like a public house than the kind of private dwelling we're familiar with today. At any given time, the house might be inhabited by dozens of relatives and servants, not to mention friends and acquaintances. The rooms themselves were large and undifferentiated. Relatives and guests often socialized, ate, and slept in the same room.

The cottages of the poor were little more than "squalid hovels." It wasn't uncommon for twenty or more family members to share a one-room cottage that barely exceeded twenty square yards. Three generations might share the same bed. People went a lifetime never really having a moment alone. In pre-Napoleonic Europe, more than three-quarters of the population lived under these kinds of horrible conditions.[19]

By the nineteenth century, however, at least for the well-to-do, the notion of privacy had gained hold. The manor houses were divided into private spaces, each with a particular function. There was now a parlor, a formal dining room, private bedroom chambers, storage rooms, and quarters for the servants. The privatization of space encouraged greater intimacy and self-reflection, feelings that were barely exercised in the public life of the late medieval household. Even the poor gained a modicum of privacy. Between the mid-sixteenth and mid-seventeenth centuries, more than half of all laborers' homes had expanded to three or more rooms.[20]

The changes in the layout of the home paralleled changes in the notion of family life. The nuclear family is a relatively new convention. In medieval times, the idea of family was a much looser affair. While the conjugal bond provided a sense of affiliation, we need to remember that families were extended institutions and included grandparents, aunts, uncles, and cousins, generally living together or close by. Even the idea of childhood was not yet developed. Children were perceived as little adults and were valued for their economic contribution to the household. Many were sent to other homes to apprentice at the age of seven or eight.

The growing sophistication and complexity of economic and social life in the early modern era required more abstract learning and specialized training of the young, which could only be passed on by formal educational training in the classroom. Schools, which in the medieval age were used almost entirely to train clerics, expanded to include more general education. Schools isolated youngsters from the adult world, resulting in their new classification as "children." Parents assumed a new responsibility of educating their children and looking after their development. For the first time, observes historian Philippe Aries, "the family centered itself on the child."[21] By the nineteenth century, the modern private family had superceded the extended communal family of the medieval era.

The increasing separation and detachment of the individual from the collective life of the community began to find expression in changes in vocabulary. The word "I" began to show up more frequently in literature by the early eighteenth century, along with the prefix "self-." "Self-love," "self-pity," and "self-knowledge" found their way into the popular lexicon. The autobiography became a new popular literary mode. Self-portraits became popular in art. Even more interesting, small personal mirrors, which were little used in the medieval era, were being mass-produced by the mid-sixteenth century. Giant wall mirrors became a popular part of the furnishings in bourgeois homes. Mirrors reflected the new sense of interest in the self. Historian Morris Berman reminds us that in the medieval period, people "were not terribly concerned with how they appeared in the view of others."[22] The increasing sense of self brought with it greater self-reflection and, not surprisingly, endless hours of solitary time before the mirror.

The new emphasis on the self and personal autonomy was particularly notable in the changing style in furniture. The chair was introduced around 1490 at the Palazzo Strozzi in Florence.[23] Before that time, people sat on wooden benches that lined the walls or on three-legged stools, or they huddled together on cushions on the floor. The only chair in medieval palaces was the throne reserved for the sovereign, denoting his elevated status. Uniform series of chairs first came into vogue in France during the height of the Renaissance, reflecting the newly elevated status of the individual. The idea of the chair was truly revolutionary. It represented an emerging feeling among an incipient bourgeois class that each person was an autonomous and self-contained being, an island unto him- or herself. Historian John Lukacs observes that "the interior furniture of houses appeared together with the interior furniture of the mind."[24] It's probably not unfair to say that with the widespread introduction of the chair in Europe, the autonomous individual of the modern era had indeed arrived.

The transformation from public to private life and the growing emphasis on the individual was very much in evidence in the bedchamber. Medieval sleeping arrangements were communal, just like every other aspect of social life. Landlords and their mistresses, relatives, friends, and even valets and chambermaids slept alongside one another in makeshift beds. Members of the same sex often shared the same bed. Michelangelo slept with his workmen, four to a bed.

The permanent bed wasn't introduced until the sixteenth century. In the seventeenth century, four-poster beds with canopies were commonplace among the nobility and burgher class. Curtains were attached to the beds to provide some small bit of privacy. Still, it was often the case that a man and woman would be making love behind the curtains while relatives and friends were socializing just a few feet away. On wedding nights, relatives and guests of the newlyweds customarily accompanied them to their wedding bed to witness the consummation of the marriage. The following morning, the bridal couple was expected to show the stained sheets to other members of the household as proof of their union.[25]

Slowly, the practice of sleeping alone in a single bed behind closed doors became more common. The kind of indiscriminate bodily contact that was so frequent in the late medieval era became a source of embarrassment. Public exhibitions of lust and sexuality, so prominent a feature of the medieval era, became taboo in the better households. Sexual relations became increasingly a private act, committed behind closed doors.[26]

The bath, which had previously been a communal activity, was also privatized and individualized. Remember, public baths were common in villages across much of Central, Western, and Northern Europe in the late medieval era. The fifteenth-century Florentine writer Bracciolini was taken aback upon his first visit to a public bath in Baden, Switzerland. By that time, Renaissance Italy had already left communal life behind. Here is how he described the event:

> Above the pools are galleries where the men sit watching and conversing. For everyone is allowed to go to other people's baths, to contemplate, chat, gambol and unburden the mind, and they stay while the women enter, and leave the water, their full nakedness exposed to everyone's view. No guard observes who enters, no gate prevents one from entering and there is no hint of lewdness. . . . The men encounter half-naked women while the women encounter naked men. . . . People often take meals in the water. . . . Husbands watched as their wives were touched by strangers and did not take offense, did not even pay attention, interpreting everything in the best light. . . . Every day they go to bathe three or four times, spending the greater part of the day singing, drinking, and dancing.[27]

The public baths were held up to scorn by Protestant Reformers, who worried that open displays of nudity invited licentious behavior. Bathing became a private affair by the eighteenth century in many parts of Europe.

Human urination and defecation were also made private during this period. In the medieval era, men would regularly relieve themselves in public places. Visitors to the Louvre during the reign of King Louis XIV "relieved themselves not only in the courtyard, but also on the balconies, staircases, and behind doors."[28] By the early modern era, the sight and smell of human waste had become a source of embarrassment and disgust, and steps were taken in cities across Europe to move these bodily functions behind closed doors. London was the first city to construct an underground sewer system, in the late nineteenth century, and to introduce flush toilets.[29]

The disgust over bodily animal smells was also used to create greater distance between the rich and the poor. Well before Marx penned his theory on the class divide, the emerging bourgeoisie was already creating its own self-justification for separating the classes. The urban and rural poor were said to emanate an animal stench, thus reinforcing the idea that they were little removed from brute animals. The emerging middle class began to use the term "the dung man" to refer to the poor. The new olfactory boundaries erected around the poor and laboring people proved far more

effective than philosophical treatises in separating the classes and justifying the continued exploitation of the masses by a new business elite. If the
poor were no better than brute animals, there was no reason why they
couldn't be exploited in like fashion, with no more concern than one
might feel in the yoking of an ox to a cart.[30]

The Making of the Bourgeoisie

Changes in table manners, living arrangements, family life, sexual activity,
and hygiene probably did more to create the sense of the rational, detached, self-possessed, autonomous individual than all of the scholarly
tomes of Enlightenment philosophers. These changes in personal behavior also effected an even more profound change in human consciousness
that is not always given sufficient attention, but without which the modern era would have been an impossibility. Although seemingly contradictory, the new bourgeois man and woman who were the products of these
fundamental behavioral changes were, at one and the same time, both
more individualized and autonomous and yet more tightly integrated into
a conformist-oriented culture than any other people in history. How was
this feat accomplished?

Periods in history follow a path not too dissimilar from the one that
individual human beings follow in their own life journeys. Passages in life
are marked by the increasing differentiation of the self from the whole—
first the infant's struggle to claim his or her own identity separate from the
mother; later the adolescent's partial separation from the family; and in
early adulthood, the individual's claim to an independent personhood.
Each stage in the differentiation process is accompanied by a new, more
complex integration into an ever more expansive set of social and environmental relationships. The passages of life are marked by a sophisticated balancing act between ever increasing individual claims and ever
greater social obligations.

The creation of the bourgeois man and woman is a good illustration of
the process at work. While differentiation has been part and parcel of human development from the very beginning of our journey, it wasn't until
the modern era that the individual claim to independence became so total-
ized. The idea of an autonomous individual whose freedom lay in the ability to accumulate wealth and exclude others from his material domain was

so extreme that it threatened the dissolution of the social nature of human life and a descent back into Hobbes's nightmarish war of all against all. While Enlightenment philosophers placed their emphasis on the merits of differentiation, they presented no vision of how such anarchic behavior could be regulated to ensure against a meltdown of the social fabric. Instead, most scholars at the time—Rousseau and his followers excluded—cast their lot with Adam Smith's glib suggestion that in a market economy, each individual pursues his or her own self-interest and that even though such behavior might appear selfish, it's only by the maximizing of such self-interest that the general welfare is advanced. A dubious proposition.

The real brilliance of the new bourgeois class was the way it balanced the potential anarchy of individualism with a new, sophisticated understanding of one's social obligations. The great twentieth-century sociologist Max Weber glimpsed the significance of the new mental acrobatics in his examination of the role that Protestant Reformation theology played in creating the internal controls that allowed unbridled capitalism to flourish without sacrificing the social order.

Recall how the Protestant theologian John Calvin replaced the external order imposed by the Church on each individual with an internally imposed order that was far more strict. Every action at every moment of a believer's life had to conform to God's glory. All personal conduct must, therefore, be perfectly controlled and ordered. Lapses, respites, and doubts were all signs of nonelection and therefore to be avoided. Calvin's doctrine transformed the unsystematic and somewhat casual way of life of medieval Europe into the methodically planned life characteristic of the new bourgeois class. Self-control replaced church control in daily affairs.

The bourgeois man and woman created their own private despotism over personal behavior. They learned to be self-controlled, self-sacrificing, and self-possessed, to be diligent and industrious. At first, these values were a way of living out their faith. Eventually, the religious intent fell by the wayside in Europe, but the values remained and became a critical element in fostering the capitalist ethos. Never before in history had people willingly imposed on themselves such utter restraints. In the past, control over people's behavior was more often enforced externally by extended family, or by governments and elites, and backed up by coercion and violence. In an era given over to the creation of the autonomous individual, each person now became his or her own ruler, governing his or her own behavior with the kind of fervor that, if imposed by an external political force, would have been considered harsh and heavy-handed. The bourgeois ethos proved effective. Everyone learned to balance his or her newly won autonomy and independence with self-imposed responsibilities to society.

In America, unlike Europe, the integration process continued to remain attached to its religious roots. Convinced that they were indeed the "chosen people," Americans were far more disposed to balancing their newly won autonomy with a shared obedience to a higher authority rather than a personal responsibility to their fellow human beings. For Americans, self-control, self-sacrifice, and industrious behavior were more likely to be exercised to please God—and self—than to fulfill one's social obligations. In this sense, many Americans remained true to the Protestant ethic, long after Europeans had passed it by. It was this divergence that set off the American Dream from its European antecedents.

Americans found no contradiction in living in two seemingly contradictory realms at the same time: one characterized by religious zeal and faith in eternal salvation, the other by Enlightenment secularism, rational behavior, and the belief in material progress—the contrary worlds of John Winthrop and Benjamin Franklin. What united both Reformation theology and Enlightenment philosophy was the premium each placed on the autonomy of the individual. Reformation theologians railed against the papal authority of the Church and admonished their fellow Christians that priests were imperfect like all other human beings and therefore could not serve as divine intermediaries. Martin Luther, John Calvin, and their successors argued that the Church's interpretation of biblical doctrine was no more authoritative than that of every other Christian and that each individual's relationship to God is ultimately a personal experience. The Protestant Reformation sought to dethrone the Church hierarchy and elevate each believer, making every human being equal in the eyes of the Lord. The Enlightenment philosophers elevated the individual as well, but their reasons for doing so were more bound up in ideas about rational human behavior. The status of the autonomous individual, however, remains to this day the common link between these two great historic streams.

Americans are arguably the most individualistic people on Earth, both because of our deep religious convictions and our materialistic ambitions. That's why Americans continue to be so anti-authoritarian in nature. We don't like bosses of any kind and refuse to humble ourselves at the feet of politicians, business potentates, or, for that matter, any higher authority, with the exception of God on high. In America, every person thinks of her- or himself as the equal of every other person.

Although the idea of the autonomous individual allows Americans to be both religious and secular, faith oriented and rationally driven, living in both the Reformation and Enlightenment worlds can play havoc with one's sense of teleology. While the Reformation side of the American character calls on each individual to experience the suffering of Christ in this world in return for salvation in the next, the Enlightenment side beckons every American to pursue happiness in the here and now in the name of human progress.

Europeans were less schizophrenic in this regard and eventually abandoned their religious zeal, leaving them only their Enlightenment ideology. And even that, in turn, was subsequently compromised by their deep misgivings about man's perfectibility and the inevitability that unfettered market forces would automatically lead to unlimited material progress for all.

It was Americans, then, who not only became the most enthusiastic disciples of the Protestant Reformation theology and the most ardent supporters of Enlightenment ideology but also the keenest champions of individual autonomy. Europeans, because of their long history of more dense spatial arrangements and paternalistic and communal ways of living, never fully embraced the idea of the lone self to the extent Americans would on the sparsely settled frontiers of a vast new continent. Americans, on the other hand, have, throughout our history, paid homage to the individual in popular myth, literature, and in virtually every human endeavor. The American Dream was never meant to be a shared experience but, rather, was meant to be an individual journey. In a peculiar sense, the American way of life became an extreme caricature of European ideas that sprang forth and enjoyed a period of influence in the sixteenth, seventeenth, and eighteenth centuries, only to be tempered by new countervailing forces in the nineteenth and twentieth centuries that reflected Europe's earlier paternalistic and collectivist roots.

The "New World," then, is a bit of a misnomer. We Americans continue to live out a dream whose roots lie deep in Europe's past, many of whose central tenets and assumptions no longer hold much sway in a world far removed in space and time from the historical conditions that gave rise to them.

6

Inventing the Ideology of Property

THE VAST CHANGES in spatial and temporal consciousness and the birth of the rational, autonomous individual transformed European life over a period of several hundred years. There is, however, one other institutional development that emerged alongside all of the other conceptual changes—an institution that gave concrete shape and meaning to the rest and provided the indispensable linchpin for the birth of the capitalist economy and the rise of the nation-state.

The invention and codification of a private property regime in the late medieval to early modern era became the foundation for the pursuit of the Enlightenment utopian vision of unlimited material progress. Private property rights became the essential legal tool for separating the individual from the human collective as well as from the rest of nature. A private property regime institutionalized the new spatial and temporal consciousness and made possible the modern notions of autonomy and mobility as well as the negative idea of freedom as personal independence and self-reliance. Its stormy development, and the equally fierce resistance to it, has continued, until very recently, to be the defining dynamic of European politics and the politics of much of the rest of the world.

The institutionalization of private property certainly would have to be considered one of Europe's most important contributions. Without a mature, regulated private property regime in place, market capitalism could not exist and the nation-state would never have survived. This last point needs to be emphasized. The very concepts of a modern market and nation-state are inseparably linked to a private property regime. The purpose of markets is to allow for the free exchange of property. The primary function of the state, in turn, is to protect the private property rights of its citizens.

Europe created the idea of the states' new role, only to have second thoughts about the matter when so many of its destitute population were systematically left out of the new economic arrangement. Americans, however, bought the idea of the states' new mission from the get-go and never wavered from the view that the primary function of government is to safeguard the private property holdings of the people. Tocqueville took note of Americans' fierce attachment to private property rights on his short visit to the new country. He asked, rhetorically,

> Why is it that in America, the land par excellence of democracy, no one makes that outcry against property in general that often echoes through Europe? Is there any need to explain? It is because there are no proletarians in America. Everyone, having some possession to defend, recognizes the right to property in principle.[1]

Once again, Americans became the purest advocates of a European idea, later partially abandoned by Europeans themselves, as they begin to rein in private property rights with a commitment to socialist reforms. Knowing, then, how the private property regime emerged and understanding its critical role in the birth of modern capitalist markets and nation-state governance, as well as the different ways it was embraced in the Old World and in America, are essential to coming to grips with the full meaning of the changes now taking place in Europe as it prepares to move beyond both these pillars of the modern age to become the first post-territorial governing region in a network-linked global economy.

The Medieval View of Property

Property meant something very different in the medieval era than it does now in the modern world. In the feudal world, the holding of property was always considered conditional in nature, whereas in industrial society, the holding of property is regarded as an absolute right that resides exclusively with the owners, subject to certain limitations imposed by the state. This is a critical distinction that separates the feudal way of conceptualizing property from the way we think about it today.

The feudal society was conceived as being part of a "Great Chain of Being," a hierarchically structured natural and social world that stretched from the lowliest creatures in nature to the princes of the Church. The entire chain was God's creation and was organized in such a way as to ensure that each creature performed his or her role as God had prescribed it, which included serving those above and below according to his or her station.

The social structure of feudal society operated in a manner similar to nature's grand hierarchy. Every rung of the social ladder is populated by a unique category of individuals who perform a specific role or function in the grand scheme of things, and each is bound to those above and below him in the chain by a complex set of mutual obligations and reciprocal relationships. From serf to knight, from knight to lord, and from lord to Pope, all are unequal in degree and kind, and yet each is obligated to the other by the medieval bonds of homage, and all together make up a perfect mirror of God's total creation.

The notion of property has to be viewed within the broader context of the Church's worldview. While Church leaders came increasingly to acknowledge a legitimate role for private property in the social schemata, it was always understood that property itself was held in the form of a trust all along the social hierarchy. Since God is the owner of his creation, all things in the earthly world ultimately belong to him. God grants human beings the right to use his property so long as they are righteous and fulfill their obligation of homage and fealty both to him and to every other person on the social ladder in the way he has preordained.

Property, then, was a rather complex phenomenon in feudal society and was tightly bound to the idea of proprietary relationships. Things were not owned outright or exclusively by anyone, but rather shared in various ways under the conditions and terms established by a rigid code of proprietary obligations. For example, when the king granted land to a lord or vessel, "his rights over the land still remained, except for the particular interest he had parted with." The result, says historian Richard Schlatter, is that "no one could be said to own the land; everyone from the king down through the tenants and sub-tenants to the peasants who tilled it had a certain dominion over it, but no one had an absolute lordship over it."[2] "The essence of the theory" of property in the medieval world, writes historian Charles H. McIlwain, "is a hierarchy of rights and powers all existing in or exercisable over the same objects or persons, and the fundamental relationship of one power to another in this hierarchy is the superiority of the higher to the lower, rather than a complete supremacy in any one over all the others."[3]

By the late eighteenth century, the feudal concept of the conditional right to use private property had given way to the modern notion of absolute ownership. While there were many factors that led to this radical change in the notion of property, none proved more important than the breakup of the feudal estates and the enclosure of the land commons into private real estate that could be bought and sold in the marketplace.

The land was transformed, first in England, and later on the Continent. After more than a millennium of history, when people had belonged to the land, new legislative initiatives, in the form of the great Enclosure Acts, reversed the spatial and temporal playing field. Henceforth, the land belonged to people and could be exchanged in the form of private property in the marketplace. Real estate could also be transformed into capital and used as a tool of credit to leverage economic activity.

It's difficult to imagine the change in consciousness brought on by the English Enclosure Acts. For centuries, people's security was bound up in attachment to their ancestral land and their duties and obligations in a Christian hierarchy that stretched from the common fields they tended to Christ's throne above. Now the land, which heretofore had been considered God's creation and administered by a complex set of rules and obligations that connected the lowliest serf to the Angels of Paradise, was severed. The land was divided up in the form of privately owned plots. Those who could not afford to purchase a lot of their own were forced off the land. Some became paid laborers working for the new owners, while others were forced to migrate to the nearest towns to find "work" in the new industrial factories.

In this detached world, one's labor became a form of property, and people sold their time in the marketplace. Daily rounds gave way to jobs, status in the community gave way to contractual agreements, and everyone, whether they wanted to or not, became responsible for making his or her own destiny.

It should be emphasized that a private property regime makes modern markets possible and not the other way around. In the medieval era, exchange was generally by way of barter between relatives, extended kin, and neighbors. Without a common law and legal code, the only way to trust the authenticity and to ensure a peaceful transfer of ownership of property was for the seller and buyer to know each other and to be a part of a tightly bound social community. For this reason, markets were always local and limited in their reach and importance. A mature private property regime, by contrast, substitutes subjective criteria like trust, with objective criteria like ownership titles, and provides enforcement mechanisms—the police and the courts—to make sure that sellers and buyers abide by their contractual agreements. Only when such a legal regime is in place and backed by the full coercive authority of the state can markets be extended in space and time to include large numbers of players—most of whom are strangers to one another—in the exchange of property.

The Protestant Reformation of Property

The Protestant Reformation figured significantly in the reformulation of private property relations. Martin Luther and his followers launched an all-out attack on the authority of the Pope and the feudal social order over which the Vatican presided. Luther argued against the idea of the Church as God's sole emissary on Earth and said that the priests were sinners like everyone else and therefore incapable of acting as intermediaries between the faithful and the Lord Almighty. He counseled that the only infallible authority on matters of faith was the Bible and that God's will was knowable to every Christian by reading the scriptures. Each man and woman, said Luther, stands alone before God. Luther's doctrine challenged the very basis of papal authority—its claim to be God's appointed representative on Earth. By doing so, Luther and his followers cast doubt on the legitimacy of the Holy Roman Empire and feudal social arrangements.

Luther was particularly harsh in his attacks on Church property, arguing that the Vatican had amassed untold wealth over the centuries at the expense of the people and had violated Christian faith, which preached abstinence and eschewed worldly luxuries.

The Reformation fervor ended up replacing one propertied class for another. Church lands were confiscated in Western and Northern Europe—even in Catholic Spain and Austria—and the lands of feudal lords were either seized or sold. The routing of the old feudal order made room for the establishment of a new bourgeois monied class of merchants, traders, and shopkeepers.

Luther's notion of "a calling" helped lay the groundwork for the natural-law theory of property and provided the all-important spiritual underpinning for the amassing of capital and wealth—which made the industrial age possible. Luther argued that all callings, even the most humble in nature, are equally sacred in the eyes of the Lord. He wrote that "what you do in your house is worth as much as if you did it up in heaven for our Lord God."[4] Luther railed against what he regarded as the elitism of priestly asceticism and argued that by faithfully discharging one's earthly duties—regardless of the calling—the believers are serving as God's stewards and the caretakers of his creation.

John Calvin, recall, went even further than Luther, calling on the faithful to continually improve their lot in life. While Calvin's doctrine was never intended to advance the notion of commerce, it had the unintentional effect of bolstering the very interests of the new capitalist class. His emphasis on unceasing work, productivity, and improving one's station proved compatible with a new class whose interest lay in hard work, expanded production, frugality, and a rational ordering of human activity in the marketplace.[5] His doctrine helped justify, though inadvertently, the idea of accumulation of wealth and the amassing of capital, the key ingredients of a modern property regime and capitalist way of life. Economic historian Richard Henry Tawney and sociologist Max Weber wrote extensively on the deep philosophical connection between the rise of the Protestant work ethos and the emergence of modern capitalism. By freeing up individuals from dependency on the Church hierarchy and arming each person with a new psychology of material self-advancement, the Reformers left behind far more than a religious legacy. Long after the religious fires had died down, European men and women retained a new sense of self-worth that was compatible with modern notions of property accumulation.

The old idea of the individual as a small part of a complex social organism made up of proprietary relations and obligations gave way to the modern notion of the individual as an autonomous being in the world, alone before his God and his fellow human beings, and exercising, by strength of personal will, his or her unique stamp on the world. The metamorphosis of the individual from a loyal servant enveloped in the bowels of a Great Chain of Being to an autonomous agent with one's own individual calling, and always improving one's material lot to the greater glory of God, went hand in hand with a change in the notion of property from proprietary rights to exclusive ownership. Property, once bound up in complex social arrangements and the conditional rights of usage, came to be seen much like the new individual, as autonomous things, each unique, and indivisible. Tawney writes that what remained after the fall of the feudal social order "was private rights and private interests, the material of a society rather than a society itself."[6] In this new world, property rights would be the social glue that bound people together. Private property and unfettered economic freedom, said Tawney, "were taken for granted as the fundamentals upon which organization was to be based, and upon which no further argument was admissible."[7]

While the Protestant ethic was born in Europe, many of its most fanatic disciples migrated to America, where they hitched Calvin's religious vision to Enlightenment notions of science, private property rights, and capitalist market relations, creating the uniquely American Dream.

The Metaphysics of Private Property

With private property ensconced as the organizing principle of society, it was left to modern scholars to create the appropriate philosophical rationale to accompany it. They found their answer in the natural-law theory of property—a concept that had developed slowly in the late medieval period and advanced more quickly during the Reformation and its aftermath.

The French political philosopher Jean Bodin began by arguing that common ownership is unnatural and a violation of divine law. Plato's commonwealth, with its adoration of communal ownership, wrote Bodin, is "against the law of God and nature, which detests not only incests, adulteries and inevitable murders, if all women should be common; but also expressly forbids us to steale, or so much as desire anything that another man's is."[8] Bodin reminded his readers that theft is forbidden by God. Why would God include the commandment "Thou shalt not steal" if he didn't mean to embrace the concept of private ownership of property? asked Bodin.

Bodin goes on to make the point that the family—a natural institution— is built on private property, and the state, in turn, is built on the family.[9]

That being the case, argued Bodin, the chief responsibility of the state is to protect each person's—and family's—"natural" God-given right to own property.

The belief that the primary role of the government is to protect each person's inalienable right to own property was a radical idea that, in time, became the rallying cry for republican reformers and others in their struggle to replace monarchic rule with democratic forms of government. Bodin was insistent on this score. If the state were to abrogate its main reason for being—the protection of private property—it would have no legitimate claim to exist. He wrote, "But the greatest inconvenience is, that in taking away these words of Mine and Thine, they ruin the foundation of all Commonweales, the which were chiefly established to yield unto every man that which is his owne, and to forbid theft."[10]

Bodin's writing pierced the church/state veil that had enveloped Europe since the fall of the Roman Empire. At a time when the prevailing orthodoxy still viewed the state as the upholder of the faith, Bodin dared to argue that the state's primary charge was far more secular in nature—to protect the natural right of private property. Individual rights—embedded first and foremost in private property—took precedence over both aristocratic privileges and deference to Church authority. In the new scheme of things, rulers exist to protect the individual rights of property holders rather than individuals existing to serve the interests of princes and kings. Tawney described the new way of thinking about the relationship of the individual and the state this way:

> What it implies is, that the foundation of society is found, not in functions, but in rights: that rights are not deducible from the discharge of functions, so that the acquisition of wealth and the enjoyment of property are contingent upon the performances of services, but that the individual enters the world equipped with rights to the free disposal of his property and the pursuit of his economic self-interest, and that these rights are anterior to and independent of, any service which he may render.[11]

Having laid out the broad intellectual groundwork for a bold new conception of private property in the fifteenth and sixteenth centuries, the unfinished business of filling in both the substance and details of the modern notion of ownership was taken up in the seventeenth century by the

political philosopher John Locke and later by a succession of theorists including Adam Smith, David Hume, Jeremy Bentham, John Stuart Mill,
and Georg Wilhelm Friedrich Hegel.[12]

Locke's theory of property was published in 1690 in *Two Treatises on
Civil Government*. His treatises quickly became the secular bible for a middle class that was beginning to climb onto the political stage in England. His
writings served as a rationale for parliamentary reforms in England and,
later, provided the philosophical foundation for the French and American
revolutions.

Like many of his predecessors, Locke argued that private property is a
natural right and unalterable. Locke's reasoning, however, is what distinguishes his theory from those who came before him. He argued that each
man creates his own property by adding his labor to the raw stuff of nature, transforming it into things of value. While Locke acknowledged that
the Earth and all of its creatures were common to all men in the state of
nature, he was quick to add that each man, in turn, "has a property in his
own person . . . and this no one has any right to but himself." Locke goes
on to assert that "the labor of his body and work of his hands . . . are properly his." That being so, Locke concluded that

> whatsoever, then, he removes out of the state that nature hath pro-
> vided and left it in, he hath mixed his labor with it, and joined to it
> something that is his own, and thereby makes it his property. It be-
> ing by him removed from the common state nature placed it in, it
> hath by this labor something annexed to it that excludes the common
> right of other men. For this "labor" being the unquestionable prop-
> erty of the laborer, no man but he can have a right to what that is
> once joined to, at least where there is enough, and as good left in
> common for others.[13]

As to the question of how much property a person might legitimately
claim for himself, Locke said, "as much land as a man tills, plants, improves, cultivates and can use the product of, so much is his property."[14]

Locke's natural-right theory of property was wildly popular with the
new generation of independent farmers, merchants, shopkeepers, and
small capitalists who were transforming English life and ridding the country of the last vestiges of feudal privilege. His treatises offered more than
a mere explanation of the natural right of property. He elevated human la-

bor and glorified acquisition as the crowning achievement of human existence. Unlike medieval churchmen, who thought of human labor as a set of necessary obligations to fulfill, Locke saw in it opportunities for which every man ought to strive.

David Hume (and, later, Jeremy Bentham and John Stuart Mill) added the notion of utility value to the ownership of property. Hume argued that the justification for private ownership lies in the idea of utility: "Examine the writers of the laws of nature," writes Hume,

> and you will always find that whatever principle they set out with, they are sure to terminate here at last, and to assign, as the ultimate reason for every rule which they establish, the convenience and the necessities of mankind. What other reason, indeed, would writers ever give, why this must be mine and that yours.[15]

The utility theory of property provided yet another rationale that could be used by the new class of merchants and traders to advance their personal and political agenda. The utility theory softened the edges of Locke's labor theory, making property not just an end in itself but rather an instrument for advancing human happiness. Philosophers of the period were in agreement that "the greatest possible happiness of society is attained by ensuring to every man the greatest possible quantity of the produce of his labor."[16]

The utilitarians were among the first of the modern theorists to make the clear distinction between ownership as a thing in and of itself, that one possessed, and ownership as an instrument to advance human happiness. Georg Friedrich Hegel, the German philosopher, picked up this distinction in a slightly different way. His theory of property—which some call the personality theory—has become as important as Locke's labor theory of ownership in establishing the notion of private property in the modern world.

Hegel argued that property plays a far more important role than most philosophers had heretofore been willing to acknowledge. Beyond its material and utilitarian value, said Hegel, property has a deeper function. According to Hegel, "property enables an individual to put his will into a 'thing.'"[17] One expresses his or her sense of personality by imprinting it into possessions. It is by way of fixing one's will onto objects in the external world that each person projects his being and creates a presence among men. Work, in Hegel's cosmology, is a creative expression rather than just an exercise of labor, and the product of that work represents an expropriation of the world and its incorporation into the projected personality of the owner. He writes:

> Personality is that which struggles to . . . give itself reality, or in other words to claim that external world as its own. To claim that external world as its own personality requires the institution of property.[18]

As one's personality is always present in the owned object, property becomes an extension of one's personality. Others, in turn, come to know and recognize one's personality through the objects one owns. Hegel, then, viewed property as more than just a way to satisfy needs. On a more profound level, property is an expression of personal freedom. By surrounding oneself with property, a person inflates his or her personality in space and time, creating a sphere of personal influence. In short, he or she creates an expanded presence in the world.[19]

Property and personhood become nearly synonymous in Hegel's mind. Each becomes an expression of the other. Nearly a century after Hegel first advanced his personality theory of property, William James lent his support to the theory in terms readily recognizable to a generation becoming comfortable with psychological notions of projection. James writes:

> It is clear that between what a man calls me and what he simply calls mine, the line is difficult to draw. We feel and act about certain things that are ours very much as we feel and act about ourselves. Our fame, our children, the work of our hands may be as dear to us as our bodies are, and arouse the same feelings and the same acts of reprisal if attacked. . . . In its oldest possible sense, however, a man's self is the sum total of all that he can call his, not only his body, and his psychic powers, but his clothes and house, his wife and children, his ancestors and friends, his reputation and work, his land and houses and yacht and bank account. All these things give him the same emotions. If they wax or prosper, he feels triumphant, if they dwindle and die away, he feels cast down . . . a great part of our feelings about what is ours is due to the fact that we live closer to our own things and so feel them more thoroughly and deeply.[20]

James goes on to observe that when something that belongs to us is stolen or destroyed or simply lost, we feel "a sense of the shrinkage of our personality" because the things we come to possess are an extension of who we are.[21]

If Hegel's theory of property seems more contemporary than Locke's, perhaps it is because the emphasis of the capitalist system has shifted substantially over the years, from a production to a consumption orientation. The labor theory of property provided an ideal philosophical backdrop for an era where the attention was focused narrowly on hard work, industrious behavior, savings, and capital accumulation. Merchants, shopkeepers, and an emerging bourgeois class looked to the labor theory of property as a justification for their own behavior. Locke's ideas became values to live by as much as explanatory theories of the nature of property relations. Today, consumption and the commodification of personal experience are far more important factors in the commercial equation. It's no wonder, then, that the notion of property as an extension of one's personality and a mark of selfhood has greater social currency. Marketing professionals have long understood the close connection between personhood and property, and have habituated several generations of consumers to the idea that who we are is a direct reflection of what we have.

Mine vs. Thine

The metamorphosis in thinking about the nature of property paralleled the many other changes that were transforming a continent from a feudal economy to a market economy and from dynastic rule to nation-state governance. The new concept of property was a way for Europeans to reorder their relationship to space and time. The new technologies opened the door to vast new spaces and dramatically quickened the human tempo. Space that had for so long been conceived of as cloistered and vertical was suddenly horizontal and wide open to the vanishing point of the horizon. Time, which for aeons had been experienced as cyclical and relatively closed, was suddenly experienced as linear and expansive. The old feudal institutions, with their spatial walls and temporal boundaries, simply collapsed in the wake of what appeared to be an endless frontier running alongside an infinite future. The development of a private property perspective was the critical mental tool for domesticating the new spatial and temporal frontier.

The whole of earthly reality was reconfigured into a single formula—"mine vs. thine." And with this formulation, Europeans set out to enclose the whole of space and time. In the new future being born, every person would become his or her own private god whose divinity lay in amassing property, inflating his or her being, and casting an ever larger shadow over existence and duration. More mine, less thine. Those who could, by talent and cunning, acquire the most property could transform it into capital and use that capital to control not only nature but the lives of other people as well. They were called "capitalists."

The modern market economy and the nation-state, in turn, became the institutional mechanisms to speed along this new reorganization of the world. The market would serve as the impartial arena where each capitalist would lock in battle against his fellow warriors in the struggle to capture space and sequester time in the form of private property. The infant nation-state, in turn, was to be the protector of every person's property by establishing legal codes and enforcement mechanisms—and, by so doing, guarantee his or her freedom.

The concept of a society based on the sanctity of private property rights is a uniquely European idea. Its champions saw private property as the one and only mechanism that could ensure individual freedom. Later, its Marxist detractors would claim that private property, far from being the guarantor of personal freedom is, in fact, the single greatest obstacle to achieving it.

For the Enlightenment philosophers and the jurists of the eighteenth and nineteenth centuries, freedom was defined in negative terms as the right to exclude others. The early modern era was a time of differentiation—the separation of the individual from the cloak of the Church, the yoke of the feudal estate, the constraints of the craft guilds, and the many other obligations and indentures that were an integral part of a dynastic order based on status and rank.

Private property was viewed as a ticket of sorts to personal liberation. To be free, in the sense that it was used at the time, was to be autonomous and mobile—to not be dependent on or beholden to others or held hostage to circumstances. The more propertied one was, the more autonomous and mobile one could be. Greater autonomy and mobility meant greater freedom. Property, then, was a border between the self and the other. Property means "mine not thine." The greater the accumulation of property and wealth, the larger the extension of one's domain and sphere of influence in the world. If one were secure in one's property, then all of the other rights would be guaranteed—the right to privacy, the right to be free of coercion, and so forth. Property rights, protected by law, ensured that no man could be bullied, oppressed, or made subject to another man's will.

An eighteenth-century Virginian, Arthur Lee, captured the high regard in which property was held on both sides of the Atlantic, declaring, "The right of property is the guardian of every other right, and to deprive a people of this is in fact to deprive them of their liberty."[22] John Locke asked, rhetorically, What was the true purpose of governments? They are instituted, said Locke, "for the mutual preservation of [our] Lives, Liberties, and Estates, which I call by the general name, Property." When one reflects on the real reason "men" unite into commonwealths, Locke mused, it is to ensure "the preservation of their property."[23]

Today, we have come to take for granted the dense legal codes and statutes, the common law, the legislative oversight, and the judicial review that enshrine private property at the very center of modern social life. But in the eighteenth and nineteenth centuries, the idea of a private property regime was still novel, and the subject of great public discussion. Kings and queens and the nobility and aristocracy of virtually every European kingdom still ruled by divine right, backed by the threat of force and coercion. The very idea that the only legitimate function of the state is to protect everyone's claim to property, equally and impartially, by rule of law, was incendiary. Thomas Paine and Alexis de Tocqueville went so far as to claim that the American and French revolutions were the product rather than the source of property relations.[24]

The central role of the sovereign state in a post-dynastic era, then, becomes one of protecting private property relations and allowing the accumulation and exchange of property to flourish. It becomes clear that this new kind of state exists primarily to ease the workings of a nascent capitalist economy. Jean-Baptiste Say, the French classical economist, made the point that if government "either practices robbery itself, or is impotent to repress it in others, or where possession is rendered perpetually insecure, by the intricacies of legislative enactments," the market can't function. It is only when property rights are secured by law and enforced by the state that "the sources of production, namely land, capital and industry [labor], attain their utmost degree of fecundity."[25]

Is this just eighteenth-century polemics, or is there some profound truth to what Jean-Baptiste Say and other Enlightenment philosophers were preaching? Hernando de Soto, the Latin American economist, writes in his most recent book, *The Mystery of Capital*, that Say and other European economists of the day were right on the money. De Soto asks the question, Why are people so poor in the developing world, especially when "the poor already possess the assets they need to make a success of capitalism?"[26] De Soto estimates the total value of just the real estate held by the poor in the third world to be more than $9.3 trillion.[27] But, he argues, "because the rights to these possessions are not adequately documented, the assets cannot be turned into capital, cannot be treated outside of narrow local circles where people know and trust each other, cannot be used as collateral for loans, and cannot be used as a share against an investment."[28]

What separates the rich from the poor and the developed from the undeveloped worlds, says de Soto, is that America and Europe established "a widespread formal property law and invented the conversion process in that law that allowed them to create capital."[29] De Soto says that Westerners "take this mechanism [a formal property rights regime] so completely for granted that they have lost all awareness of its existence."[30]

De Soto and other third-world economists have come to understand that a private property regime is the very source of market capitalism. But for eighteenth-century utilitarian philosophers, it was much more. A private property regime was to be the means to replace the older, theologically inspired utopian vision of the Church with a new materialist-driven utopian dream. Divine salvation in the world to come would become secondary to material salvation here and now on Earth. "Property is human liberty exercised over physical nature," wrote Raymond-Théodore Troplong, the president of the French Senate between 1852 and 1869.[31] Using the scientific method, all of nature could be expropriated, harnessed, and reduced to productive private property. Mixing one's labor to nature's resources—making something of it—not only transformed it into man's property but also made it more productive, thus increasing its value.

The accumulation and exchange of property would make the dream of an earthly cornucopia a reality. At a time when much of the Earth's surface was still unexploited frontier, the framers of the new vision understandably believed that property accumulation could be expanded almost indefinitely into the future. Eternal salvation slipped from the ascendant position that it had enjoyed for more than eleven centuries in Europe to make room for the radical new idea of material progress. During the French Revolution, the French aristocrat Marquis de Condorcet confidently predicted:

> No bounds have been fixed to the improvement of the human faculties . . . the perfectibility of man is absolutely indefinite; . . . the progress of this perfectibility henceforth above the control of every power that would impede it, has no other limit than the duration of the globe upon which nature has placed us.[32]

Not everyone agreed. The naysayers, and there were many, argued that a society organized almost exclusively around a private property regime and a "mine vs. thine" attitude would be the ruination of civilization. They envisioned a world of unrelenting competition and struggle in which the more powerful would prevail and the rest become indentured or cast aside. Jean-Jacques Rousseau, in his *Discourse on the Origin of Inequality*, published in 1755, wrote:

> The first person who, having enclosed a plot of land, took it into his head to say *this is mine* and found people simple enough to believe him, was the true founder of civil society. What crimes, wars, murders, what miseries and horrors would the human race have been spared, had someone pulled up the stakes or filled in the ditch and cried out to his fellow men: "Do not listen to this impostor. You are lost if you forget that the fruits of the earth belong to all and the earth to no one!"[33]

Nearly one hundred years later, Karl Marx published his *Communist Manifesto*. He attacked the philosophical and historical roots of private capital formation, calling it a scourge on civilization, and beseeched his fellow European countrymen to abolish the privatization of the means of production.

Although Europe was the seedbed for advancing a private property regime, there was opposition from the start. For every follower of John Locke, there were others who preferred to cast their lot with Rousseau. If, for some, private property was the path to utopia, for others it was a dystopian nightmare. Europe was caught between two very different conceptions of society. The older tradition favored a more communitarian approach to organizing economic activity, social life, and political rule. The emerging bourgeois class, however, was more anxious to let every man loose to go it on his own. An entrenched aristocratic class went along with the bourgeoisie. The nobility proved to be quite flexible in adapting to the new republican regimes and were often able to take advantage of their deep pockets and social connections to make their own killings in the marketplace.

Working people, however, didn't experience much of the material gains promised by the Enlightenment philosophers and their successors. Life in the urban industrial shops and factories was draconian. Dangerous working conditions, long hours of toil at the workbench, and later on the assembly lines, near starvation wages, and squalid and overcrowded living environments were a far cry from the world offered up by Condorcet. Millions of desperate Europeans simply picked up stakes and fled to America in hopes of finding a better life. Of those who stayed behind, many found the socialist critique of capitalism compelling, and more than a few became willing converts. European trade unions, cooperative associations, and socialist political parties gained increasing support among the working class in countries across Europe in the nineteenth and early twentieth centuries.

The idea of a welfare state became acceptable in Europe around this time. It was a grand compromise, a way to appease the rising bourgeois class and the remaining aristocracy on the one hand, and Europe's working class and poor on the other hand. The idea of a private property regime would be upheld in return for a promise that some of the excesses of unbridled market capitalism would be redistributed, in the form of government social benefits. The welfare state would become a way to balance the books and prevent class divisions from turning into open warfare and revolution in the streets. For the most part, the great European compromise succeeded.

Americans' Love Affair with Property

America didn't follow Europe's example. Socialism never really took hold on American soil. The German economist Werner Sombart laid the blame on the fact that American laborers enjoyed three times the amount of beef as German workers. He wrote, "On the shoals of roast beef and apple pie, all socialistic utopias founder."[34]

The unadulterated European vision of a utopian society formed around the protection of individual property rights found its most enthusiastic supporters in the new world. Geography played an important role. There was so much cheap and free land for the taking. For millions of European newcomers moving on wagon trains west across the Appalachian Mountains and into the fertile fields of the American Midwest and on to the great prairies of the American plains, it certainly seemed like Eden. They wrote home and expressed their amazement about all of the available land. Listen to this description of the American wilderness by one newcomer:

> The seemingly interminable line of trees before you, the boundless wilderness around, the mysterious depths amid the multitudinous foliage, where foot of man hath never penetrated, which partial gleams of the noontide sun, now seen, now lost, lit up with a changeful, magical beauty; the wondrous splendour and novelty of the flowers; the silence, unbroken but by the low cry of a bird, or hum of an insect or the splash and croak of some huge bullfrog; and the solitude in which we proceeded, no human being, no human dwelling, in sight.[35]

From the very beginning, the young republic gave away vast tracts of land to settlers. The Public Land Act of 1796 allowed settlers to buy land at two dollars an acre and provided a year's credit for half of the total purchase. By 1800, the government was selling off 320-acre sites and allowing the buyer to put down only 25 percent of the purchase, the rest to be paid over the course of four years. For less than $160, a European could lay claim to hundreds of acres of prime land, something out of reach in Europe, except for the wealthiest merchants and aristocrats. By 1811, more than three million acres of land had been sold to farmers.[36]

The government sale of millions of acres of public land continued throughout the century. There was the Homestead Act of 1862, which provided 160 acres of public land to every farmer. This single act turned over 270 million acres of public land—10 percent of the entire landmass of the U.S.—to settlers. The clarion call of "free land" echoed back East and all the way to Europe. The Homestead Act spawned one of the greatest migrations in history. Easterners, newly arrived immigrants, and freed slaves who were anxious to find new opportunities out West all rushed out onto the American frontier. The homesteaders needed only pay a filing fee of ten dollars to claim the land along with an additional six dollars for the final title, and a two-dollar commission to the land agent. To take final possession, the claimant had to build a home and farm the land within five years of making the claim. If the requirements were met, the title to the land was transferred from the government to the claimant.[37] Millions of Americans became property holders. In 1873, the government passed the Timber Culture Act, in 1887 the Desert Land Act, and in 1916 the Grazing Homestead Act.[38]

In 1890, the U.S. Census Bureau officially announced the close of the American frontier. The Bureau wrote:

> Up to and including 1880 the country had a frontier of settlement, but at present the unsettled area has been so broken into by isolated bodies of settlement that there can hardly be said to be a frontier line. In the discussion of its extent, its westward movement etc., it can not, therefore, any longer have a place in the census reports.[39]

In less than a century, millions of acres of public land had been transformed to private property holdings. Even with the closing of the American frontier and the increasing waves of immigrants arriving each year from all over the world, the ratio of population to land continued to be sparse compared to Europe. In America, we still have far fewer people and far more unused land than Europe. The result is that we feel less crowded and more autonomous, less interdependent and more independent, less communitarian and more individualistic. Even New York City, our most dense urban environment, has only one-third the number of persons per square mile as Frankfurt, Germany.[40]

The differences in human population relative to landmass have had a profound impact on how we Americans perceive the world around us and how Europeans do. When Americans travel to Europe, we always notice how compact everything is, how narrow the streets are, how close together all of the buildings are, how crowded the cafés are, and how small the portions of food are in the cafés. Even the elevators are cramped. An obese American can barely squeeze into one of them. Everything seems squished, tiny, parsimonious.

Americans are used to more space, much more. We may have officially closed the frontier more than a century ago, but we still live out the frontier spirit. We want to feel free, and freedom for many Americans means expanding the personal space we can control.

In the twentieth century, suburban home ownership became the way to keep the American Dream alive. The idea of living in a detached home, surrounded by wide expanses of garden and lawn was, and still is, rare in the urban residential communities of Europe. In the medieval era, crowding provided a sense of mutual security. As late as the eighteenth century, the Dutch were still building row houses, which had been the custom throughout Europe since the days of the Roman Empire. Even in the United States, early European settlers favored the European housing model. Over 71 percent of the residential population in the nation's capital, Washington, D.C., still lived in European-style row houses in the 1920s. In many Eastern cities, row-house construction was the norm until the end of World War II.[41]

The suburbs, by contrast, offered a different kind of security, less communal and more individualistic in bent. After 1870, says sociologist Kenneth Jackson, "the new idea was no longer to be part of a close community, but to have a self-contained unit, a private wonderland walled off from the rest of the world."[42]

The suburban home personified the American belief that freedom means autonomy; that is, the right to exclude others and to exercise near total control over one's immediate environment. European visitors to America can't help but notice how different America's suburban neighborhoods are from those in residential areas of Europe, where people huddle much more closely together.

Europeans are surprised by the sheer size of the American home, which, on the average, contains more than twice the floor space of the average European home. The average floor space in American homes is about 2,300 square feet. In France, it's 946 square feet, in Germany 932 square feet, in Spain 917 square feet, and in Britain only 817 square feet.[43]

Europeans are even more surprised by the amount of land each home occupies in America. Even with a growing population, we have far less human density today than eighty-five years ago. We are becoming more, not less, spread out. How did we pull this off? By moving out into the countryside and turning farm and pastureland into suburban housing tracts. According to the U.S. Census Bureau Report of 1920, the average density of urbanized areas, which include cities, suburbs, and towns, was a little less than ten persons per acre. By 1990, the number of people had halved to four persons per acre. More important, the average density of all new housing developments in the U.S. since 1960 is a little more than two persons per acre. That's less than one-fourth the average number of people per acre in 1920. We did this by occupying eight times more developed land than we did more than eighty years ago.[44]

The amount of land occupied per household is continuing to go up as well. This is happening even though the number of persons per household is declining. With single-parent households, smaller families, and empty nesters, household size has declined from 3.28 persons in 1940 to fewer than 2.48 persons in 2000.[45] While the number of households is increasing, so is the amount of space they are occupying. In Massachusetts, for example, there was one-half an acre of land per person in the 1950s, and by 1985 there was 1.83 acres of land per person.[46] In Maryland, lots of one acre or more per household are the most popular development category and make up three-quarters of all the land converted to housing in that state in the 1980s.[47]

By contrast, metropolitan areas in Europe are, on the average, three to four times more dense than in America. Even Europe's suburban areas are four times as dense as ours in the States.[48]

The American penchant to own land is matched by our desire to own the houses that go on the land. Federal government policies have long encouraged home ownership over rental in the American housing market. The Federal Housing Administration (FHA) and the Veterans Administration (VA) mortgage guarantees have underwritten the financing of one-quarter of all the single-family homes constructed in the past half century.[49] Federal tax deductions on mortgage titles, accelerated depreciation, and other incentives have also encouraged home ownership over rentals in America.

European government policies favor apartments over houses and encourage renting rather than ownership. In Germany, Italy, and Spain, more than 50 percent of families live in flats, and in France, 41 percent live in flats.[50] Home ownership throughout most of Europe is significantly less than in the United States. While 68 percent of Americans own their homes, only 54 percent of the French and 43 percent of Germans own their homes. In the Netherlands, only 44 percent of households own their own homes, and in Switzerland, less than 30 percent of households own their own homes.[51] (Only in the U.K., Italy, and Spain is home ownership as high as in the U.S.)

Publicly funded housing is also much higher in Europe than in the U.S. And, unlike in the U.S., public funding of housing since World War II has included much of the middle class as well as the poor. The number of people in publicly funded housing is two to three times as high in Europe as in the United States. In the U.K. and France, for example, approximately 20 percent of households live in social housing.[52]

In America, freedom means independence, and independence means private control over space. Being self-contained and self-reliant has been the recurring theme of the American psyche since well before the American Revolution. We like to keep our distance from our neighbors. Not surprisingly, then, there is little sense of community in the average American suburb, certainly less than one experiences in the residential neighborhoods surrounding European cities. Jackson makes the pointed observation that "there are few places as desolate and lonely as a suburban street on a hot afternoon."[53]

More than 60 percent of all U.S. metropolitan residents live in the suburbs, and their numbers are growing.[54] As shocking as it might seem to most Europeans, two-thirds of America's 86.4 million homes are single-family domiciles.[55] And while we seek autonomy inside our self-contained suburban homes, we also retain that nervous energy and restlessness that are also so much a part of the American Spirit. For Americans, freedom means both autonomy and mobility. It's no wonder, then, that in any given five-year period, 25 to 35 percent of all households change residence.[56]

Europeans do not share the American restlessness, perhaps because they experience the place where they live as more than a house, as a community. With community comes deeper roots and less willingness to pick up and move to some unknown new place. The average European moves only half as often as the average American.[57] I have a young Italian friend in her early thirties who had lived in Rome for several years. She told me she was about to move back to the small community outside Bologna where she grew up and her parents still had their ancestral home. In America, it is unusual for children to return home to their childhood neighborhoods to live out their adult lives. Quite the contrary in Italy and other parts of Europe. My friend told me that many of her friends spent a few years in the "hot" cities of Europe at the beginning of their careers only to find their way back to their childhood communities when they chose to raise families of their own.

There's an old American saying, "There is no such thing as a free lunch." We've paid a heavy price for our penchant for autonomy and mobility. The desire for ever bigger houses and more private space coupled with our sense of rootlessness and constant changing of residence has cost us dearly, in terms of the aesthetics of daily living. An increasing number of Americans live in cookie-cutter housing tracts plopped down on former agricultural lands stretching as far as sixty to seventy miles from metropolitan beltways. More than 60 million people—one-quarter of the population of the lower forty-eight states—now live in what planners call "exurbs." The mass exodus of population from older cities into suburbs and exurbs has occurred rapidly, and with little or no long-term spatial planning to guide the migration. Nearly one-sixth of all the land developed over our nation's history occurred in just ten years between the early 1980s and the 1990s.[58] The net result of this chaotic and undirected dispersion of population is what we call "sprawl." It has become a defining characteristic of the American landscape.

Sprawl is easy to identify. It consists of scattered housing developments, often isolated from one another, and from places of employment, schools, and commercial areas; commercial strip malls along roads adjacent to interstate highways; few if any pedestrian paths connecting housing developments; a lack of public transportation, and wall-to-wall automobile traffic. Worse still, these residential areas generally lack a sense of organic development, or any kind of history. Some—not all—are communities in name only. An increasing number of Americans live in "bedroom communities," an obvious oxymoron. Culturally barren and nondescript, American suburbs can be isolated places to live. In a sense, they represent the final chapter of the American Dream. Each person is surrounded by his or her possessions and isolated from his or her surroundings—millions of autonomous personal spheres, virtually cut off from one another. Few Americans could likely name half of their neighbors within a three-minute walk of their houses.

What zoning restrictions that do exist in American counties are often weighted toward wide-open residential and commercial development. Coordinated long-term spatial planning between adjacent counties and at the state or federal level is virtually nonexistent. It's everyone for themselves, and the effect is blight, writ large, across the width and breadth of the American landscape.

It's not that way in Europe, because the rights of individual property holders, whether they be home owners or commercial businesses, are continually balanced against the customs, social norms, and goals of the community as a whole. Any American that's ever driven across Europe notices the difference almost immediately. Each community has its own history and story to tell. Communities seem to follow an organic plan. There is a sense of purposefulness and order. In the big cities as well as in the outlying metropolitan areas, there is a sense of neighborhood and of community. People seem to belong.

None of this came about by chance. Spatial planning is far more developed throughout Europe. And now, the governments of Europe have gone a step further, developing an ambitious continent-wide spatial development plan. In September 2000, the European Conference of Ministers Responsible for Regional Planning (CEMAT) adopted what they call "Guiding Principles for Sustainable Spatial Development of the European Continent." The aim is to bring the economic and social development of each region into harmony with its ecological surroundings and cultural heritage in a "long-term, large-scale and balanced spatial development."[59] The forty-five member states of the Council of Europe have agreed to work cooperatively at the local, regional, national, and continental levels, to make sure that future spatial planning across the European landmass is compatible with Europe's dream of inclusivity, diversity, sustainability, quality of life, universal human rights, the rights of nature, and peace among people.

Try to imagine the people of the United States ever agreeing to commit ourselves to a similar coordinated long-term spatial planning effort for the country. As long as undeveloped land is still widely available, the cost of gasoline is relatively cheap, home mortgages are affordable, and tax deductions on mortgage payments continue to exist, there is little chance we will reverse our present developmental course. Those who can afford it will have to make due with an occasional vacation in Europe, where they can enjoy a short respite walking streets that go from somewhere to somewhere and that feel lived in.

The Collision of Property and Democracy

On July 12, 1893, a young American historian, Frederick Jackson Turner, read a paper before a meeting of the American Historical Association in

Chicago on the closing of the American frontier, announced by the U.S. Census Bureau of 1890. Turner reflected on the two dreams that animated American life over the course of its short history as a nation. The first "was that of individual freedom to compete unrestrictedly for the resources of a continent—the squatter ideal." Turner noted that, to the pioneer, "government was evil."[60] Americans were, and remain to this day, suspicious of government, always worried that it might encroach on or limit their right to accumulate property and remain free. "Don't tread on me" was one of the early mottos of the American revolutionaries in their struggle against the British crown. The spirit of that message continued to live on in the life of the young republic after the American Revolution.

The other dream, writes Turner, "was the ideal of democracy—government of, by, and for the people."[61] These two dreams coexisted "with the passing into private possession of the free public domain and the natural resources of the United States." Turner cautioned, however, that "American democracy was based on an abundance of cheap and free lands; these were the very conditions that shaped its growth and its fundamental traits."[62]

As long as cheap and free land was available, Americans would not have to be overly worried about class conflict. The exploited and destitute masses of immigrants and the native-born could escape the oppression of the East by continuing to move westward. The West, in effect, became a safety valve, a way to ensure equality of opportunity without having to worry about equality of condition. On the frontier, every person was equal in the sense that he or she was on his or her own, unencumbered by government edicts or, for the most part, the long hand of Eastern commercial interests. Now, however, noted Turner, "the age of free competition of individuals for the unpossessed resources of the nation is nearing its end."[63] Turner worried about the fate of a people whose "nervous energy" had for so long been almost singularly dedicated to the task of taming the wild environs of a vast continent and transforming its natural abundance into a store of private property.

American president Calvin Coolidge once remarked that "the business of America is America's business." Thirty years earlier, intellectuals such as Turner were already beginning to have doubts about what the future might bring for America, if that was all there was to the American Dream. In his paper, Turner cites the French intellectual Emile Gaston Boutmy, who observed,

The striking and peculiar characteristic of American society is that it is not so much a democracy as a huge commercial company for the discovery, cultivation, and capitalization of its enormous territory.[64]

Turner ended his paper with a lament that, in hindsight, more than one hundred years later, appears eerily prescient. He wrote,

So long as success in amassing great wealth for the aggrandizement of the individual is the exclusive or the dominant standard of success, so long as material prosperity, regardless of the conditions of its cost, or the civilization which results, is the shibboleth, American democracy, that faith in the common man which the pioneer cherishes, is in danger. For the strongest will make their way unerringly to whatever goal society sets up as the mark of conceded preeminence.[65]

Most of my European friends and acquaintances are quick to ridicule America's love affair with "the almighty dollar." "All you Americans think about is money" has become a standard mantra in virtually every opening discussion about the American character and the American way of life. In reality, the American condition is more complex. It's not the money per se. Rather, it's the search for personal security that comes from being propertied, the belief that our possessions will make us free. For many Europeans who have opted for less wealth and more play, the American obsession with creating propertied wealth appears more like a kind of pathology. They say that "our possessions end up possessing us."

But the point is, it was the American people that became the purest advocates of the European Enlightenment idea that equates private property with freedom. So fervent has been our belief that when the U.S. Congress adopted a new version of the federal income tax in 1894, it was declared unconstitutional by the courts. The U.S. Constitution had to be amended before the new tax could be adopted.[66] The very idea that government might take away a portion of one's propertied wealth to be used for other purposes was anathema to many Americans weaned on the frontier tradition of rugged individualism and self-reliance.

By the end of the first decade of the twentieth century, with the frontier closed and cheap public land no longer there for the taking, questions of economic justice and redistribution of wealth began to be heard, especially among immigrants and the native-born laboring in the new foundries and factories in the Eastern and Midwestern cities. The rise of a small coterie of super-rich and powerful robber barons like Andrew Carnegie, John D. Rockefeller, and Cornelius Vanderbilt, whose wealth rivaled the great aristocratic families of Europe, did not sit well with millions of American men and women toiling in wretched conditions in the factories and sweatshops that these new men of commerce controlled.

President Theodore Roosevelt was the first head of state to challenge the American preoccupation with property. In 1910, he told the American people,

> We are face to face with new conceptions of the relations of property to human welfare, chiefly because certain advocates of the rights of property as against the rights of men have been pushing their claims too far. The man who wrongly holds that every human right is secondary to his profit must now give way to the advocate of human welfare, who rightly maintains that every man holds his property subject to the general right of the community to regulate its use to whatever degree the public welfare may require.[67]

America's flirtation with the redistribution of wealth picked up steam during the global depression in the 1930s. President Franklin D. Roosevelt's administration's New Deal programs were America's first real foray into balancing property rights with human rights. The American dalliance continued through the 1960s and ended abruptly with the demise of President Lyndon B. Johnson's Great Society programs.

By 1980, America had all but abandoned the idea of redistributive justice. The election of Ronald Reagan, a transplanted Westerner, as president signaled a return to the earlier American Dream, the one that glorified the rags-to-riches theme and held up property rights as the foundation of American freedom.

Now, however, the rationale that spawned private property relations is beginning to fray in the wake of new technologies that are once again fundamentally altering our sense of space and time. The quickening connection of the central nervous system of every human being to every other human being on Earth, via the World Wide Web and other new global communication technologies, is forcing us into a global space and a new simultaneous field of time. The result is that property exchange in national markets is going to increasingly give way in the twenty-first century to access relationships in vast global networks.

Diminished attachment to a private property regime has great potential import for the future of commerce and governance. After all, market capitalism is based on the idea of exchanging property in the form of goods and services between sellers and buyers. If the psychological and ideological attachment to private property continues to weaken, what will be the eventual fate of the marketplace?

The change from ownership to access has equally important implications for nation-state governance. Enlightenment philosophers and economists never tired of making the connection between a private property regime and the legitimacy of the nation-state. It was always assumed that the mission of the nation-state was largely to secure the private property of its citizens. If private property relations were to be subsumed by new commercial relationships—whose modus operandi is less wedded to market exchanges inside a territorially defined political unit and more geared to access in globally connected networks—what might be the effect on the future of the nation-state itself?

The conundrum is that the very commercial and political institutions that are attempting to accommodate these new spatial and temporal realities are the ones whose own futures are in doubt because of the far-reaching changes now taking place in the world. The capitalist marketplace and the nation-state are the defining institutional paradigm of the modern era, just as the Church and the feudal order were in the medieval era. And just as new spatial and temporal changes led to the demise of the medieval arrangement, now, once again, dramatic spatial and temporal changes are leading to the weakening of national markets and nation-states and the emergence of global commercial networks and transnational political spaces like the European Union. Rethinking a world beyond capitalist markets and nation-states will likely be as contentious and bitterly fought as was the struggle that led to the fall of Christendom and feudal society and the rise of the market economy and nation-state. Understanding what historian Karl Polanyi called the "Great Transformation," the twists and turns that gave birth to modern capitalism and nation-state formation, can provide a much-needed perspective on the challenges facing our current generation as it wrestles with defining a new consciousness and new institutional models better suited to a globalized space and time.

7

Forging Capitalist Markets and Nation-States

THE MARKET ECONOMY has become such a pervasive force in modern life that we have come to think of it as almost like a force of nature. If the truth be known, we Americans would be utterly lost were the marketplace not the centerpiece of our existence. We forget that the market economy is a relatively new institution in human history. While markets existed far back into antiquity, they were always marginal to social life. Most economic activity was traditionally based in the household. In fact, the very term "economy" comes from the Greek *oikos*, which means "home." Members of an extended family produced what they needed for themselves, bartered with nearby neighbors, and occasionally sold any surplus production in open-air markets, which were held infrequently. Large markets, like the great Frankfurt Fair in late medieval times, were annual events that drew itinerant merchants from far afield. At the bigger fairs, one could purchase more exotic goods. Silk, books, parchment, drugs, and spices, mostly from the Far East, were among the more popular goods available for sale.

But the idea of a fully integrated modern market economy extends well beyond the notion of merchants setting up their stalls and selling their wares to local buyers. For modern markets to work, all of the elements that go into making things—land, human labor, and technology—have to be dislodged from the traditional household setting and be converted into a form that can be rationalized, abstracted, quantified, and made into property negotiable for a price in the marketplace.

Even though the concept of the modern market economy originated in Europe, it found its fullest expression in America. Europeans, early on, had mixed feelings about capitalism. Americans never did. America has long been regarded as the bastion of capitalism. So unwavering has been our faith in capitalist dogma that the idea of America and capitalism has come to enjoy a tautological status.

Americans may be the only pure capitalists left in the world. Adam Smith's idea of an unfettered marketplace where individual sellers and buyers compete to maximize their property holdings is the primary playing field for living out the American Dream. Were the capitalist arena to be seriously compromised, the American Dream would suffer. That's why Americans are so fiercely loyal to the tenets of capitalist theory. They are the alpha and omega of our way of life, without which the American Dream would be an impossibility.

The capitalist market is not held in as high esteem by Europeans. It is the very different set of historical circumstances that led Europeans to temper their enthusiasm for capitalism while Americans became its most ardent champion.

The Struggle for Free Markets

As mentioned earlier, a spate of new technologies in the early modern era in Europe shortened distances traveled, sped up exchanges, and decreased transaction times, making possible much bigger markets. Feudal governing institutions were too small and parochial to manage the new potential reach of human activity. In fact, these same institutions, for the most part, saw larger markets as a potential threat and acted to thwart them.

By the late medieval era, more than one thousand towns had sprung up throughout Europe. The towns had graineries, shops, and inns, and were served by local craftsmen. They produced a variety of goods and services requiring expertise not available on every manorial estate. Masons, fine weavers and dyers, metalworkers, and armorers, and later the broiderers and glovers, the scriveners, the upholsterers, and the hatters, clustered together in these prototype urban areas, establishing "free cities"—regions independent of the reach of the local lords. If a serf, for example, were to escape his lord and flee to a city and remain there for a year and a day, he was deemed to be free, having passed from the jurisdiction of his lord to the jurisdiction of the city burghers.[1]

Each craft industry established a guild to regulate the activity of its members. The guilds were responsible for maintaining quality standards for their industry, determining how much would be manufactured and sold, as well as the fair price for the sale of their goods and services. The guild economy operated by custom, not by market forces. The point was not to make a profit but, rather, to maintain a way of life. Guilds opposed an open market, free labor, the commercialization of land, and competitive prices—all of the essential hallmarks of a modern economy. For more than four centuries, the guilds fought off the emerging capitalist class by using city codes and regulations to enforce their will. Craft guilds were not abolished in France until 1791, England in 1813 and 1814, Austria and Germany in 1859 and 1860, and Italy in 1864.[2]

In the sixteenth century in England, an independent merchant class was beginning to challenge the guilds' control over the production of goods and services. Economic conditions in England, and later on the Continent, were making the guild system increasingly untenable. The wave of land enclosures was freeing up peasants, providing a new exploitable workforce. Advances in transportation—the laying down of better roads and improvements in river navigation—were making it easier to move raw materials and finished goods between the countryside and towns. A burgeoning population was demanding more goods at cheaper prices.

The textile guilds were the first to be hurt by the new market forces being unleashed. Rogue merchants began to skirt guild controls and urban jurisdictions by dispersing work to cheaper labor in the countryside—called the "putting-out" system. New breakthroughs in technology and the organization of work led to a "division of labor," substantially reducing the costs of manufacturing goods and the time necessary to produce them. The new production model was better able to meet the upsurge in consumer demand.[3]

The new method of doing business had a second, more profound effect. Under the guild system, the masters and journeymen owned their own tools, giving them control over production. The new class of independent merchants began to "take possession directly of production," providing the tools and machinery used by their rural labor force.[4] Poor cottagers engaged in the putting-out system for weaving were among the first to feel the full effects of the new capitalist way of conducting business. Living at the very margins of poverty, a cottager was often unable to pay for the purchase of material in advance of the sale of his cloth and had to seek credit from the merchant employer. That generally meant pledging his most valued asset, his loom, as security against a money advance for the raw material he needed. If unable to pay off the debt, he would have to forfeit his loom to the merchant employer, putting the means of production directly into the hands of the capitalist—further strengthening his position vis-à-vis the craftsmen.[5]

By providing the raw material and the tools necessary for production and by controlling the transport of supplies and finished products between country and town, the new merchants were able to exercise far greater control over labor costs. Already destitute, desperate, and without any other means to make a livelihood, peasant workers had little choice but to accept the conditions of employment imposed on them by a fledgling capitalist class. The guilds, for their part, could not compete with either the pace or the volume of production or the price of the finished products.

The introduction of the factory into Europe further eroded the power of the master craftsmen and their guilds. In the latter half of the sixteenth century, factory manufacture came to England. Paper mills, ironworks, cannon factories, and, later, textile factories introduced the idea of centralizing all of the production tasks under one roof with a common energy source—first using water and windmills, and later using coal and steam-powered machinery. Factory manufacture required large sums of capital—often several thousand pounds or more—well beyond the means of even the wealthiest master craftsmen. Only the new class of merchant capitalists could afford the cost of this new kind of manufacturing model.[6] Historian Maurice Dobb makes the point that "the subordination of production to capital, and the appearance of this class relationship between capitalist and the producer is, therefore, to be regarded as the crucial watershed between the old mode of production and the new."[7]

Master craftsmen were finding it difficult to stem the capitalist tide. Many simply gave up and became paid employees in the new capitalist factories. Others fought back by putting up as many firewalls as they could in an effort to prevent the new merchant capitalists from breaking out of the countryside and into larger trading markets. For example, notes the late economist and historian Robert Heilbroner, "Over a journey of a hundred miles, a traveling merchant might fall under a dozen different sovereignties, each with different rules, regulations, laws, weights, measures, money."[8]

Toll stations added still another formidable obstacle to regional and national trade. At every border and jurisdiction there were toll stations. In the fourteenth century, reports Heilbroner, "there were said to be more than thirty toll stations along the Weser River and at least thirty-five around the Elbe; along the Rhine, a century later, there were more than sixty such toll stations . . . "[9] Along the Seine in France, there were so many toll stations in the late fifteenth century "that it cost half its final selling price to ship grain two hundred miles down the river."[10] Heilbroner makes the telling point that only England enjoyed a unified internal market in the late Middle Ages, which in large measure accounts for its emergence as Europe's first great economic power.[11]

Still, while the guilds and local towns could more effectively control the conditions of commerce within their city walls and immediate surroundings by exclusionary and protectionist tactics, it proved far more difficult to control external trade. Towns and guilds banded together in an effort to curtail the new capitalist enterprise burgeoning in the rural countryside. The nascent merchant capitalists fought back using every means at their disposal to break through the barriers and create national markets.

Europe found itself in the throes of a great struggle between a new commercial order and an old economic regime. New technologies were radically altering spatial and temporal realities. The old social economy, based on controlling production, fixing prices, and excluding competition from the outside, was too provincial to accommodate the range of new technologies that were making possible greater exchange of goods and services between more people over longer distances. The new technologies gave birth to a capitalist class hell-bent on exploiting their full potential. They found their commercial model in self-regulating free markets.

What was missing was a new, more expansive, and agile political framework that could impose its will on the thousands of local municipalities and force the elimination of local tolls and tariffs and countless other statutes and codes that maintained an aging medieval economy. In addition, there was a need to establish a common language, a unified educational system, a single police force, and other centralized mechanisms to make viable a nationwide internal commercial trading market. It was this need, says Karl Polanyi, "which forced the territorial state to the fore as the instrument of the 'nationalization' of the market and the creator of internal commerce."[12]

The Rise of the Nation-State

The nation-state is a relatively new institution for governing human society. Some scholars date its origins no further back than the American and French revolutions in the late eighteenth century, while others suggest that its roots extend even further back to England in the twelfth and thirteenth centuries. The popular conception of the nation-state is of an organic creation rooted in common culture, language, and customs that evolved over time into a modern state formation. Although there is a germ of truth to the notion, in reality the nation-state is more of an "imaginary community"—an artificial construct largely created by political and economic elites to foster more expansive national trading markets and to secure overseas colonies. That's not to say that there aren't exceptions to the rule. Certainly, some of the nationalists' ethnic struggles in the postcommunist era in Central and Eastern Europe have less to do with expanding markets than with preserving ethnic identities. Still, for the most part, the nation-state and national markets emerged together, each feeding the other in a symbiotic relationship. National markets increased the pace, speed, flow, and density of exchange of property between people, while the territorial nation-state created and maintained the rules and regulations necessary to ensure an efficient flow of property over a unified and expansive geographic plane.

The genius of the nation-state lay in its ability to provide a new collective identity for the growing numbers of autonomous free agents who made up the world of private property relations in self-regulating markets. It did so by establishing itself as a near mirror image of the self-interested market maximizing individuals of the nascent capitalist economy. Like each of the autonomous individuals who claimed sovereignty over his own personal property domain, the nation-state claimed a similar right of sovereignty over the larger territory of which all the individual free agents were a part. And, like its citizens, the nation-state claimed its autonomy as an equal among nations and defended its right to protect the property under its control as well as to compete with other nation-states—through trade or war—for contested territory.

The difficult challenge for the budding nation-state was how to eliminate all the internal pockets of resistance to free trade in a national market while at the same time enlisting the emotional support of its subjects—later its citizens—in the collective tasks of society, including the collection of taxes and the conscription of armies to protect its national interests. This was no easy matter since, in many ways, the Enlightenment idea of the detached, self-interested, autonomous agent—operating only with his own material self-interest in mind and determined to optimize his own property holdings—seemed strangely at odds with an effort to forge a collective sense of common purpose and identity. How does the nation-state convince millions of newly emancipated individuals to give up some of their autonomy and freedom to the state?

The answer was to create a compelling story about a common past, one convincing enough to capture the imagination of the people and convince them of their shared identity and common destiny. The architects of the modern nation-state understood the magnitude of the task ahead of them. After Italian state unification in 1861, Massimo d'Azeglio, the former prime minister of Piedmont, was said to have remarked, "We have made Italy, now we have to make Italians."[13]

Every nation-state in the modern era has created a myth of origins complete with its own heroes and heroines and past moments of trials and tribulations often memorialized in elaborate rituals. In an increasingly disenchanted secular world, the nation-state had to establish a powerful new image of a people who shared a noble past and were destined for future greatness. At the same time, the nation-state had to create a convincing enough utopian vision of what lay ahead to win the loyalty of its subjects and, later, citizens. If the road to immortality no longer lay with accepting Christ as savior, then at least it could be found in the relentless pursuit of unlimited material wealth in the form of the accumulation and exchange of property. In return for giving one's allegiance to the state—the litmus test being whether the citizen would be willing to give his or her life for their country—the state would uphold its side of the covenant by protecting each person's right to own and exchange private property in a free marketplace.

Creating a shared identity was also essential to making viable an unobstructed national market. Before there was an England, France, Germany, and Italy, what existed was a thousand different stories and traditions being lived out in little hamlets, nestled in valleys and on mountainsides across the continent. Each story was passed on in a separate language or, at least in a distinct dialect.

A myriad of local languages, customs, and regulations for conducting commerce kept the transaction costs high for producing and trading goods and services over a wide geographic terrain. Suppressing or even eliminating pockets of cultural diversity was an essential first step in creating an efficient and seamless national market. Creating a single homogenized national myth required the often ruthless destruction or subordination of all the local stories and traditions that existed for centuries of European history.

The success of the nation-state model owes much to the adoption of rational processes for marshaling far-flung activities. To begin with, it was necessary to establish a single dominant language in each country so that people could communicate with one another and understand shared meanings. It's often thought that sharing a common language was indispensable to bringing people together under the aegis of the nation-state. However, that's not generally the case. Take France, for example. In 1789, on the eve of the French Revolution, less than 50 percent of the people spoke French, and only 12 to 13 percent spoke it correctly. In northern and southern France, it would have been virtually impossible to find anyone who spoke French. At the time Italy was unified in 1861, only 2.5 percent of the population used the Italian language for everyday communication. In eighteenth-century Germany, fewer than 500,000 people read and spoke in the vernacular that later came to be the official German language, and many of them were actors who performed new works on stage or scholars writing for a small intellectual elite.[14]

Much of the impetus for creating national languages had less to do with nation-state formation and more to do with the demographics facing the early print industry. Printers in the fifteenth and sixteenth centuries were anxious to expand the markets for the mass production of books. The problem was that while Latin was the official language of the Church and was used among European scholars and government officials in the palace courts, it represented too small a reading market for the new communications revolution. On the other hand, there were so many languages and dialects spoken across Europe that each one, by itself, would be too small a market to be commercially viable. The answer, in most countries, was to choose a single vernacular language, usually the most dominant in a region, and establish it as the language for reproduction—first in Bibles and later for works of literature and science.

Even here, the languages that eventually became standard French, German, Spanish, Italian, and English are, in part, invented. They were usually the result of combining elements of all the various idioms spoken in a region and then standardizing the grammar.[15] However, once a common language became accepted, it created its own mystique of permanence. People came to think of it as their ancestral tongue and the cultural tie that bound them together.

Getting everyone to speak and read the new vernacular necessitated the creation of a national educational system in each country. A single educational system, in turn, created reliable and predictable standards of what was to be learned and how. Standardized national education was a wholly new phenomenon of the modern era and helped forge a national consciousness. With each generation of schoolchildren learning the same subjects, in the same way, in a common language, it wasn't long before people began to believe that they were, indeed, part of a shared experience and a common destiny. A French minister of education, reflecting on the success of French public education, remarked that "he could consult his watch at any moment of the day and say whether every child in France, of a given age, would be doing long division, reading Corneille, or conjugating . . . verbs."[16]

There were often more subtle effects of national education besides creating a shared language and a sense of common cultural identity. State-administered public education inculcated students into the new spatial and temporal consciousness of the modern era. Schools were designed to resemble factories, and students were made comfortable with the idea of spending an entire day in a large, centralized facility with different rooms set aside for specialized learning tasks, mirroring the kind of specialization of labor and work environment they would graduate into after their education was completed. Students were also taught the virtues of punctuality and efficiency, making and keeping schedules, and being industrious, disciplined, and competitive with one another. They were made to believe that learning was an acquisitive activity, the goal being to possess knowledge that could be used to advance one's self-interest. The curriculum was designed to prepare students for the economic tasks that awaited them in the emerging market economy. Turning out "productive citizens" became the primary responsibility of national education in every modern state.

The nation-state's intervention into the affairs of its citizens merely began with the establishment of a common language and a universal educational system. The modern state's mission is to create a totally rationalized environment that can optimize the free play of property exchange in a market economy. Records have to be kept on every citizen. Birth certificates, school registrations, marriage licenses, death certificates, and passports all have to be issued. Taxes have to be collected, and government revenues need to be distributed. Full-time armies need to be trained, equipped, quartered, and sent into battle. Standards have to be set to regulate everything from the quality of food and medicine to the quality of the environment. Even reproducing the culture itself is no longer just left to chance or to the whims of local communities. Museums have to be built, memorials financed, historic dates recognized and celebrated, and parks set aside for recreation and entertainment. The list is nearly endless.

Medieval political institutions were far more lax and less involved in the day-to-day affairs of their own subjects. Creating a "productive" society requires the kind of total mobilization of human life that would have been unthinkable in any previous period of history. The irony here is that the Enlightenment philosophers favored a world populated by autonomous agents, seeking only to optimize their own self-interests in the marketplace. To make that possible, however, nation-states had to create giant bureaucracies to oversee the game, and make sure that all of that "self-interest" didn't disintegrate into a nightmarish Hobbesian "war of all against all." In the end, the price of securing individual freedom in the marketplace was more government intervention and involvement in the most intimate aspects of people's personal lives. By the first decade of the twentieth century, more than 700,000 Austrians were employed by their national government and more than 500,000 people in France worked in government bureaucracies, as did 1.5 million in Germany and 700,000 in Italy.[17]

Consolidating Power

Nations and states both existed before the modern era. A nation is a community of people who share a particular lived experience, while a state is a political institution that controls or possesses a geographic region for the purpose of exploitation and does so by manipulating the means of violence to maintain obedience to its rule. What is unique in the modern era is the coming together of the nation and the state in a single schema.

In medieval Europe, there were literally thousands of small, isolated communities whose shared lived experience was local and barely extended beyond the nearest mountain range or river basin. These communities were loosely bound to larger institutional authorities that included kingdoms, dynasties, and the papacy in Rome. Rule, in medieval Europe, however, was experienced more over peoples than territories. In fact, territories were vague and fluid, rather than precise and fixed. Even local rule was rather spotty and more arbitrary. Government in medieval Europe was personalized, even to the extent that it was often portable. That is, the royal families would often establish residence in an area and make visits to the various estates, taking their entire government entourage along with them. Representatives would be dispatched to collect rent and taxes from the villagers of the district, creating a more personal relationship between ruler and ruled. In the fourteenth century, this kind of makeshift arrangement began to slowly give way to more rationalized forms of rule exercised from a distance.[18] But the point, says historian David Held, is that in the medieval era, "empires were *ruled* but they were not *governed.*"[19] They simply lacked the means to administer an entire kingdom from a centralized location.

The introduction of the cannon in the mid–fifteenth century fundamentally changed the nature of political rule. More powerful lords, with sufficient funds to finance the new military technology, were able to, literally as well as figuratively, destroy the walls and fortresses of local rulers and consolidate their holdings over a larger territory. Between 1450 and 1550, many of the thousands of independent principalities and duchies were weakened or eliminated altogether as central governments became more powerful.[20] Eventually, the monarchies succeeded in disarming the old medieval warrior-dynasties and replacing them with a single sovereign rule. By the middle of the seventeenth century, Europe was no longer ruled by feuding local families but rather by centralized monarchical states.[21]

The amassing of economic power in the hands of the monarch was often welcomed by a peasant class tired of being caught up in the ceaseless warfare between feuding local nobles. The people, at least for a time, were willing to subject themselves to strong rule from above if it meant making day-to-day life in their locality a little less precarious and slightly more bearable.

Rousseau, however, caught the deeper political significance of the shift from ruling people to governing territory. In *The Social Contract*, he wrote,

> It is understandable how the combined lands of private individuals become public territory, and how the right of sovereignty, extending from the subjects to the ground they occupy, comes to include both property and person. . . . This advantage does not appear to have been well understood by ancient kings who, only calling themselves kings of the Persians, the Scythians, the Macedonians, seem to have considered themselves leaders of men rather than masters of the country. Today's kings more cleverly call themselves Kings of France, Spain, England, etc. By thus holding the land, they are quite sure to hold its inhabitants.[22]

By claiming sovereignty over territory, the monarchies were able to broaden their claim to power to include power over all the property within their jurisdictional boundaries, including the property people held over their own labor, as well as their other worldly holdings. Henceforth, loyalty to the king became a critical litmus test for securing one's property and, by extension, one's freedom. The centralized authority was now the only force that could both assure one's property and take it away.

The first formal recognition in international law of the sovereign rights of territorial states came in the form of a peace agreement in 1648 that ended the thirty-year war between Lutherans, Calvinists, and Catholics. The Peace of Westphalia recognized the irreconcilable differences between the various branches of Christianity and granted territorial rulers sovereign authority within their own domains to establish matters of religion, while restricting the rights of other countries to intervene in what was hereafter to be considered an internal matter within each respective country. The essential points laid out in the Peace of Westphalia, although modified over the course of the next three centuries, remained pretty much the same until the end of World War II.[23]

The treaty recognized that the world is made up of autonomous and independent states and that each state is sovereign over the internal affairs within its fixed territory. Moreover, each state is equal to every other state, and no superior authority exists over them. Finally, territorial states are each expected to preserve their own self-interests, and while free to enter into diplomatic relationships and bilateral or multilateral agreements with one another, they also have the right to use force to settle disputes, if necessary.[24]

For a time, the interests of the new territory-based monarchical rulers and the emerging capitalist class and bourgeoisie coincided. The new state powers, anxious to consolidate their rule, needed to generate revenue. Armies had to be raised, ships had to be built, weapons had to be manufactured, and administrative bureaucracies had to be set up both to control their own territory and to colonize new territories abroad. It was, therefore, in the interest of the monarchies to stimulate domestic economic activity.

For their part, the merchants and manufacturers were desirous of reforms that would help speed the transition to free trade in national markets. They sought the elimination of legal and customary restrictions that hampered labor mobility, pushed for legal enforcement of commercial contracts backed by the police power of the monarchy, and pressed for improvements in roads, waterways, and communication to speed commerce and expand the geographic range of trade. They also wanted the centralized political authority to standardize weights and measures and create a single coinage to reduce transaction costs and expedite commercial activity. The monarchical authority was more than willing to facilitate the changes and back up the reforms with the full coercive force of the state because the state, too, had an interest in creating favorable conditions for the flourishing of a national market.

Eventually, however, the mercantilist policies pursued by the new regimes threw an irreconcilable wedge between the nascent capitalist class and the government. The states were intent on accumulating precious metals—gold and silver—to finance their domestic spending and foreign adventures. They reasoned that the best way to increase their money holdings was to favor foreign over domestic trade. The strategy was to heavily regulate domestic production so they could secure high-quality goods at low prices and then sell the goods abroad for higher prices and be paid in precious metals.

Under the scheme, their overseas colonies would be restricted to producing only cheap raw materials for export back to the parent country and be forced to buy their finished manufactured goods from the home country at inflated prices. Any effort in the colonies to manufacture their own goods for domestic use or for trade abroad was forbidden, and any infractions were harshly punished.

Many states established their own foreign trading companies to conduct business on their behalf in their colonies. The most powerful and notorious of these were the Dutch and British East India companies. The latter boasted its own private army and, at one point, administered most of India as a surrogate for the British government.

The emphasis on foreign trade greatly benefited the export merchants, but at the expense of the domestic manufacturers. While, at first, the increase in foreign trade helped expand the home market for manufactured goods, the restrictions that governments like Britain's eventually placed on the volume of domestic production that could be produced in order to keep export prices artificially high worked to the disadvantage of the manufacturers.[25]

The young capitalist class preferred open markets and free trade, believing that it was the best way to increase output, optimize their margins, and improve their profits. The peasantry, the urban working poor, and the rising middle class all felt the sting of higher prices on domestic products. They also suffered under the burden of increased taxes to finance government spending on armies, weaponry, and wars.

By the late eighteenth century, the breach between the emerging capitalist class and the monarchies was irreversible. On June 17, 1789, deputies of the third estate defied King Louis XVI by establishing their own National Assembly and demanding a French constitution. A few months later, the radicals issued the Declaration of the Rights of Man and the Citizen, which stated, among other things, that "the source of all sovereignty resides essentially in the nation: no body of man, no individual can exercise authority that does not emanate expressly from it."[26]

In a stroke of the pen, government ruled by divine authority, and passed on by royal inheritance, was dethroned. Henceforth, sovereignty was to lie with "the nation." Who comprised "the nation"? The citizens. And who were the citizens? Those who shared a common lived experience and were bound together by a collective past and future destiny. The citizen, the nation, and the state were conjoined as a single governing entity for the first time in history. From now on, government was to be of, by, and for the people.

The French Revolution was heavily influenced by the United States of America, which had already fought and won its own revolution to secure the rights of the people. The Americans and French were engaged in a radical new kind of political experiment, for which there was little precedent. Historian Anthony Smith writes,

There was no question in earlier epochs of mobilizing the people to participate in politics at the center, nor of the need for men, let alone women, to become politically aware and active "citizens." Nor, as a result, was there any interest in providing an infrastructure and institutions, which would cater to all the needs and interests of the citizens.[27]

After the euphoria of declaring themselves sovereign died down, the French settled on a more restrictive definition of the citizen, "limiting political rights to men of property and education."[28] The Americans, the British, and most other new nation-states in the eighteenth and nineteenth centuries did so as well. Since it was assumed that the nation-state's raison d'être was to protect the property rights of its citizens, it made sense to extend the vote to only those "men" in society who owned property.

The great shift to modern nation-states, which began with England, the United States, and France, spread rapidly to other parts of Europe in the nineteenth and early twentieth centuries. Two developments were particularly important in hastening the transition: the confiscation of Church land by the emerging bourgeois class, and the coming of the railroad and the telegraph.

France and Spain had begun seizing Jesuit properties as early as the 1760s. The forced sale of Church properties continued in Italy, Germany, and elsewhere. Much of the land was purchased at the auction block for rock-bottom prices by wealthy bourgeois lawyers. The new landowners joined forces with the older aristocratic class in the 1850s and 1860s in support of a private property regime, free trade, national markets, and centralized nation-state governance.[29]

Of all the developments that facilitated the transformation to the modern nation-state, none proved more important than the introduction of the railroad and the telegraph. These two technologies alone broke through the ancient spatial and temporal barriers that had kept Europeans relatively isolated from one another since the fall of the Roman Empire. In 1780, a stagecoach made the trip from London to Manchester in four to five days. By 1880, the train could travel the same route in under five hours.[30] The railroad allowed for the quick dispatch of troops across vast distances, the fast and efficient shipment of raw materials and finished products to distant markets, and the dramatic increase in the mobility and range of travelers. The telegraph created instantaneous communication between people over great distances and enabled railroads to coordinate freight and passengers and make tracks safe.

Britain in 1840 had laid down only 2,390 kilometers of track. By 1900, it had laid out more than 30,079 kilometers of track, connecting every hamlet, village, town, and city into a national grid. Similarly, France went from 496 kilometers of track in 1840 to 38,109 kilometers by 1900.[31]

Principalities and city-states were just too small to handle the potential "economies of scale" made possible by these revolutionary new transportation and communication technologies. Only expanded national markets operating across a wide terrain and secured by territorial nation-state governments could reap the full potential of technologies that were beginning to annihilate space and time. In the sixteenth century, Europe was governed by more than five hundred separate entities. By 1900, twenty-five nation-states governed over most of Europe.[32] None of the political leaders of the time could have imagined the possibility that just a half century later, the nation-states of Europe, pressed by new spatial and temporal realities, would begin a new journey, fusing their commercial and political interests in a union that would eventually subsume much of the sovereignty of nation-state regimes.

The Last True Believers

What becomes clear in even a cursory examination of the evolution of capitalist markets and nation-state governments in Europe is that their development has been anything but smooth. The history of these two pillars of European modernity is checkered with struggle and compromise all along the way, as competing interests have sought to impose their own beliefs and agendas onto the process.

Europeans often wonder why we Americans, by contrast, have been so unquestioning of capitalist theory and so patriotic and loyal to our country. The difference is that America wasn't faced with all the labyrinthine conflicting interests that often impeded the evolution of free markets and nation-state development in the Old World. The American economic and political experiment emerged on virgin soil. There were few remnants of feudalism in the colonies, although one could make the case that the plantation system and slave labor was a close facsimile. Still, we were spared having to spar with an entrenched nobility and aristocracy. Moreover, craft guilds never became a force to reckon with in America. Free labor existed from the very outset. Capitalists never had to contend with a pre-existing set of economic relationships that favored set prices over market prices and placed restrictions on production so that craftsmen could maintain control over their respective trades.

Equally important, mercantilism never really took hold in America. The United States of America was born in rebellion to the mercantilist policies of the British crown. We fought a revolution to free ourselves from what we regarded as an intolerable exercise of economic tyranny by the state, and although we toyed with our own brand of mercantilism in the early years of the republic, it was a short-lived affair.

Nor did Americans have to wrestle with competing cultural affiliations in the forging of a national identity. Immigrants that fled to America from Europe were anxious to leave many of the old ties behind. Starting over meant accepting the American Dream—free markets and representative government. That's why they came here. The fact that English was established as the lingua franca made assimilation easier among immigrants who, in their native lands, had long been separated from one another by language barriers.

The Americanization of the New World wasn't friction-free. There were already Native Americans here when Europeans arrived. The genocide of the American Indian and the internment of their remaining numbers have continued to haunt Americans, undermining any claim we might have about our special moral status among the peoples of the world. So, too, with regard to slavery. The forced transport and enslavement of millions of Africans in the American South all but nullified any pretense we might have entertained about the nobility of the American experiment.

By and large, however, the American project was as free of traditional encumbrances and conflicting interests as it is possible to be. The capitalist class and the government of the country were rarely at odds. It was simply assumed that the primary role of government was to protect the private property interests of its citizens, which meant safeguarding a capitalist free-market economy. In Europe, however, governments eventually, if not reluctantly, took on the role of tempering the excesses of the market by redistributing wealth more equitably to ensure that no one was left behind.

So, if Americans are the most passionate capitalists and the most patriotic people on Earth, it's because we view our free-market economy and

American government as the guarantors of the American Dream. Were either of these two institutions to begin to fail, or were Americans to come to believe that either the capitalist system or our representative form of government were no longer fostering the American Dream but, rather, undermining it, the stability of the system itself would be cast in doubt— which is just what's beginning to happen in the wake of increasing corporate influence over the political affairs of government, the growing divide between rich and poor, and the steady downward mobility of middle- and working-class Americans.

Political observers worry that increasing numbers of Americans are alienated from the American political process and have come to believe that special interests—especially big business—run the country. They are forever pouring over election turnouts for signs of whether Americans are disengaging from the political process. The numbers are not encouraging. Nearly 70 percent of all eligible adults voted in the national election in 1964. By 2000, only 55 percent of eligible adults cast a vote in the national election.[33] More important than the slippage in the number of people voting is the steep decline in the number of people who still believe in the American Dream. Recall that one out of three Americans say they no longer believe in the American Dream. If that figure continues to free-fall, America is in deep trouble. Without the American Dream to bolster us, there is little left of the public psyche to maintain the American bond.

The problem, however, is that the fall of the American Dream may be inevitable. In a world that is moving beyond the kind of eighteenth-century ideological assumptions that gave rise to the American Dream, we Americans may find ourselves like the proverbial "odd man out," grossly out of step with the changes taking place all around us as the human race enters a global era.

THE COMING

GLOBAL ERA

8

Network Commerce in a
Globalized Economy

HUMANITY FINDS ITSELF, once again, at a crossroad between a dying old order and the rise of a new age. Revolutionary new technologies are forcing a fundamental change in our spatial and temporal consciousness. After two hundred years of living under the dominion of national markets and territorial nation-states, human relationships are bursting out of the old institutional seams. A new man and woman are emerging whose sense of self and perception of the world are as different from the autonomous, propertied individual of the modern age as the latter was to the communal individual of the medieval era. The new consciousness is far more expansive and global in outlook.

The national market and the nation-state suddenly feel a bit too small and limited to accommodate a world where more and more human activity—both economic and social—spill over the old edges and spread out onto the entire globe.

The birth of a new economic system is driving the changes in governance models, just as it did in the early modern era, when market capitalism uprooted the feudal economy and forced a shift in governing models from city-states and principalities to modern nation-states. This time around, it's the national market economy that is being challenged by a global network economy and the nation-state that is being partially sub-sumed by regional political spaces like the European Union. Network commerce is too quick, too dense, and too globally encompassing to be constrained by national borders. Nation-states are too geographically lim-ited to oversee inter-regional and global commerce and harmonize the growing social and environmental risks that accompany a globalized world.

Every country is facing the pressures of an ever more connected and interdependent world. But it is European society that appears to be at the vanguard of the changes taking place, making it the world's classroom for rethinking the future.

What's pushing all of these institutional changes is a communication revolution that is increasing the speed, pace, flow, density, and connectiv-ity of commercial and social life. Software, computers, the digitalization of media, the Internet, and mobile and wireless communications have, in less than two decades, connected the central nervous system of nearly 20 per-cent of the human race, at the speed of light, twenty-four hours a day, seven days a week. Today, one is instantaneously connected, via the World Wide Web, to literally a billion or more people, and able to communicate directly with any one of them. Incredibly, the total amount of information a peasant farmer or an inhabitant of a small village might have been exposed to in a lifetime two hundred years ago would not be as great as the informa-tion contained in a single online Sunday edition of *The New York Times*.

It's not only the expanded reach and greater access to information that have been so fundamentally altered but also the speed of exchange be-tween people. Recall that the standard hour didn't come into play in people's lives until the thirteenth century. Before that time, economic and social exchange was not dense enough to warrant the segmentation of the day into twenty-four standard units of measurement. In the medieval era, one's daily rounds were as limited and unhurried as they might have been in antiquity and required only a handful of natural benchmarks to mark the passage from one activity to another—the medieval day was divided into sunrise, high noon, and sunset. As human population grew, scattered hamlets metamorphosed into larger towns and cities, and commerce, trade, and social intercourse quickened, making it necessary to establish the hour and then the minute and the second, to organize the dramatic in-crease in the density and volume of human exchanges.

Over the past decade, two new time segments have been introduced into social life, both the result of the quickened pace of communication between people brought on by the computer and telecommunications revolutions. The nanosecond and picosecond are so short in duration that they exist far below the realm of human perception. One second in duration represents the passage of one billion nanoseconds. While it's impossible for the human mind to grasp a nanosecond experientially, information is now flowing at that speed everywhere in the world.

The market-exchange economy and territory-bound nation-state were not designed to accommodate a communication revolution that can envelop the globe and connect everyone and everything on the planet simultaneously. The result is that we are witnessing the birth of a new economic system and new governing institutions that are as different from market capitalism and the modern territorial state as the latter were from the feudal economy and dynastic rule of an earlier era. (We'll turn our attention to new governing institutions in the next chapter.)

The Birth of a New Economic System

The market economy is far too slow to take full advantage of the speed and productive potential made possible by the software, communications, and telecom revolutions. Nor is it just a matter of finding new organizational formats to upgrade the conduct of business in a market economy. It's the market-exchange mechanism itself that is becoming outmoded.

Markets are linear, discrete, and discontinuous modes of operation. Sellers and buyers come together for a short moment of time to exchange goods and services, then part. The lapsed time between the completion of one exchange and the introduction of the next exchange represents the lost productivity and added cost of doing business that eventually make markets obsolete.

The new communication technologies, by contrast, are cybernetic, not linear. They allow for continuous activity. That means that the start-and-stop mechanism of market exchanges can be replaced with the idea of establishing an ongoing commercial relationship between parties over time.

For example, consider the Amazon.com way of selling versus the new music company models for marketing music. Amazon.com operates in a conventional market-exchange relationship with customers even though the computer and World Wide Web are used to make the purchase. The buyer pays for an individual compact disc, and the seller ships it by mail.

By contrast, in the new network model used by music companies such as Napster, the user pays a monthly subscription fee that gives him unlimited access to the music company's library. In the old Amazon.com model, the physical CD—the property—is exchanged between seller and buyer, whereas in the new network model, the user is paying for the time for which he has access to the music.

In pure networks, property still exists, but it stays with the producer and is accessed in time segments by the user. Subscriptions, memberships, rentals, time-shares, retainers, leases, and licensing agreements become the new medium of exchange. The music company creates a 24/7 commodified relationship with the client, making him part of a music network. Now the user is paying for access to the music when he is asleep, awake, working, as well as when he is listening to the music. The music company prefers commercializing an ongoing relationship with the user over a period of time, rather than having to sell each CD as a separate market transaction. It's a matter of time and cost.

The music companies maintain a fast, efficient, smooth, and continuous relationship with the client over time, while Amazon.com is slogging along, having to negotiate each and every transaction as a discrete closed-end process. In a world where everyone is connected via cyberspace and information is being exchanged at the speed of light, time—not materials— becomes the most scarce and valuable resource. In pure networks, providers and users replace sellers and buyers, and access to the use of goods in extended time segments substitutes for the physical exchange of goods between sellers and buyers.

The music companies also favor the network model over discrete market transactions because the relationship with the user is more likely to be sustained into the future. In other words, users are less likely to take their business elsewhere, as they would were they to enter into a discrete market-exchange transaction. That's why automobile companies such as General Motors and DaimlerChrysler, if they had their way, would never sell another car again. They would much prefer to keep the car and have the user pay for access to the driving experience through a leasing agreement. This way, they create a relationship with the client that is more likely to be sustained than if the buyer purchased an automobile. At Ford, the renewal rate for leasing cars is nearly 50 percent, while 24 percent of customers who bought their last car from Ford are likely to buy their next car from the company.[1]

Transaction costs and margins also come into play in the shift from market-exchange models to network models. In a market-exchange economy, sellers make profit on their margins, and margins are dependent on transaction costs. But most corporate executives I work with tell me that their margins are continuing to go down, mainly because of the introduction of new communications and production technologies, as well as new methods of organization that are reducing their transaction costs. When transaction costs approach zero, margins virtually disappear, and market exchanges are no longer viable ways of conducting business.

Book publishing is a case in point. In a market, I sell my book to a publisher, who then sends it to a printer. From there, it is shipped to a wholesaler and then to a retailer, where the customer pays for the product. At each stage of the process, the seller is marking up the cost to the buyer to reflect his or her transaction costs. But now, an increasing number of publishers—especially of textbooks and research books, which require continuous updating—are bypassing all the intermediate steps in publishing a physical book and the transaction costs involved at each stage of the process. While Encyclopedia Britannica still charges $1,395 for its twenty-two-volume set of books, the company sells far fewer physical books. Instead, the company puts the books' contents on the World Wide Web, where information can be updated and accessed continuously. Users now pay a subscription fee to access the information over an extended period of time. Encyclopedia Britannica eliminates virtually all the remaining transaction costs of getting the information to its subscribers. The company has made the transition from selling a physical product to a buyer to providing the user access to a service over time. How does a physical book compete with an online book in the future, when the latter has reduced the transaction costs so dramatically? The same process is at work across many industries. (See *The Age of Access* for a more detailed analysis.)

In every industry, there are scattered operational examples of "pure" network models. There are many more instances in which partial networks already exist. In these cases, multiple parties come together to share expertise, knowledge, research facilities, production lines, and marketing channels. The idea behind the networks is to pool resources and share risks while improving quality and reducing the time necessary to get goods and services to end users.

What all these networks have in common is a way of doing business that differs fundamentally from the market-exchange model articulated by Adam Smith and the classical economists and their neoclassical successors in the twentieth century. The operational assumptions that guide networks turn much of orthodox market-based economic theory on its head and open up a new window for rethinking political governance as well.

Recall, Adam Smith argued that the superiority of a market-exchange economy lies in the ability of each individual to pursue his or her own self-interest. In *An Inquiry into the Nature and Causes of the Wealth of Nations*, Smith writes:

> Every individual is continually exerting himself to find out the most advantageous employment for whatever capital he can command. It is his own advantage, indeed, and not that of society which he has in view. But the study of his own advantage naturally, or rather necessarily, leads him to prefer that employment which is most advantageous to the society.[2]

Markets, by their very nature, are adversarial forums. They are arm's-length exchanges where each party enters into the negotiation with the idea of maximizing his own self-interest at the expense of the other party. Buy cheap, sell dear, and *caveat emptor*—let the buyer beware—have been guiding behavioral principles from the very beginning of modern market relations.

Networks operate on an entirely different principle. Each party enters into the relationship based on the supposition that by optimizing the benefits of the other parties and the group as a whole, one's self-interest will be maximized in the process.

Networks are made up of autonomous firms that give up some of their sovereignty in return for the benefits of sharing resources and risks in an extended field of operations. In a network, each party is dependent on resources controlled by another party. The parties become, in effect, a single entity engaged in a common task for a period of time.

The film industry was one of the first to shift into a network way of conducting business. The big studios disaggregated their operations in the late 1940s and early 1950s. Skilled craftsmen and creative personnel, who were previously employed in-house, set up their own independent companies. Now, when a film is done, the major movie studios partially finance the film and market it, while the executive producers bring together all of the individual subcontracting firms—the cinematographers, set designers, editors, etc.—in a short-lived network to make the movie. Often, the risks are distributed among the key entities, and they each share in the revenue stream once the film is released.

Sociologist Manuel Castells identifies five primary kinds of networks: supplier networks, in which firms subcontract for a range of inputs from design operations to the manufacturing of component parts; producer networks, composed of companies that pool their production facilities, financial resources, and human resources to expand their portfolio of goods and services, broaden geographic markets, and reduce up-front risk costs; customer networks, which link together manufacturers, distributors, marketing channels, value-added resellers, and end users; standard coalitions, which bring together as many firms as possible in a given field with the purpose of binding them to the technical standards established by an industry leader; and technology cooperation networks, which allow firms to share valuable knowledge and expertise in the research and development of product lines.[3]

Cooperative Commerce

The keys to a successful network are reciprocity and trust. Each member of the network operates out of a sense of "goodwill," feeling an obligation to cooperate and assist rather than take advantage of the other parties. Trust is at the core of network relationships. Caveat emptor is replaced with the notion that none of the parties "will exploit the vulnerabilities that partnerships create."[4] When companies enter into networks, they give up some of the control they enjoy in markets. They have to share knowledge, make their operations transparent, and allow their partners to know a lot more about how they conduct business. In short, they give up some of their autonomy to become part of an extended commercial activity. In the process, they become exposed and vulnerable. In the market arena, by contrast, sharing knowledge and making one's operations transparent would be seen as an error in judgment, allowing competitors to take advantage of one's weaknesses. In a network, however, vulnerability is considered a strength, not a weakness, a signal of trust and a willingness to work together to everyone's mutual benefit.

Networks rely as much on the informal social ties of the participants as on the formal arrangements between the parties. The more embedded individual players become with each other, the more likely they will be willing to open up and share valuable knowledge, expertise, and often vital business data with others. One prominent CEO put the value of embeddedness this way:

> Of course [opportunism] can be a problem, but do you think that I would ever have made such a close relationship with this guy over so many years if I thought he would screw me if he had a chance? That's why he has so much business. I can trust him.[5]

The close relationships between the players in a network often give them the lead over companies engaged in old-fashioned adversarial arm's-length market exchanges. Brian Uzzi, writing on the value of structured embeddedness in the *American Sociological Review*, notes,

> Embedded ties promote, and enable the greatest access to, certain kinds of exchanges that are particularly beneficial for reducing monitoring costs, quickening decision-making, and enhancing organizational learning and adaptation. These benefits not only accrue to the individual firms of a network connected via embedded ties, but to the network as a whole.[6]

The advantages of embeddedness become apparent when many companies work together on a common project that is complex and requires putting everyone's heads together. The more each knows about the others' expertise, perspectives, and approaches, and the more each member is willing to share his or her own ideas, the greater the likelihood of success. In cutting-edge high-technology industries and in the retail sector, where being first to market with an innovation is critical to success, being able to pool knowledge among a broad group of players, each of whom understands a specific part of the process, can result in quicker problem-solving. Said another CEO,

> When you deal with a guy you don't have a long relationship with, it can be a big problem. Things go wrong and there's no telling what will happen. With my guys [referring to embedded ties], if something goes wrong, I know we'll be able to work it out. I know his business and he knows mine.[7]

Networks also facilitate the exchange of vital industry information that would not necessarily be available to a firm operating as an autonomous agent in an adversarial market. Uzzi reports on one manufacturer who "passes on critical information about next season's hot sellers only to his close (network) ties; thus giving them an advantage in meeting future demands."[8]

In a global economy where competition is stiff and the difference between success and failure often hinges on subtle variations in the quality of goods and services, networks often enjoy an advantage over individual market players. One clothing manufacturer said,

> If we have a factory that is used to making our stuff, they know how it's supposed to look. They know a particular style. It is not always easy to make a garment just from the pattern, especially if we rushed the pattern. But a factory that we have a relationship with will see the problem when the garment starts to go together. They will know how to work the fabric to make it look the way we intended.[9]

A sense of indebtedness is at the heart of the network model. It's the feeling that "we're all in this thing together" and need to go the extra mile to support others in the network, in good times as well as bad. One CEO explained what indebtedness means in his own firm's relationships with its network partners.

> I tell them [subcontractors] that in two weeks I won't have much work. You better start to find other work. [At other times] . . . when they are not so busy we try to find work . . . for our key contractors. We will put a dress into work . . . to keep the contractor going . . . where we put work depends on [who] needs to work [to survive].[10]

What's ultimately driving the shift to a network model is time scarcity. Organizational theorists Candace Jones and Stephen Borgatti of Boston College and William Hesterly of Utah's David Eccles School of Business observe that the old economic model that relies on sequential market exchanges between clients, suppliers, and distributors to coordinate complex tasks and get new products to end users is just too slow and outdated. Networks that coordinate the expertise of all the players in the commercial mix, from suppliers upstream to distributors and even end users downstream, in a single team approach, have the clear edge in reducing the lead time in getting new products and services out the door. Certainly that has been the case in the semiconductor, computer, film, and fashion fields, where product life cycles are often measured in weeks and months rather than years. Networks are also better positioned to reduce costs in competitive markets like the auto industry.[11]

Networks spawn greater creativity and innovation for the simple reason that they have a larger pool of the best minds to draw from. Walter W. Powell says that when one compares the advantages and disadvantages of the various business models, it becomes clear that

> passing information up or down a corporate hierarchy or purchasing information in the marketplace is merely a way of processing information or acquiring a commodity. In either case the flow of information is controlled. No new meanings or interpretations are generated. In contrast, networks provide a context for learning by doing. As information passes through a network, it is both freer and richer; new connections and new meanings are generated, debated, and evaluated.[12]

When commercial transactions were fewer, when the lead time for a new product introduction was longer, and when there was still plenty of untapped and unexploited consumer market potential, market exchanges and hierarchical ways of organizing business made sense. Giant, vertically configured companies with hierarchically controlled management could produce standardized products with long life cycles, allowing them to amortize their costs while maintaining centralized control over research and development, production schedules, and distribution channels. And the slow pace of discrete and discontinuous market exchanges was still sufficient to keep up with consumer demand.

In the past twenty years, a number of factors have changed the commercial context. The dramatic increase in the cost of energy, the escalating costs and risks associated with research and development, the ever shorter life cycle of goods and services, increased labor costs, the consumer preference for more customized just-in-time products, global competition, and smaller profit margins have all contributed to making the market-exchange and hierarchical models increasingly obsolete.

Global commerce is becoming more dense and sped up. No single firm can effectively compete as an autonomous agent working solely through a market-exchange mechanism. Today, going it alone is a prescription for extinction. Only by pooling resources and sharing risks and revenue streams in network-based relationships can firms survive. This means giving up some autonomy in return for the entrepreneurial advantages and security that come with networked arrangements. While competition still exists among firms—markets aren't disappearing any time soon—cooperation in the form of outsourcing, co-sourcing, gain-sharing, and shared saving agreements are increasingly becoming the norm.

In a globalized economy where everyone is connected and ever more interdependent, the idea of autonomous free agents maximizing their individual self-interests in simple exchange transactions in markets seems woefully out of date. A network, in a very real sense, is the only corporate model capable of organizing a world of such speed, complexity, and diversity.

Although the network model is becoming more popular, little attention has been paid to the way networks change our very concept of the role of property and the philosophy of commerce. There has been even less discussion of the long-term implications that flow from a deep change in personal behavior that goes with the transition to the new economic model.

The first thing to understand about the shift from markets to networks is that borders become less fixed and more porous. In markets, borders are critical. A possession is an extension of one's personal territory. It is exclusive to the owner. Sir William Blackstone, in his *Commentaries on the Laws of England*, wrote that property is "that despotic dominion that one man claims and exercises over the external things of the world, in total exclusion of the right of any other individual in the universe."[13]

In a market-based regime, property is rarely meant to be shared but only possessed or exchanged. The status of property is unimpeachable. It is either "mine or thine." The time and place of the exchange between seller and buyer represent the frontier where the property leaves one hand and is transferred into another. The negotiation of the transaction is an adversarial event. Both parties hope to gain at the other's expense. That's why it's called competition. To win is to come away from the exchange with greater value in personal holdings. The goal of market exchange of property is to enlarge one's territorial dominion.

In networks, both physical and intellectual property stay with the producer and are shared with one or more other parties. Knowledge, information, and know-how, which are all forms of property, are similarly shared. What's mine is also thine. The clear territorial boundaries that mark private property regimes in an age of market transactions melt. What was once a frontier separating the parties becomes common ground. Unlike market exchanges, which are expected to result in winners and losers, in network relationships, shared activity is expected to result in what is now called "win-win" situations.

The more conventional idea that competition for scarce resources is the essential nature of human behavior—the Hobbes/Darwin ethic—gives way to the radical notion that cooperation is more vital to one's survival and advancement. If that is the case, then what are the implications for how we define personal freedom?

Belongings vs. Belonging

Recall that in the market era, freedom is defined as autonomy. One is free to the extent one is not dependent or beholden on another. To be independent, one needs to be propertied. With property, one can enjoy exclusivity and freedom. How does one secure property? By competing with others in an adversarial market setting. Network commerce suggests the very opposite definition of freedom. One's freedom is secured by belonging, not by belongings. To belong, one needs access. With access, one can enjoy the freedom that goes with inclusivity. Freedom is found in shared relationships rather than isolation.

If freedom means the power to experience the full potential of one's being in the world, is that potential fulfilled by being walled off from others and surrounded by territorial boundaries, or by deep communion with others on common ground? The "deathbed" test is the best judge of which of the two definitions of freedom is closer to the mark. Contrast the man or woman who spent a lifetime collecting possessions and pursuing autonomy with the man or woman who spent a lifetime exploring relationships and pursuing intimacy. Which of these two can be said to have optimized the full potential of their being, resulting in the most freedom?

Network commerce has consequences that go far beyond just a business model. Its assumptions about how best to optimize the individual good are deeply at odds with how we have come to define appropriate behavior and the good life in the modern era. Markets are based on mistrust, networks on trust. Markets are based on the pursuit of self-interest, networks on shared interest. Markets are arm's-length transactions, networks are intimate relationships. Markets are competitive, networks are cooperative.

The changing nature of how we think about our relationship to property is forcing a fundamental re-appraisal of the human condition, just as it did in the early modern era, when our ideas about property radically changed. The "great transformation" from proprietary obligations on the feudal commons to property exchange in a market economy marked a watershed in our thinking about the nature and purpose of human intercourse. Likewise, today the transition from property exchange in markets to access relationships in networks is again changing the assumptions about the nature of human activity.

Unfortunately, there's been scant discussion, either in academia or in public policy circles, about how to reconstruct our theories of property relations to bring them in line with the reality of network commerce operating in a globalized economy. A few scholars, however, have made attempts at revising our notions of property. The most important contribution to the discussion, thus far, comes from the late University of Toronto professor Crawford MacPherson, considered by many of his colleagues to be one of the distinguished contemporary authorities on the philosophy and history of property. (I first introduced MacPherson's ideas in *The Age of Access*, published in 2000.)

MacPherson starts his analysis by reminding us that our current concept of property is largely an invention of the seventeenth and eighteenth centuries. We are so used to thinking of property as the right to exclude others from the use or benefit of something, says MacPherson, that we've lost sight of the fact that in previous times, property was also defined as the right not to be excluded from the use or enjoyment of something. MacPherson resurrects the older sense of property, the right of access to property held in common—the right to navigate waterways, walk along commonly used country lanes, and enjoy access to the public square.

While this dual notion of property still exists, the right of public access and inclusion is becoming increasingly marginalized and diminished by the right of private ownership and exclusion, as the market economy comes to dominate more and more of the social domain. Consider the example of the changing pattern of home ownership in the U.S. Over the past forty years, growing numbers of Americans have taken up ownership in what are called common interest developments (CIDs). In these gated communities, not only are the homes privately owned, but even the streets, sidewalks, town squares, and parks are privately owned by the members who live there. Nonmembers often must seek permission at the gates to drive down the streets, walk on the sidewalks, stroll in the parks, or visit shops in the square. More than forty-seven million Americans—nearly one-sixth of the American population—already live in these private communities, and the numbers are growing dramatically.[14] CIDs may become the dominant living arrangement by mid-century.

We Americans have, in just two centuries, come up against a basic contradiction that lies at the heart of the American Dream. We have long sought both autonomy and mobility and believe that the two are mutually reinforcing. Now millions of Americans have transformed large swaths of America's public space into privatized communities, denying millions of other Americans access to and mobility through whole parts of America. A country that once prided itself on its openness and expansiveness—its lack of boundaries—is being systematically walled off into exclusive domains at an alarming rate, changing the very character of the American landscape and the American experience. There is nothing comparable to this vast privatization of living space in Europe.

MacPherson notes that a private property regime was used for structuring human relationships in a world of physical scarcity. Now, notes MacPherson, at least for the top 20 percent of income earners, securing the right to a material revenue has been solved, and therefore their interest is turning to the more expansive and deeper issue of securing a quality of life. MacPherson argues, in turn, that property needs to be redefined to include the "right to an *immaterial* revenue, a revenue of enjoyment of the quality of life."[15] He suggests that "such a revenue can only be reckoned as a right to participate in a satisfying set of social relations."[16]

In a society of true abundance, the idea of excluding others becomes increasingly unimportant in structuring property relationships. If everyone has more than he or she needs, then what practical benefit is there in excluding others? In a society that has vanquished scarcity, immaterial values assume greater importance, especially the pursuit of self-fulfillment and personal transformation. The right not to be excluded from "a full life" becomes the most important property value people hold. Property in the new era, argues MacPherson, "needs to become a right to participate in a system of power relations which will enable the individual to live a fully human life."[17]

Of course, for the four-fifths of the human race who still labor under conditions of abject poverty or bare subsistence, economist Hernando de Soto's plea to catch up with the wealthy nations by establishing a private property regime, like the one Europe and America have enjoyed for the last two hundred years, makes some sense.

There is, however, another reason why the developed societies find themselves between an old property regime based on the exchange of products in markets and a new property regime based on the right of access to one another's assets in networks—that is, the increase in vulnerability that inevitably accompanies the change in the complexity and density of human interactions and the shrinking of space and time in a globalized world.

I had the opportunity, twenty-three years ago, to visit with the late Ilya Prigogine, the Belgian physical chemist. His theory of "dissipative structures," for which he won a Nobel Prize, offers some guidelines as to why our thinking about property relations and our notions of freedom are radically changing.

Prigogine brings together assumptions from thermodynamics and cybernetics in his analysis. He observes that all living things as well as many nonliving things are dissipative structures. That is, they maintain their structure by the continuous flow of energy through their system. The flow of energy keeps the system in a constant state of flux. The fluctuations are generally small and can be adjusted to by negative feedback. However, occasionally, says Prigogine, the fluctuations may become so great that the system is unable to adjust, and positive feedback takes over. The fluctuations feed off themselves, and the amplification can easily overwhelm the whole system. When that happens, the system either collapses or reorganizes itself. If it is able to reorganize itself, the new dissipative structure will exhibit a higher order of complexity and integration and a greater flow-through than its predecessor. Each successive ordering, because it is more complex than the one preceding it, is even more vulnerable to fluctuations, collapse, or reordering. Prigogine believes that increased complexity creates the condition for evolutionary development.

Our complex, high-energy flow-through global economy is a prime example of Prigogine's dissipative structures. A dramatic change in energy flux anywhere in the system can traumatize the entire system and lead to

either collapse or reorganization to a higher, more complex level of performance. In the modern era, when distances were still significant, time
was more plentiful, and density of exchange less tight, energy fluctuations
anywhere in the world were generally localized in their impact, rarely affecting the entire planet. That is no longer the case. In a globalized economy where space and time are increasingly dense, and everything is more
interdependent, any event occurring anywhere in the system can make
everything else in the system vulnerable. Networks are the only business
models that can accommodate a vulnerable high-risk global economy.
Networks bring together interested parties with the specific objective of
pooling resources and risk to mitigate losses. Only by cooperating in extended business-to-business and business-to-consumer networks can firms
enjoy the kind of just-in-time information, knowledge, and response capacity to adjust rapidly to fluctuations anywhere across the entire global
economy.

In the modern era, when there was still an expansive frontier of untapped resources, labor, and potential wealth to tap all over the world, the
combative, autonomous individual—the cowboy mentality—was the ideal
commercial prototype, and the market mechanism was the most effective
arrangement to expropriate and exploit the many economic possibilities.

In the new global commercial playing field of increasing complexity
and interdependence, opportunities are increasingly modeled around
shared vulnerabilities and pooled risks rather than around exclusive self-
interest and individual entrepreneurial gambles. In a global risk economy,
trust, reciprocity, and cooperation become more important survival values
than go-it-alone rugged individualism and adversarial behavior.

THE SAME GLOBAL CONDITIONS that are forcing a new cooperative
economic model to the fore, based on network architecture, are affecting
the political arena as well. Nation-states can no longer go it alone in a
dense, interdependent world. Like transnational companies, they are
slowly coming together in cooperative networks to better accommodate
the realities of a high-risk globalized society. The European Union is the
most advanced example of the new transnational governing model, and
for that reason, its successes and failures are being closely watched in
every region of the world as nation-state leaders rethink the art of governance in a global era.

The "United States" of Europe

T HE EUROPEAN UNION is the third-largest governing institution in the world. Its 455 million citizens are spread out over a landmass that is half the size of the continental United States. In the course of the next two years, its people will ratify a constitution, pledging their lives and fortunes, and tying their personal and collective destiny to its political success.

What Is Europe?

All in all, the EU is a remarkable feat, especially when one stops to reflect on the fact that even its architects are unsure of exactly what the EU represents. The problem is that there has never been any governing institution like the EU. It is not a state, even though it acts like one. Its laws supercede the laws of the twenty-five nations that make it up and are binding. It has a single currency—the euro—that is used by many of its members. It regulates commerce and trade and coordinates energy, transportation, communications, and, increasingly, education across the many national borders that make it up. Its citizens all enjoy a common EU passport. It has a European Parliament, which makes laws, and a European Court, whose judicial decisions are binding on member countries and the citizens of the EU. And, it has a president and a military force. In many of the most important particulars that make up a state, the EU qualifies. Yet, it cannot tax its citizens, and its member states still enjoy a veto on any decision that might commit their troops to be employed.

Most important of all, the EU is not a territory-bound entity. Although it coordinates and regulates activity that takes place within the territorial boundaries of its nation-state members, it has no claim to territory and is, in fact, an extra-territorial governing institution. This is what makes the EU unique.

Nation-states are geographically defined governing institutions that control specific territory. Even dynasties and empires claimed ultimate control over the territory of their subject kingdoms. The only faint historical parallel to the EU is the Holy Roman Empire of the eighth to the early nineteenth centuries. In that period, the Vatican claimed ultimate sovereignty over the principalities, city-states, and kingdoms of much of Western and Northern Europe. In reality, the Holy See's actual influence over territory-related matters was more moral and ethereal than enforceable.

The member states of the European Union still control the territory they represent, but their once absolute power over geography has been steadily eroded by EU legislative encroachments. For example, the Schengen Agreement, an EU agreement forged in 1985, gives the European Union the power to create a Europe-wide set of rules governing immigration into the EU, and even includes a European police force to protect the EU's members' borders. The individual states, however, still retain the right to decide how many immigrants to allow into their country and to designate which countries outside the EU they can emigrate from. Once an émigré becomes a citizen in a member country, he or she is allowed full reign to take up residence anywhere else in the Union and be granted the full protection of whichever host country he or she settles in. Citizens of EU member countries not only have the right to establish residence in another member country but can even vote and run for office in local elections and European parliamentary elections, only not in the national elections of any second country they may be living in.

Because the EU itself is not bound by territorial constraints, it can continue to bring new states under its umbrella. Indeed, the EU's criteria for membership is value-based rather than geographically conditioned. In theory, any country can apply for membership and, if it fulfills the qualifications, be admitted into the Union. The open-ended and inclusive nature of this new kind of governing institution has caused concern among existing members and tensions among prospective candidate nations. Some argue that even though membership is value-based, it ought to be limited only to those countries that make up "historical Europe." The problem is, historians disagree as to exactly what constitutes historical Europe. Geographers say there is no such thing as the European continent. Yet others argue that Europe begins at the edge of the Atlantic Ocean and extends across Europe into Russia and even to Turkey to the southeast. Is Russia part of Europe or Asia? Is Turkey part of Europe or the Middle East? Recall, the Ottoman Empire controlled parts of Europe at various times. So is Europe part of the Middle East?

Many claim that Europe is tied by a common cultural thread and point to its Greco-Roman roots, Christendom, and the eighteenth-century Enlightenment as proof that Europe exists. Europe, they say, is a state of mind that results from a shared past and common destiny. Again, the problem is that history has not unfolded in the tidy fashion that Euro-enthusiasts project. For example, in the ancient Greco-Roman world, the idea of Europe never extended north of Gaul and the British Isles. Certainly the Nordic countries were not considered part of what the ancients regarded as "Europa."

The Catholic Church argues that Christianity is the cultural glue that constitutes Europe. But how do we explain the fact that Islam ruled over parts of Europe from the eighth century to the early twentieth century?

Nor are these simply academic questions. There is a heated debate, both inside the Union and out, on whether to admit Turkey and eventually even Russia to membership. And there is the related question of broadening the Union's associational ties to include North Africa and the Middle East.

Where, then, does the European Union end? No one knows. EU observers use the term "variable geometry" to encompass all of the possible combinations that might make up this new governing experiment. If it's hard to grasp exactly what the EU is, it is because it is continuously metamorphosing into new forms as it adjusts to fast-moving new realities. The EU is, in actuality, the first really post-modern governing institution. If it seems amorphous and less fixed, that's because it is navigating in a world of perpetual novelty. In the global era, duration has shortened to near simultaneity, and history has given way to an ever changing now. Geography, in turn, is no longer experienced contiguously and in terms of distances but rather as a patchwork of patterns that brings disparate places together in shared activities. For example, regions like Baden-Württemberg, Rhônes-Alpes, Lombardy, and Catalonia are now united in close commercial, social, and political networks that leapfrog across their existing nation-state borders.[1] Many regions of Europe now have more intimate activity with consort regions far removed from their own geography.

Unlike past states and empires, whose origins are embedded in the myth of heroic victories on the battlefield, the EU is novel in being the very first mega-governing institution in all of history to be born out of the ashes of defeat. Rather than commemorate a noble past, it sought to ensure that the past would never be repeated. After a thousand years of unremitting conflict, war, and bloodshed, the nations of Europe emerged from the shadows of two world wars, in the span of less than half a century, decimated: their population maimed and killed, their ancient monuments and infrastructure lying in ruins, their worldly treasures depleted, and their way of life destroyed. Determined that they would never again take up arms against one another, the nations of Europe searched for a political mechanism that could bring them together and move them beyond their ancient rivalries.

In 1948, at the Congress of Europe, Winston Churchill pondered the future of a continent wracked by centuries of war and offered his own vision of a European Dream. He said, "We hope to see a Europe where men of every country will think of being a European as of belonging to their native land, and . . . wherever they go in this wide domain . . . will truly feel, 'Here I am at home.'"[2] Jean Monnet, who more than any other single individual was responsible for creating the idea of a common European community among formerly divided peoples and countries, understood how difficult it would be to fulfill Churchill's dream. The problem, noted Monnet, is that "Europe has never existed; one has genuinely to create Europe."[3] This meant making people aware of their Europeanness.

The preamble to the 1957 Treaty of Rome, which established the European Community, states unequivocally that the aim is "to lay the foundations for an ever closer union among the peoples of Europe."[4] The grand hope was "to substitute for age-old rivalries the merging of their essential interests; to create, by establishing an economic community, the bases of broader and deeper community among peoples long divided by bloody conflicts; and to lay the foundations for institutions which will give direction to a destiny henceforward shared."[5] Here was the first political entity in history whose very reason for existence was "to build peace."[6]

Today, two-thirds of the people living across the European Union say they feel "European." Six out of ten EU citizens say they feel very attached or fairly attached to Europe, while one-third of European youth between the ages of twenty-one and thirty-five say they "now regard themselves as more European than as nationals of their home country."[7] The World Economic Forum's own survey of European leaders found that 92 percent of them see their "future identification as mainly or partly European, not national."[8] Although difficult to fathom, this extraordinary change in how people perceive themselves has occurred in less than half a century.

Forging a Union

From the very beginning, the process of forging a common European community ran up against the other side of a paradox: that the architects of the new, more interdependent, and expansive governing model were nation-states, whose very reason for existence was based on exclusive control of territory, the contestation and seizure of other countries' lands, and the sequestration of people within their borders who owed their allegiance and loyalty to the state. Breaking open the nation-state container to allow "a closer union among the peoples of Europe" threatened the long-standing sovereignty of nation-states, undermining their hegemony and rule. The question has always been, Would there be more to be gained than lost in sacrificing a degree of national sovereignty in return for a greater measure of security and opportunity? At each turning point in the fifty-year development of the Union, the nations and peoples of Europe have narrowly voted yes to a rewriting of the political contract, conferring more authority to the Union, while giving up an increasing share of their national sovereignty in the process.

The journey to union began with the creation of the European Coal and Steel Community (ECSC) in 1951.[9] Many European intellectuals and political leaders argued that the long-standing economic rivalry between Germany and France was at the heart of the lingering conflict in Europe, and a major cause of war that periodically engulfed the continent. Jean Monnet proposed the idea of merging the coal and steel production of Germany and France, especially along the long-contested industrial corridor that bordered the Ruhr and Saar rivers. The ECSC Treaty of Paris, signed by France, Germany, Italy, Belgium, the Netherlands, and Luxembourg, provided for the creation of a supernational high authority with broad regulatory powers, a council with legislative powers, a political assembly, and even a European Court of Justice.[10] The new entity would have the power to bind the member states under the umbrella of a higher authority for the very first time. The intent was to set the stage for a broader union.[11]

In 1957, the six member states of the ECSC signed the Treaty of Rome, broadening their mission to include the creation of a European Economic Community. The EEC's mandate called for the establishment of a common market and included the harmonization of taxation, the elimination of internal customs barriers, and the enactment of rules governing capitalism and the free deployment of labor. A legislative body was set up comprised of representatives of each member state, a commission was created and given executive power, a European Parliament was established with limited advisory and legislative oversight, and the European Court of Justice was given broad judicial review power. The new European Economic Community enjoyed an international legal identity. It could enter into diplomatic relations and negotiate treaties on behalf of its member countries just like nation-states. The Treaty of Rome and the establishment of the European Economic Community meant that member states no longer had the right to act alone in economic matters.[12]

The six states also entered into a separate agreement to create a cooperative venture to develop nuclear power across their territories. The European Atomic Energy Community (EURATOM) came about because the six countries realized that only by pooling their investments and sharing the technology could they afford to compete with the U.S. and the USSR in the nuclear power field.[13] In 1965, the ECSC, EURATOM, and the EEC merged.

The EEC Treaty gave the body the power to set a common agricultural policy for the member states, as well as to establish a common transport policy, a customs union, and a common policy to govern external trade.[14] The architects of the EEC were mindful that greater economic union would necessitate a more free and mobile labor force that could seek employment and take up residence across national boundaries. The treaty created four basic rights: the right of citizens to move between states; the right to establish residence in another state; the right to work in another state; and the right to move capital between countries.[15]

Until very recently, most Americans, and possibly an equal number of Europeans, viewed the European Economic Community and its successor, the European Union, as little more than a common market that could give its member states the advantages that come with a larger unified internal trade zone. Its early architects and visionaries even promoted the idea publicly in order to gain acceptance for the Union. Privately, however, they were clear, from the very beginning, that they had a far more ambitious agenda in mind. Jean Monnet, the founding father of the Union, declared early on that "we are not forming coalitions between states, but union among people."[16] Monnet and others believed that the only long-term solution that could guarantee a peaceful and prosperous Europe was the surrendering of more national sovereignty to a broader political union. They realized, however, that sporting an overt political agenda would backfire and create resistance by the member states—all of whom were anxious to increase their economic clout by joining together in common cause in the commercial arena. For the most part, national leaders saw the union as a way to further national objectives, strengthen their own domestic agendas, and secure their national sovereignty. In a world dominated at the time by two superpowers, the U.S. and the USSR, the six member nations reasoned that only by pooling their economic resources could they hope to compete. It was the fear of being swallowed up that pushed the member states along to greater levels of economic integration.

But big-picture players like Monnet, Robert Schumann, German chancellor Konrad Adenauer, and, later, Jacques Delors, the president of the European Commission, saw the Union in far more visionary terms. Their strategy was to move incrementally with technical and economic measures designed to increasingly bring member states together in a seamless, interdependent, commercial web of relationships. Each small step of economic integration would result in a slight, sometimes imperceptible erosion of their national sovereignty. None of the steps alone, they figured, would be enough to arouse the ire of member states and threaten the furtherance of the Union. The upshot of this piecemeal strategy would be that "one day the national governments would awaken to find themselves enmeshed in a 'spreading web of international activities and agencies,' from which they would find it almost impossible to extricate themselves.

To a large measure, the strategy paid off. Economic pressures in the post-world War II era propelled European countries toward union. The United States provided the main stimulus. The Bretton Woods Agreement, which also set up the International Monetary Fund and World Bank, was an attempt to create a global commercial market to foster U.S. economic development. Anxious to impose a global set of rules that would encourage free trade, the U.S. established the General Agreement on Tariffs and Trade (GATT) in 1947.

The U.S. was particularly concerned with the dire straights of wartorn Europe. With the Soviet Union already occupying Central and Eastern Europe, and with powerful Communist political parties in France and Italy, the U.S. worried that much of Europe might fall to the Soviets. To ensure against a Communist takeover, the U.S. embarked on a twoprong program to secure Western Europe in the post-war era. It established the North Atlantic Treaty Organization (NATO) in 1949, whose mission was to create and deploy an integrated American and European military force that could defend Western Europe from Soviet aggression. The U.S. also launched an economic recovery initiative to resurrect the economies of Western Europe, in the belief that it would be the best means of slowing the advance of Communist political parties in France, Italy, and elsewhere, and lowering the threat of Soviet influence.

The Marshall Plan, named after its architect, Secretary of State George Marshall, provided more than $25 billion of economic development assistance to Europe in the late 1940s and early 1950s.[18] But the funds came with conditions. To continue receiving aid, European nations would need to prepare the ground for "the formation of a single large market within which quantitative restriction on the movements of goods, monetary barriers to the flow of payments and, eventually, all tariffs are permanently swept away."[19]

European countries were also favorably disposed to creating a common market, but for different reasons. Worried that they would be squeezed by the superpowers and risk becoming a satellite to one or the other, they saw the pooling of their economic resources and talents as a way to gain sufficient advantage to claim a measure of economic independence.

Both parties served to gain from the creation of a European common market. A strong Western European economy would hold off the Communist menace and create a market for U.S. investment abroad. A European common market would give European nations the security and freedom they needed to revive their ailing national economies and assure their continued existence. And underlying these more strategic economic considerations was the belief that by joining together, the nations of Europe might at long last put an end to centuries of warfare among themselves.

The European Economic Community expanded in the 1970s and 1980s, adding the United Kingdom, Ireland, Denmark, Spain, Greece, and Portugal to its ranks. While the economic devastation of World War II provided an impetus to create a European community, the oil shock of 1973 added new urgency to efforts aimed at integration. The global recession that followed on the heels of the spike in oil prices imposed by the Organization of Petroleum Exporting Countries (OPEC) threatened to undermine the carefully designed social welfare regimes put in place in Western European nations. The Thatcher-Reagan economic revolution of the 1980s, with its emphasis on deregulation of government-owned businesses and the further liberalization of global trade, put additional pressure on member nations of the European community. Greater integration was the only viable means for member countries to stay afloat in troubled times.

The Single European Act (SEA) of 1987 brought the member states a giant step closer to union, while subtly eroding the national sovereignty of the individual countries. Among its many sweeping provisions was the extension of new powers to the European Parliament. For the first time, the parliament was to be consulted before the adoption of new legislation by the European community. The parliament was also given the power of veto on the admittance of new states and on agreements made with states outside the community. Equally important, qualified majority voting was introduced in many areas where unanimous votes of member states were previously required. Finally, the community established the idea of "Exclusive Community Competence," which prohibited member states from acting alone in a number of critical areas that had previously been the prerogative of national governments, including matters related to economic and monetary union, social cohesion, research and technology development, and environmental policies.[20]

The SEA effectively weakened the power exercised by the council, which was made up of the heads of the member states. Why would member governments willingly surrender their sovereignty and cede more power to the Union? Because the SEA was presented as a purely technical treaty designed to further economic and fiscal integration, member states all found something to bolster their vision of the role of the community. The arch-confederalists, who favored economic but not political union, hoped that a more integrated market would strengthen their national economies and shore up their political regimes. Those who supported a more federal political union hoped that closer economic integration would make the individual member states more interdependent and reliant on the Union, eventually drawing more political power away from their respective states and toward Brussels.[21]

The fall of the Berlin Wall and the collapse of the Soviet Empire in Central and Eastern Europe in 1989 forced the community to revise its mission once again. Recall that the Cold War and the division of Europe into two competing blocs after World War II played a key role in the initial formation of the European community. It was to be an economic and political bulwark against Russian aggression. Now that the Cold War was over, Europe had to turn its attention to the prospects of a reunited Germany and an integrated Europe that stretched from the Atlantic seaboard to the Russian border. Again, external events pushed the member states even closer to union.

The Maastricht Treaty of 1992 transformed the European Economic Community into the European Union. The sweeping provisions of the treaty made clear, once and for all, that the Union was to be far more than a common economic market. The newly constituted European Union was to be built upon three pillars.[22] Member nations agreed to the introduction of a single EU-wide currency—the euro—by January 1, 1999. Member states agreed to extend intergovernmental cooperation to include a Common Foreign and Security Policy (CFSP). Finally, the members agreed to establish regulations governing Justice and Home Affairs (JHA), including the granting of common rights to all European citizens, furthering police cooperation among the states, and harmonizing immigration and asylum policies across the Union.[23] The states also agreed to broaden EU membership and began entertaining applications from Central, Eastern, and Mediterranean European states. (Austria, Sweden, and Finland joined the Union in 1995, and ten Central, Southern, and Eastern

European countries—the Czech Republic, Cyprus, Estonia, Hungary, Latvia, Lithuania, Malta, Poland, Slovenia, and Slovakia—officially joined in May 2004.)[24]

The treaty created new bodies. The Committee of the Regions gave the regions of Europe an official voice, for the first time, in European community affairs. Recognition of the regions served to further weaken nation-state sovereignty. Now, 222 regions from Catalonia to Lombardy were to be officially represented in Brussels, giving them direct access to one another, the member states, and the EU governing machinery, without having to be represented exclusively by their nation-states.[25] The Cohesion Fund was established to assist states whose economic development lagged behind the rest of the Union's members.

The Maastricht agreement also introduced the concept of Europe-wide citizenship and gave the European Parliament additional powers.[26]

The Maastricht Treaty was clarified and strengthened with the passage of the Treaty of Amsterdam in 1997. This treaty reinforced the Union's commitment to human rights and required applicant countries to uphold the provisions of the European Convention on Human Rights as conditions for acceptance into the community. The Amsterdam agreement gave the EU the legislative power to act against discrimination based on sex, race, religion, ethnic background, disabilities, or age, anywhere within the Union. The Union was also given the power to act on employment issues affecting its member states. The Union was even granted some power to enact broad standards governing public health policy, although the organization and delivery of health care remained the responsibility of the member states.[27]

At a follow-up conference in Nice in December 2000, Union members agreed on further reforms of the council—narrowing the range of issues on which individual member states could impose their veto power. Votes of the big countries on the council were tripled in weight, while those in the smaller nations were merely doubled. Passage of council proposals would henceforth require 73.29 percent of the weighted votes, a two-thirds majority among the member states and a majority of 62 percent of the Union's total population.[28]

At Nice, as at earlier summits, both those who championed a more federal union and those who preferred to retain as much power as possible at the state level could argue, with some justification, that their interests were partially met. At every juncture of the Union's existence, the public perception has been one of maintaining a delicate balancing act that would retain nation-state sovereignty while further empowering the community. Whether the individual countries really believe this to be the case is doubtful. It is true that each step forward to a closer union of the peoples of Europe has been met with a half-step back to preserve nation-state powers. Still, the cumulative effect has been a slow, irreversible trek toward the vision first laid out by the Union's early architect, Jean Monnet.

Lest there be any doubt on this score, the EU's draft constitution, which is currently being considered for ratification by its member states, makes clear that a new transnational political institution is being born that, in its every particular, is designed to function like a state. It is possible that a number of member nations might vote against ratification of the constitution, forcing a crisis and a re-evaluation of a Europe-wide governing body. Although, if public opinion polls are in any way a bellwether, the constitution is likely to be ratified by the member states. According to a Eurobarometer poll conducted in February 2004, a sizable 77 percent of the people in the member states support an EU Constitution. Opposition to the EU Constitution is only 15 percent overall, while somewhat higher in Austria, Sweden, Denmark, and the U.K. Still, even in these countries, opposition is still low, ranging from 23 percent to 30 percent of the population. Equally important, 62 percent of those polled said they favored national concessions to ensure that the constitution is adopted, and in only one country, Slovenia, did a majority say they would rather not make concessions.[29]

But even if the new constitution were to be rejected, the Union itself is already so far along toward integration that no one really believes it will ever dissolve back into separate nation-state governments, each going it alone in the global era. Rather, most political observers believe that if this particular constitution runs into serious trouble, the member states will merely resurrect its various particulars in other treaties and directives until the substance of the covenant becomes binding on the community.

The adoption of the European Union Constitution gives the EU the legal stature of a country, despite the fact that this new governing institution has no claim on territory—the traditional hallmark of statehood. While its provisions allow it to regulate activity within the territories of its members, including activity that affects property rights and relations, it's worth emphasizing that the EU is not, in itself, a territory-bound government. It is, rather, the first transnational government in history whose regulatory powers supercede the territorial powers of the members that make it up. This fact alone marks a new chapter in the nature of governance. The EU's very legitimacy lies not in the control of territory or the ability to tax its citizens or mobilize police or the military force to exact obedience but, rather, in a code of conduct, conditioned by universal human rights and operationalized through statutes, regulations, and directives and, most important, by a continuous process of engagement, discourse, and negotiation with multiple players operating at the local, regional, national, transnational, and global levels.

The New EU Constitution

Under the proposed constitution, which includes a Charter of Fundamental Rights, the Union will be able to sign treaties in its own right, binding its member nations. It might ultimately be granted a seat on the Security Council of the United Nations—replacing the United Kingdom and France. It will have a president elected by the European Council who will serve for up to five years and be responsible for setting the EU's agenda. Currently, the EU presidency rotates every six months, and the office is held, in turn, by each of the presidents of the member nations.

The EU will also have a single foreign minister responsible for conducting foreign and defense policies. The constitution calls for a single foreign and security policy, and member states are called upon to "unreservedly support the Union's foreign and security policy in a spirit of loyalty and mutual solidarity."[30] However, member states are given an escape clause. They can either abstain from voting or vote no, which would allow them to block a foreign policy proposal from even being taken up by the council.[31] In addition, while the European Union is charged with the task of creating a rapid-reaction strike force, national governments will still retain control over their own armed forces. Valéry Giscard d'Estaing, the former French president who oversaw the constitutional drafting process, said he believed that it would take twenty years before the Union had a unified and integrated foreign policy and spoke with a single voice in the international arena.[32]

The national governments will retain control over taxes. While the

EU budget currently exceeds 100 billion euros a year, the member states have steadfastly refused, until now, to grant it the right to raise taxes independently of the states—making it dependent on the members for its budget.[33]

The member states will also still retain control over decisions of whom they grant citizenship, although, as mentioned earlier, any citizen of a member state will have the right to take up residency in another member state, and work, and vote in local and European parliamentary elections, and even run for office in either venue. Moreover, under the new constitution, broad policies designed to harmonize immigration along with refugee and asylum issues will be decided by majority vote. Under the old rules, any country could exercise a veto.[34]

The constitution also grants the Union the right to establish at least minimum rules concerning judicial procedures dealing with the rights of the accused, the rights of victims, and the admissibility of evidence in court proceedings. EU changes in criminal law would require only a majority vote.

Those favoring a stronger EU hoped that any future changes in the constitution itself would be made by a majority of the states, if four-fifths of the states agreed. They lost, however, to the confederalists who were successful in imposing a unanimous agreement provision for any proposed constitutional changes.[35]

The EU Constitution is being sold as a kind of grand compromise, with something for everybody. For countries like the U.K. and France, who believe that the EU should exist as an extension of but not a substitution for the nation-state, the constitution provides some relief. The new rules strengthen the voting power of big countries in the Council of Ministers.[36] Under the new provisions, the council can pass legislation when half of the members, representing 60 percent of the EU population, vote for it. This gives the bigger nations—Germany, U.K., France, and Italy—more potential power to steer the legislative agenda. On the other hand, the Council of Ministers' power is somewhat diminished because of the new powers ceded to the commission.

For the smaller nations, who would like to see a more federal union, the constitution strengthens the European Commission. The commission has a monopoly over the right to propose new legislation, which is tantamount to veto power over prospective legislation that might be taken up by the Council of Ministers and the European Parliament. The commission's president, who will be elected by the European Parliament, will enjoy greater executive and enforcement powers.

The parliament will also get new budgetary and law-making powers. Most EU legislation voted by the Council of Ministers will be subject to parliamentary approval.

My first impression in reading over the European Constitution was that large chunks of it would never be acceptable to the majority of the American people, were it to be submitted for ratification in the U.S. Although there are passages throughout that would no doubt resonate with many Americans—including sentiments cribbed largely from our own Declaration of Independence and the Bill of Rights of the U.S. Constitution—there are other ideas and notions in the 265-page document that are so alien to the contemporary American psyche that they might be considered with suspicion or even thought of as somewhat bizarre.

To begin with, there is not a single reference to God and only a veiled reference to Europe's "religious inheritance." God is missing. Strange, in a continent where great cathedrals grace the central plazas of most cities, and small churches and chapels appear around every corner. Still, most of the ancient sanctuaries are visited primarily by tourists nowadays. One would be hard-pressed to see more than a scattering of local people at a Sunday morning mass. As mentioned in the opening chapter, for the most part, Europeans—especially the post-war generations—have left God behind. Europe is arguably the most secular region in the world. That's not to say that there wasn't a heated debate over the absence of God in the document. Pope John Paul II and the Vatican lobbied publicly for "a clear reference to God and the Christian faith" in the preamble.[37] Others argued that not to mention Christianity, when it played a pivotal role in the history of Europe, was unforgivable. Most, however, agreed with Anna Palacio, Spain's former foreign minister, and a member of the drafting convention, who argued that "the only banner that we have is secularism."[38] A French diplomat put it even more bluntly: "We don't like God."[39]

God is not the only consideration to be given short shift. There is only a single reference to private property, tucked deep inside the document, and barely a passing mention of free markets and trade. The Union's objectives, however, include a clear commitment to "sustainable development . . . based on balanced economic growth," "a social market economy," and "protection and improvement of the quality of the environment."[40] The Union's other objectives are to "promote peace . . . combat social exclusion and discrimination . . . promote social justice and protection, equality between men and women, solidarity between generations, and protection of children's rights."[41]

Much of the constitution is given over to the issue of fundamental human rights. It might even be said that human rights are the very heart and soul of the document. Giscard d'Estaing declared with pride, on the unveiling of the document, that "of all the men and women in the world, it is the citizens of Europe who will have the most extensive rights."[42]

The rights outlined in the Charter of Fundamental Rights of the European Union go far beyond the rights contained in our own Bill of Rights and subsequent constitutional amendments. They include the Right of Life: "no one should be condemned to the death penalty, or executed." Everyone has the right to have his or her physical and mental activity respected. In the fields of medicine and biology, the individual's right to free and informed consent is protected. Eugenics practices are prohibited, "in particular, those aiming at the 'selection' of a person." Selling human body parts is also prohibited, as is the reproductive cloning of human beings. Everyone has "the right to the protection of personal data concerning him or her." Similarly, "everyone has the right to access the data which has been collected concerning him or her, and the right to have it rectified." Everyone has "the right to marry and the right to found a family." Everyone has "the right to form and to join trade unions for the protection of his or her interests." "Everyone has the right to education and to have access to vocational and continuing education." While discrimination based on sex, race, color, and ethnic or religious background is prohibited, other discriminations, based on genetic features, language, and opinions, are also prohibited. The Union "shall respect cultural, religious, and linguistic diversity" as well. Children are granted the conventional rights "to such protection and care as is necessary for their well-being," but they are also guaranteed the right to "express their views freely." "Such views shall be taken into consideration on matters which concern them in accordance with their age and maturity." In addition, "every child shall have the right to maintain, on a regular basis, a personal relationship and direct contact with both his or her parents, unless that is contrary to his or her interests."[43]

There are still other rights that do not exist in our U.S. Constitution. For example, the EU Constitution grants everyone "the right of access to a free placement service," as well as "the right to limitation of maximum working hours, to daily and weekly rest periods, and to an annual period of paid leave." The constitution also guarantees the right to paid maternity leave and parental leave following the birth or adoption of a child. The Union "recognizes the right to social and housing assistance so as to ensure a decent existence for all those who lack sufficient resources." The constitutional guarantees also include "the right of access to preventive health care and the right to benefit from medical treatment." The EU even guarantees "a high level of environmental protection and the improvement in the quality of the environment . . . in accordance with the principle of sustainable development."[44]

Many of the rights guaranteed by the new European Constitution remain controversial in the United States. While they have their advocates, and enjoy some measure of popular support, public sentiment remains far too divided to elevate them to the status of universal human rights. And the U.S. is not alone. Few countries outside Europe would likely subscribe to most of the universal human rights guaranteed by the new EU Constitution. To this extent, the EU has become the undisputed leader in championing new human rights among the governing regimes of the world.

The EU Constitution is something quite new in human history. Though it is often weighty—even cumbersome—and does not enjoy the eloquence of, say, the French and U.S. constitutions, it is the first document of its kind to expand the human franchise to the level of global consciousness, with rights and responsibilities that encompass the totality of human existence on Earth. (While the United Nations Charter and subsequent United Nations human rights conventions also speak to universal human rights, the UN itself is not a governing institution representing individual citizens, as is the EU.)

The language throughout the text is one of universalism, making it clear that its focus is not a people, or a territory, or a nation, but rather the human race and the planet we inhabit. If we were to sum up the gist of the document, it would be a commitment to respect human diversity, promote inclusivity, champion human rights and the rights of nature, foster quality of life, pursue sustainable development, free the human spirit for deep play, build a perpetual peace, and nurture a global consciousness. Together, these values and goals, which appear in many different forms throughout the constitution, represent the warp and woof of a fledgling European Dream.

Government Without
a Center

D REAMS REFLECT HOPES, not achievements. To this extent, the European Constitution represents a future to be filled in. And, like the U.S. Constitution of more than two hundred years ago, one can point to the many hypocrisies and contradictions that belie the noble sentiments contained in the new European covenant. Nonetheless, the framers of the European Constitution have forthrightly set to paper a vision of the kind of world they aspire to and would like to live in and the rules to oversee the journey.

For the past half century, Europe's political elites have engaged in a running struggle to define the limits of power of the emerging European Community. While the federalists have argued for ceding more power to the Union, the confederalists have attempted to retain power in the hands of the member states and have thought of the European Union more as an intergovernmental forum to coordinate national objectives and strengthen each member's own self-interests. Former French prime minister Lionel Jospin put the confederalist position this way: "I want Europe, but I remain attached to my nation. Making Europe without unmaking France, or any other European nation, that is my political choice."[1] In other words, the Union is to be a "Europe of States." All of the compromises along the way have reflected the tensions between these two divergent forces.

While the powers that be continue to jostle back and forth between federalism and confederalism, the very technological, economic, and social realities that gave rise to the European Community and that continue to push it along its journey to union have created a political dynamic of a different sort. Rather than becoming a superstate or a mechanism to represent the enlightened national self-interests, the EU has metamorphosed into a third form. It has become a discursive forum whose function is to referee relationships and help coordinate activity among a range of players, of which the nation-state is only one. The EU's primary role has become orchestral. It facilitates the coming together of networks of engagement that include nation-states but also extend outward to transnational organizations and inward to municipal and regional governments, as well as civil society organizations.

The EU is a response to a peculiar kind of globalization—one that the visionaries of the post–World War II era never anticipated. Between 1945 and the late 1980s, the world was divided into two powerful political blocs, the United States and the Soviet Union. Each attempted to expand its sphere of influence by exercising a measure of centralized control over countries, regions, and global commercial forces. Likewise, the post–World War II era saw the rise of several hundred transnational corporations who sought to extend their reach and influence by transborder mergers and acquisitions and the establishment of vast global value chains. This was the era of centralized and hierarchical command-and-control operations, at both the political and economic levels.

What neither the politicians nor business leaders foresaw was the advent of a new kind of technology revolution whose modus operandi is, at the same time, both highly connective and decentralized. The software revolution, the digitalization of media, personal computers, the World Wide Web, and wireless information flows transformed communications from a vertical to a horizontal plane and from centralized command-and-control to decentralized interactivity. Similarly, the shift in the global energy regime, which is just now getting under way, from elite energy sources such as oil, coal, natural gas, and nuclear, which are centrally organized and vertically distributed, to more dispersed renewable energy sources such as the sun, wind, biomass, geothermal, and hydro stored in the form of hydrogen, and generated locally at end sites in a decentralized fashion, is changing the very nature of how energy is shared. Power, both literally and figuratively, will be increasingly decentralized in the coming century.

The EU was born into the old world of vertical organization and centralized control. The community was an effort to pool nation-states' economic, social, and political resources and create "economies of scale" that could compete with the larger political and commercial forces around it. While one of the two political superpowers still exists and transnational corporations continue to expand their reach to every corner of the globe, counterforces at the local and regional levels are emerging that are both challenging global, political, and commercial hegemony and, at the same time, attempting to assert their places in an increasingly connected world.

The new decentralized technologies are being exploited in two opposite directions—toward greater concentration as well as greater dispersion of power. For example, while Microsoft has attempted to be the gatekeeper to cyberspace by imposing its operating system on most owners of personal computers, the scrappy upstart company Linux, a firm started by social activists dedicated to the free sharing and sourcing of code between computer users, is now threatening Microsoft's dominance.

Likewise, while global corporations are using the new decentralized forms of communication to create business-to-business partnerships and establish a tighter grip on their respective industries and the communities in which they do business, local activists around the world use the same connective communication technologies to organize global resistance movements to what they regard as unbridled corporate power.

The point is, the rise of the new decentralized information and communication technologies in the late 1980s unleashed powerful new forces and countervailing forces and brought many new players onto the public stage. The new connective technologies helped corporations transcend national boundaries and disperse their production and distribution activities around the globe. The same connective technologies, however, helped cities and regions, cultural and ethnic groups, and social and environmental movements to leapfrog national boundaries and begin exercising influence on a broader global playing field.

The EU suddenly found itself in the midst of a whirlwind of contending forces vying for power and recognition, each with its own resources to bring to bear and its own agenda, and none powerful enough to dominate the political process alone. This was a far more complicated political game.

Previously, the EU merely had to negotiate its external relationships with the two superpowers, the U.S. and USSR, and its internal relationships among the contending member states. The member states, in turn, contained the myriad of subnational forces within their own territories. The global information and communication revolutions decimated nation-state boundaries just as the cannon once toppled the city-state walls of the feudal era. And, like the former era, new forces were let loose onto the political landscape, this time beyond the reach of the nation-state itself.

The Feedback Revolution

The first inkling that politically centralized command-and-control mechanisms were too antiquated to accommodate the vast changes in spatial and temporal orientation brought on by the new information and communication technologies came with the sudden fall of the Soviet Empire. The new technologies ran havoc over the rigid bureaucratic style of governance in Central and Eastern Europe and the former Soviet Union. The inability of Communist governance, at every level, to respond to the liberating power of decentralized global information and communication technologies helped seal its doom. The old walls of repression and censorship were too thin to withstand the media invasion. The penetration of MTV (Music Television), rock music, and Western lifestyles behind the iron curtain, via the new information and communication technologies, proved too much for a creaky governmental apparatus whose methods of governance were borrowed from technologies and organizational styles popular in the early twentieth century.

The old centralized forms of governance—both in the Soviet Union and in the West—were modeled after Frederick Taylor's Principles of Scientific Management. Taylor, whom we touched on in chapter 4, was the first to introduce a rationalized, hierarchical command-and-control mechanism into American industry in the first decade of the twentieth century. His model was quickly taken up by governments around the world.

Taylor argued that management should assume complete authority over how work is carried out on the factory floor and front office. He reasoned that if laborers retained some control over how their work was to be executed, they would conspire to work as little as necessary to perform the tasks assigned to them. Taylor's organizational model depended on sever-

ing any independent judgment on the part of the workers and giving them
exact orders along with precise instructions on how they were to perform
their work.

> The work of every workman is fully planned out by the management
> at least one day in advance, and each man receives in most cases
> complete written instructions, describing in detail the task which he
> is to accomplish, as well as the means to be used in doing the
> work. . . . This task specifies not only what is to be done, but how it
> is to be done and the exact time allowed for doing it. . . . Scientific
> management consists very largely in preparing for and carrying out
> these tasks.[2]

Governments, like companies, relied on this kind of top-down bureaucratic model of governance for most of the twentieth century. In this
schema, the ideas, feelings, and expertise of those delivering government
services, as well as the affected citizenry, are largely ignored. The most efficient organization is deemed to be the one where the civil servants perform like soldiers and the citizenry are treated as passive recipients. The
old form of rationalized command-and-control mirrored the machine
mentality of the era. Both machines and men were thought of as passive
instruments wound up by an outside prime mover and made to repeat
simple actions over and over again. The rationalized model made little or
no room for input from those executing the tasks or from those receiving
the services. It was assumed that they had little value to contribute up the
line of command.

The introduction of intelligent information and communication machines with feedback loops changed the nature of technology and created
new metaphors for rethinking the art of governance.

The philosophical inspiration for the new technology revolution dates
back to the early years of the twentieth century and the scientific writing
of Alfred North Whitehead, the father of process philosophy. He was the
first to eliminate the ancient wall separating space and time—being and
becoming—and reduce all phenomena to pure activity. Before Whitehead, most philosophers believed that phenomena was divided into two
realities: what something was and what it did. There was structure and
function, the "being" of a thing and its "becoming." Whitehead, one of
the first modern philosophers to live during the transition to electricity,

came to view behavior as pure process in which space and time melded together into a single extended field of pure activity. What something is, proclaimed Whitehead, can't be differentiated from what it does. All phenomena represent continuous patterns of activity responding to changes in the patterns of activity around them. Because everything is in continuous flux, novelty is present at every instant. Whitehead believed that all living things are continuously anticipating novelty in their surrounding environment and making adjustments to those changes in order to secure their duration—what we now call "feedback." Whitehead called this anticipation-response mechanism "subjective aim" and said that it was really what "mind" was about.

A half century after Whitehead's insight, Norbert Wiener introduced a mechanical analogue of process philosophy with the concept of cybernetics. Wiener and his colleagues were working on improving the sighting and targeting of anti-aircraft gunnery in World War II. Wiener's engineering insights on how machines and humans communicate transformed process philosophy into a new technological format, which soon thereafter gave birth to modern information and communications technology.

Wiener inaugurated the new field of cybernetics research. Cybernetics comes from the Greek word *kyberneties*, which means "steersman." Cybernetics reduces purposeful behavior to two components, information and feedback, and postulates that all processes can be understood as amplifications and complexifications of both. Wiener defined information as

> the name for the content of what is exchanged with the outer world as we adjust to it, and make our adjustment felt upon it. The process of receiving and of using information is the process of our adjusting to the contingencies of the outer environment, and of our living effectively within that environment.[3]

Cybernetics is the theory of the way these messages or pieces of information interact with one another to produce predictable outcomes.

According to cybernetics theory, the "steering mechanism" that regulates all behavior is feedback. Anyone who has ever adjusted a thermostat is familiar with how feedback works. The thermostat regulates the room temperature by monitoring the change in temperature in the room. If the room cools off and the temperature dips below the mark set on the dial, the thermostat kicks on the furnace, and the furnace remains on until the room temperature coincides once again with the temperature set on the dial. Then the thermostat kicks off the furnace, until the room temperature drops again, requiring additional heat. This is an example of negative feedback. All systems maintain themselves by the use of negative feedback. Its opposite, positive feedback, produces results of a very different kind. In positive feedback, a change in activity feeds on itself, reinforcing and intensifying the process, rather than re-adjusting and dampening it. For example, a sore throat causes a person to cough, and the coughing, in turn, exacerbates the sore throat.

Cybernetics is primarily concerned with negative feedback. Wiener points out that "for any machine subject to a varied external environment to act effectively it is necessary that information concerning the results of its own action be furnished to it as part of the information on which it must continue to act."[4] Feedback provides information to the machine on its actual performance, which is then measured against the expected performance. The information allows the machine to adjust its activity accordingly, in order to close the gap between what is expected of it and how it in fact behaves. Cybernetics is the theory of how machines self-regulate in changing environments. More than that, cybernetics is the theory that explains purposeful behavior in machines.

Today's intelligent technologies all operate by cybernetic principles. Continuous negative feedback—and occasional positive feedback—take us from a much slower technological era organized around linear, discrete, and discontinuous actions to a vastly sped-up age of pure process and uninterrupted flows.

Process Politics

Smart technologies were coming of age in the early 1980s, just at the time when governments everywhere were under intense scrutiny by an increasingly leery and cynical public. Government bureaucracies were accused of being bloated, inept, uncaring, and slow. A deep worldwide recession in 1973–75 and again in 1980–82—occasioned by the oil shock—added billions of dollars to government deficits in the U.S. and elsewhere, forcing a discussion about the appropriate size of government and the extent to which it could be counted on to provide a broad social net for its citizenry. Prime Minister Margaret Thatcher in Britain and President Ronald Reagan in the U.S. led a political rebellion against big government, preaching the value of deregulation of industry and privatization of government services. The idea was to disperse as much government activity as possible into the commercial arena and the not-for-profit third sector, where it was supposed that the marketplace and the civil society would provide more efficient means for delivering value. "Bigger is better" lost its cachet, and decentralization became vogue.

Process philosophy and the principles of cybernetics, which were already making heady inroads in technology, commerce, and even psychology—personal therapy relies heavily on process-oriented mental reconditioning—began to find their way into discussions of governance. Political scientists argued that the rational top-down bureaucratic approach to public policy does not allow for appropriate feedback or input by all the actors involved—both the agents and the affected constituencies. A new generation of political scientists and policy analysts favored a process approach to governance that would replace the old closed hierarchical model with a new open-systems model. They argued that effective governance is less a matter of imposing, from on high, predetermined decisions on passive recipients at the bottom than of engaging all the actors—government, business, and civil society players—in an ongoing process of deliberation, negotiation, compromise, and consensus with the radical suggestion that the best decisions are the ones reached democratically by everyone affected. The process itself—with its emphasis on continuous feedback—becomes the new governing model. In the process-oriented model, networks become the best mechanism for continuous engagement between the parties.

The idea that governance encompasses a broader range of players and activity than just government was revolutionary in its implication. While the modern nation-state, especially the French and U.S. models, gave homage to the idea of government of, by, and for the people, in practice, as government took on greater responsibilities and their bureaucracies ballooned, the political game narrowed to a binary relationship of the governors and the governed. Government was seen as a self-contained activity, separate and distinct from all the other activities that occur in society.

The 1968 student rebellion played a seminal role in loosening up the idea of governance. Students argued that the university was a community of shared interests and that they ought to enjoy some say in how it is to be governed. They sought to break out of the narrow container that kept all decision-making in the hands of a remote board of trustees and university bureaucracy. Governance, they declared, stretched far beyond the confines of academic rules and institutional protocols to include the totality of relationships and activities that make up the life of the university community. They demanded an ongoing process approach to university decision-making that would include all of the actors engaged in relationships within the university—trustees, administrators, faculty, support staff, students, and even the grounds-keepers and other workers who service the community, as well as members of the broader surrounding communities in which the universities were embedded. Governance, said the student reformers, was not edicts and rules passed down from the top, but an open-ended deliberative process entered into by equal players, each with their own interests and aspirations, but all interdependent and ultimately responsible for one another's shared welfare.

A similar upheaval occurred at the state level a decade after the student revolt. Philosophers such as Michel Foucault argued that in a post-modern world of increasing complexity, density, and interdependence, every action of every player affects the nature, quality, and distribution of power across the entire system. He wrote that government

> refers to all endeavors to shape, guide, and direct the conduct of others, whether these be the crew of a ship, the members of a household, the employees of a boss, the children of a family, or the inhabitants of a territory.[5]

Foucault and others claim that the old model did not make room for feedback and inclusion of all the potential actors. In the new way of thinking, every level of governance is embedded with every other level in a continuous process of engagement—what Foucault calls "governmentality." Sociologist Mitchell M. Dean defines governmentality as "the relationship between the government of ourselves, the government of others, and the government of state."[6]

Government becomes only one player, among many diverse players, in the political game. The state is no longer sovereign. It loses its power as the exclusive agent responsible for disciplining its citizenry. The exercise of power becomes much more diffuse and decentralized. Dean calls this new kind of governance "government without a centre, a form of administration in which there is no longer a centrally directing intelligence."[7]

The new communication technologies figure prominently in the deconstruction of state sovereignty. Now the players that were once isolated and powerless at the bottom of the old nation-state governing pyramid have the means of communication at their disposal to connect with their kind and with others who share mutual interests in a field that crisscrosses, penetrates, and transcends the nation-state container. Governance is reconceived as the management of communication flows, and players position themselves at strategic nodes, embedded in multiple interacting networks, where their every decision and action has consequences that flow across the network and beyond.

The dramatic growth in global connectedness, made possible by the new communication technologies, so increases the interdependence of everyone that the old nation-state governing unit is simply incapable, on its own, of managing the sheer volume and flow of human exchange and interactivity that is generated.

Network Governance

In the early 1990s, the EU began to look to the new decentralized information and communication technologies that were remaking commerce and social life as well as to the new network models being used to organize the increasingly complex exchange activity brought on by the new technologies, with the idea of making them the centerpiece of a new approach to governance. There was widespread agreement that the European Union had to catch up to the new technologies that were revolutionizing society.

In 1994, the European Commission published a report entitled *Europe's Way to the Information Society: An Action Plan*. The report spelled out a series of initiatives for making the European Union the first fully integrated information society in the world. The plan called for integrating a host of EU cross-border activity into interactive networks and included proposals for a network of universities and research centers, a teleworking network, a distance-learning network, road-traffic and air-traffic control networks, health-care networks, and a trans-European public administration network. In a 1996 follow-up report entitled *Europe at the Forefront of the Global Information Society: A Rolling Action Plan*, the EU honed and refined the earlier vision, placing more emphasis on extending the new technologies across industry and establishing the proper regulatory regime and stimuli to make network ways of doing business viable and effective. The plan also emphasized the integration of the new information and communication technologies and network practices into the educational system, as well as making them part of the everyday life of European citizens. Most important of all, the EU began to reinvent its style of governance to accommodate the many changes being introduced to usher in an information society.[8]

The various EU government agencies and organizations were encouraged, and even required, to establish "high levels of inter-action and networking between European level agencies, state, provincial and local governments, NGOs, business and corporate actors, educational organizations, research institutes and a variety of user-groups."[9] EU government agencies were tasked with facilitating the networks and becoming a co-member with other interested parties. Emphasis was placed on creating networks that transcend nation-state boundaries. The idea was to establish a European frame of reference. For example, research institutes applying for EU grants are required to establish transnational networks of players to qualify for funds. Many of these networks operate in a generally informal manner. Their activities often take place outside or alongside the more formal protocols and procedures that characterize the older top-down kind of governance that still exists.[10]

Each year, more and more of the daily work of EU governance is being given over to these more informal networks of players, changing the very way government is perceived. The old centralized top-down model of governance, with its rational performance standards and tight command-and-control mechanisms, is slowly giving way to a process-oriented model of governance, made operational in horizontally structured networks. The new information and communication technologies are driving the political changes as they did in commerce.

When the density of human activity leaps from a regional geographic plane to a global electronic field and from mimetic, linear, discrete exchanges to continuous novelty, feedback, and flow, hierarchical command-and-control mechanisms become too slow to govern activity. Statutes become outdated almost as soon as they are enacted, and old-fashioned top-down governing institutions prove too snail-like to manage the cascade of novelty and, as a result, experience a form of political gridlock.

The European Union is the first governing experiment in a world metamorphosing from geographic planes to planetary fields. It does not govern property relationships in territories, but rather manages open-ended and continually changing human activity in global networks. It has even become popular in the European Union to talk about "polycentric" governance in contrast to conventional government. Traditional government is associated with territorial rule. Polycentric governance is decentralized and is not just about what governments do. Rather, say the late social theorist Paul Hirst and political theorist Grahame Thompson, "it is a function that can be performed by a wide variety of public and private, state and non-state, national and international institutions and practices."[11] With polycentric governance, the governing franchise is expanded to include non-state players. It is a new political game that is far more complex and sophisticated, in which no one player can dominate the field or determine the outcome, but where everyone has some power to affect the direction and flow of the process.

The polycentric governing style is characterized by continuous dialogue and negotiations between all the players in the many networks that make up its ever changing economic, social, and political field of influence. The new genre of political leader is more like a mediator than a military commander. Coordination replaces commands in the new political scheme of things.

In a technological era where space is becoming a single unified global field, duration is shrinking to near simultaneity, and everything is compressed and sped up, historical consciousness characterized by great utopian visions, well-defined political ideologies, established bureaucratic procedures, and long-term social goals steadily gives way to a more therapeutic consciousness characterized by continually changing scenarios and expedient short-term strategic options. The EU is, as mentioned before, a post-modern political institution. Its world is one of ever changing contours and fleeting realities where only novelty itself is permanent and where duration has narrowed to an ever present now. If ancient dynasties were designed with the purpose of commemorating and ritualizing the past, and modern nation-states were charged with organizing an open-ended future, new political institutions such as the EU are designed to cope with a continually changing present.

So if the EU seems, at times, to represent many different faces depending on changing conditions and circumstances, it's because its persona is continuously re-adjusting to the ever changing patterns of activity around it. Its chameleonlike ability to reinvent itself is its strong suit.

Unlike nation-states, then, the EU is perceived not as an agent of destiny but, rather, as a manager of momentary conflicts and competing agendas. In the new era, grand meta-narratives—the kind that motivated citizen loyalty in the nation-state era—are passé. In their place are numerous smaller stories, each reflecting the perspectives and aims of the different constituencies. Finding some common ground between the disparate players and forging an ongoing dialogue and periodic consensus that can move them together as a community, even as they retain their individual identities, becomes the mandate and mission of the European Union. "Unity in diversity" is the unofficial moniker of the new European Constitution.

The EU has continued to confound its critics and expand and deepen its political influence precisely because its organizational model has been more "process-oriented" over the past half century of its existence. The EU's political success has been all the more impressive given the fact that its primary architects, the French, are known for their more conventional, hierarchical, and centralized way of exercising political control. Even though the old nation-state way of governing has attempted to put its stamp on EU governance at every step of the way—and continues to do so today—the new disaggregated technological, commercial, and social realities of a global era have forced the EU to manage more by process than by edict and statute.

"Multilevel governance" is the unexpected synthesis that has emerged out of the contest waged between the federalists and confederalists to define the community's future. The continuous give-and-take between those favoring a more centralized approach and those preferring an intergovernmental approach resulted in countless compromises along the way that began to fundamentally alter the political dynamic in a manner neither side foresaw. For example, the introduction of the Subsidiarity Principle has become a mainstay of EU governance. The principle represented a compromise, of sorts, between the confederalists and the federalists. The principle, which has been incorporated into the new constitution, states that, whenever possible, governing decisions ought to be made as far down and as close as possible to the communities and constituents most affected by the decisions. The intergovernmentalists hoped that the Subsidiarity Principle would keep governing decisions tucked deep inside the nation-state container. The federalists hoped that the Subsidiarity Principle would free local regions from nation-state authority and give them greater license to bypass the state and work directly with Brussels. As mentioned earlier, a Committee of the Regions was established in 1994 to represent regional interests within the EU. The upshot of subsidiarity is that the regions have now become a kind of third force, and they play off their relationships with both host countries and the EU to advance their goals. And, they often bypass both governing institutions and create networks among themselves as well as with transnational global institutions to meet their objectives. They have added a new level of engagement to the European political potpourri. Now, the governance networks are increasingly made up of local, regional, national, transnational, and global players, in a myriad of shifting alliances, each attempting to influence the direction of the political game.

The net result of the protracted struggle between the confederalists and federalists over pushing political authority further down into the states, or pushing it beyond national territorial boundaries to the Union itself, has been that neither the member states nor the Union has been strengthened. Rather, there has been a balkanization of authority, with the entrance of new players and a multiplication of competing agendas.

The EU has ended up becoming the rule-maker and gatekeeper. It establishes the directives that govern the play, brings together the players, and helps facilitate the political process among the parties. The EU is the first purely regulatory state whose function is to serve as an arbiter among contending forces.

It's often said that the United States is unique among nations because it owes its existence to an idea—the belief in the inalienable rights of persons to life, liberty, and the pursuit of happiness. The EU is an even more ethereal political experiment. The U.S. government's legitimacy is, at least, still grounded in the conventional notion of control over territory, the ability to tax, and the right to exercise force, if necessary, to assure obedience to its laws. The EU enjoys none of the conventional requisites of states. Its legitimacy is based exclusively on the continued trust and goodwill of the members who make it up and the treaties and directives—and soon a new constitution—they have pledged to uphold.

We are so used to thinking of citizenship as something that goes hand in hand with a territory and a nation that it is difficult to fathom the idea of also being a citizen of a transterritorial governing body bound not in traditional property relations but rather in universally accepted codes of human conduct. The late British sociologist Ernest Gellner captures the inherent difficulty of belonging to a shared ideal that transcends geography. He writes,

> The idea of a man without a nation seems to impose a strain on the modern imagination. . . . A man must have a nationality as he must have a nose and two ears. . . . All this seems obvious, though, alas, it is not true. But that it should have come to *seem* so very obviously true is indeed an aspect, or perhaps the very core, of the problem of nationalism. Having a nation is not an inherent attribute of humanity, but it has now come to appear as such.[12]

Some post-modern political theorists suggest that in the new world of dense, overlapping, and ever changing relationships, governance is really more about association and connectivity than about controlling a specific physical space.[13] Scholars refer to the political reconfiguration of Europe as "the new medievalism," a term coined by the late Hedley Bull of Oxford University in an essay he wrote back in 1977. Even then, Bull sensed the emergence of a new political landscape in Europe. He thought it "conceivable that sovereign states might disappear and be replaced not by a world government, but by a modern and secular equivalent of the kind of universal political organization that existed in Western Christendom in the Middle Ages."[14] Bull pointed out that "in that system no ruler or state was sovereign in the sense of being supreme over a given territory and a given segment of the Christian population; each had to share authority with vassals beneath, and with the Pope and (in Germany and Italy) the Holy Roman Emperor above."[15] Bull noted that "all authority in mediaeval Christendom was thought to derive ultimately from God."[16] He suggested that

> if modern states were to come to share their authority over their citizens, and their ability to command their loyalties, on the one hand with regional and world authorities, and on the other hand with substate or sub-national authorities, to such an extent that the concept of sovereignty ceased to be applicable, then a neo-mediaeval form of universal political order might be said to have emerged.[17]

Bull used his own country as a model. He wondered what would happen if the United Kingdom had to share its authority with the authority of Wales, Wessex, and Scotland at a subnational level, as well as with authority in Brussels and world bodies such as the United Nations in New York "to such an extent that the notion of its supremacy over the territory and people of the United Kingdom had no force."[18] Bull believed that reconfiguring the political world into "a structure of overlapping authorities and crisscrossing loyalties that hold all peoples together in a universal society"[19] would be far superior either to the existing system of competing sovereign states with their propensity to war or to the prospect of a single world government whose monopoly over the means of coercion and violence would heighten repression and oppression on a grand scale.[20] Bull's thesis proved to be remarkably prescient.

What, then, is the EU? Sociologist Ulrich Beck says it is a "negotiation state, which arranges stages and conversations and directs the show."[21] The EU, then, is less a place than a process. While it maintains many of the fixed physical trappings of a state—an EU passport, a flag, a headquarters—its genius is its indeterminacy. Unlike the traditional nation-state, whose purpose is to integrate, assimilate, and unify the diverse interests inside its borders, the EU has no such mission. To the contrary, its role is just the opposite of what nation-states do. The EU's political cachet is bound up in facilitating and regulating a competing flow of divergent activities and interests.

The EU may appear to some as weak and vacillating and without sufficient coercive authority—the ability to tax and police. To others, however, it is the very model of a new kind of governing institution, suited to processing the multiple interests that proliferate and interconnect across every imaginable boundary in a globalized environment. Political scientist Tim Luke views the EU as

a more dynamic, more interconnected, yet more fragmented and fluid milieu for enacting authority and managing flows of influence from multiple sources, than can be contained by the Euclidean geometry and identity spaces of territorialized or super-territorialized modernity.[22]

Despite its ephemeral nature, the EU packs a wallop. Its statutes and directives have untold impacts on its member countries. The U.K., for example, estimates that over 80 percent of the environmental legislation governing its citizenry comes from directives issued by the European Environmental Agency.[23] Other EU statutes and directives governing such things as consumer product safety, drug testing, medical protocols, financial services, and competition, all flow from Brussels to the states. But the important thing to remember is that the regulatory decisions made in Brussels are themselves the result of a polycentric process of negotiation, compromise, and consensus, involving many parties at the regional, national, transnational, and global levels.

The whole process ultimately works because the people of Europe want "problems without frontiers" to be addressed by the whole European community. The questions of whether or not to introduce genetically modified (GM) food crops and label GM food products, develop guidelines for quarantining cattle to prevent the transmission of bovine spongiform encephalopathy (BSE), sign treaties to reduce global-warming gases and protect biodiversity, outlaw human cloning, and the consideration of countless other initiatives are best handled at the Europe-wide level because the very nature and consequences of such activities transcend national boundaries and can only be effectively addressed by the whole community working in concert.

Sharing Power

Although government policy networks share many attributes with commercial networks, there are differences in their goals. Commercial networks are dedicated to optimizing the income stream of their players. Public networks have a different purpose—to propose and deliberate on legislative initiatives and help implement policy decisions made in the political arena.

To some extent, the proliferation of public networks has been largely defensive in nature. The public's increasingly negative opinion of government effectiveness in delivering services helped spawn the move to deregulation, privatization, and decentralization of public activity. There is, however, another side to this story. Some argue that the private sector played an up-front role in fanning the flames of citizen discontent—even to the point of creating a crisis of public confidence that was not entirely justified—in order to capture enormous new commercial opportunities that came with the privatization of large swaths of vital human services.

Motivations aside, public policy networks have been introduced as a way to stop the hemorrhaging that was leading to a wholesale deconstruction of government-related activity. There was a real sense of dread among policy leaders in the 1980s and 1990s that government was quickly imploding and that the capitalist marketplace might eventually end up as the unchallenged arbiter of human relationships. Many warned that the notion of democracy was being upended and that political choices that used to be made by citizens at the ballot box were increasingly being made by consumers in the marketplace. Neoliberals and libertarians favored just such a course, arguing that the market mechanism was far superior to the political process as a way of representing the collective will of the people and assuring the future well-being of society.

Government policy networks were seen as a means to meet the criticism halfway. Governments everywhere sensed the real need to reach out and involve both the private sector and the civil society in the initiation as well as the implementation of government policy. That recognition represented a revolution in political thinking. Up until the advent of public policy networks, the political arena had been divided into two separate realms. The citizenry voted for their elected leaders who, in turn, passed legislation reflecting the will of their constituents. Government bureaucracies, in turn, were responsible for implementing the political will. Their role was considered to be neutral and purely administrative in nature. The establishment of public policy networks was an admission, of sorts, that the politics of representative democracy doesn't begin and end with the election of officials and the passage of legislation and that the question of advocacy and implementation is as politically charged and in need of active involvement as the question of voting for leaders and passing bills.

Public policy networks became a way for government to jump back in and re-invigorate the political process before devolution shifted too much activity to the marketplace. The reasoning behind such networks was Whiteheadian. The social environment is continually in flux and often changes considerably at every stage of the political process. Nor are the interests of the affected constituencies frozen in time. Their priorities and goals are also continually shifting as they anticipate and adjust to changes in their environment. Public policy networks are a way for the government to keep political deliberation, decision-making, and implementation alive and relevant by ongoing dialogue and negotiation between all the affected constituencies. Governance is no longer divided into discrete and separate stages but becomes a "continuous process" of engagement.

Realizing that government would no longer be able to monopolize the governing process, public officials urged a compromise—a joint sharing of the political domain with both the commercial and civil society sectors. Henceforth, the government would be a facilitator of the political process rather than an overseer. The hope was that a more open communication between all the players and a willingness to search for common ground would deepen the democratic process, expedite consensus-building, and streamline the implementation of political decisions. Public policy networks, it was argued, would create a new win-win politics as opposed to the win-lose outcome of more traditional adversary-based politics. Public policy networks would also provide an organizational means of handling the quickening pace of change and the growing density of exchange in a globally connected world.

Sociologist Andrew Barry makes the point that the network, in the European Union, has become

> a way of both transcending the political conflict between welfarism and neo-liberalism, and as a way of developing a form of public intervention which *animates* social and economic actors instead of creating a dependent or protective relation between the state and its clients.[24]

It should be added that public policy networks are also a way of ensuring that unbridled market forces don't gain inordinate sway over the affairs of society.

With public policy networks, politics becomes a 24/7 affair, just like commerce. In the new world of instantaneous information and communications and continuous feedback loops, there are no longer beginnings or endings to political engagement, but only relentless political discourse. The density of exchange and the multiplicity of interests mitigate against any downtime. Governance ceases to be a bounded activity and metamorphoses into an open-ended process. Politics, in the new European sense of the term, has come to mean all of the purposeful activity that people and organizations engage in, through either formal or informal networks, to effect their interests and goals. Participatory democracy migrates to the far edges of space and envelops duration, becoming an all-consuming human endeavor. Everything in society becomes politicized, and anyone left out of the governing networks risks falling far behind the political process, with little chance of catching up to the flow of the game.

11

Romancing the
Civil Society

POLITICS IN the nation-state era operates along two poles—market and government. EU politics, by contrast, operates between three nodes—commerce, government, and civil society. The shift from two-sector to three-sector politics represents a radical progression in the evolution of political life, with profound import for how we human beings organize our future. If two-sector politics made the Enlightenment vision viable, three-sector politics makes the new European Dream realizable.

The Forgotten Sector

The civil society is the realm perched between the marketplace and government. It is composed of all the activities that make up the cultural life of individuals and their communities. The civil society includes religious institutions, the arts, education, health care, sports, public recreation and entertainment, social and environmental advocacy, neighborhood engagement, and other activities whose function is to create community bonds and social cohesion. The civil society is the meeting place for reproducing the culture in all of its various forms. It is where people engage in "deep play" to create social capital and establish codes of conduct and behavioral norms. The culture is where intrinsic values reign. The civil society is the forum for the expression of culture and is the primordial sector.

Despite the civil society's importance in the life of society, this realm has been increasingly marginalized in the modern era by the forces of the market and nation-state governance. Economists and business leaders, in particular, have come to view the marketplace as the primary institution in human affairs. Both capitalist and socialist theorists argue that human behavior is, at its core, materialist and utilitarian and that the moral values and cultural norms of a society are derivative of its economic orientation— or, to quote Madonna, "We are living in a material world, and I am a material girl."

The materialist philosophy lies deep in the pre-Enlightenment and Enlightenment past. As we discussed in chapter 4, Locke, Descartes, Smith, and other early modern philosophers mounted a roundabout assault on the faith-based worldview of the Church. While some among their ranks still professed their allegiance to a higher divine authority, they often favored reason over faith and put as much store in material progress and the vision of an earthly cornucopia as on eternal salvation. The modernists came to believe that the marketplace is the wellspring of the human spirit and that the culture is the beneficiary. They have put work before play and substituted utilitarian values for intrinsic values.

The materialists view the marketplace as the critical social institution and primary arbiter of human relations. The problem is that their analysis is at odds with the history of human development. There is not a single instance I know of in which people first came together to establish markets and create trade and then later took on a cultural identity. Nor are there any examples of people first coming together to create governments and only later creating culture. First, people create language to communicate with one another. They then construct a story about themselves. They ritualize their origins and envision their collective destiny. They create codes of conduct and establish bonds of trust—what we now call "social capital"— and develop social cohesion. In other words, they engage in "deep play" to establish their common identity. Only when their sense of solidarity and cohesion is well developed do they set up markets, negotiate trade, and establish governments to regulate activity. Even in the early modern era, when the emerging capitalists and bourgeois class erected an imaginary nationalism to unite formerly disparate peoples in a new political configuration, the nation-state, they had to dig deep into the past and borrow bits and pieces from various local cultural stories to craft a new unified myth of national origins.

The introduction of new technologies into a society is also conditioned, in large part, by the cultural consciousness. For example, in 1831, Europeans invented chloroform for use in surgery. Centuries earlier, the Chinese invented acupuncture and used it as an anesthetic. Why did the Europeans never discover acupuncture and the Chinese never discover chloroform? Because European and Chinese ideas about space, time, and reality were so utterly different.

The Chinese culture, because of its emphasis on context, holistic thinking, the complementarity of opposites, and harmony with nature, predisposed it to discoveries like acupuncture. The European mind, being more reductionist, analytical, and detached, was predisposed to discoveries like chloroform. That's not to suggest that cultural consciousness rigidly predetermines specific evolutionary advances in technology, but only that it conditions the mind to view the world in a certain way and therefore leads to new discoveries that conform with a people's mental perception of the scheme of things.

Of course, cultural consciousness is not static. New discoveries and inventions continually modify spatial and temporal consciousness and can lead to a shift in the cultural paradigm itself as well as to fundamental changes in economic and political arrangements. But, I would suggest that throughout history, people's experience of reality begins with creating a story about themselves and the world and that story acts as a kind of cultural baseline DNA for all the evolutionary permutations that follow.

The point is that the culture is not and never has been an extension of either the market or the government. Rather, markets and governments are extensions of the culture. They are secondary, not primary, institutions. They exist by the grace of the cultures that create them. Jean Monnet sensed as much, admitting in the late 1960s that "if the European construction process had to be started again afresh, it would be better to start with culture."[1]

After a long period of being colonized at the hands of the market and nation-state, the civil society—along with the deeper cultural forces that underlie it—is pushing to re-establish its central role in the scheme of public life. And like all liberation movements, the first prerequisites for re-asserting its prominence is casting out much of the language that has come to define its very being. Advocates complain that the civil society is not "the third sector," as many academicians claim, but rather the first sector. Similarly, categorizing civil society groups as "not-for-profit organizations" or "nongovernmental organizations" makes them appear as less significant or even just shadows of commercial or governmental institutions. A new generation of activists prefer to think of their institutions as civil society organizations (CSOs). They also define their activity as service rather than volunteering, to connote its importance in developing and reproducing the culture.

The reach of the civil society is impressive. A study conducted by the Johns Hopkins Comparative Nonprofit Sector Project, covering twenty-two nations, estimates that the civil society sector is a $1.1 trillion sector employing more than nineteen million full-time paid workers. "Nonprofit" expenditures in these countries average 4.6 percent of the gross domestic product, and nonprofit employment makes up 5 percent of all nonagricultural work, 10 percent of all service work, and 27 percent of all public employment.[2]

Several European nations now boast an employment level in the "nonprofit" sector that exceeds that of the United States. In the Netherlands, 12.6 percent of total paid employment is in the nonprofit sector. In Ireland, 11.5 percent of all workers are in the nonprofit sector, and in Belgium, 10.5 percent of workers are in this sector. In the U.K., 6.2 percent of the workforce are in the not-for-profit sector, and in France and Germany, the figure is 4.9 percent. Italy currently has more than 220,000 nonprofit organizations, and its not-for-profit sector employs more than 630,000 full-time workers.[3]

The growth in employment in the nonprofit sector was stronger in Europe in the 1990s than in any other region of the world, expanding by an average of 24 percent in France, Germany, the Netherlands, and the U.K.[4] The expansion in nonprofit employment in these countries alone accounted for 40 percent of total employment growth, or 3.8 million jobs.[5]

It is interesting to note that in the ten European countries where revenue data was available, fees for services and products accounted for one-third to one-half of the income in the nonprofit sector between 1990 and 1995. Globally, of the twenty-two countries for which data is available, 49 percent of nonprofit revenue comes from fees for services and products. In the U.S., 57 percent of all nonprofit revenue comes from fees for services and products.[6] The share of funds coming from the philanthropic and public sectors, however, has declined in many countries, thus dispelling the long-harbored myth that the nonprofit sector is virtually dependent on government or private charity to sustain itself.

Community service is very different than labor in the marketplace. One's contribution is meant to advance the social capital of the community. While economic consequences often flow from the activity, they are secondary to the social exchange. The goal is not the accumulation of wealth but, rather, social cohesion and well-being.

Unlike market capitalism, which is based on Adam Smith's notion that the common good is advanced by each person pursuing his or her own individual self-interest, the civil society starts with the exact opposite premise—that by each person giving of him- or herself to others and optimizing the greater good of the larger community, one's own well-being will be advanced.

In a globalized economy of impersonal market forces, the civil society has become an important social refuge. It is the place where people create a sense of intimacy and trust, shared purpose and collective identity. The civil society sector is the antidote to a world increasingly defined in strictly commercial terms.

Civil society organizations have exploded across the world in the past twenty years. In large part, they are a reaction to a new globalized economy where market forces are more remote and less accountable to local communities, and governments have become both too small to address issues that cross borders and affect the whole world—such as global warming, illegal immigration, computer viruses, and terrorist threats—and too big to accommodate needs of local neighborhoods and communities. Civil society organizations empower people to champion their own interests in a world where corporations and governments are less likely to do so. Civil society activists argue that over-reliance on a deregulated global marketplace has led to unbridled capitalist greed and exploitation while diminishing the traditional role of government as a redistributive agent and provider of essential social services. The authors of the Johns Hopkins study on the dramatic growth of civil society institutions conclude that the success of civil society organizations is attributable to their ability to fill the vacuum left by market and government failures.

CSOs are more flexible than governments and more deeply anchored in geography than corporations. The civil society's clarion call is "think globally and act locally." Civil society organizations often organize across national boundaries while representing the interests of local neighborhoods and communities. They are able to be transnational and global, as well as communal and local, making them the ideal social agents to address the plethora of issues that confront humanity in a more dense and interconnected world.

Making Room for a New Political Partner

CSOs have pushed for greater representation in every country as well as at global institutions such as the United Nations, World Bank, IMF, and World Trade Organization. The participation allowed, however, has rarely been more than perfunctory and advisory in nature. The EU has become the first government to formally acknowledge CSOs as full-fledged partners in public policy networks. The European Union has recognized the civil society as the "third component" of European Union governance, viewing it as serving "an intermediary function between the State, the market and citizens."[7] There is a growing understanding that the very success of the EU as a new kind of regulatory state depends, to a great extent, on the effectiveness of civil society organizations in representing the interests of real constituencies whose concerns span the local, regional, national, and even EU boundaries. The CSOs bring true "participatory democracy" to the governing process, making them critical players in the new political experiment. Officials understand that without their active and full participation, the EU is likely to fail. The Economic and Social Committee (ESC) of the EU observed that "one of the biggest challenges for European governance is ensuring effective participation of organized civil society."[8]

Romano Prodi, the president of the European Commission, underscores the significance of the new political partnership. He envisions "EU institutions, national governments, regional and local authorities and civil society interacting in new ways: consulting one another on a whole range of issues; shaping, implementing and monitoring policy together."[9] This process is what President Prodi calls "network Europe."[10]

Although formal representation of CSOs in public policy networks is still weak, the very fact that the EU acknowledges a three-sector partnership is of great historic significance. Recall that the nation-state has been, from the very beginning, a handmaiden of commercial interests. Its mission has been to protect property rights and create conditions favorable to the geographic extension of market forces. Two-sector politics—commerce and government—has been the ever present reality of the modern era.

Now that commercial forces have broken through their national container and taken their activity to a global playing field, they are far less dependent on nation-states to protect their property interests. Indeed, global companies can now play states off against one another—threatening to relocate their operations elsewhere if their interests are not accommodated—making states hostage and increasingly subservient to their commercial agendas. And, if states fail to come in line with global commercial interests, regulating bodies such as the IMF, World Bank, and WTO can impose sanctions and force compliance.

The decoupling of the commerce-state partnership has weakened the state and diminished its power. The EU's courtship of the civil society is an attempt to re-assert political influence in an era of global commerce. By giving up some of their remaining sovereignty and pooling their interests with one another and civil society organizations, nation-states can play collectively on a broader geographic playing field and, by so doing, more effectively negotiate the terms of engagement with global corporate institutions whose power eclipses most individual nation-states and whose influence spans the globe.

Finding Common Ground Between Universal Human Rights and Local Cultural Identity

The most remarkable political change of the past three decades has been the growing involvement of the civil society sector in the political process. There are three broad strains in the civil society. First, there are all of the organizations and activities that promote religion, education, and the arts; provide social services; care for neighborhoods and communities; and foster recreation, sports, and play. For the most part, these activities fall inside national boundaries and are not generally overtly political. Second, there are the "rights" organizations, whose objectives are much more politically oriented and whose activity is, more often than not, directed beyond national boundaries and toward more universal concerns. Third, there are the many organizations that represent the interests of local cultures and ethnic subgroups, whose purpose is to maintain their traditions, rituals, and values and represent their groups' interests, both domestically and internationally, to ensure their survival and growth.

The civil rights movement, the environmental movement, the women's rights movement, the human rights movement, the poor people's campaigns, the peace movement, the disability rights movement, the gay rights movement, the animal rights movement, the consumer rights movement, and the anti-eugenics movement have remade the political landscape. These civil society movements transcend the territorial boundaries of nation-states. Their vision is universal. Their goals are global. They seek a transformation in human consciousness itself—a new awareness of the rights of every individual being and the indivisibility of the Earth's living community. The European Union has become the place where these movements are beginning to make their voices heard, inside as well as outside the corridors of political power.

It's worth pointing out that the new politically active rights-oriented transnational CSOs were not the first to break the hold of nation-state prerogatives in the international arena. An earlier genre of technical- and professional-based international nongovernmental organizations seeded the path for the new players. The International Bureau of Weights and Standards, the International Union for the Protection of Literary and Artistic Works, the International Bureau of Commercial Statistics, the International Labor Office, the International Institute of Agriculture, and the International Association of Seismology were among the thousands of nongovernmental organizations that proliferated from the turn of the century to the 1960s.[11]

Like their rights-oriented successors that began to take root in the late 1960s, in the aftermath of the student rights movement, these older INGOs were based on individual participation, voluntary association, and democratic practices. Their goal was to establish universal standards governing a particular field, endeavor, or activity. They sought to influence political and commercial behavior by having their standards accepted and adopted by relevant institutions in both arenas. They represented a third force with a nonbinding agenda whose influence was based largely on professional or technical expertise and rational norms of behavior.

The new rights-oriented transnational movements also seek to establish universal codes of conduct, not of a technical or professional nature but rather governing human behavior itself. Their legitimacy is not grounded on professional expertise but flows from a deeply felt sense of human conscience. They appeal to human empathy rather than rational calculation. Their sights are set on intrinsic values, not on utilitarian concerns. Their goal is less materialistic and more idealistic. Their efforts are designed to advance not merely economic growth but quality of life. For them, personal transformation, not just material advance, becomes an equal measure of progress.

While the rights-oriented CSOs often focus their attention beyond national borders, the ethnic-oriented CSOs' attention is generally focused below national borders, in particular regions. At some times, the ethnic CSOs' agendas are complementary to the EU's, and at other times, they are at odds. Despite the fact that the EU's motto is "unity in diversity," the subcultures across Europe are often insular and xenophobic and frightened about the effect of Europeanization and globalization on their own communities. If universal human rights–oriented CSOs are more cosmopolitan and worldly in their orientation, local subcultures can often be defensive and reactionary and more directed toward building walls rather than eliminating boundaries.

The difficulty with the many subcultures that dot the European landscape is that their history is deeply embedded in territory. In a globalized world of fast-disappearing boundaries and increased mobility, territory-bound subcultures often feel under siege. Their fear and rage are frequently directed at immigrants and asylum seekers who they see as a threat to their ability to maintain their cultural identity. The feeling of being "invaded" often leads to hatred of foreigners and ultra-right political movements.

Still, local subcultures, especially those that exist as minorities within a larger culture that claims to represent the national identity, have found reason to create common cause with the EU. The Scottish and the Catalonians, for example, view the EU as a liberating force of sorts. Being part of a larger transnational political body has given them greater maneuverability within their own nations. Now, local subcultures, attached to specific geographic regions, can often bypass nation-state constraints and establish political, commercial, and social ties at the EU level, affording them a greater degree of independence and autonomy than they have known under nation-state rule.

EU architects began to sense a potential ally among cultural groupings and opened up direct political channels with local subcultures as a way to soften the influence of nation-state players. Antonio Ruberti, the former commissioner for Science, Research, Technological Development and

Education at the European Union summed up much of the mixed feelings in Brussels about the status of local cultures. "Although it is a handicap in some respects," notes Ruberti, "for the most part European diversity represents a 'trump card.'"[12]

The rights groups and ethnic groups often overlap and share common agendas. For example, global human rights organizations support the Tibetan people's struggle to maintain their identity and autonomy against Chinese political encroachment and repression that threaten their very existence. But rights groups and ethnic groups are just as often at odds with one another. That's because the former ultimately represents the global interests of free individuals while the latter's concern is with the more traditional interests of communities. For example, some cultural groups in Africa still practice female genital mutilation and consider it a rite of passage to adulthood. Women's groups in the first and third world have sought an end to the procedure, claiming that it violates women's basic human right to control their own bodies. They charge that the practice is a way for men to hold women in bondage.

What makes the European Dream so interesting and problematic is that it seeks to incorporate both universal human rights and more parochial cultural rights under the same political tent. This is quite different from the nation-state agenda, whose aim was limited to the protection of individual property rights and civil liberties and the assimilation and integration of sub-groups into a single national identity. Accommodating multi-culturalism and human rights at the same time is no easy task. Remember, cultural communities are rooted in family, extended kin ties, and/or shared religious experiences and are generally anchored in physical settings. The various human rights movements, by contrast, are universal, not particular. Their emphasis is on the individual, not the group. Their setting is the biosphere, not territory.

The real question at hand for Europe is whether or not its people can stretch their affiliations and aspirations from the particular to the universal and from the local to the global. Is it possible to coexist and even flourish in a world of so many divided loyalties? Can one be a Catalonian and at the same time a Spaniard, a European, and a global citizen? To the extent that local cultures feel threatened by larger national, transnational, and global forces, they are likely to view their cultures as "possessions to defend" and sink deeper into the old "mine vs. thine" mentality. On the other hand, to the extent that they see Europeanization and globalization as a way to liberate themselves from the older nation-state yoke and to gain greater independence, maneuverability, and access to the outside world, they may come to view their culture more as "gifts to share," bringing them into a less adversarial and more cooperative relationship with others. Certainly, the idea of a "networked Europe" fits more comfortably with the latter scenario.

Which course is likely to prevail? Right now both the xenophobic and pluralistic cultural schools are at play. The question of future outcomes depends largely on whether ethnic-based interests and rights-based interests can find common ground with one another and with the European Union over an extended geographic field, stretching from the local to the transnational arena. If the European Union can facilitate the coming together of these varied interests in Europe-wide governing networks, the stage will be set for a new kind of politics more suited for the challenges of a globalizing world. The success of the European Dream depends, in no small measure, on the ability to make cultural identity, universal human rights, and European governance a seamless rather than a contradictory relationship.

The new partnership between the EU and civil society organizations is going to prove difficult to manage. We need to bear in mind that CSOs are often at odds with government over official policies. Governments, in turn, often perceive CSOs as threats to their authority and seek to undermine their credibility and discredit their legitimacy.

It's not surprising, then, that the EU has not always greeted the participation of the third sector with open arms. It has been the combination of relentless public pressure and mobilization of popular support behind their agendas that has forced government recognition and secured them a place in the formal public policy debate.

Former United Nations secretary-general Boutros Boutros-Ghali characterizes civil society organizations and movements as "a basic form of popular representation in the present-day world." He says that "their participation in international relations is, in a way, a guarantee of the political legitimacy of those international organizations."[13]

Boutros-Ghali's opinion, while widely shared, is still controversial in many quarters. Although the UN General Assembly allows for greater formal input by CSOs at international gatherings, the UN Security Council bars civil society participation, as does the WTO. Some global organizations, such as the World Bank and the IMF, give lip service to

CSO representation but generally limit participation to an advisory role, often several steps removed from official proceedings. Nation-states and provincial and local governments are also ambivalent about how much formal participation by CSOs ought to be sanctioned. Most governments would probably prefer to limit CSO involvement to a monitoring and feedback function and to mobilizing support behind government initiatives, with formal partnerships limited to just the delivery of services. The CSOs, understandably, would like to be at the decision-making table, with an equal voice and vote in policy decisions. The tensions between the two sectors often flare up and spill out onto the streets. Civil society protests at global political forums and at the EU, as well as at national- and regional-level conferences and meetings, have increased dramatically in recent years.

Much of the ambivalence on the part of government actors and the rising sense of frustration and anger by the activists have to do with conflicting political agendas. Transnational civil society movements use their clout to gain increasing recognition of the universal rights of individuals—as well as nature—under international laws and seek to hold governments accountable to said laws. Their ultimate aim is to create a new planetary political sphere connecting individuals and nature directly to global covenants and conventions. Civil society organizations that represent local subcultures eat away at national sovereignty from the other end. They are constantly in search of new ways to secure greater regional and local autonomy and a more independent voice in decisions that affect their communities. Nation-states sense that the goals of rights-oriented and subculture-oriented civil society organizations, at times, threaten their own sovereignty and hegemony and attempt to either absorb or ignore activist efforts to gain a foothold into the political process.

The European Union, on the other hand, has shown itself to be somewhat more open on the matter of integrating the civil society into its political sphere, although even in Brussels, there are pockets of resistance to the idea of advancing greater CSO participation. The reason the EU is willing to share at least some governing power with civil society organizations is that they bring with them the kind of local, grassroots credibility that Brussels so desperately needs to effectively maintain its legitimacy in a world torn between local, national, regional, and global forces.

A recent study conducted by Edelman PR, one of the world's leading public relations firms, found that among public opinion leaders, especially in Europe, civil society organizations are more favorably regarded and enjoy higher levels of trust than either the commercial or government sectors. While 41 percent of European opinion leaders were favorably disposed toward CSOs in Europe, only 28 percent regarded businesses favorably, and a mere 17 percent were favorable to government.[14] Opinion leaders in the U.S., however, were more favorably disposed to business and government, with 40 percent favorable to commerce and 46 percent favorable to political institutions. Only 34 percent were favorable to CSOs.[15]

When it comes to trust, again European opinion leaders said they have greater trust in CSOs than either business or government. The figures are compelling. Fifty-one percent of opinion leaders say they trust CSOs, only 41 percent say they trust business, and a meager 26 percent say they have trust in government. Again, the United States' opinion leaders express greater trust in government and business than CSOs, but the difference in trust levels between the three sectors is only slight.[16] Other surveys confirm similar findings.

It's not hard, then, to understand why the European Union has embraced, at least tentatively, the idea of sharing governance with CSOs in European policy networks. CSOs enjoy widespread public support and bring a new sense of participatory democracy to the political process. The EU is often criticized for a failure to narrow what observers call the "democratic deficit." With European public opinion polls showing lukewarm support of the European Union, the bureaucrats in Brussels have everything to gain and little to lose in embracing CSOs as partners in Europe-wide policy networks.

Equally important, CSOs are the social engine for preserving cultural diversity throughout the European Union and for mobilizing public support behind universal rights agendas. They are both embedded in geographic communities and, at the same time, connected in their activities beyond regional and even EU boundaries. They are local, transnational, and global players and the essential political partner for an EU regulatory state dedicated to advancing both cultural diversity and universal human rights.

What's becoming clear is that in a world increasingly dominated by global corporate interests, governments at every level—municipal, regional, national, and transnational—will have to establish deep interlinking policy networks with civil society organizations if either are to amass enough political power to provide an effective counterbalance to the commercial arena.

12

The Immigrant Dilemma

EUROPE IS A KALEIDOSCOPE of cultural diversity. The Union's inhabitants break down into a hundred different nationalities who speak eighty-seven different languages and dialects, making the region one of the most culturally diverse areas of the world.[1]

For a long time, the business community and Europe's political elite viewed these cultural enclaves as impediments to progress, historical backwaters that resisted change and fostered traditional prejudices against other groups, especially immigrants and foreigners. Nation-states tried to assimilate them into the dominant national cultures but had only mixed success. Local cultures proved quite resilient.

The early EU visionaries, like their nation-state political counterparts, were uneasy with the idea of accommodating distinct cultures. They worried that local cultures would be unfriendly to Europeanization and, therefore, made little room for them at the table. By the 1970s, however, multiculturalism was experiencing a makeover of sorts. A new generation of post-modern scholars took up their cause, arguing that the Enlightenment project, with its emphasis on grand meta-narratives, nation-state hegemony, and monolithic ideologies, was the real impediment to change. The post-modernists contend that the emphasis on single-perspective and unified visions only supports a colonial agenda that breeds intolerance of other views and spawns repression and violence against minorities at home and subject peoples abroad. In a world increasingly dominated by global commercial forces and remote and impersonal political bureaucracies, the post-modernists champion an antidote in the form of multicultural perspectives and the reification of local cultures.

If, in the nation-state era, the struggle was a class one and centered on the question of possession and distribution of capital and the protection of private property rights, in a global era the struggle is over diversity and centers more on preserving one's cultural identity and enjoying access rights in a densely connected, interdependent world.

What most people fear in a globalizing age, where all the old boundaries are being torn down, is both getting lost and being left out. One's cultural affiliation provides a larger group identity and is a way of being heard, of securing a safe haven in the new multilayered world. Having access is a way of being included in the larger flow of activities that is inexorably moving the human race into a shared commercial arena and global public square. The resurgence of cultural identity, then, serves a dual function. It both establishes a boundary to differentiate oneself from the outside world and provides a strong social vehicle that can be used to assert one's right to access to the global flows that surround.

From Class Politics to Cultural Politics

Managing cultural diversity would be tough enough, if it were only a matter of accommodating the often competing agendas of existing European subcultures. The situation is exacerbated by the dramatic increase in immigrant cultures from outside the European Union.

The globalization of capital flows creates new divides. The world's poor are forced to migrate to wherever capital takes up residence. It's a matter of finding work. In Europe, companies are anxious to recruit cheaper immigrant workers in order to cut their labor costs and remain competitive in world markets. Immigrant groups will often take menial jobs that the native population refuses to do. Cheap immigrant labor also has the effect of dampening wages for everyone else. And, in a depressed labor market with high structural unemployment, Europeans worry that immigrant groups will grab the few available manufacturing and service jobs, at the expense of the native-born.

There is also the concern that immigrant cultures will strain an already overburdened welfare system by taking up precious social services. In an era characterized by heavy taxes and diminishing welfare benefits, native populations, and especially less endowed local cultural communities, are loath to have their taxes spent on educating "foreigners" and providing welfare benefits to support their families.

Lastly, native cultural communities claim that poor immigrants pose a real threat to public safety. It is true that a disproportionate number of immigrants commit crimes and end up in prison. In Germany, for example, foreigners make up a startling 33 percent of the prison population, even though they comprise less than 9 percent of the country's population. In France, 26 percent of the prisoners are immigrants, while foreigners make up only 8 percent of the population.[2]

The main reason for the high crime rate is the high unemployment rate among foreigners living in the EU countries. In Germany, 15 percent of the immigrant work population is unemployed, compared to 7 percent of the native-born population. In France, the unemployment rate among male immigrants is 20 percent, compared to 9 percent of the native-born population. Europeans are growing increasingly apprehensive. In a recent poll conducted by the European Commission, 39 percent of EU residents said that legal immigrants should be sent home if they're unemployed. The immigrants counter that they would like to work but are systematically excluded from employment in many industries. In France, there are more than fifty professions that exclude non-EU nationals from employment, including airline pilots, pharmacists, funeral-home directors, midwives, and architects. Foreigners are even denied the right to obtain licenses to sell alcohol and tobacco. Other countries sport similar employment restrictions.[3]

Immigrants are frequently discriminated against by their adopted country. The discrimination, in turn, perpetuates the cycle of dire poverty and alienation and fans the flames of social unrest among immigrants, creating a kind of vicious cycle that's difficult to break. Then, too, immigrant parents often are unable to exert the same kind of parental control over children that they were able to command in their native land. The breakdown of family authority combined with abject poverty and a sense of rootlessness make for a powerful mix of escalating antisocial behavior and crime.

Europeans, by and large, feel inundated and overwhelmed by the immigrant crush. The resentment has been building up slowly over the course of the past half century and now threatens to undo the process of Europeanization. Only 21 percent of Europeans polled in 2000 considered themselves to be "actively tolerant" of immigrants. More than half of the EU population surveyed said that the quality of education suffers if the immigrant percentage of the school population "is too high."[4] Moreover, one half of the EU population agreed that "people from minority groups abuse the social welfare system."[5]

Even in the United Kingdom, which has long been known for being somewhat more tolerant of immigrants, two-thirds of those surveyed said that there were just too many foreigners in their country.[6] Similarly, according to a German poll, two-thirds of the population favor stronger immigration controls.[7] The growing resentment toward immigrants has encouraged the birth of anti-immigration parties on the extreme right, many of whom enjoy widespread popular support. The Italian Northern League, the Swiss People's Party, the Austrian Freedom Party, and the French National Front have all met with success at the polls with their populist appeals attacking immigrants.[8]

The EU as a Land of Immigrants

Although European countries have experienced migratory waves in the past, the numbers, until late, have been relatively small compared to those of the United States. America is a nation of immigrants. Everyone—with the exception of Native Americans—came from somewhere else, and most immigrants, at least for the first three centuries, arrived from Europe. European cultures, by contrast, have existed often in the same region for millennia of history. Welcoming newcomers has proved to be challenging.

The modern wave of immigrants began arriving in Europe after World War II. Labor shortages brought on by the losses of so many young men and women in the war led Germany, France, Belgium, and Switzerland to recruit cheap labor from Southern Europe in the late 1950s and 1960s, and Turkey and North Africa in the 1950s, 1960s, and 1970s.[9] Most of the foreign workers were characterized as guest workers and deemed to be temporary rather than permanent residents. The U.K., France, and the Netherlands drew immigrant labor from their foreign colonies. Italy and Spain soon followed suit, by bringing in guest workers to fill menial jobs within the agricultural sector.[10] Labor shortages throughout Europe were so acute at the time that immigrants were welcomed with open arms. They were regarded as essential to the effort to rebuild the war-torn economies of the continent. In the 1970s, the dramatic post–World War II economic growth began to cool down. The OPEC oil embargo in 1973 led to a worldwide recession and growing unemployment lines across Europe. Fear over job loss ignited native political resentment and spawned anti-immigrant movements in virtually every European country.

Immigration picked up again in the aftermath of the collapse of the Soviet Empire and the tearing down of the Berlin Wall. The economic boom in Western Europe in the 1990s brought in more immigrants. Many were asylum-seekers and illegal aliens from Central and Eastern Europe and especially war-ridden Yugoslavia.

The successive waves of immigrants into Western Europe over the past five decades has nearly equaled the intensity of the great migrations to America at the turn of the last century. Germany took in 24.5 million immigrants between 1950 and 1988, while France opened its doors to 21.9 million immigrants. The U.K., Switzerland, and Scandinavia, as well as the low countries of Holland, Luxembourg, and Belgium, accounted for an additional 25 million immigrants.[11]

The European Commission reports that in 1999, nineteen million people, or 5.1 percent of the total population of the fifteen member states, were non-nationals. Thirty percent of the migrants, or six million people, were from other EU member states. The remaining thirteen million immigrants, totally 3.4 percent of the total population of Europe, were from outside the EU. By way of contrast, in 1985 there were only 8.4 million third-party immigrants (non-EU nationals) living in Europe, or 2.3 percent of the total population. In Austria, non-nationals make up 9 percent of the population, and in Germany they make up nearly 7 percent of the population. In France and Sweden, non-nationals comprise 6 percent of the population.[12]

The sociological effects of this kind of rapid immigration can be boggling. For example, in Germany in 1960, nearly everyone who married was German. In only one marriage out of every twenty-five was a foreign national one of the partners. By 1994, in one out of every seven marriages, one or both of the spouses were foreign born. Births are even more illuminating. In 1960, only 1.3 percent of births had a foreign father or mother. By 1994, 18.8 percent of newborns had a foreign father, mother, or both.[13] Mixed cultural marriages seem to have two contradictory effects. They often deepen the sense of diminution of German culture and lead to a more bitter cultural retrenchment and reprisals against foreigners. At the same time, the fusing of cultural traditions opens up new channels of communications between the cultures and lessens some of the cultural barriers, at least among the grown children of mixed marriages.

The mounting tensions over the influx of new immigrants led the International Organization for Migration to conclude, in a report published in the summer of 2002, that there is a prevailing view in Europe "that immigration pressures have reached intolerable levels."[14] The report warned that Europeans feel that their identities are being jeopardized by the onslaught of foreign nationals.[15]

Still, to put all of this into perspective, the net migration rate into Europe between 1990 and 1998 was 2.2 percent, while U.S. net migration during the same period was 3 percent, and Canada's was 6 percent.[16] The fact of the matter is that, whether justified or not, many—not all—Europeans feel beleaguered by immigration, and their angst is not likely to abate anytime soon.

Repopulating the Old World

The immigration backlash portends serious consequences for the long-term well-being of Europe itself. The sad truth is that without a massive increase in non-EU immigration in the next several decades, Europe is likely to wither and die—both figuratively and literally.

According to the European Commission, total EU population is expected to peak around 2022. In just the next fifteen years alone, the population over the age of sixty-five in Europe will increase by 22 percent. The population over the age of eighty will grow even faster. The number of very old people will rise by 50 percent, to more than twenty million. Europeans between the ages of fifty-five and sixty-four will grow by 20 percent, and in France, Luxembourg, the Netherlands, and Ireland the number of citizens between the age of fifty-five and sixty-four will grow by more than 40 percent. Currently, elderly people make up 16 percent of the total EU population, but by 2010 they will represent 27 percent of the entire population.[17] The demographics become even more dire as we head further into the century. By 2050, the population of older persons will increase to 35 percent. There will be 2.4 old people for every child, and one-third of the entire population of Europe will be over sixty years old.[18] The result is that the median age in Europe, which is now 37.7 years, will be 52.3 years in 2050. By contrast, in the U.S. the median age in 2050 will have risen only slightly, to 35.4 years.[19] Europe's overall population is expected to fall by a startling 13 percent between 2000 and 2050.[20] Some individual countries fare even worse. Italy is projected to lose one-fifth of its total population by 2050.[21] (Italy already has the world's oldest population. Twenty-five percent of its citizens are over sixty years old.) Spain's current population of 39.9 million is expected to drop to 31.3 million by 2050.[22]

At the heart of the problem is the continent's frighteningly low fertility rate. Europe has the lowest fertility rate of any region of the world. In Spain, Sweden, Germany, and Greece, the fertility rate has dropped to 1.4 percent or lower, according to the World Health Organization. In Eastern European countries such as Bulgaria, Latvia, and the Ukraine, the fertility rate is even lower, at 1.1 percent.[23]

Historical comparisons tell the story. Among women born in West Germany in 1950, 14.9 percent were childless. Of the women born in West Germany in 1965, however, 31.2 percent were childless.[24]

The European Commission warns that "after centuries of continuous expansion the end of European population growth is now in sight."[25] *Financial Times* columnist Martin Wolf put it more bluntly, saying that "Europe is becoming a vast old people's home."[26]

The only saving grace in all of these dismal statistics is the fact that when the EU enlarges from twenty-five to an expected twenty-eight countries, its total population will be upward of 550 million people. The U.S., which has a higher fertility rate, still won't reach 550 million citizens until at least 2050.[27]

Adding more countries with additional people won't solve the problem of an aging population. Governments are worried. They have embarked on a number of programs to encourage more births. They have provided handsome tax breaks for parents, paid maternity leave, free child care, a reduction in utility rates for large families, and financial assistance for young parents to purchase homes. Still, these policy initiatives, to date, have had little or no effect.[28]

There are a lot of reasons why fertility rates continue to drop. Europeans stay in school longer and marry later. Women with careers are deferring decisions about having children. Many couples require both partners to work to maintain the standard of living they enjoyed when they were growing up. Contraception, abortion, and divorce have also played a role in keeping down the number of births. Moreover, many of the younger generation prefer to be less tied to parental obligations and more free to enjoy their lives.

An aging population is likely to result in Europe losing its competitive edge in the world economy over the course of the first half of the twenty-first century. Already the warning signs are ominous. Across Europe, younger workers are organizing for what they call "generational justice."[29] They are feeling the burden of having to finance retirement benefits for an aging older population. Recently, thirty thousand young people took to the streets in Paris to protest what they regard as the overly generous pension benefits enjoyed by their parents' generation.[30]

By 2006, more people will be retiring from the French workforce than will be entering it. With fewer working people left to provide tax revenue to finance retirement benefits, the French government, like other European nations, is suggesting radical changes in its pension program. Under newly proposed legislation, workers would be required to work for forty years rather than the current 37.5 years to secure full benefits.[31] The unions have vigorously fought the reforms and have staged several nationwide one-day work stoppages.[32] Prime Minister Jean-Pierre Raffarin vows, however, to continue to push for pension reforms, saying that "this is my duty to future generations."[33]

In Germany, entitlements for retirees already account for 15 percent of the nation's GDP and by 2040 are expected to be as high as 26 percent of the GDP.[34] In Austria, the government has cut pension benefits by 10 percent and is gradually raising the retirement age from sixty to sixty-five.[35]

Fewer younger workers paying for the retirement of an increasing number of older workers—many of whom retire at age fifty-five and live on pensions for more years than they worked—is clearly untenable. Economists warn that the drag on the European economy from having to support more and more retirees is likely to be catastrophic. The European Commission estimates that the EU share of world gross product could plunge from its current 30 percent to less than 10 percent, making Europe a second-tier economic region by the second half of the twenty-first century.[36] Any way you cut it, Europe's aging population is going to prove to be an increasing burden on the European economy.

The demographic reality places Europe in the throes of a dilemma. The only way out, short of a miraculous rise in fertility—which is highly unlikely—is to open the floodgates to millions of new immigrants. In an article on the subject of Europe's changing demographics that appeared in *Science Magazine* in 2003, the authors, Wolfgang Lutz, Brian C. O'Neill, and Sergei Scherbov, write that "there is a fear that just as the world is entering its most competitive stage ever, Europe will be less competitive vis-à-vis the United States and the Asian economies, which are much younger and are benefiting from what you might call a demographic window of opportunity."[37] The researchers conclude that Europe would have to take in more than a million immigrants a year to be equivalent to European women having, on average, one more child.[38] Germany alone would have to welcome 500,000 young immigrants every year for the next thirty years, or double its birthrate, to avoid a steep demographic decline from its current eighty-three million people to fewer than seventy million people, and to reverse the aging of its population, which is expected to rise from a current average age of forty-one to forty-nine by 2050.[39]

The question of immigration puts the European Dream to the ultimate test. While it's relatively easy to talk about encouraging diversity and promoting inclusivity, it's rather more difficult to open one's door to outsiders with whom native-born would have to share their own space and fortunes.

Europeans find themselves, to some extent, caught between a rock and a hard place. Without a massive influx of immigration over the next several decades, Europeans will age and the European project will die. On the other hand, a flood of immigration—and that's what would be required for the European economy to hold its own on the world stage—threatens to overwhelm already strained government-welfare budgets and people's sense of their own cultural identity.

Unlike America, where accommodating waves of immigrants was relatively easy because of the availability of cheap and free land, in Europe every nook and cranny has long since been filled by different cultural groups. There are few empty spaces to absorb newcomers. Most of the new immigrants stream into already tightly congested urban and suburban areas, where they jostle with other immigrant groups and native populations for a place to live their lives.

It's difficult to imagine fifty million immigrants coming into Europe between now and 2050.[40] Even these numbers, says the European Commission, would make only a marginal difference in the old-age dependency ratio in 2050.[41] According to the commission, "Immigration can contribute to filling certain specific gaps in the European labour market, but it can in no way stop or reverse the process of significant population ageing in Europe."[42] To make a real difference, robust immigration would have to be combined with a dramatic increase in fertility. That means bringing the number of births back up to 2.1 percent, the level at which Europe would be able to exactly reproduce its population.[43]

The strangest aspect of what's unfolding in Europe is the seeming disconnect between an aging population and a young dream. In the past, civilizations flushed with the vitality and dynamism of youth were the ones that created powerful new dreams to guide them into the future. The French and American revolutions were made by young men and women. It was Thomas Paine, the great revolutionary leader, who fought in both the American and French revolutions, who said, "Every age and generation must be as free to act for itself, in all cases, as the ages and generation which preceded it."[44]

The new European Dream is of a far different sort. It does not share the passion of the early American Dream, with its vision of a young chosen people destined for greatness. It is less evangelical and more patient. Its goal is harmony, not hegemony. It speaks to a future world where people can live in peace with one another, enjoy a quality of life, and have the opportunity to fulfill a more private dream of personal transformation. In short, it is not the exuberance of youth but is rather the wisdom of age that propels the European Dream.

Dreams are always about expectations for the future. Immigrants to America were willing to sacrifice to make a better world for their children. Their hopes were enshrined in the birthrate. Having children represented a kind of litmus test of their faith in the future. Can there really be a European Dream, then, without a heartfelt commitment to reproducing the population who will be its beneficiaries?

Increasing the fertility rate and making room for new immigrants requires sacrifice. The question, then, is this: In a post-modern world where quality of life and personal transformation in the here and now often take precedence over sacrifices that will benefit others in the far-off future, how likely are Europeans to compromise their present options on behalf of creating opportunities for others not yet here? I would suggest that the success or failure of the emergent European Dream hinges, to a great extent, on how the current generation of Europeans address the issues of fertility and immigration. What good is a dream if there is no one left in the future to benefit from its promise? For the European Dream to live on and be fulfilled, Europeans will need to address the two most critical challenges before them: reproducing their numbers in a sustainable fashion and welcoming new strangers into their midst.

Cultural Diasporas and Multi-Allegiances

There is a fundamental difference in the way immigration manifests itself in Europe compared to what we have traditionally experienced here in the U.S. In America, immigrants quickly assimilated into the dominant culture. Many were anxious to leave their pasts behind. Their dream was to become an American. The children of immigrants were, more often than not, embarrassed by their parents' customs and ways and did everything they could to shed their past. "Starting over" was part and parcel of the American Dream.

The immigration dynamic in Europe is of a quite different nature. Immigrants are not as anxious to assimilate. Quite the contrary. Most take their culture with them, much like gypsies have for centuries. Cultural diasporas have forced a rethinking of the very idea of immigration and, in so doing, created new challenges and opportunities in Europe and throughout the rest of the world.

Ethnographers have identified more than two thousand separate nation-peoples in the world today. Because there are only two hundred territorial nation-states recognized under international law, the vast majority of distinct peoples live as minorities in their own countries or as displaced people wandering around the world in search of a home.[45]

Globalization of financial flows, communications, and transportation has sped the global flow of human labor. The world is experiencing a great migratory upheaval as individuals and whole peoples pick up stakes and journey to catch up to the flow of capital. Millions of human beings are in transit each year, most moving from south to north and east to west to find new economic opportunities in more affluent lands. Whole peoples have become like the wandering Jews of the last two millennia. Many, like the ethnic Chinese, exist in tight-knit communities designed to re-create their cultures abroad. It is estimated that fifty million Chinese now live outside China.[46]

The very notion of a diaspora is that one's allegiances and loyalties are still partially attached to one's traditional homeland. A homeland is often territorial but is also defined in terms of shared customs and traditions, common language, folklore, and religion.

Communications and transportation, in particular, have allowed people to be in two worlds at the same time. In past centuries, land migrations and journeys across oceans to distant lands were usually permanent. Few ever returned to their native land. And communication by letters back home was so unpredictable and took so long that little contact was maintained with family and friends in the old country. While the old cultural ways stayed alive for a time in the hearts and in the practices of immigrants, they invariably faded after two or three generations in a new land.

Today, an Egyptian immigrant to America can watch television programming twenty-four hours a day from his native country. Sports, entertainment, and news keep the immigrant abreast of the latest developments back home. The Internet, landlines, and cell phones provide instant contact with kin. Cheap airline travel allows for frequent personal trips back and forth between both homes. One can engage in a rich network of commercial, social, and even political activity with members of the same culture strung out in cultural pockets all over the world. These diaspora public spheres create a new dimension to culture. No longer strictly bound by geography, cultures are becoming increasingly de-territorialized and mobile. One's sense of being is less anchored to a place than to a state of mind. Cultures are becoming transnational and global, just like commercial and political activity.

People live their culture "both here and there," notes the German sociologist Ulrich Beck.[47] Nowhere is this more evident than in the recent migratory flows between Mexico and the United States. A detailed study of Mexican communities in the U.S. by the American sociologist Robert Smith reveals how different the new twenty-first-century post-modern immigration is from the earlier assimilationist, or "melting pot," models of the nineteenth and twentieth centuries.

Smith reports on the establishment of support committees in New York made up of Mexican migrant workers who donated money for the laying down of drinking-water pipes and for the reconstruction of churches, buildings, and even town squares back in their native villages in Mexico. The sums collected by Mexican migrants living in the U.S. were often greater than the public expenditures on infrastructure in their villages back home. Mexican immigrants living in the U.S. also participated actively in decisions on how the funds were to be deployed and were in continual dialogue with officials in their native communities vis-à-vis teleconferences.[48] Mexican mayors even traveled to New York to submit community investment proposals before migrant associations.[49]

Transnational businesses also enmesh Mexican migrants in the States with their counterparts in Mexico. For example, La Puebla Food Corporation, a small family-run tortilla-producing businesses in New York, connects its production and marketing operations with business and markets back home, creating its own version of transnational commerce.

Moreover, the increasing number of Mexican immigrants living in the U.S. gives them additional political clout. Politicians running for office in much of the Southwest part of the U.S. cannot hope to be elected without the support of Mexican-American voters. That gives Mexican-American associations the political muscle to influence political decisions in the U.S. that affect the vital interests of Mexico.[50] Nor is the Mexican-American immigrant unique. It is estimated, for example, that just the flow of funds from immigrants back to their native communities amounts to more than $100 billion per year, with 60 percent of the funds going to developing countries. That exceeds official development assistance to third-world countries.[51]

In many instances, the proliferation of cultural diasporas with split allegiances and loyalties has proved to be vexing and even threatening to the native-born population. The influx of Muslims into Europe, and especially France, is a good case study. Muslims now make up 8 percent of the French population. Many of the nearly five million Muslim immigrants—mostly from Algeria, Morocco, and Tunisia—are second and third generation.[52] They consider themselves both French and Muslim. Sometimes, however, the two loyalties collide.

In 2003, in the city of Lyon, a sixteen-year-old Muslim girl wore a head scarf—the traditional garb among Muslim women—to public school, igniting a political firestorm across France about what should be regarded as appropriate behavior of immigrants living in the country. Teachers at the school saw the girl's act as provocative and divisive and refused to let her attend class. A 1994 government policy ruling allows schools to prohibit "ostentatious displays" of religious symbols within the schools. France's official head-scarf mediator, Hanifa Cherifi, attempted to mediate between the girl's family and local school authorities and eventually succeeded in arranging a compromise between the parties—but not before the French public weighed in on both sides of the issue in a highly charged and polarized debate.[53]

The Muslim community argued that the girl's right to practice her religion and customs was being violated. Government officials, however, made the point that French policy, ever since the founding of the republic, has emphasized the indivisibility of French citizenry, and therefore does not recognize the existence of minorities or separate nations in its midst. Roger Fauroux, president of France's High Council on Integration, an independent body that advises the government on integration issues, spoke for many of his fellow countrymen, arguing that "there has been one obsession since the French Republic was created: The unity of the French people is fragile so let's not make it more fragile."[54] On February 12, 2004, the French National Assembly voted by an overwhelming margin of 494 to 36 to ban the wearing of Muslim head scarves and other religious symbols including Christian crosses and Jewish skullcaps in public schools. While the new law reflects the sentiment of the vast majority of French citizens, it served to further anger an already deeply alienated Muslim community living in France.[55]

The French assimilationist ideal has been under increasing attack in recent decades, as Muslims and other immigrants have flooded into France. In Marseille, France's second largest city, where 10 percent of the population is Arab and 17 percent Muslim, the question is becoming, What is authentic French culture? "We are no longer a France of baguettes and berets, but a France of 'Allah-u akbar' and mosques," quipped Mustapha Zergour, the head of a French-Arab radio station in Marseille.[56]

The Muslim diasporas are transforming parts of France into a multicultural transnational sphere. Many of the immigrants are poor, discriminated against, jobless, and living in squalid urban and suburban ghettos with high crime rates. They are regarded with increasing suspicion and fear among the older entrenched French population. At the same time, the dire plight of many young Muslims is pushing some toward extreme religious fundamentalism. Al Qaeda and other militant Muslim groups have been successful in recruiting Muslim youth into terrorist cells, casting fear among Frenchmen everywhere in the country.

In 2003, the French government established the French Council of the Muslim Faith, an organization whose function is to represent the Muslim community at the national level. France is also experimenting, for the first time, with affirmative action programs in an effort to lift the prospects of poor Muslim youth.[57]

France is not the only country in Europe confronted with a growing population of Muslim immigrants. There are now more than ten million Muslim immigrants living inside the European Union, in addition to another five million Muslims who have lived in places like Bosnia, Albania, and Kosovo for centuries. Europe is expected to take in ten million more Muslims in the next ten years alone, and if Turkey becomes part of the Union, sixty million more Muslims will join the ranks of EU citizenry. As the native population of Europe ages, demographers estimate that a younger Muslim population sporting larger families will soon come to make up more than 10 percent of the European population, and maybe much more by mid-century. Already, Muslim Turks in Germany, Muslim Pakistanis in the U.K., and Muslim Moroccans in Spain make up sizable cultural diasporas.[58] Their presence is transforming their new homelands. Writing in *The New York Times Magazine*, Timothy Garton Ash reflects on how pervasive the Muslim immigrants' influence is becoming. He writes, "I have just bought my newspaper from a Muslim news agent, picked up my cleaning from a Muslim cleaner, and collected my prescription from a Muslim pharmacist, all in leafy North Oxford."[59]

The Muslim influence is particularly challenging because Islam has traditionally viewed itself as a universal brotherhood of the faith. One's allegiance to Islam is supposed to supercede allegiances to any particular culture, place, or political institution. Many devout Muslims believe that one's first loyalty must be directed toward upholding the faith and expressing solidarity with other Muslims. Loyalty to nation-states has been far less central to the thinking of the Muslim world than in the Christian world. In the post-9/11 era, the uncovering of global Muslim networks channeling financial assistance, political support, and even paramilitary support to terrorist networks was unsettling.

Growing concern over possible terrorist attacks on European soil became real on March 11, 2004, when Muslims from the Moroccan Islamic

Combatant Group, with suspected links to Al Qaeda, blew up commuter trains in downtown Madrid, killing 200 people and injuring more than 1,500 people. The worst terrorist attack in more than a half century in Europe sent the continent reeling. Within days of the strike, Spanish voters went to the polls in a national election and cast out the center-right Popular Party in favor of the Socialists, in large part to express their opposition to Spain's decision, a year earlier, to support the U.S. by committing Spanish troops to the Iraqi war. The incoming Socialist Prime Minister, José Luís Rodríguez Zapatero, announced that Spain was withdrawing its troops from Iraq and declared the Iraqi war "a disaster" that "hasn't generated anything but more violence and hate."[60]

Only one of the suspected terrorists in the Madrid bombings was a Spanish citizen. Still, the Spanish public, and Europeans in general, worry that terrorists from outside the Union might find safe havens among local Islamic populations living in Europe, allowing them to recruit new members and establish home-grown cells.

Although the vast majority of Muslims are peaceful, law-abiding citizens of the countries in which they reside, it is probably fair to say that there are at least some whose loyalty to the state is thin in comparison to their loyalty to Islam. (The same might be said of certain Orthodox Jewish sects and fundamentalist Christian communities.) Interestingly, their very universalism makes the Muslim world potentially more comfortable in a globalized society than many others. The challenge is whether the Muslim faith can reinstate the kind of tolerant acceptance of other religions and cultures that was the religion's moniker at the peak of its influence in the thirteenth, fourteenth, and fifteenth centuries.

Cultural diasporas are undermining the traditional relationship between a people, property, and territory. For aeons of history, the three were virtually inseparable. No longer. Cultures exist in multiple domains, both virtual and real. As cultural communities disperse throughout the world, they begin to reorganize themselves in ways that more closely resemble nodes in networks. Sophisticated communications and transportation technologies allow members of shared cultures to stay linked socially and commercially across myriad national boundaries. Cultural diasporas provide a vehicle that allows a people to retain their sense of identity while negotiating their way in an increasingly globalized world. In the new era, everything is more mobile. Even property, in the form of capital, credit, and investment, is no longer rigidly attached to territory but free to circulate between nodes within worldwide diaspora networks.

Seen in a broader perspective, the proliferation of cultural diasporas marks the beginning of the end of the more geographically limited notion of the "public sphere" as a boundaried system inside a nation-state container. Cultural diasporas open the door to the possibility of a truly global public sphere made up of diverse cultural communities that exist both inside and across national boundaries and are no longer determined by territory.

Yale University anthropologist Arjun Appadurai makes the argument that much of the violence unfolding between cultural groups is the result of not being able to escape the old political logic that ties nation to territory and state.

> This incapacity of many deterritorialized groups to think their way out of the imaginary of the nation-state is itself the cause of much global violence because many movements of emancipation and identity are forced, in their struggles against existing nation-states, to embrace the very imaginary they seek to escape.[61]

According to Appadurai, cultural diasporas have yet to create a language "to capture complex, nonterritorial, postnational forms of allegiance." He concludes by suggesting that "neither popular nor academic thought . . . has come to terms with the difference between being a land of immigrants and being one node in a postnational network of diasporas."[62]

What happens, then, in an era of global labor flows, when people switch from one region of the world to another with the same ease that people used to shift residence from one town to the next? And, if they take their cultural identity with them wherever they take up residence in the world, so they can be "both here and there" at the same time, how are we to go about redefining the politics of geography? Diaspora politics is, by its very nature, transnational and global in its frame of reference and outlook. A Europe made up of cultural diasporas from all over the world becomes, in effect, a global public square.

The old conventional idea of swearing exclusive allegiance to one's new land becomes increasingly problematic in a world of cultural diasporas. Can Americans or, for that matter, French, German, or British citizens, ever feel really comfortable sharing their land with people whose allegiances are split? In a world where people take their culture with them, don't expect immigrants to be readily disposed to make the ultimate sacrifice expected by nation-states—to bear arms in defense of the state and be willing to give one's life to one's country.

But absent this kind of unswerving loyalty to a territorially anchored nation-state, bound by a commonly accepted meta-narrative and ideology to live by, how do disparate peoples get along? What unites them, if not shared territory, loyalty to the state, and a common ideology?

The answer to the question begins with a willingness to rethink our notion of political space and time in a globalized world. While we've discussed various aspects of the spatial and temporal re-orientation occurring in the wake of globalization, two further considerations warrant discussion.

Living in Multiple Spaces and in Deep Time

For starters, in a world increasingly made up of cultural diasporas, political space is more complex. Borrowing from Hedley Bull's idea of a neomedieval political arrangement, theologian John Milbank of the Univesity of Virginia argues that the idea of "enlightenment simple space" is too limited a notion in a dense, layered, and highly embedded world of contending and overlapping lived realities.[63] The space of the Enlightenment, with its emphasis on abstract measurement, location, extension, and boundaries, is unable to accommodate the crosscutting loyalties and competing agendas of real communities bumping up against one another in lived spaces. Milbank suggests that the older idea of "gothic complex space" might be a more appropriate metaphor for rethinking spatial categories.[64] In the medieval world, space was more relational than territorial, and boundaries were less fixed and more porous. There were fewer borders separating public and private lives, and human activity was entangled in a complex set of stories that overlapped. Michel Foucault explained the medieval sense of space this way:

> In the Middle Ages there was a hierarchic ensemble of places; sacred places and profane places; protected places and open, exposed places; urban places and rural places (all these concern the real life of men). In cosmological theory, there were the supercelestial places, as op-

posed to the celestial and the celestial place was in its turn opposed to the terrestrial place. . . . It was this complete hierarchy, this opposition, this intersection of places that constituted what could very roughly be called medieval space: the space of emplacement.[65]

Cultural diasporas, because they are lived simultaneously both "here and there," are attached in time, not in space, and are therefore not containable by geography. With people increasingly living in multiple places, with multiple loyalties, political space needs to be redefined in a way that loosens up the old rigidity of bounded territory. Some scholars talk about introducing the idea of Maze Europe, suggesting that fixed borders give way to zones of interactivity, fuzzy or rolling borders held together by multilevel regulatory arrangements.[66] That's beginning to happen in the EU as regions, CSOs, and cultural diasporas interact across traditional nation-state boundaries. It's also happening at the periphery of the EU. Many countries bordering the EU and even those somewhat removed have entered into various "associational arrangements" with the EU. As commercial, political, and cultural exchanges between the EU and its neighbors increase in density, borders become even fuzzier. Harvard's John Gerard Ruggie argues that the EU's very mission, at least in the past, is to unbundle territory.[67]

On the other hand, the EU is taking strong measures to ensure its borders against the illegal flow of immigration into the community. The earlier mentioned Schengen Agreement, to develop a unified approach to policing the EU borders and to block the flow of illegal immigration, is being zealously pursued. If it all sounds a bit contradictory, it is. The EU is caught between the old politics of bounded territory and the new politics of global space. It's trying to accommodate emergent global, political, and commercial realities within the constraints imposed by its members, whose authority and legitimacy are attached to territoriality. It's no wonder that Jacques Delors, the former European Commission president, referred to the EU as "an unidentified political object."[68]

The EU's confusion about what constitutes geography in an era of cultural diasporas and globalized commercial flows becomes all the more obvious when the question of bringing new members into the fold is raised. Some of the EU's architects remember back to their student days in the spring of 1968 when French radicals declared "to hell with borders."[69] The EU claims to be inclusive and says that membership ought to be based on shared universal principles, which leads some observers to suggest a "Europe without shores."[70] While no one seriously entertains the idea of a Europe that potentially envelops the globe, there is a growing recognition that the EU "represents a break with the modern conception of political territoriality."[71]

The most difficult point of trying to establish a politics that transcends territoriality is figuring out how to unite all of the contending forces in a new sense of shared purpose that is as powerful as the age-old territorial imperative. Jean-Marie Guéhenno, the former under-secretary-general for Peacekeeping Operations at the United Nations, put it best: "Having lost the comfort of our geographical boundaries, we must in effect rediscover what creates the bond between humans that constitute a community."[72]

If the new spatial reality is far more complex than the simple geometry of the Enlightenment permits, the changing temporal reference is equally complicated. While the temporality of the older American Dream is all future-directed, the temporality of the emergent European Dream combines all three temporal domains—past, present, and future—in a single gestalt. For Americans, the only real consideration was how to improve one's lot by making something out of oneself. Striving for a better future, both material and emotional, has been at the root of the American Dream. Most American immigrants chose to forget their past and sacrifice their present for future rewards. The European Dream, by contrast, is far more ambitious. Europeans want to preserve and nurture their cultural heritage, enjoy a good quality of life in the here and now, and create a sustainable world of peace in the near or not too distant future. And, on top of all this, they seek to establish a politics based on inclusivity—that is, honoring everyone's individual dream equally—a difficult challenge by any stretch of the imagination.

What we have, then, is a radical new spatial and temporal orientation and a new European Dream that is emerging out of it. Still, missing from the equation is a new social glue that's powerful enough to bind 455 million people together in common cause. That glue has to be even stronger and more cohesive than the existing social glue that binds people to territorial and nation-state loyalty, if the European Dream is to become a reality.

13

Unity in Diversity

THE EUROPEAN DREAM is compelling but seems a bit utopian
and out of reach. It's hard to imagine hundreds of millions of
people coalescing around such a grand vision. But, then, the idea
that people might come together around democratic values and nation-
state ideology would probably have seemed equally fanciful and far-fetched
in the late medieval era. The question is, What kind of new-shared bond
would propel people to transcend their old loyalties and make the European Dream a viable universal dream? Put simply, although it's no simple
task, we'd have to be willing to broaden our sense of attachment from
property rights and obligations grounded in territory to universal human
rights and obligations grounded in our collective participation on a shared
Earth.

Shared Vulnerabilities and Global Consciousness

Before the skeptics and cynics dismiss such notions as utterly unachiev-
able, let me say that globalizing forces make such a prospect less unlikely
now than in any other period of human history.

First, the increasing mobility of the human race and the de-spatialization of culture in the form of dispersed cultural diasporas as well as the emergence of a global public square make property rights and narrow territorial interests at least less important in human affairs than in the past.

Second, the contours of vulnerability have changed dramatically for the human race. In ancient times, when life was lived in local space and time, vulnerability of all kinds was similarly local. Threats to one's survival and security were generated close to home. The surrounding wild, warring lords, and disease and pestilence rarely had effects beyond the region. For this reason, the political institutions needed to provide a sense of security were local and regional. In the modern era, when improvements in communication and transportation brought people together across greater distances and in more dense patterns of activity, threats to one's survival and security also expanded. Commercial activity extended to broader geographic markets, human mobility increased dramatically over far greater distances, and the pace and flow of human activity quickened. Vulnerability, in turn, expanded in direct proportion to the compression of space and time and the acceleration of human interactivity. Local principalities and city-states were too parochial and narrow in their reach to protect their subjects. The result was the formation of nation-states.

Today, the compression of space and time is giving rise to a global flow of human activity. The dramatic increase in the density of human exchange, in turn, is creating new threats to security whose effects are often immediate and global in scale. Terrorism, the threat of nuclear war, global warming, computer viruses, the cloning of human beings, the death of the oceans, the loss of biodiversity, the growing ozone tear, a scandal in regional trading markets, and any number of other events can tip the world into chaos.

Nation-states are too geographically constrained to effectively deal with global threats and risks. Moreover, nation-states are designed to protect property and defend territory. They are exclusive, not inclusive, governing institutions. They were never conceived of as vehicles to manage global risks and threats.

What would happen, however, if millions—even billions—of human beings were to really believe that global threats to their security were at least as real and dangerous as the more localized threats that they face each day? Addressing these threats would require a new covenant among human beings that extended their commitment and allegiances, as well as their sense of security, beyond the narrow limits of territory, and the more limited protection afforded by property rights and civil rights.

Universal human rights is the next political chapter in the evolving history of our species. Some champions of universal human rights mistakenly believe that support of human rights ultimately stems from altruism and is motivated by goodwill alone. While altruism and goodwill play a role, there is another side to human rights—one that finds cause in a sense of vulnerability and the need for security. David Beetham writes that "it is as much the exposure to common threats as the sharing in a common humanity that justifies the claim that the human rights agenda is universal."[1]

The first real awareness of humanity's shared vulnerability came with the dropping of the atomic bombs on the populations of Hiroshima and Nagasaki, Japan, in 1945. We quickly came to realize that our common humanity was at risk in the event of an all-out nuclear war. Ulrich Beck writes that "with nuclear . . . contamination, we experience the 'end of "the other.'"[2] Today, we are subject to a host of global problems that affect all of humanity. Solutions, in turn, require a collective effort.

Cambridge University political scientist Bryan Turner argues that the notion of "human frailty" and "vulnerability" and the accompanying feeling of sympathy are the only universally shared emotions that have the power to unite humanity and provide a foundation for acceptance of universal human rights.[3] Turner notes that rights have traditionally been tied to Lockean notions of property. These kinds of rights, by their very nature, cannot be regarded as universal, because they establish, from the get-go, the idea of "mine vs. thine." Individual property rights and, by extension, the territorial rights of nation-states are meant to be exclusionary. While one might make the case that everyone has the right to acquire property, it's not the kind of right that brings all of humanity together in some deep, fundamental way.[4] On the contrary, the struggle between the possessed and the dispossessed over property rights has probably done more to divide our species than any other socially constructed phenomenon. Even the more vague right espoused by Thomas Jefferson in our Declaration of Independence, the right to pursue happiness, is "notable for its cultural diversity," observes Harvard sociologist Barrington Moore. "Only misery," notes Moore, "is characterized by its unity."[5]

Borrowing from the earlier works of Arnold Gehlen and Helmut Plessner, Turner makes the point that "human beings are ontologically frail, and . . . that social arrangements, or social institutions, are precarious."[6] People are subject to natural disasters, hunger and disease, the wrath of their fellow human beings, and natural decay and death. Now these frailties are compounded by the unpredictability brought about by the increased density of human exchange and the introduction of powerful new technologies whose negative impacts can be felt quickly and on a global scale.

Turner's views about the "human condition" differ substantially from those of Thomas Hobbes, who argued that people were inherently aggressive and acquisitive, rather than frail and dependent. Hobbes believed that people entered into a social contract to ensure a certain kind of security— their right to acquire property without fear of expropriation by others. Turner, however, believes that what unites people is not acquisitiveness— How could greed be a uniting force?—but participation in a "community of suffering." His thoughts might be regarded as a secularization of the Christ story.[7]

People require political institutions, according to Turner, because they are open and vulnerable, not because they are cunning and aggressive.[8] By reconfiguring the universality of the human condition in this way, Turner opens up the possibility of advancing a new vision for the human race to embrace. In the medieval world of Christendom, humanity's fallen nature was considered its universal condition, and eternal salvation was offered up as the dream to unite humanity. In the modern era, humanity's utilitarian and acquisitive nature was thought of as its universal condition, and material progress was embraced as a unifying dream. In the global era, frailty and vulnerability become humanity's universal condition, and global consciousness becomes the sought-after dream. Likewise, proprietary obligations structured the faith-centered salvationist worldview of Christendom, property rights structured the utilitarian era of material progress, and in the new world coming, human rights become the indivisible norm to advance global consciousness and foster a sustainable stewardship of the Earth.

Frailty and vulnerability are arguably a universal condition. But that doesn't mean that everyone is going to automatically embrace universal human rights. For that to happen, human beings would need to internalize a sense of empathy with the same passionate commitment that earlier generations felt when they substituted reason for faith. Only by empathizing with another's plight—their suffering—does one come to value the notion of universal human rights.

From the Age of Reason
to the Age of Empathy

The social glue that kept the Christian dream of eternal salvation alive and vibrant was faith. In the modern age, reason became the coveted behavior to secure material progress. In the new era, empathy is the human response to shared vulnerability and the key to global awareness.

To empathize is to cross over and experience, in the most profound way, the very being of another—especially the other's struggle to endure and prevail in his or her own life journey. Even though empathy has deep biological roots, like language, it, too, has to be practiced and continually renewed to be of use. Empathy is the ultimate expression of communication between beings.

In the long sweep of human history, what becomes clear is that the human journey is, at its core, about the extension of empathy to broader and more inclusive domains. Parents' empathy for their child is the first classroom. At this stage, the process is both biologically driven and socially constructed. Each step beyond this most biologically rooted connection requires patient revelation. Empathy is something that reveals itself to us if we are open to the experience. And we are most often open when we have experienced personal hardships and travails in our own individual journeys to endure and prevail.

While the human journey, then, is often littered with defeats and failures and suffering of immense magnitude, the saving grace is that the hardships we endure, both individually and collectively, can prepare us to be open to the plight of others, to console them and champion their causes.

"Do unto others as we would have others do unto us" is the operational expression of the empathetic process. At first, the Golden Rule extended only to kin and tribe. Eventually, it was extended to people of like-minded values—those who shared a common religion, nationality, or ideology. Today, the global risk society has become like a giant classroom for the extension of empathy. Modern communications and transportation allow us to witness the frailty, vulnerability, and suffering of our fellow human beings, as well as our fellow creatures and the Earth we inhabit, on a daily basis. We begin to experience the plight of others as our own. When, for example, an American parent watches a television interview with a bereaved parent in some distant part of the world who just lost her child to the ravages of AIDS, the connection is immediate and heartfelt. We think, That could be my child.

Turner's point is that "human beings will want their rights to be recognized because they see in the plight of others their own (possible) misery."[9] Altruistic feelings don't run as deep as empathetic ones. So while altruism may be a basis for some people believing in universal human rights, it doesn't penetrate deep enough to the core of our being like empathy and therefore is less powerful an emotional force in engendering a transformation of human consciousness.

If utilitarian reason wed us to a world of "mine vs. thine," encoded in property rights, then empathy takes us into a new world of "we," embedded in universal human rights.

Empathy is the new social glue and universal human rights the new legal code of behavior for promoting a global consciousness. That's not to imply, however, that the older social glues of faith and reason that wed humanity to a transcendent quest and material progress are therefore no longer relevant and ought to be abandoned. Rather, a fully articulated global consciousness makes room for all three social clues but in a nonhierarchical fashion. Faith, reason, and empathy are all critical to a mature human consciousness. One does not preclude the other but, rather, suggests the other. St. Thomas Aquinas, the great thirteenth-century scholastic of the Church, struggled to find an accommodation between faith and reason—the so-called "delicate synthesis." The urgent intellectual task of the coming global era is to create a new synthesis that unites faith, reason, and empathy in a powerful mix that allows each to be a door to the other.

Enforcing Universal Human Rights

Universal threats require the adoption of universal rights and obligations. While the shrinking of the world is helping to expand our notion of vulnerability and empathy, how do we create an institutional vehicle to give universal human rights the same enforceable status that property rights have enjoyed in the nation-state era?

We'd have to begin by rethinking citizenship. Traditionally, the rights people enjoyed were by dint of their status as citizens of a sovereign country. In recent years, however, the state's right to confer citizenship and be the ultimate arbiter of the rights of each citizen has steadily eroded. The proliferation of multiple identities has significantly weakened the state's hegemony over citizenship. For example, historically, a person could not claim citizenship in a new country unless he or she renounced his or her previous citizenship in the country from which he or she emigrated. This view held sway in most countries until after World War II. The U.S. State Department would regularly inform dual citizens living abroad that if they reached maturity while still living outside the U.S., they would forfeit their U.S. citizenship. Governments were leery of citizens whose loyalties might be compromised, especially in times of war.

In the more mobile world of global labor flows and cultural diasporas, dual citizenship is no longer an anomaly but is, rather, a fact of life. Most Americans would be surprised to learn that 90 percent of the more than one million people who immigrate to our shores each year come from countries that allow multiple citizenship. (More than half the nations in the world honor multiple citizenship.) Currently, some forty million Americans are eligible to claim citizenship in another country.[10] That means that one out of every seven Americans could potentially vote in another country, run for office, and even serve in its armed forces.

The concept of citizenship is changing dramatically to meet the needs of a globalizing world. In his now famous essay *Citizenship and Social Class*, published in 1950, T. H. Marshall, the British political philosopher, outlined three stages in the history of citizenship and the rights and duties conferred by it. Citizenship, he wrote, conferred civil rights in the eighteenth century, political rights in the nineteenth century, and social rights in the twentieth century.[11] Civil rights guaranteed the right to private property and other associated rights, including the right to privacy, the right to bear arms (in the case of America), as well as the rights to freedom of expression, religion, and press. Political rights extended the franchise from white male property owners to women, minorities, and the poor. In the twentieth century, citizenship included social rights, including the right to health care, education, and pensions. The evolution of citizens' rights was meant to allow each person the opportunity to pursue a full and meaningful life.

Now, the notion of what a full and meaningful life means has broadened and deepened once again, suggesting the need for a further metamorphosis in the idea of citizenship and the rights and obligations that go along with it.

Sociologist John Urry lists six new categories of citizenship emerging in the post-modern era. First, there is cultural citizenship, which recognizes the right of every culture to preserve and nurture its identity. Second, there is the right of minorities to take up residence and remain in other societies and receive the full rights as well as undertake the full responsibilities of the native-born population. Third, there is the right of ecological citizenship. Every human being has the right to live in a sustainable and harmonious relationship with the Earth and to enjoy the fruits of the natural world. Fourth, there is the concept of cosmopolitan citizenship—the right of every human being to enter into relationships with other citizens, societies, and cultures without interference by state authorities. Fifth, there is consumer citizenship, by which we mean the rights of people to open access to goods, services, and information flowing across the world. Sixth is mobility citizenship, which covers the rights and responsibilities of visitors and tourists in the passage through other lands and cultures.[12]

All of these new kinds of citizenship exist below and beyond as well as within nation-state borders. Each in its own way undermines nation-state territoriality as the exclusive realm of citizen engagement. The new forms of citizenship are de-territorializing rights and making them universal in nature and scope. The rub, notes Urry, is that "there is an increasing contradiction between rights, which are universal, uniform and globally defined, and social identities, which are particularistic and territorially specified."[13]

Citizenship is becoming increasingly international as human activity becomes increasingly global. The old idea of tying citizenship to nationality appears almost quaint in a world of global commerce, transnational civil society movements, and shifting cultural diasporas.

Even the very word "citizen" is grossly inadequate to define the new rights and obligations that are emerging in a globalized society. "Citizen" comes from the Latin root *civis*, which means "to be a member of a city." One's rights and obligations, therefore, are tied to a place. Universal human rights eclipse any particular place. They exist independent of territory. That's why rights activists use the term "human rights" as opposed to "citizen rights," to make clear the difference between the old idea of tying rights to territory and the new idea of de-territorializing rights and making them universal.

The Charter of the International Military Tribunal, which governed the Nuremberg war crimes trials after World War II, was the first multilateral government agreement to acknowledge rights and duties in a moral community that transcends sovereign states. The U.S. and its allies put Nazi war criminals on trial for "crimes against humanity." While Nazi officials argued that they were just following the orders of their government and were protected from prosecution because of their rights as German citizens, the Allies disagreed. They argued that under the Nuremberg Doctrine, Nazis had the right and obligation to disobey "unlawful orders" from superiors—which they defined as orders that denied people their basic rights as human beings. If Nazis carried out unlawful orders, they could be tried for crimes against peace and humanity.

The human rights era began in earnest with the formation of the United Nations in 1945. The UN Charter states that one of the main purposes of the UN is to promote and encourage "respect for human rights and for fundamental freedoms for all without distinction as to race, sex, language, or religion."[14] In 1948, the UN General Assembly adopted the Universal Declaration of Human Rights, the first international agreement to articulate the idea of the inalienable rights of all human beings and to establish a list of particulars outlining the specific rights and freedoms of all human beings. In that same year, the UN adopted the Convention on the Prevention and Punishment of the Crime of Genocide. It would be forty years before the United States finally ratified the treaty.

A number of other human rights conventions and agreements followed in the wake of the first UN declarations. The Convention on the Right to Organize and Collective Bargaining was adopted by the International Labor Organization (ILO) in 1949. In 1951, the UN Convention on the Status of Refugees was adopted. In 1957, the ILO Convention Covering the Abolition of Forced Labor was adopted as well as the Convention Concerning Indigenous and Tribal Populations. A year later, the ILO adopted the Convention Concerning Discrimination in Employment and Occupation. In 1965, the UN adopted the Convention on the Elimination of All Forms of Racial Discrimination. The following year, the UN adopted two human rights agreements: the International Covenant on Civil and Political Rights and the International Covenant on Economic, Social and Cultural Rights. The two conventions were finally ratified and went into force in 1976. In 1979, the UN adopted the Convention on the Elimination of All Forms of Discrimination Against Women. In 1984, the UN adopted the Convention Against Torture and

Other Cruel, Inhumane or Degrading Treatment or Punishment. The Declaration on the Right to Development was adopted in 1986. The UN Convention on the Rights of the Child was adopted in 1989. In 1993, the UN formally established the post of High Commissioner for Human Rights.[15]

Once ratified, all of these conventions have the force of international law behind them. The member states and every citizen of every country can be held liable for any violations of the statutory safeguards contained in the treaties. Nation-states lose their absolute control over questions regarding the treatment of their citizens and are now subject to a higher authority. Unfortunately, the enforcement mechanisms are weak. Because the UN has no independent enforcement power of its own, it must rely on intergovernmental agreement for the imposition of any sanctions on violations of human rights. Without the consent of the UN Security Council, the UN body is powerless to act. Often, member states are juggling competing strategic interests and agendas and are reluctant to impose tough sanctions, even in the case of extreme violations of human rights, including genocide. And herein lies the dilemma. Universal human rights are meant to supercede the laws of the nation-states. Yet, under the current UN system, nation-states retain the power—via their vote in the UN Security Council and General Assembly—to thwart the implementation of human rights laws. This means that the UN is left with little recourse short of garnering worldwide public support for sanctions and hoping that the pressure will push member nations to act responsibly and wisely.

From the very beginning, international CSOs have played a critical role as catalysts in the preparation and adoption of human rights conventions as well as monitors in the enforcement of the agreements. Women's organizations were instrumental in framing the 1979 Convention on the Elimination of All Forms of Discrimination Against Women. Amnesty International and the International Commission of Jurists made important contributions to the UN Declaration and Convention Against Torture. Environmental organizations were instrumental in helping shape the 1992 UN Treaty on Biodiversity.[16]

Although the UN does not yet enjoy extraterritorial authority to enforce universal human rights, the European Union does—making it the first nonterritorial political institution in history with the power to compel compliance to universal human rights statutes among its member countries and the 455 million people living within its jurisdiction.

The member states of the European Union are bound by the provisions of the European Convention on Human Rights, a sweeping document covering universal human rights. With the impending ratification of the European Union Constitution, additional universal human rights will be adopted as official law. The European Court of Human Rights is vested with the authority to arbitrate the provisions of the European Convention, and the European Court of Justice is responsible for judicial oversight in regard to member state compliance with the Charter of Fundamental Rights of the European Union. The judicial powers of both the Court of Human Rights and the European Court of Justice supersede the judicial authority of any of the member states of the Union. Moreover, all EU citizens have the right to appeal decisions made against them in a domestic court in the European Court of Human Rights.[17]

By decoupling human rights from territoriality, the European Union has ventured into a new political frontier, with far-reaching consequences for the future of the human race. While the world has watched attentively as the EU created a seamless commercial zone and trading market, complete with a common currency, to bind its member nations more closely together, of far greater long-term impact is the EU's success in establishing a full range of universal human rights and subjecting its member states and citizens to strict compliance, backed up by the power of legal enforcement. There is no precedent for this decoupling. As political scientist Carlos Closa Montero observes, "The defining and primordial element of citizenship is the enjoyment of political rights."[18] But citizenship, heretofore, has always been attached exclusively to a nation-state. What happens, then, to the very idea of the state, when the political rights of its members are conferred and guaranteed by an extraterritorial body? Philosopher Roger Scruton goes to the heart of the matter. He writes, "International law does not recognize the distinction between citizenship and nationality and regards the first as completely determined by the second."[19]

By granting European Union citizenship to the 455 million citizens of its twenty-five member countries, the EU has created a new nonterritorial but nonetheless legally binding form of political representation. Add to this the fact that the European Convention on Human Rights, backed up by the European Court of Human Rights and the European Court, affords every "EU citizen" universal human rights that override their traditional nation-state political rights, and we begin to understand the profound significance of the EU experiment. Sociologist Yasemin Soysal sums it up this way: "What we have is a trend towards a new model of membership anchored in deterritorialized notions of person rights."[20]

This transnational idea of citizenship may help create a new sense of belonging for all of the disparate individuals and groups who no longer feel comfortable thinking of themselves exclusively as citizens of a particular country with all of the political limitations and constraints that go along with territorial affiliation in a global age. The EU citizen is the first in the world to be fully guaranteed universal human rights enforceable by law. The EU's example, however, will likely be followed by others, as globalization forces a concomitant expansion of rights to include enforceable universal human rights.

Sociologist Gerard Delanty argues that the new kind of de-territorialized citizenship may be the only way to rebundle the multitude of competing interests and agendas that currently divide people into a more coherent whole. He writes, "Since a collective European identity cannot be built on language, religion or nationality without major divisions and conflicts emerging, [European] citizenship may be a possible option."[21] The more difficult part is convincing Europeans to feel as passionate about their human rights as past generations have felt about their civil rights, political rights, and social rights.

The former rights weren't suddenly articulated and embraced whole cloth. Rather, they were the embodiment of a long struggle to redefine human aspirations. In a very real sense, these earlier rights represent the codification of the last great human dream that emerged in the Enlightenment and matured with the spread of market capitalism and the coming of age of the nation-state. That dream, which is still very much alive in the U.S., has all but run its course in Europe. Now Europeans have a new dream, one more expansive than the one they left behind: to enjoy a quality of life, to respect one another's cultures, to create a sustainable relationship with the natural world, and to live in peace with their fellow human beings. Universal human rights are the legal articulation of the new European Dream. The European Dream and universal human rights come together as a single package. The Dream is the aspiration; the rights are the behavioral norms for fulfilling Europeans' hopes for the future.

The real issue is how deep Europeans' yearning is for a new story about themselves. Can the European Dream find an accommodation between the particularity of older, more diverse, and often divergent cultural traditions and values on the one hand, and universal human rights on the other, when the two often clash? How effective will international civil society movements likely be at "thinking globally and acting locally"? Can they serve as a political bridge between local cultures and global values? Will the EU experiment with de-territorialized citizenship—subject to universal human rights statutes—survive? How likely is it that this radical new approach to the notion of citizenship will be extended to other regions of the world in the twenty-first century, or will it remain a European curiosity?

The success of the European Dream will depend as much on political acumen as on human psychology. The older American Dream, grounded in Reformation theology and Enlightenment philosophy, owed its success, in large part, to the effective welding together of property rights, markets, and nation-state governance. Property rights made predictable market relations possible. Nation-states, in turn, were the regulatory vehicles, which, by dint of their monopoly over the enactment and enforcement of legal codes, taxation, and police power, were able to exact broad compliance to a private property regime and the Enlightenment project of material progress.

The new European Dream brings together a different mix, made up of universal human rights, networks, and multilevel governance. Human rights are the norms that govern network activity. The European Union, in turn, is the regulatory mechanism whose managerial authority and moral legitimacy make possible the continuous dialogue among the parties to advance the dream of global consciousness.

The older Enlightenment vision and the new European Dream reflect two very different notions of freedom. As we mentioned in previous chapters, in the old dream, freedom is defined negatively as autonomy. To be free is not to be dependent on others. To be self-possessed requires sufficient property. With property, one can enjoy exclusivity and be free from the encroachment of others. The struggle for freedom in the modern world, not surprisingly, has been fought along class lines, and claims over capital have become the heart of the struggle to be free. Civil rights, political rights, and social rights were all designed, in one way or another, to advance property interests. They were norms of behavior whose primary reason for being was to narrow the divide between the possessed and the dispossessed.

In the new European Dream, freedom is defined in the exact opposite manner. To be free is to be enmeshed in interdependent relationships with others. The more inclusive and deeper the relationships, the more likely one will be able to fulfill his or her ambitions. To be included, one requires access. The more access one enjoys, the more relationships one can enter into and the more freedom one experiences.

If property rights are essential to achieving autonomy, universal human rights are critical to securing inclusion. Human rights are all about inclusion. They speak to the rights of women, minorities, cultural groups, the disabled, children, our fellow creatures, to all have their interests equally included. Universal human rights are a guarantee that a person's very being will be considered and not left out. The struggle for freedom in a globalizing world is fought over identity claims and access to others. Universal human rights are behavioral norms that narrow the divide between the connected and the unconnected, the included and the excluded.

But if every group has its unique identity and competing and conflicting claims on the world, what motivates people to agree to other people's demands to be recognized and included? Empathy. Recognizing in the frailty, vulnerability, and struggle of others one's own life struggle. While people have different outlooks on the world and seek different paths in life, what we all share in common is the struggle to be recognized. "To be or not to be." How does one operationalize empathy? By "doing unto others as we would have others do unto us" or, just as important, "by not doing unto others as we would not have others do unto us."

The Politics of Empathy

As already mentioned, empathy is not only an innate predisposition but also a learned process. It requires constant and continuous engagement with others. One's empathy matures and deepens in proportion to one's active involvement with others. And this is where the new network multilevel approach to governance plays a pivotal role. It's the forum for people to be represented and recognized and to have their interests accommodated. But for network multilevel governance to work for some, it must also work for others. Networks are based on the notion that every player counts and that no player alone can dictate outcomes. Networks require a letting go, a willingness to trust, listen to others, reciprocate and compromise. One enters a network with the idea that optimizing the welfare of the whole is essential to optimizing one's own individual interest. In other words, unlike markets, which are adversarial and competitive, networks are interdependent and cooperative. One surrenders some authority to the group, not necessarily out of a sense of benevolence but rather out of a shared frailty and vulnerability. In a complex, multilayered, densely interactive world, no one can go it alone. Like it or not, everyone is vulnerable and at risk. The threats are global, and no one can be truly isolated from the consequences. In a world of risk, cooperation ceases to be a luxury and becomes a necessity for survival.

Network governance, then, is a way to pool risks in order to advance everyone's interests. But in the very process of engaging with others in multilevel governance, each player becomes aware of the others' struggle to be counted and recognized. Multilevel governing networks are like giant laboratories for the exploration of empathy. This new form of governance succeeds only to the extent that all the players can reach out and empathize with the aspirations and plight of others. The reconciling of disparate interests depends, first and foremost, on the acceptance of the shared struggle for recognition. Universal human rights, in turn, codify recognition. They are nothing more or less than statements of acceptance of "the other," whether it be women, minorities, different cultures, children, our fellow creatures, or the Earth we jointly inhabit.

Recognizing "the other" is a tough and painful process. It requires giving up a measure of hegemony. For example, how does a devout Muslim or Orthodox Jewish male learn to surrender his control over his community and recognize the equal right of women to fully participate in that community and in the world at large? A tall order, and not something likely to be accepted overnight. But multilevel governance at least provides a meeting place, a playing field, for engaging one another. If one wants to be recognized and have his or her agenda met, he or she has to be willing to listen to and accommodate the interests of others in the network. Of course, one can choose not to play at all, but the price of not participating is isolation, which is the ultimate expression of nonrecognition. The struggle for recognition in a globalizing world is likely to be as vigorously championed and hotly contested in the twenty-first century as the class struggle was in the twentieth century.

The European Dream is a delicate Aristotelian balancing act between the desire for greater differentiation and deeper integration, the two poles that have characterized human development from the very beginning of the human journey. Negotiating the unfolding dialectic between differentiation and integration has been the central mission of every governing arrangement in history. Slaves and empires, subjects and kingdoms, citizens and states, and now persons and global governing institutions are each milestones along the evolutionary journey to greater individuation and integration of the human species. Universal human rights in the global age, like the earlier property rights regime of the nation-state era and the proprietary obligations of the feudal era, are the legal embodiment of the existing relationship between individuating and integrating forces. They are the connective tissue between the particular and the universal.

In every period of history, the struggle between individuating and integrating forces has been the core battleground of politics. Slaves want to be liberated, subjects want to be freed, citizens want to be represented, and persons want to be recognized. On the other hand, kingdoms want to rule, states want to govern, and multilevel governing institutions want to manage. Fealty codes, civil rights, political rights, social rights, and now human rights have each, in their own way, prescribed codes of behavior to maintain that sensitive balance between human differentiation and integration. And that is why people fight so passionately to articulate, secure, and shore up these codes. There is a deep unstated realization that they are the lifelines that connect the individual with the larger social forces at each stage of the human journey.

The new European Dream represents the next stage in the deepening human story of individuation and integration. The European Union is the first governing experiment to attempt an accommodation between the new forces of individuation and integration that are stretching human consciousness inward to the multiple identities of the post-modern persona and outward to the globalizing forces of the economy. Expect the struggle over human rights to broaden and deepen in Europe as hundreds of millions of people rethink their identities in an increasingly globalized society.

14

Waging Peace

AMERICAN HARD-LINERS like to say that while the European Union might be an economic superpower, it is a political dwarf when it comes to the rough-and-tumble world of global geopolitics. It is fair to say that the conservative right, including most of the insiders in the Bush White House, loathe the "Brussels" mentality. There is the perception that the EU is soft, almost feminine in character, and unable and unwilling to fight for itself. Whenever the conversation turns to geopolitics in Washington, invariably the comment is made that Brussels whines about U.S. strong-arm tactics and bullying behavior but appears quite comfortable letting us sacrifice our young men and women in uniform around the world to protect European security interests.

Some say that the problem is that with the end of the Cold War, American and European interests have begun to diverge. The struggle to defend the West against Soviet aggression united our peoples in common cause for more than half a century. The fall of the Soviet Empire makes the American-European bond less salient. Moreover, now that the European Union rivals the U.S. in raw economic power, it's understandable, argue "the realists," that competitive pressures between the two superpowers create strains in the relationship and risk fissures in the Atlantic alliance. On the other hand, more moderate voices would argue that the American and European economies are so intertwined that, despite areas of contention, we have much more to gain than to lose by continuing close ties with our friends across the Atlantic.

My own belief is that the growing divide between America and Europe is more visceral than pragmatic. It has to do with very different sensibilities about how each superpower perceives its relationship to the world and the kind of vision of the future each holds.

Taking a Life

If we really want to understand how deep the chasm in thinking is between America's perception of how to conduct foreign policy and the European Union's, the best place to start is with analyzing the very different way each society views the question of capital punishment. It's here that we come face-to-face with two very different ideas about whether the state can ever be justified in taking the life of a human being. Since war is all about taking lives and sacrificing lives, the European position on capital punishment offers insight into its approach to foreign policy and security matters.

No issue more unites Europeans than the question of capital punishment. For them, opposition to the death penalty is as deeply felt as opposition to slavery was for the American abolitionists of the nineteenth century. Indeed, for a society so used to muting its passions, Europeans express a raw emotional disgust of capital punishment that is not evident anywhere else in the world. Whenever a prisoner on death row in the United States is executed, it is barely noticed in America but elicits vehement protest across Europe. Make no mistake about it: Europeans are the abolitionists of the twenty-first century, and they are determined to evangelize the world and will not rest until capital punishment is abolished across the Earth.

Americans would find it incredible that candidate countries for EU membership must abolish capital punishment as a condition for entry into the Union. It tops the list of conditions for acceptance into the fold. Try to imagine the United States making opposition to the death penalty a condition for citizenship.

Why so fervent? Europeans have experienced, firsthand, so many human deaths and so much destruction at the hands of governments over the course of the twentieth century that the thought of the state retaining formal power to execute a human being is greeted with repulsion. More than 187 million human beings were killed in the century just passed, many of them in Europe.[1] The death penalty, for Europeans, is a constant reminder of the dark side of their past, a period in which states regularly ordered the deaths of millions of human beings in the battlefields and in concentration camps stretching from Auschwitz to the Gulag.

In 1983, the Council of Europe adopted Protocol No. 6 to the European Convention for the Protection of Human Rights and Fundamental Freedoms, outlawing the death penalty, except in respect to acts committed in time of war or imminent threat of war. In 2002, the Council of Europe amended Protocol No. 6, barring the death penalty unconditionally, even including crimes committed during times of war or the imminent threat of war.[2]

The amended protocol has been the subject of growing controversy. Tempers flared between the U.S. and its European allies after the World Trade Center and Pentagon attacks when France, the U.K., Spain, and Finland indicated that they would not extradite Al Qaeda terrorist suspects to the United States if they were tried under the proposed military tribunals and made subject to the death penalty.[3] White House and State Department officials were livid, as were many Americans, at the prospect that a terrorist suspect, perhaps responsible for the brazen murder of three thousand people, would be afforded the legal protection of European countries.

Even if a person commits the most heinous of crimes against his fellow human beings, including genocide, he or she enjoys, in the official words of the European Union, "an inherent and inalienable dignity."[4] The death penalty, according to the EU, is "a denial of human dignity, which is a fundamental basis of the common heritage of the European Union as a union of shared values and principles."[5] That means that if Adolf Eichmann, for example, the architect of the Nazi plan to exterminate the Jews and others, were to be tried today in Europe and found guilty, he would be spared the death penalty. (Eichmann was tried by an Israeli court in 1961 for crimes against humanity and found guilty and hanged in 1962.)

While many Americans oppose the death penalty and are as committed to its abolition as Europeans, the vast majority of Americans—two out of three—do not, and would likely argue that a mass murderer forfeits his or her right to be considered part of the human race.[6]

The Europeans see their position on the death penalty as going to the very heart of their new dream, and hope to convince the world of the righteousness of their cause. Here's how the EU put it, in an official memorandum on the death penalty:

> Long ago European countries, either in practice or in law, made a choice for humanity, abolishing the death penalty and thus fostering respect for human dignity. And this is an ultimate principle that the EU wishes to share with all countries, as it shares other common values and principles such as freedom, democracy, and the rule of law and safeguard of human rights. If it succeeds in reaching this goal, both the EU and those countries will have furthered the cause of humanity."[7]

The EU memorandum goes on to say that it "invites the USA to equally embrace this cause."[8]

The irony of all this is that the European Union, whose peoples have, for the most part, long ago eschewed any devout Christian affiliation, seem to be taking up where Christian doctrine left off, in regard to the inviolability of every human life.

Many Europeans might be reluctant to acknowledge their debt to Christianity, but the fact of the matter is that opposition to the death penalty is rooted in New Testament doctrine. In his Sermon on the Mount, Jesus says to the faithful, "Ye have heard that it hath been said, An eye for an eye, and a tooth for a tooth: but I say unto you, That ye resist not evil: but whosoever shall smite thee on thy right cheek, turn to him the other also."[9]

Christ goes even further, saying, "Ye have heard that it hath been said, Thou shalt love thy neighbor, and hate thine enemy. But I say unto you, Love your enemies, bless them that curse you, do good to them that hate you, and pray for them which despitefully use you, and persecute you."[10]

Contrast the European opposition to the death penalty with American sentiment. Here, in the most avowedly devout Christian country in the world, most Americans favor the Old Testament approach to punishment. Thirty-seven percent of those who favor the death penalty say they do so based on the Old Testament adage of "an eye for an eye."[11]

Despite the fact that while dying on the cross, Christ pleaded with God to forgive his executioners, "for they know not what they do," Americans are far less forgiving. American sentiment on crime is much more retributional in nature. Surveys show that many Americans believe that people sentenced to death deserve it. Some observers of the American psyche, including psychologist Richard Nisbett at the University of Michigan and psychologist Dov Cohen of the University of Illinois, believe that Americans' predisposition for retribution stems, at least in part, from the need to protect possessions on the frontier when property rights were less secure.[12] Every American youngster grows up watching Hollywood Westerns where cattle rustlers are hunted down by sheriffs' posses or vigilantes and hung from the nearest tree.

Europeans, on the other hand, deeply oppose the idea of retribution. The European Union makes clear that "capital punishment should not be seen as an appropriate way of compensating the suffering of crime victims' families, as this view turns the justice system into a mere tool of illegitimate private vengeance."[13]

At the heart of Christian doctrine is the belief in redemption—that even the worst sinner can be saved. The European Union embraces this most basic of Christian beliefs in its support of rehabilitation. The EU states that "maintaining capital punishment would not fit the philosophy of rehabilitation pursued in the criminal justice systems of all EU member states and according to which one of the penological aims of penalties is that of rehabilitating or resocializing the offender."[14]

In fairness, it should be pointed out that rehabilitation continues to be the stated aim of the American penal system, and many Americans support that premise. But surveys show that many other Americans are beginning to turn away from that doctrine and are hardening their views on the role of the criminal justice system. The reversal in attitudes in just a few decades is striking, considering how basic the question of rehabilitation vs. retribution is to how a people define themselves and the moral codes by which they live. While Europe—and virtually the rest of the industrial world—has abolished capital punishment over the past three decades, America has gone in the opposite direction. Thirty-eight states now permit the death penalty, and in the past twenty-nine years, more than eight hundred people have been executed. More than 85 percent of the executions have occurred in the past decade alone.[15]

Americans' support of the death penalty reflects not only our frontier tradition of swift and decisive Old Testament justice but also the American apocalyptic vision of a world divided between good and evil forces. In the end, good triumphs, but only if backed up by the righteous might of the state. While Europeans also recognize that there are bad guys in the world and that the might of the state occasionally has to be deployed to secure the general peace and welfare, they start from the premise that the imposition of state violence is a last resort and ought to be entertained only in the most extraordinary of circumstances.

It ought to be acknowledged that not all Europeans are opposed to the death penalty. A sizable number of people, in some countries, feel much like a majority of Americans do on the issue. But the political elite, opinion leaders, as well as the professional and middle class have long since tipped the scale in favor of abolition of state-sanctioned executions.

So, Americans accuse Europeans of coddling criminals or, worse, appeasing evil behavior. Europeans accuse Americans of being ruthless and uncivilized in sanctioning state executions. Behind all of the heat is the very real difference in the perspective that the two superpowers have about the kind of world they live in and the future they embrace.

Europe's zeal to abolish the death penalty is inextricably linked to its dream of universal human rights. If the older Enlightenment dream was about establishing civilized norms of behavior, the new cosmopolitan dream is about establishing empathetic codes of conduct. Were Europeans to accept the notion that the state has a legitimate right to take the life of any human being, it would undermine the very idea of universal human rights that supersede states' prerogatives.

The problem facing Europe, however, is that it has to live in two worlds simultaneously: the everyday world of realpolitik and the dream of a better world to come. Keeping its commitment to the future without losing sight of the very real dangers posed by the present is the demanding task. Nowhere is that challenge more taxing for the EU than when it comes to framing a foreign-policy agenda. How do Europeans square their position on not taking the life of a criminal with waging war against an enemy?

Going It Alone

The Bush Administration's response to Europe's "perceived pacifism" is "Get real." In a country where a majority of the people believe in "an eye for an eye," it's not surprising that American foreign policy is based on different criteria for dealing with adversaries. The American approach combines old-fashioned paternalism with tough justice. Reward our friends and punish our enemies.

To really understand the roots of American foreign policy, Europeans need to appreciate America's near obsession with autonomy. For our country, long bounded by two great oceans, freedom has meant autonomy in a hostile and unpredictable world. Not to be dependent and beholden to others but, rather, to be self-reliant has been the leitmotif of American foreign and security policy from the very early days of the young republic.

American foreign policy before the two world wars was always expansionist in the Americas and isolationist in the world. The U.S. didn't even enter World War I until 1917, three years after the fighting commenced and just a year before cessation of conflict. Similarly, the U.S. joined with the Allies in World War II two years after the commencement of war, and then only after the Japanese surprise attack on our naval and air fleets at Pearl Harbor in Hawaii.

Before World War II, most countries subscribed to the Hobbesian doctrine that human behavior was, by its very nature, aggressive and acquisitive, and, therefore, if left unchecked would lead to a "war of all against all." Only by establishing a sovereign authority that could impose a single, unified will on the people would violence be abated and material progress be secured. The same behavior exists among states. Therefore, the only way to keep the peace was either for one country to gain hegemony and impose its will on the rest, in the form of an empire or federation, or, barring that possibility, for countries of relatively equal strength to join together in an alliance to maintain a balance of power that would prevent any one country from dominating the rest. The history of the past three centuries is riddled with attempts by one power to gain hegemony over others—the Spanish Empire, the Austro-Hungarian Empire, the Bourbon and Napoleonic empires, the German Third Reich, and the Soviet Union all come to mind. Each of these attempts invariably led to countermoves in the form of alliances by other states to challenge the hegemony. The Peace of Westphalia settlement of 1648, which we discussed briefly in chapter 7, curtailed the power of the Hapsburg Empire, and later, the Congress of Vienna imposed a similar balance of power after Napoleon's defeat.

The classic liberal theory of foreign relations offers an alternative, of sorts, to the Hobbesian vision. It begins with the Enlightenment idea that material self-interest is best promoted by open markets and the liberalization of trade, both at home and abroad. Liberal theorists were at odds with the Hobbesian idea that war was the natural human condition. They preferred to think that rational self-interest is the prime mover and economic efficiency the driving force of human behavior. They bound their ideas to Locke's theory of property rights, Adam Smith's notion of the invisible hand, and the bourgeoisie faith in representative democracy. Liberals viewed the free market as the natural order of things and believed that if it was left unencumbered and allowed to flourish, it would prevent nations from plunging into a nightmarish Hobbesian world. The British were the first to employ liberal theories to foreign policy. In the name of "free trade," the British became a hegemonic world power in the late nineteenth and early twentieth centuries, only to raise the ire of others, especially Germany, which was determined not to be marginalized on the world stage.

After World War II, the United States and the Soviet Union emerged as great world powers. Neither was able to enforce its will on the other and become hegemonic. Both, however, realized that their fortunes lay in mobilizing as much of the world as they could under their banner. While each sought alliances in Asia, Africa, and the Middle East, the primary struggle for influence was fought in Europe. The Soviet Union imposed its will in Central and Eastern Europe by force of arms. The Americans, by contrast, relied on the liberal doctrine of advancing open markets and free trade and began to implement a series of initiatives to resurrect the economies of Western Europe with an eye toward building a vibrant Atlantic partnership that could hold the Soviets back and foster the economic interests of America. (We discussed the various institutional initiatives, including the Marshall Plan and the creation of the United Nations, the IMF, the World Bank, NATO, etc., in chapter 11.)

With the collapse of the Soviet Empire in the late 1980s, the U.S. government deepened its commitment to a liberal foreign policy. Both President George Bush and President Bill Clinton pushed for further liberalization of trade, hoping to create, at long last, a global capitalist marketplace, dominated by America's economic prowess.

America's commitment to a multilateral foreign policy, based on alliances, took an abrupt turn with the election of President George W. Bush in 2000. Conservative politicians and ultra-right-wing ideologues had been preparing the groundwork for years. Many former operatives of the Reagan Administration set about the task of crafting a shadow foreign policy in the 1990s. They established think tanks, published books and articles, set up task forces, and issued white papers, all critical of what they regarded as failed foreign and security policies. The conservatives believed that America's interests were ill served— and even undermined—by the government's entering into multilateral global treaties, alliances, and commitments that bound us to the will of others whose interests were not always commensurate with our own. The conservatives favored a return to the older American foreign policy based on autonomy, backed up by military might. They argued that it had served us well in protecting our vital interests in the American hemisphere in the nineteenth and twentieth centuries and could do so again in the global theater because of our unmatched economic and military superiority.

Some critics warned out loud that if the "neoconservatives" were to regain power, America would cast its lot with a "radical" foreign policy, at odds with America's historical role. The critics got it wrong. For most of American history, the conservative view of how America ought to conduct foreign policy was the standard. Only in the brief fifty-year span from the end of World War II to the end of the Cold War did America depart from its historical legacy and enter into multilateral relationships with the rest of the world.

When European intellectuals accuse current American leaders of conducting a "cowboy diplomacy," they are right. The American tradition in foreign policy follows close on the heels of the American Dream. Our vision of the noble American is a man or woman alone in a hostile and unpredictable world but able, by sheer perseverance and will, to tame the wild, keep evil forces in check, create an island of order, and make the world a safe place to be. Every American Western novel and movie glorifies this story. This is who we think we are: an uncomplicated, good-hearted people who stand up against evil and champion the right of every person to be free— which we define as autonomous and independent. Why would we pursue a foreign policy at odds with our own basic sense of who we are?

Even before the terrorist attacks on the World Trade Center towers and the Pentagon, the George W. Bush Administration was beginning to steer American foreign policy back to its earlier vision of "going it alone." The United States began to unbundle itself from previous global commitments, while rejecting new global initiatives.

In a series of stunning reversals, the U.S. government refused to sign the Kyoto Protocol to curb greenhouse gases, it said no to the Land Mine Treaty and to the comprehensive Test Ban Treaty, and it withdrew from the Anti-Ballistic Missile Treaty, even though virtually every other nation gave its support to these covenants. And, in a final rebuff of world public opinion, the U.S. refused to support the International Criminal Court, which bound the nations of the world to an enforceable standard for securing universal human rights.

The "great reversal" was a long time in the making. In 1992, when now vice president Dick Cheney was the secretary of defense, the Pentagon prepared a draft document outlining what would become the cornerstone of U.S. foreign policy a decade later. The Pentagon white paper bluntly stated that the U.S. government must "discourage the advanced industrial nations from challenging our leadership or even aspiring to a larger regional or global role."[16] The Pentagon report said that it was critical that the United States "retain the preeminent responsibility for addressing . . . those wrongs which threaten not only our interests, but those of our allies or friends, or which could seriously unsettle international relations."[17]

The attacks on the World Trade Center towers and the Pentagon gave the Cheney forces the opportunity to operationalize the vision of American foreign policy they had laid out a decade earlier. The new national security strategy, put out by the White House, said that the U.S. government would maintain whatever military capabilities were needed to ensure that no other state could impose its will on America or its allies and would discourage and even prevent any potential adversary from attempting to build their military capability to challenge our own.[18]

In a commencement address at the U.S. Military Academy at West Point in June 2002, President Bush made clear that "America has, and intends to keep, military strengths beyond challenge—thereby, making the destabilizing arms races of other eras pointless, and limiting rivalries to trade and other pursuits of peace."[19] The president's remarks were calculated to let the world know that, henceforth, America would use its vast military machine to be the unchallenged hegemonic power and that it would not allow itself to be weighed down by multilateral commitments and treaties or be burdened by alliances that required shared deliberation and consensus prior to taking action.

Much of the rationale for the new unipolar policy was driven by the new circumstances in which the U.S. found itself in the post-9/11 period.

The Bush Administration argued that in an era punctuated by global terrorism, "a military . . . must be ready to strike at a moment's notice in any dark corner of the world."[20] Because it's impossible to know when terrorists will strike, or where, the U.S. must be able to exercise the option of preventive action as a form of self-defense. Secretary of Defense Donald Rumsfeld put the new situation facing America and the world this way: "We don't know what we don't know."[21] That being the case, America might have to attack before being attacked. The White House's new post-9/11 security strategy is unequivocal on this point. In its now famous September 2002 directive on national security, the Bush Administration stated that "to forestall or prevent . . . hostile acts by our adversaries, the United States will, if necessary, act preemptively."[22]

Worried that terrorists might be able to secure weapons of mass destruction and strike at will, the U.S. government said that it had no choice but to determine, on its own, if necessary, when the sovereign rights of the U.S. are in jeopardy and to act accordingly without having to consult or receive prior permission by other governments. By the new policy, the U.S. assumes virtually carte blanche authority to invade any country it suspects of harboring or financing terrorists or developing weapons of mass destruction that might find their way into terrorists' hands. The new foreign policy, then, is what can be euphemistically referred to as "anticipatory self-defense." Critics argue that the policy is an oxymoron and threatens to undermine the entire post–World War II set of agreements, embodied in Article 2 and Article 51 of the UN Charter, which makes it illegal for one country to attack another unless first attacked, and then only in self-defense.[23]

The U.S. counters that if it were forced to wait until it had sufficient evidence of wrongdoing, or until it could muster up a consensus in the UN Security Council, it might be too late to defend itself. The problem, as G. John Ikenberry points out in an article in *Foreign Affairs*, is that if "the United States feels it can take such a course, nothing will stop other countries from doing the same."[24] Ikenberry asks rhetorically whether the United States would want "this doctrine in the hands of Pakistan, or even China or Russia."[25]

When political observers wonder whether the U.S. and its closest ally, the European Union, are beginning to diverge and grow apart in some kind of fundamental way, the answer is an unqualified yes. American foreign policy seeks to resurrect the realpolitik of an earlier era and rests its claims on its sovereign right and duty to protect and defend its territory and citizenry as it sees fit. Nor does it feel obligated to demure to international arrangements that might impede what it perceives to be its vital interests. Stalwarts in the Bush Administration have even gone so far as to claim, according to Harvard's Stanley Hoffman, that "the United States Constitution allows no bowing to a superior law, such as international law, and no transfer, pooling or delegation of sovereignty to any international organization."[26]

Many in the U.S. government would not subscribe to such overly heated rhetoric. Still, the reality is that the Bush doctrine, if taken to its logical extreme, does relegate all international covenants and commitments secondary to its sovereign right to be the ultimate arbiter of its country's actions.

Divergent Views of the World

The U.S. foreign policy is light-years away from the foreign policy orientation of the twenty-five member states that make up the European Union. These countries have increasingly shed the historical legacy of nation-state sovereignty in favor of working in concert, under international laws, to which they are bound. The European Dream is one of inclusivity, not autonomy. They seek to live in a world governed by consensus. The "go it alone" policy of the U.S. is anathema to them because it threatens to unravel all of the painstaking small steps they have taken to pool their interests and share a collective destiny. They worry that U.S. flouting of international norms and agreements opens the door to the very Hobbesian world of "war of all against all" that they had hoped to leave behind in the ashes of the last world war.

Some will say, Hold on . . . Didn't many European Union member nations act in possible violation of international law, not to mention the EU's own governing principles, by joining the U.S. in its "coalition of the willing" in Iraq? Perhaps. But the interesting point was that the split inside the EU was the subject of much soul-searching in the aftermath of the Iraqi invasion. Instead of leading to irreconcilable fissures and the disaggregation of the Union, as some predicted it would, it had the opposite effect. Member states began asking how they might strengthen their common foreign and security policy to make sure that they didn't suffer a repeat of the spectacle that unfolded in the days leading up to the U.S. invasion of Iraq.

The sovereignty issue is what ultimately divides the U.S. and the EU, and an older American Dream from the new dream shared among most Europeans. To whom do we owe our ultimate allegiance? Where does authority lie in a globalized world? The U.S. is reverting back to an earlier era where allegiance is to the nation-state and final authority rests with the sovereign government. The state confers all rights upon its citizens and determines the nation's role in the international community. There is no higher authority. Within the nation-state container, people are granted civil, political, and social rights, which allow them the opportunity to acquire property and pursue happiness.

The European Dream is far more cosmopolitan. While the EU member states retain a modicum of sovereignty, their citizenry are also bound to universal human rights that supersede sovereign state prerogatives. If the American doctrine of unqualified state sovereignty were to prevail, the whole notion of universal human rights, the very edifice upon which the new European Dream is built, would collapse. Universal human rights are a sham in a world where the highest authority rests with the sovereign state. If the nation-state is the ultimate sovereign authority, as many in the Bush Administration believe, then human rights can't possibly be universal, because their very viability would depend on the whims and caprices of a territory-bound political institution.

It's a strange paradox that in a world that is increasingly globalized and in which geographic boundaries of all sorts are loosening or disappearing altogether, the U.S. government is hardening its notion of sovereignty in contradistinction to everything going on around it. But that's because dreams die hard. We are a people who don't like to be told what to do by anyone. We like to think that we are capable of making our own way in the world without outside interference. We don't even like our own government to tell us what we can and can't do. Why would we be any more disposed to having a foreign power dictate the terms of our behavior? Our sense of self-reliance and autonomy runs deep, to the very marrow of our being.

The mere thought of being constrained by the will of others goes against the grain of the American spirit. Constraints are not our strong suit. In fact, it is the lack of constraints, the openness of the American way of life, that has allowed us to realize our dreams. Bowing to the will of others seems too subservient, too submissive for the American mind. President Bush, for whatever our European friends think of his intellectual credentials, understands the American psyche. In his State of the Union Address in 2003, President Bush told the American people that "the course of this nation does not depend on the decisions of others."[27]

Americans, by and large, have mixed feelings about international law. Polls show that a majority of Americans support our membership in the United Nations and favor the U.S. being party to international agreements. A comprehensive poll conducted by the German Marshall Fund in the fall of 2002—a year after the attacks on the World Trade Center towers and the Pentagon—found 61 percent of Americans favoring a multilateral approach to foreign policy, and 65 percent of Americans saying that the U.S. should invade Iraq only with UN approval and the support of its allies.[28] I'd suggest, however, that American sentiment in this regard is thin compared to our friends in Europe. Just six months after the poll was conducted, a firm majority of Americans rallied behind President Bush's decision to send troops into Iraq without a UN resolution. At the time of the U.S. invasion of Iraq, 72 percent of the American public said that they favored sending in troops, and only 25 percent said that they opposed the invasion.[29] While some Americans took to the streets in protest, the numbers were relatively small compared to the outpouring of sentiment across Europe in opposition to the U.S. invasion.

The reality is that Americans are deeply divided on how best to conduct foreign policy. A sizable minority, primarily in the northeastern and northwestern regions of the country, think more like Europeans when it comes to foreign policy. Their views tend to be more cosmopolitan. The southern, southwestern, midwestern, and Rocky Mountain regions—whose population makes up a solid majority—are more likely to identify with America's frontier mentality and favor a "go it alone" approach, if necessary, to secure American self-interests abroad.

Similarly, the German Marshall Fund reported that 75 percent of Americans believe global warming is a serious issue, and a majority favor the U.S. joining the EU in ratifying the Kyoto Protocol.[30] Yet here, too, the reality is somewhat different. American voters are opposed to government legislation that would force automakers to increase fuel-efficiency standards if it meant having to drive smaller cars, and a majority oppose even a moderate increase in the gasoline tax—the U.S. has the lowest gasoline taxes of any major industrial country.

Or, consider the American view of the International Criminal Court. Seventy-one percent of the American people say they favor ratification of the treaty. Yet barely a whisper of disagreement could be heard on the hustings when the Clinton Administration signaled that U.S. approval of the agreement had to be conditional on American troops being immune from prosecution by the judicial body—which makes a mockery of the very idea of the institution.[31] The vast majority of Americans agree with the Clinton Administration stance. While 71 percent of the French electorate, 65 percent of the German public, and 52 percent of the British people say the International Criminal Court should have authority to try their nation's soldiers for war crimes, only 37 percent of Americans say the International Criminal Court should have jurisdiction over U.S. troops accused of war crimes.[32] I have a hard time imagining the American public ever allowing the International Criminal Court to try American soldiers for war crimes.

Political scientist Francis Fukuyama writes that "Americans . . . tend not to see any source of democratic legitimacy higher than the nation-state."[33] Europeans think differently. While European states are ceding more and more sovereignty to the EU and international bodies, the U.S. is going the other way. That's because Europeans feel that their freedom is enhanced by inclusivity and embeddedness with others, while Americans feel that transferring sovereign rights to extraterritorial agreements and institutions diminishes our sovereignty and results in loss of personal freedom.

Europe's Dream of Perpetual Peace

What, then, does a European foreign and security policy look like? For beginners, it's so utterly different from anything that came before it in human history that it requires a leap of human imagination to even entertain it. European foreign policy is built on spreading peace rather than amassing power.

Europeans reject the kind of power politics that has dominated foreign policy for centuries and has led to so much death and destruction in the world. European leaders ask rhetorically: Who knows better than us the terrible consequences that can result from nations attempting to assert their will over others by means of coercion and force? And to those who say that human behavior will never change, Europeans retort, Look at what we've accomplished in Europe. After centuries of fighting among ourselves, twenty-five nations have put down their arms, joined with one another, and vowed never to go to war with one another again. German foreign minister Joschka Fischer speaks for many in Europe who are determined to never again allow national rivalries to descend into open warfare. Looking back at the checkered history of the modern nation-state, Fischer says that Europe is now steering a different course into the future: "The core of the concept of Europe after 1945 was and still is a rejection of the European balance-of-power principle and the hegemonic ambitions of individual states that had emerged following the Peace of Westphalia in 1648."[34] Fischer and other European leaders are committed to replacing the old ideology, steeped in the Hobbesian vision of a "war of all against all," with a new vision of perpetual peace.

The new European Dream has ancient roots. In 1795, the German philosopher Immanuel Kant published an essay entitled *Perpetual Peace: A Philosophical Sketch*. Although it received little attention at the time, the piece was resurrected in the post–World War II era, and has become an almost biblical reference for the new European vanguard. Kant envisioned a "state of universal peace" brought about by the creation of "a world republic." Kant believed that such a state would be possible once the nations of the world accepted representative forms of governance. The spread of democratic principles, thought Kant, encourages cooperation over conflict and lays the groundwork for a cosmopolitan order.

While Europeans don't espouse a world government, they do believe that the deepening of the democratic impulse can lead to a new way for people to behave with one another—one based on mutual respect, empathy, and a recognition of "the other." That's why European leaders favor negotiation over ultimatums, reconciliation over recrimination, and cooperation over competition.

Romano Prodi, the president of the European Commission, says that the EU's goal is to establish "a superpower on the European continent that stands equal to the United States."[35] Many American political observers worry that remarks like these signal a new era of conflict between Europe and America and warn that the United States needs to remain watchful and on guard lest Europe become a new hegemon and a threat to America's self-interests. They misunderstand what Mr. Prodi means by the term "superpower." Europeans have a very different idea in mind of what ought to constitute a superpower in a globalized society. Listen carefully to how President Prodi explains the success of the European experiment. He writes,

> The genius of the founding fathers lay in translating extremely high political ambitions . . . into a series of more specific, almost technical decisions. This indirect approach made further action possible. Rapprochement took place gradually. From confrontation we moved to willingness to cooperate in the economic sphere and then on to integration.[36]

For Prodi and other European leaders, superpower status is derived from expanding cooperation rather than enlarging sovereignty. It's not force of arms, but negotiating skills and openness to dialogue and conflict resolution that are the distinguishing characteristics of this new kind of superpower. That's why "process" is so important to the new politics. The essence of the European Dream is the overcoming of brute power and the establishment of moral conscience as the operating principle governing the affairs of the human family.

Most Americans find such sentiments a bit gooey and unrealistic. Europeans say that the opposite is the case. The new Europe was not born of naïveté and inspired by Pollyannaish fantasies but, rather, developed out of a sense of utter repugnance at the kind of barbaric behavior human beings are capable of inflicting on their fellow human beings. The new European experiment is an attempt to transcend the worst vestiges of humanity's past and is guided not by wishful thinking but by a sober assessment of the human condition.

Now that Europe has shown that its new approach to politics can work for twenty-five nations, representing 455 million human beings, it is anxious to share its experience with the rest of the world. President Prodi's idea of a European superpower is something quite new and extraordinary. He believes that the European Union "has a role to play in world 'governance'"— to make the European experience a model for the rest of the world to emulate. Prodi notes with pride that in Europe, "the rule of law has replaced the crude interplay of power . . . power politics have lost their influence." He believes that by "making a success of integration we are demonstrating to the world that it is possible to create a method for peace."[37]

In a survey of public opinion over whether the European Union should become a superpower, 65 percent of the European public said they favor the EU becoming a peer of the United States. But when asked why they favor such a course, the answer they gave was that it would allow Europe to more effectively cooperate rather than compete with the United States. Even in France, a country most Americans feel to be occasionally at odds with the U.S., 90 percent of the public favored the EU becoming a superpower, and the overwhelming majority said that if it were on a more equal footing with America, Europe would be able to work much more closely with the United States.[38]

Americans, by contrast, have a very different attitude on the question of whether the EU should be a superpower. Fifty-two percent of Americans say the U.S. should be the world's only superpower, and only 33 percent say they favor the European Union enjoying a superpower status.[39] While Europeans see their superpower status as a way to deepen cooperation on the world stage, Americans perceive superpower status as a potential threat to American dominance in the world.

Robert Kagan, of the Carnegie Endowment for International Peace, sums up the growing schism in the way Europeans and Americans view their roles in the world. He writes,

> On the all-important question of power—the efficacy of power, the morality of power, the desirability of power—American and European perspectives are diverging. Europe is turning away from power, or to put it a little differently, it is moving beyond power into a self-contained world of laws and rules and transnational negotiation and cooperation. It is entering a post-historical paradise of peace and relative prosperity, the realization of Immanuel Kant's "perpetual peace." Meanwhile, the United States remains mired in history, exercising power in an anarchic Hobbesian world where international laws and rules are unreliable, and where true security and the defense and promotion of a liberal order still depend on the possession and use of military might.[40]

Understandably, when Europeans are asked about spending money on defense, only 19 percent favor increasing expenditures, while 33 percent would like to cut military spending and 42 percent want to maintain the current low defense budgets. Forty-four percent of Americans, on the other hand, are willing to increase military spending.[41] That doesn't mean that Europeans aren't willing to spend money—but they want the funds to be used to support their very different idea about how to conduct foreign and security policies.

Chris Patten, the EU commissioner in charge of external relations, outlined the European vision of a twenty-first-century foreign policy in a speech delivered in June 2000. He said that the EU foreign policy should be true to values that animate its domestic relations and that it should play to its strengths. Patten reminded his fellow Europeans that the EU, for all of its exalted rhetoric about building bridges to peace, was powerless to stop the fighting in neighboring Bosnia or Kosovo in the 1990s, and had to rely on American military intervention to stop the conflict. How does Europe prevent future Bosnias and Kosovos from occurring? Patten says the answer is to be more pre-emptive in the future and draw troubled countries and regions into effective dialogue and active cooperation with the EU before hostilities break out. "This requires," says Patten, "the application of tools such as trade, external assistance, environmental cooperation, competition policy and so on, which are matters of Community competence."[42]

Like Prodi, Patten believes that the European Union should apply its regional experience of multilateral cooperation on a wider world stage. Patten notes that the European model of integration "is inspiring regional experiments from Asia to Latin America," and says that "the EU's ambition must be to reflect abroad what is best about our own model. Our sense of civil society."[43]

American foreign policy analysts don't buy the idea that bad guys can always be reasoned with, and they ask how Mr. Patten would suggest dealing with rogue regimes like North Korea and Iraq, or trouble spots where long-held prejudices and animosities are so deeply entrenched that they appear irremediable, such as the Israeli-Palestinian conflict. Patten counters by using Europe's own past experience as an example. He makes the rather convincing argument that "European integration shows that compromise and reconciliation is possible after generations of prejudice, war and suffering."[44]

Harvard professor Joseph Nye Jr. describes Europe's new approach to a common foreign and security policy as the exercise of "soft power," which he defines as co-opting people rather than coercing them. Nye says that when it comes to conducting foreign policy,

> a country may obtain the outcomes it wants in world politics because other countries want to follow it, admiring its values, emulating its

example, aspiring to its level of prosperity and openness. In this sense, it is just as important to set the agenda in world politics and attract others as it is to force them to change through threat or use of military or economic weapons.[45]

For a long time, America's soft power was a magnet for the rest of the world. Our democratic values, our multicultural origins, our openness, our can-do attitude, our optimism, our innovation and creativity, our prosperity, drew the world to our shores. We served as an inspiration for others. Today, much of America's soft-power assets have begun to depreciate in value. Others began to lose faith in the American model during the Vietnam War. In the post-9/11 era, world public opinion has turned dramatically against the American government's policies in the world. Many see America, whether justified or not, as an arrogant bully, insensitive to other voices and opinions and unresponsive to a range of concerns that affect the rest of the world. According to a TimeEurope.com poll, 87 percent of Europeans think the U.S. "poses the greatest danger to world peace in 2003."[46] Similarly, a Gallup International poll conducted in thirty-three countries in 2002 reports that in twenty-three of the countries surveyed, "the population is more likely to say U.S. foreign policy has a negative rather than a positive effect on their country."[47] Most Americans are blown away by such attitudes. We've always thought of ourselves as champions of justice, as peacemakers. How could the whole world be so wrong in their assessment of us?

It should be noted that while world public opinion is overwhelmingly negative in its assessment of the U.S. government, it is more favorable to the American people and our way of life, although even here, our soft power is eroding. While there is much that attracts others to America, there is a growing unease over what is perceived to be American selfishness and brutishness. I am forever asked by Europeans, for example, why Americans insist on driving big, gas-guzzling automobiles that pollute the world. Or why America, the richest country on Earth, does so little to help the poor. Or why Americans have so many guns, and why there is so much violence and bloodshed on American streets.

It goes without saying that people all over the world enjoy American music, American movies and television, American dress and consumer lifestyles, and American education. They are less favorably disposed, however, to the way America gets on with the rest of the world and are leery of what they perceive to be a sense of narcissism and lawlessness permeating American culture.

Europe's soft power, by contrast, appears to be appreciating in value. Even many of my American friends will occasionally say, "Why can't we be more like the Europeans in our values and attitudes?" It's not all that simple. There are plenty of things not to admire in Europe. Scratch the surface, and one can detect a sense of elitism and superiority among many Europeans, especially among the professional class, that is absent among their professional peers in America. And while there is far less violence on the streets of Europe, youth gangs are becoming more prevalent and crime is escalating. And when it comes to discrimination against minorities, Europeans more than hold their own with Americans. The dramatic increase in anti-Semitism and intolerance of immigrant populations is unsettling. Still, Europeans appear to be closer to the pulse of the changes that are transforming the world into a globalized society. More than two hundred years ago, it was the young United States that captured the world's attention with its dream of democracy and the inalienable right of every human being to pursue happiness. Today, the world's attention is being drawn more to the new European Dream with its emphasis on inclusivity, cultural diversity, universal human rights, quality of life, sustainable development, and peaceful coexistence.

A New Kind of Military

European foreign and security policy rests on two operational pillars: first, redefining the role of military engagement away from the old nation-state idea of territorial defense and toward the new transnational idea of peacekeeping and humanitarian intervention; second, employing economic assistance as a foreign policy tool to secure greater cooperation among peoples and countries.

Crisis conflict resolution is the centerpiece of European military preparedness. Over the past half century, EU member states have provided 80 percent of the peacekeeping forces in conflicts around the world, as well as 70 percent of the funds for reconstruction.[48] The aim of European military operations, sometimes called "robust peacekeeping" or "second-generation peacekeeping," is to stop the violence between the warring parties and create the conditions for establishing a workable peace accord. This kind of military intervention requires a complete rethinking of military strategies. New military terms such as "safe havens," "no-fly zones," and "humanitarian corridors" have become part of the lexicon in recent years.

The new military formula starts from the opposite assumption of conventional military engagement. In the old military scheme, the idea was to impose maximum casualties on the enemy. In the new military scheme, the goal is to minimize casualties on all sides of the conflict. The soldier's orders are no longer to risk his or her life and to kill the enemy. Peacekeeping troops have a different mission—risking their lives in order to save the lives of civilians. Mary Kaldor, professor of Global Governance and Human Rights at the London School of Economics, puts it succinctly: "Whereas the legitimate bearer of arms, the soldier, had to be prepared to die for his country, the peacekeeper risks his or her life for humanity."[49] The EU member countries contribute ten times the number of peacekeeping troops as the U.S., belying the oft-heard American contention that Europe lets America shoulder, alone, the task of being the world's policeman.[50]

The very idea that the European Union could dispatch troops to any member state's territory to restore order if it were in violation of the European Convention on Human Rights is revolutionary. The purpose of military action is no longer to confiscate land, indenture populations, and accumulate property but, rather, to protect people's universal human rights. Writing in the journal *Foreign Affairs*, Leslie H. Gelb and Justine Rosenthal point out the historical significance of this new kind of military thinking. States and governing institutions such as the EU are signaling a fundamental change in how they perceive the very purpose of the military. "Just think of it," say the authors of the article, "states endorsing the principle that morality trumps sovereignty."[51]

The other pillar of the European Union's foreign and security policy is development assistance. Most Americans believe that the U.S. is far and away the most generous country in the world when it comes to assisting the less fortunate in developing countries. Not true. U.S. foreign aid is a mere 0.1 percent of our Gross National Income (GNI), or one-third of European levels.[52] Europeans now provide more than 50 percent of all civilian development assistance in the world.[53] The EU also provides 47 percent of all the humanitarian assistance in the world. (The U.S. only contributes 36 percent.)[54] In 2002, EU humanitarian aid amounted to nearly €1.2 billion. Humanitarian assistance includes aid to refugees and displaced persons and emergency aid to assist victims of natural disasters and civil and ethnic conflicts. The U.S., however, is the leading provider of food aid.[55]

An increasing proportion of European development assistance is being transferred from the member states to the EU itself. The EU now administers 17 percent of all the development assistance funds generated by its member countries.[56]

It's not only the amount of economic aid that's important but also the quality of the assistance. The U.S., for example, has long been criticized for tying its aid programs to strategic military objectives rather than just to need. In 2003, the Center for Global Development and *Foreign Policy* magazine published the results of a lengthy study ranking the world's richest countries according to how much their development assistance helps or hinders the economic and social development of poor countries. The Commitment to Development Index, or CDI, is designed to look beyond foreign aid programs and examine how generous is their aid-giving, how hospitable are their immigration policies, how sizable are their peacekeeping operations, and how hefty is their foreign direct investment in developing countries. The index also penalizes financial assistance to corrupt regimes, practices that harm the environment, and barriers to imports from developing countries.[57]

The United States ranks near the bottom of the index. Of the twenty-one richest countries, only Japan fares worse than the U.S. Sixteen of the top nineteen countries are all European. Nine European nations rank in the top ten countries in the index. There are a number of reasons for the dismal performance of the U.S. vis-à-vis European countries in the Development Index. While the U.S. distributes a high amount of foreign aid to developing countries, it ties nearly 80 percent of its aid resources to agreements to purchase U.S. goods and services. The U.S. also performs poorly on environmental policies and contributions to peacekeeping.[58]

For all of its talk about fielding a different kind of military force—one dedicated to conflict resolution and peacekeeping functions—Europe has, at best, enjoyed a spotty record. By and large, European forces have fallen short in conflict intervention and the ability to actually stop hostilities, while they've been shown to be more effective in policing the peace once overt hostilities ended.

The intervention into the Bosnia conflict in 1992 and the Kosovo War at the end of the last decade proved embarrassing. European military forces were virtually powerless to impose their will on a ragtag army of thugs under the command of Serbian leader Slobodan Milosevic. The Kosovo conflict was particularly painful for the European military command. Were it not for U.S. military intervention, it's unlikely that Europe could have mustered the military might necessary to stop the hostility. Having to rely on American military forces for what was essentially a low-grade military action was humiliating. If Europe could not keep the peace in its own backyard against a less than formidable foe, how could the EU expect to maintain the peace and security of 455 million people living in twenty-five different nations?

The Kosovo War demonstrated just how lame the European military machine had become. The European forces were so ill trained, their weaponry so outmoded, and their surveillance and command-and-control structures so inadequate that they couldn't even be effectively integrated into what was essentially an American-led war effort. In the end, the European contribution to the war effort actually hindered the execution of the war.

The American military command was frustrated not only by the military shortcomings of the Europeans but also by what it perceived to be battlefield ineptness by European generals. Politics often got in the way, sending ambiguous messages to Milosevic about the Allies' intentions and willingness to fight. General Wesley Clark, the commander of NATO forces, complained that military decisions were continually being second-guessed and put on hold as Europeans fretted over the legal and political ramifications. "It was always the Americans who pushed for the escalation to new, more sensitive targets," said Clark, ". . . and always some of the Allies who expressed doubts and reservations."[59] Clark offered a sobering assessment of the "joint" NATO operation in Kosovo: "We paid a price in operational effectiveness by having to constrain the nature of the operation to fit within the political and legal concerns of NATO member nations."[60] As for the Europeans, they wondered out loud what they would do in some future conflict on European soil if the United States were not there to bail them out and take command.

The difference in the relative military effectiveness of the U.S. and the EU is almost mind-numbing. The American military machine has no match in history. American military spending alone is more than the next nine largest defense budgets combined. The U.S. now accounts for 80 percent of the world's military R&D and 40 percent of the world's total military spending.[61] If the U.S. government continues to increase its military budget at the current rate, its military expenditures will shortly be equal to the combined military expenditures of the rest of the world.[62]

European defense spending, by contrast, is only €155 billion, or less than half that of the United States.[63] Although far behind in technological preparedness, the European Union actually has more soldiers under arms than the U.S.—some 2 million troops.[64] The U.S. has only 1.4 million troops in uniform.[65]

One would expect that with half of the military budget of the United States, the EU combined forces would enjoy at least half the military capability. Unfortunately, that's not the case. Europe's strategic reconnaissance capability is a mere 10 percent of the U.S.'s, it's airlift capacity is only 20 percent of America's, and its precision-guided air-deliverance ordnance is approximately 10 percent of our own.[66]

According to public opinion surveys, more than 70 percent of Europeans support a common defense and security policy for the European Union.[67] But, as already mentioned, when it comes to the question of paying for the increased military expenditures that would be required to modernize the EU's military machine, the public is less enthusiastic. As of 2001, the amount spent by the EU and the Organization for Security and Cooperation in Europe on conflict prevention was less than the cost of one fighter jet.[68]

A RAND study done in the 1990s estimated that the cost of training, arming, and deploying a fifty-thousand-soldier force with state-of-the-art military capabilities over the next twenty-five years would run the EU somewhere between $18 and $49 billion, with an additional cost of between $9 and $25 billion if it wanted to create satellite intelligence capability.[69] To even hope to approach American military readiness, the European Union would need to increase its overall military spending from its current level of approximately 2 percent of GDP to over 4 percent of GDP.[70] No one, on either side of the Atlantic, expects that will happen.

Defense budgets have actually been shrinking in all of the EU countries, with the exception of Ireland and Greece.[71] In a period of slow economic growth and tighter government budgets, it's unlikely that member countries of the EU will choose to increase military spending at the same time they are being forced to cut social benefits. Karl Zinsmeister, of the

American Enterprise Institute, a conservative American think tank, sums up the feeling of many fellow conservatives in the United States. He writes,

> Until Europe demonstrates an equivalent willingness to commit its sons and its treasure to national defense, all talk of building a formidable independent military force in Europe is merely hot air. Wishful thinking will not man and equip a carrier battle group, build a missile shield, or otherwise instill the necessary awe in the world's tyrants.[72]

Many American government officials and military analysts, not to mention political observers, have run out of patience with what they regard as a silly EU foreign policy buttressed by a virtually nonexistent military presence. And they are not alone. British political observers have joined the rising chorus of disenchantment here in the U.S. over "fuzzy" foreign policy thinking among European elites. The British conservative Michael Gove's acid comments on the subject are typical of the talk among the "realpolitik" crowd. In his opinion,

> Europe's leaders seek to manage conflict through the international therapy of peace processes, the buying off of aggression with the danegeld of aid or the erection of a paper palisade of global law, which the unscrupulous always punch through. Europeans may convince themselves that these developments are the innovations of a continent in the van of progress, but they are really the withered autumn fruits of a civilization in decline.[73]

Americans and Europeans, then, sport two very different ideas of the way foreign policy and security ought to be handled. The Europeans seek security in strengthening international laws, and especially laws governing universal human rights. The aim is to minimize hostilities among foes and to use military intervention selectively to separate warring factions. The EU puts a high premium on conflict resolution rather than military victory. It uses economic assistance as a means of empowering the poor, spreading democracy, and bringing potential trouble spots into the community of civilized people. The current Bush Administration and a vast number of Americans—whether a majority or not is difficult to ascertain—are of a different mind. Many would agree with President Bush's national security adviser Condoleezza Rice, who wrote, at the time of the 2000 presidential election campaign, that America would be best off by proceeding "from the firm ground of the national interests, not from the interest of an illusory international community."[74]

A growing number of American critics of the European Union's foreign and security policies argue that the only reason Europe can present itself to the world as a "good guy idealist" is because the U.S. has to play "big daddy realist" and lean on the "bad guys" to preserve peace and order in Europe and elsewhere. The oft-heard refrain is that America is carrying Europe's water.

More tempered voices are likely to acknowledge that there is a role for both strategic approaches to foreign policy and security and that they might even complement each other—kind of like a foreign policy analogy of the bad cop, good cop model. The idea is that the United States, with its superior military capabilities, uses its unchallenged dominance to act as a sort of global disciplinarian, punishing wrongdoers for their transgressions and evil ways. The European Union, with its conflict-resolution and peacekeeping abilities, can serve as the rehabilitator, helping the wrongdoers, through a combination of peacekeeping and economic assistance, to see the error of their ways and reform their behavior. That dual scenario has played out in numerous occasions already in troubled regions of the world. America "does the hard war-fighting and Europe picks up the burden of peaceful reconstruction afterwards."[75] In political circles, the way they often put it is this: "America does the cooking, Europe does the washing up."[76] Not surprisingly, when Europeans and Americans were asked whether they would support such a dual formula, 52 percent of Europeans said they agreed with the division of labor, while only 39 percent of Americans concurred.[77]

From the European perspective, American taunts about Brussels' childish idealism ring hollow. Europeans have shown that they can use the tools of dialogue, process, and consensus-building to create bridges among people and put an end to age-old rivalries. The EU's twenty-five member nations are proof, on a large scale, of the wisdom of their approach. They reason that if 455 million Europeans of different persuasions and contending interests can transcend their ancient animosities and join together as an extended community in pursuit of peace and economic prosperity, why not beyond Europe?

Europeans are somewhat more circumspect when it comes to the second charge, of freeloading on the coattails of America's military might. European leaders and the European public know, deep down, that there is truth to the charge. They also worry that a unipolar world dominated and controlled by the United States might ultimately prove to be a less safe place for everyone—not because America has evil intentions but, rather, because whenever a single power can act as a hegemon, however noble its intentions, it invites countermeasures and retaliatory responses. French president Jacques Chirac voices the concerns of many other world leaders when he warns that "any community with only one dominant power is always a dangerous one and provokes reactions."[78]

Taking Responsibility for Its Own Defense

The European Union is beginning to realize that it has to create a credible military operation if it is to ensure the safety and security of its citizenry. There is a recognition that America is likely to be less willing to commit American troops in or around Europe in the future, even under NATO's umbrella, to fight battles that should be fought by Europe itself. However, it should be noted that the U.S. government appears to be of two minds on the matter. On the one hand, it continues to nudge the European Union to take more responsibility for the defense of Europe. On the other hand, it has repeatedly warned the European Union in recent years not to attempt to build its own military organization independent of NATO, fearing that if this were to happen, the U.S. might lose its ability to dictate the terms of any potential military engagement in the European theater. In other words, the U.S. would like the EU member countries to pony up greater military expenditures and to ratchet up their commitments to the defense of Europe, but within the NATO rubric, so as to maintain U.S. military dominance in that part of the world.

The idea for a Common Foreign and Security Policy (CFSP) was agreed upon as far back as 1993 in the Treaty on the European Union signed at Maastricht. But the plans to implement the CFSP languished for much of the remainder of the decade. The EU member countries had long been split on the question of whether or not to create a truly independent military force of their own. The French favored an EU fighting force accountable only to EU member nations. French president Chirac reiterated the French position in a speech to the European Parliament in the year 1999. He told the MPs that the European Command "cannot fully exist until it possesses autonomous capacity for action in the field of defense."[79]

The British, however, worried that a bid for European military autonomy might undermine NATO and anger its American ally. Britain's commitment to the EU has always been more tentative than that of other EU countries. Caught between a special relationship with the U.S. and its ancient ties to Europe, it has sought refuge in both camps and has often found itself torn between loyalties and not sure where its ultimate self-interests might lie.

The U.K. began to soften its stance on a European military force in the late 1990s, in part to assuage the feeling of other EU members for its refusal to adopt Europe's single currency. The Balkan crisis also convinced the U.K. that the EU's military weakness had to be addressed. Great Britain came to believe that a European military force could serve two masters, NATO and the European Union. It would address U.S. concerns that Europe was not doing enough to shoulder its weight in the defense of Europe. And, if the European forces were subsumed under NATO, it would strengthen the North Atlantic alliance rather than weaken it. The French saw the new British willingness as an opening wedge to its long sought-after goal of an independent military presence.

In December 1998, a Franco-British summit was convened in St. Malo, France. The two countries established the terms for what was to become the European Security and Defense Policy.[80] France and the U.K. signed a declaration that would commit the European Union, for the first time, to becoming a military as well as civil power. The declaration stated that the EU needed the "capacity for autonomous action backed up by credible military forces, the means to decide to use them and a readiness to do so in order to respond to international crisis."[81] The declaration made clear that the new proposed EU military force would act only in those situations where the whole of NATO was not involved and that it would not duplicate NATO operations.[82]

As timing would have it, just months after the St. Malo declaration was signed, NATO began a three-month air-bombing campaign over Kosovo. As in the earlier military engagement in Bosnia, European forces proved to be inept, having to rely on American air power and command to win the day. Anxious to finally come to terms with the security deficit, the EU convened a summit in June 1999 in Cologne, Germany. At the meeting, it was decided to establish a European Security and Defense Policy (ESDP), whose mission would be to field military actions for humanitarian and rescue tasks, peacekeeping, and crisis management.[83] The three mission objectives were called the Petersberg Tasks, named after a hotel in Bonn where Europeans had first laid them out back in 1992.[84] The summit participants also agreed to establish a political and security committee to coordinate EU foreign and security policy, an EU military committee made up of national chiefs of staff of the member countries, and an EU military staff to help manage the deliberations and execute the decisions of the other two committees. In a follow-up summit in Helsinki in December 1999, the EU put teeth into its plan by agreeing to field a fully operational rapid-reaction force of sixty thousand soldiers capable of carrying out the three mission objectives by 2003.[85]

The Helsinki Agreement reiterated and formalized the earlier intentions set forth by the U.K. and France in St. Malo. It called for "the Union to have an autonomous capacity to take decisions, and where NATO as a whole is not engaged, to launch and then conduct EU-led military operations in response to international crises."[86] To reassure the United States, the signatories emphasized that "NATO remains the foundation of the collective defense of its members and will continue to have an important role in crisis management. . . . Further steps will be taken to ensure full mutual consultation, cooperation and transparency between the European Union and NATO."[87]

The U.S. saw the EU initiative as a deliberate provocation designed to undermine the North Atlantic alliance and was particularly critical of the use of the term "autonomous" in referring to the new European rapid reaction force. U.S. Secretary of Defense William Cohen complained that if the EU were to create an independent defense structure outside the alliance's control, NATO would become "a relic of the past."[88] U.S. senators Jesse Helms and Gordon Smith were less measured in their reaction. They cautioned European leaders to "reflect carefully on the true motivation behind ESDP, which many see as a means for Europe to check American power."[89] Then they took off the gloves and made a stern warning: "It is neither in Europe's nor America's interests to undermine our proven national relationship in favour of one with a European superstate whose creation is being driven, in part, by anti-American sentiment."[90]

In November 2000, then secretary of state Madeline Albright voiced

the official policy of the Clinton Administration on the matter, with the is-
suing of what were called the "3Ds." The ESDP must not result in the *decoupling* of European defense from NATO; the new military organization
must not *duplicate* NATO's capabilities; and the European rapid reaction
force must not *discriminate* against NATO member countries that do not
belong to the EU.[91]

The reality is that for the American government, any European military operation is acceptable only on the condition that it be part of the
North Atlantic Treaty Organization. Then undersecretary of state Stuart
Eizenstein made the U.S. position crystal clear to its European allies. He
told them that the U.S. would "continue to celebrate the dream of a continent united through the European Union, but we must also hold before
us another essential vision—that of the transatlantic partnership."[92] It's
important to note that these statements are coming out of a White House
presided over by a liberal Democratic president. I say this because some
critics of the Bush Administration hope that a regime change in the White
House might invite a rethinking of America's long-standing security policy vis-à-vis Europe and the world. They are mistaken. Even if a liberal
Democrat were to become president again, it is unlikely that America
would diverge much from its stated position of exercising hegemony in its
foreign policy, which includes maintaining ultimate control over European security interests.

Despite vigorous U.S. objections, the European Union has forged
ahead with its plans for a rapid-reaction force, but always with the caveat
that NATO would remain the primary security organization for Europe.
The sixty thousand troops are organized into five brigades of infantry, ar-
mor, and artillery, as well as combat engineers, with full command, control, and intelligence capabilities. When fully operational, the troops will
be supported by fifteen warships and five hundred military aircraft. The
EU member states have also agreed to purchase two hundred Airbus jet
aircraft to be used as military transports.[93] The rapid-reaction force is
supposed to be capable of maintaining an expeditionary force in the field
for at least a year. To accomplish this, 200,000 troops will have to be put
on European command for standby to replace units in the field.[94]

With American troops stationed in Europe continuing to decline,
from 335,000 in the late 1980s to less than 100,000 in 2000, Europeans
are convinced that the defense of Europe and its immediate surroundings
will increasingly fall to the EU in the coming century, regardless of what

the U.S. says publicly about its continued commitment to defend Europe through the North Atlantic alliance.[95]

The idea of an EU armed forces enjoys widespread public support. Forty-two percent of EU citizens believe that European defense policy should be the responsibility of the EU, while only 24 percent believe the responsibility should be left to national governments, and a mere 20 percent believe that NATO should be in charge of European defense.[96]

On March 31, 2003, the EU launched its first military mission, committing peacekeeping troops to ethnic-torn Macedonia. The 400-member force replaced the NATO-led force that had been stationed in that Balkan nation since 2001.[97] Just two months later, in June 2003, the EU committed its first troops outside Europe, dispatching 1,400 soldiers to the Congo, where tribal conflicts had led to more than 500 deaths.[98]

While there is likely to be continued wrangling between the U.S. and the EU over the prospects for a European armed forces, at least for the foreseeable future the reality is that the NATO alliance, which proved to be so important in protecting the vital security interests of the West during the forty years of the Cold War with the Soviet Union, is increasingly a military organization in search of a mission. Its relevance is difficult to fathom. The idea that a united Europe will continue to have to be dependent on NATO, and ultimately subject its security interests to U.S. conditions and permissions, is simply untenable. Europe, of course, will have to pay a price for its desire for military independence. It's going to have to be willing to provide the necessary funds to secure its own defense. Many Americans welcome that prospect. Then again, if Europeans are going to pay their way, they ought to have their say. I suspect just as many of my countrymen are less sanguine about Europe making its own military decisions, independent of the long arm of American foreign policy interests.

We're going to have to get used to the idea that the European Union has its own global agenda and its own dream about the kind of world it would like to fashion—that dream won't always coincide with our own. Indeed, in many respects the European Dream is so utterly different from our own that the two superpowers are likely to find themselves, at times, at odds on the world stage, as we journey deeper into the century.

15

A Second Enlightenment

S IR MARTIN REES is one of the world's distinguished astronomers. The famed Cambridge University professor caused a brief ripple in scientific circles in 2003 with the publication of his book *Our Final Hour.* Rees warned that a new genre of high-risk scientific experiments and pursuits threatened the very existence of life on Earth and even the existence of the universe itself. He said he thought that "the odds are no better than fifty-fifty that our present civilization on Earth will survive to the end of the present century."[1] Ordinarily, such bombastic claims would be ignored altogether or dismissed as the ravings of a fool, but in this instance, the warnings earned a hearing in the media and became the subject of some controversy within the scientific community because of the impressive credentials of the messenger.

Questioning Unbridled Scientific Inquiry

Rees is an authority on black holes, and his theories on the origin and evolution of the universe are considered by many of his peers to be, if not the last word, at least the best word on the why and how of existence itself.

So when Rees suggested that some current and proposed new avenues of scientific pursuit perhaps ought not to be entertained because of the great potential risk they pose to existence, his words blew through the scientific community like an ill wind, threatening the very canons of science. After all, the notion of unfettered scientific inquiry is the very foundation of modern science. Enlightenment science is based on the idea of relentless pursuit of nature's secrets. To attempt to limit that pursuit or put constraints on avenues of inquiry is regarded by many in the scientific community as tantamount to squelching the scientific spirit itself. "Man's" very nature is inquisitive, argued the architects of the Enlightenment. We are a Promethean creature in constant search of understanding the grand scheme of things so that we can amass power over the forces of nature and command our own destiny. The idea of progress, so fundamental to the thinking of the modern world, is rendered moot if human beings were to accept self-imposed limits on what the mind could explore. Moreover, the entertainment of doubt about our ability to use reason to control and direct the forces of nature and our own future would put an end to the cherished utopian dream of the perfectibility of life on Earth. For all these reasons, the scientific community has, from the very outset of the Enlightenment, argued that virtually all human inquiry is worthy of pursuit.

Rees well understood the implications of his statement. Still, he asked, do we have obligations that now transcend the Enlightenment catechism? Is freedom of inquiry, experimentation, and technological application sacrosanct, even if it means the possible demise of life as we know it, maybe even of existence?

Rees put this question to a real-life test on the subject he knows the most about. He pointed to a project begun at the Brookhaven Laboratory on Long Island in 2000. Physicists there are using a particle accelerator to attempt to create a "quark-gluon plasma," a hot soup of dense subatomic materials that replicate conditions believed to exist at the time the "big bang" gave birth to the cosmos more than 13.7 billion years ago. Some scientists worry that a high concentration of energy of the type being pursued at Brookhaven could conceivably lead to three doomsday outcomes. A black hole might form—an object with such gravitational pull that even light could not escape. A black hole could "suck in everything around it."[2] It is also possible that quark particles could form a compressed object known as a "strangelet," which is "far smaller than a single atom" but could "infect" surrounding matter and "transform the entire planet Earth into an inert hyperdense sphere about one hundred metres across."[3] Or even worse, the subatomic forces of space itself could be transformed by the experiment. If that were to happen, the effect might be to "rip the fabric of space itself."[4] The result, warns Rees, could be that "the boundary of the new-style vacuum would spread like an expanding bubble," eventually devouring the entire universe.[5]

Rees and other scientists admit that the chance of any of these events occurring is exceedingly low. But while it's "very, very improbable," says Rees, "we cannot be 100 percent sure what might actually happen."[6] Rees then asks the question, Even assuming that the odds of something going wrong on this scale are as high as one in fifty million, would the potential benefit be worth the remote possibility of destroying the Earth and the entire universe?[7]

Rees goes on to warn of a number of current experimental pursuits that pose the threat of disastrous consequences for life on Earth, including the construction of small nanobots that replicate like viruses and that could race out of control, devouring matter and turning the Earth's surface to a "gray goo."[8] Rees worries about similar threats posed by genetic engineering and computer technology—especially as knowledge in the high-tech fields spreads, increasing the likelihood that someone will, by accident or intent, cause irrevocable harm. He concludes by saying that the risk attendant to these powerful new scientific and technological pursuits ought to engender a global discussion about the limits of scientific inquiry.

The immediate rejoinder by most scientists is that if we had entertained the same misgivings and fears about the harnessing of fire because it caused harm as well as good, we might never have enjoyed the vast benefits of progress and would instead have remained in a primitive state of being. The big difference, however, is that the effects of past scientific pursuits were always felt locally and were of limited duration. Today's cutting-edge scientific technology is of a different ilk. The effects and consequences of computer technology, biotechnology, and, soon, nanotechnology are global in scale and potentially long in duration.

The first realization of the vast difference in scale and duration of the new scientific endeavors and technologies came with the splitting of the atom and the dropping of the atomic bombs over human populations in Japan in the last days of World War II. Although some of the scientists engaged in the top-secret U.S. government project—the Manhattan Project—had misgivings about pursuing the research and applying the results, and expressed their concerns, the weight of scientific orthodoxy prevailed, and nuclear weapons and, later, nuclear power continued to be developed unabated. The reasoning, until this day, has been that while nuclear weapons and nuclear power plants pose a potential threat to the continuance of human life on Earth, the benefits of military security and adequate energy supplies exceed the potential threat posed by misuse and abuse or negligence. The belief has always been that the potential for wrongdoing or accidents could be "rationally" avoided, controlled, or at least mitigated.

Although Americans, by and large, continue to champion the European Enlightenment vision, putting their unswerving faith in scientific advances and technological pursuits, Europeans are beginning to have doubts about the wisdom of uncritical acceptance of the old shibboleths. As in the case of governance and foreign policy and security matters, Europe is beginning to diverge, in a fundamental way, from the American approach to science and technology. At the heart of the difference is the way Americans and Europeans perceive risk.

We Americans take pride in being a risk-taking people. We come from immigrant stock who risked their very lives to journey to the New World and start over, often with only a few coins in their pockets and a dream of a better life. When Europeans and others are asked what they most admire about Americans, our risk-taking, can-do attitude generally tops the list. We are often willing to gamble it all on a whim, a hope, or just a gut feeling. That's why Americans are so incredibly inventive, innovative, and entrepreneurial. Where others see difficulties and obstacles, Americans see opportunities. One of the traits that Americans most dislike in a person is the defeatist attitude that something can't be done or isn't worth attempting for fear of failure or unintended deleterious consequences. "You don't know until you try" is a refrain that reverberates throughout American history. If people elsewhere really want to know what irks Americans the most, it's this. We can't abide pessimism, a quality often perceived in our European friends. We are eternal optimists—although many Europeans I know say we are just plain naïve.

Our optimism is deeply entwined with our faith in science and technology. It has been said that Americans are a nation of tinkerers. When I was growing up, the engineer was held in as high esteem as the cowboy. He was viewed as a rugged individualist willing to cut against the grain, always in search of creating a better machine. The engineer was admired for his efforts to improve the lot of society and contribute to the progress and welfare of civilization. I remember seeing the lights on late at night in my neighbor's garage, as father and son experimented with various machines and engines at their homemade workbench, dreaming of a breakthrough invention that might change the world.

It's hard to give all that up. It's too ingrained. It's who we are. But on the other side of the water, the sensibilities are different. It's not that Europeans aren't inventive. One could even make the case that over the course of history, Europe has produced most of the great scientific insights and not a few of the major inventions—although certainly the Chinese might justifiably lay claim to some of the accolade. Still, Europeans are far more mindful of the dark side of science and technology. They've had longer histories with the negative as well as the positive consequences of science and technology and are, therefore, less starry-eyed. Moreover, until the post–World War II era, science and technology in Europe were largely in the hands of an educated elite and associated with control over society and the perpetuation of class divisions, whereas in America, science and technology were always more democratically dispersed. The founder of my own alma mater, the University of Pennsylvania, Benjamin Franklin, as well as Thomas Paine, Thomas Jefferson, and many of the other founding fathers, fancied themselves as scientists and inventors as much as revolutionaries and spent endless time working on scientific pursuits and the creation of new inventions. They envisioned America as a nation of inventors. Thomas Jefferson, our third U.S. president, fashioned the first modern patent laws to reward the prowess of American inventors. He hoped that the patent laws would encourage the democratization of the inventive spirit. They did.

Just as Americans took up the European Enlightenment dream of material progress, the pursuit of self-interest, and individual autonomy, and ran with it in its most pure form, while European attachment was more tentative, so, too, with the Enlightenment notions of science and technology. The Brits come closest to the American sensibilities when it comes to our unflagging faith in the pursuit of Enlightenment science and technology. But, even they temper their enthusiasm with an occasional romantic and sometimes class-directed reaction from the likes of a Samuel Taylor Coleridge or the Luddites. We have our Thoreaus and our anti-technology populist traditions as well, although these countercurrents don't run as deep in America as they do in Europe.

The divergence in views on science and technology between Americans and Europeans is growing and is now coming to the fore in a myriad of public policy debates, threatening a schism as significant as the divide over our different sense of how best to pursue foreign policy and domestic security.

Burden of Proof

In recent years, the European Union has turned upside down the standard operating procedure for introducing new technologies and products into the marketplace and society, much to the consternation of the United States. The turnaround started with the controversy over genetically modified (GM) foods and the introduction of genetically modified organisms (GMOs) into the environment. The U.S. government gave the green light to the widespread introduction of GM foods in the mid-1990s, and by the end of the decade, over half of America's agricultural land was given over to GM crops. No new laws were enacted to govern the potential harmful environmental and health impacts. Instead, existing statutes were invoked. Nor was any special handling or labeling of the products required.

In Europe, the response was quite different. Massive opposition to GMOs erupted across the continent. Farmers, environmentalists, and consumer organizations staged protests, and political parties and governments voiced concern and even opposition. A de facto moratorium on the planting of GM crops and the sale of GM food products was put into effect. Meanwhile, the major food processors, distributors, and retailers pledged not to sell any products containing GM traits.

The European Union embarked on a lengthy review process to assess the risks of introducing GM food products. In the end, the European Union established tough new protections designed to mitigate the potential harm of GM food crops and products. The measures included procedures to segregate and track GM grain and food products from the fields to the retail stores to ensure against contamination; labeling of GMOs at every stage of the food process to ensure transparency; and independent testing as well as more rigorous testing requirements by the companies producing GM seeds and other genetically modified organisms.

The U.S. government charged the EU with foul play and suggested that the Union was using GMOs as a ploy to win concessions on other trade-related issues to which the two superpowers were at loggerheads. The U.S. trade representative even threatened to challenge the EU GMO policy at the World Trade Organization, suggesting that its restrictive policies violated existing free-trade agreements.

What the U.S. didn't understand is that Europe's opposition to the introduction of GMOs was not just a political maneuver to gain a bargaining chip with the U.S. on trade, but something far more important. For Europeans, the introduction of GMOs cuts much deeper, challenging many of the fundamental assumptions that underlie the nascent European Dream. The European public worries about the potential unforeseen environmental impacts of introducing large volumes of genetically modified organisms into the biosphere. They also worry about the possible consequences to human health that might result. The argument one hears over and over again by men and women on the streets of Europe, as well as by governing elites, is that while millions of dollars have been spent on readying the new products for market, far less care, attention, and funds have been committed to assessing the potential ecological and health risks that might accompany the introduction of this radical new agricultural technology. Europeans argue that because GMOs are alive, reproduce, mutate, proliferate, and can contaminate and create irreversible niches, they pose potential threats that are global in scale and therefore require a different level of oversight.

Europeans also express concern over the impact that GM foods may have on their cultural identity. In Europe, unlike America, food plays a critical role in defining culture—many would argue that food is as important or even more important than language in maintaining the social cohesion of Europe's many cultures. Americans have a difficult time understanding the close cultural relationship Europeans have toward rural life, farming practices, food cultivation, processing, and consumption because we gave all that up long ago to become a fast-food, commercial culture. For Europeans, GM foods represent a potential threat to deeply held beliefs about sustainable development and the protection of cultural diversity, principles that go to the very heart of the European Dream. According to public opinion surveys, 89 percent of the French public, 81 percent of the German public, and 74 percent of the Italian public oppose the introduction of GM foods. On average, two out of three Europeans oppose GM foods, while in America, nearly half (48 percent) of all consumers support GM foods.[9]

Nor is the GMO issue an anomaly. The European Union is forging ahead on a wide regulatory front, changing the very conditions and terms governing how new scientific and technological pursuits and products are introduced into the marketplace, society, and the environment. Its bold initiatives put the Union far ahead of the United States, and the rest of the world, in procedures and protocols overseeing scientific and technological endeavors. Behind all of its newfound regulatory zeal is the looming question of how best to model global risks and create a sustainable and transparent approach to economic development.

In May 2003, the European Commission proposed sweeping new regulatory controls on chemicals to mitigate toxic impacts on the environment and human and animal health. The proposed new law would require companies to register and test for the safety of more than thirty thousand chemicals at an estimated cost to the producers of nearly €8 billion.[10] Under existing rules, 99 percent of the total volume of chemicals sold in Europe have not passed through any environmental and health testing and review process.[11] According to the EU environmental commissioner, Margot Wallstrom, "There is no control whatsoever of the 400 million tons of chemicals sold in the European Union each year."[12] In the past, there was no way to even know what kind of chemicals were being used by industry, making it nearly impossible to track potential health risks. The new regulations will change all of that. The REACH system—which stands for Registration, Evaluation, and Authorization of Chemicals— requires the companies to conduct safety and environmental tests to prove that the products they are producing are safe. If they can't, the products will be banned from the market.

The new procedures represent an about-face to the way the chemical industry is regulated in the United States. In America, newly introduced chemicals are generally assessed to be safe, and the burden is primarily put on the consumer and the public at large or the government to prove that they cause harm. The European Union has reversed the burden of proof. Margot Wallstrom makes the point that "no longer do public authorities need to prove they [the products] are dangerous. The onus is now on industry" to prove that the products are safe.[13]

The new EU policy represents a sea change in the handling of risks. In the United States, regulation is designed, for the most part, to address environmental problems once they occur. The Toxic Substances Control Act (TOSCA), passed in 1976, is America's primary governmental tool for regulating toxic chemicals but is generally regarded as "being weak and too deferential to industry."[14] The vast majority of non-pesticide chemicals are not screened or tested at all before introduction into the marketplace. Even though the National Environmental Policy Act (NEPA) requires environmental-impact statements in advance of some scientific experiments and technological applications, it has been narrowly applied by the federal courts and restricted in its use. Even when it has been used, the threshold criteria for fulfilling NEPA requirements is so weak as to be largely ineffective in most instances. The European Union's regulatory approach, in stark contrast, is designed to prevent harm before it occurs.

Making companies prove that their chemical products are safe before they are sold is a revolutionary change. It's impossible to conceive of the U.S. entertaining the kind of risk-prevention regulatory regime that the EU has rolled out. In a country where corporate lobbyists spend literally billions of dollars influencing congressional legislation, the chances of ever having a similar regulatory regime to the one being implemented in Europe would be nigh on impossible.

What makes the new risk-prevention regime even more impressive is that the European Union is the largest chemical producer in the world and makes up 28 percent of the entire world output of chemical products.[15] The industry, which is the third largest in the European manufacturing sector, with annual sales of €519 billion, employs 1.7 million people, and is responsible for an additional 3 million jobs related to the industry.[16] Even so, the European Commission drove the regulatory process forward.

The U.S. government and chemical industry—as well as European chemical companies and associations—have fought the new regulations. The U.S. says the EU chemical regulations threaten the export of more than $20 billion in chemicals that the U.S. sells to Europe each year.[17] Undeterred, the European Commission endorsed the proposed regulations in October 2003. It is estimated that implementing REACH will cost the chemical industry about €2.3 billion over the next eleven years.[18] The cost to downstream users (manufacturers who use chemical substances in their products) is expected to be around €2.8 to €3.6 billion over a similar time period.[19] While some environmental organizations complain that the final regulations were watered down and needed to be strengthened, the very fact that the European Union has become the first political unit in the world to transfer risk to the companies, making them responsible for proving the safety of their products, represents a new departure in addressing the question of how best to regulate environmental and health risks that accompany new scientific and technological pursuits. The new proposals still have to be acted upon by the European Parliament and the European Council.

GMOs and chemical products represent just part of the new "risk-prevention" agenda taking shape in Brussels. In early 2003, the European Union adopted a new rule prohibiting electronics manufacturers from selling products in the EU that contain mercury, lead, or other heavy metals.[20] Another new regulation requires the manufacturers of all consumer electronics and household appliances to cover the costs for recycling their products. American companies complain that compliance with the new regulations will cost them hundreds of millions of dollars a year.[21]

All of these strict new rules governing risk prevention would come as a shock to most Americans, who have longed believed that the United States is the most vigilant regulatory oversight regime in the world for governing risks to the environment and public health. Although that was the case thirty years ago, it no longer is today.

The new attention to risk prevention in Europe reflects a new sensibility to sustainable development and global stewardship of the Earth's resources and environment. Some observers note that at least some of the impetus for strengthening regulatory oversight is the result of recent past failures of Europe's regulatory procedures in handling the BSE outbreaks in cattle in the U.K. and other countries, the contamination of the blood supply with the HIV virus in France, the Perrier benzene scare in Europe, and other environmental and health calamities. While these incidences contributed to the heightened concern for better regulatory oversight, larger forces at work, well before these recent events, helped shape a new risk-prevention approach across the continent.

The long-term effect of acid rain on the Black Forest in Germany; the release and spread of a deadly radioactive cloud over much of Europe in the wake of the Chernobyl nuclear-power-plant meltdown; the heightened fears over violent weather-pattern changes, including floods in Central and Eastern Europe, which many attribute to the impacts of global warming; and the proliferation of chemical and biological weapons have all sensitized Europeans to the growing global environmental and health risks attendant to the new era. Europe's new sensitivity to global risks has led it to champion the Kyoto Protocol on climate change, the Biodiversity

Treaty, the Chemical Weapons Convention, and many other treaties and accords designed to reduce global, environmental, and health risks. As mentioned in chapter 14, the U.S. government has refused, to date, to ratify any of the above agreements.

The European Union is the first governing institution in history to emphasize human responsibilities to the global environment as a centerpiece of its political vision. Nation-states have a very different mission. Their aim has always been to expand territorial reach, exploit the Earth's largesse, and advance material wealth. The Earth, in the nation-state era, has been viewed primarily as a resource. Science and technology, in turn, have been the tools used to probe nature's secrets and harness her potential wealth. The goal was—and still is—economic growth and accumulation of property.

While the member states of the EU are still very much wedded to the older nation-state mission, with its emphasis on the right to exploit nature's resources, the people of Europe find themselves, at the same time, inexorably pulled toward a new global center of gravity where obligations to preserve the integrity of the Earth itself are of equal priority. The new crosscutting loyalties to both material self-interests and global environmental responsibilities represent the emergence of a new frame of mind for which there is no historical precedent. That's not to say that others, elsewhere, don't feel a similar tug. But in the U.S., for example, my sense is that global environmental concerns have somewhat less resonance among the public at large—although it's hard to quantify—and far less attraction to political elites and policymakers.

In Europe, intellectuals are increasingly debating the question of the great shift from a risk-taking age to a risk-prevention era. That debate is virtually nonexistent among American intellectuals. The new European intellectuals argue that vulnerability is the underbelly of risks. To the extent that individuals, and society as a whole, perceive greater opportunities than negative consequences in taking risks, they are "risk takers." Americans, we've already noted, are risk-taking people. Europeans, on the other hand, are far more risk-sensitive. Much of their outlook is conditioned by a checkered past history where risk-taking resulted in significant negative consequences to society and posterity. Risk-sensitivity, however, has a silver lining. A sense of vulnerability can motivate people to band together in common cause. The European Union stands as a testimonial to collective political engagement arising from a sense of risk and shared vulnerability. A sense of vulnerability can also lead to greater empathy for others, although it can also generate fear and retaliation toward outsiders, especially if they are perceived to be somehow to blame for one's compromised circumstances.

The severing of the individual from the collective in the industrial era created a new sense of risk exposure and vulnerability. Private and public insurance were ways of pooling risks to provide for one another. Insurance became a means of reducing vulnerability in an otherwise atomized, autonomous world. Although many Americans enjoy private insurance and the government provides insurance in the way of the Social Security fund, the idea of insurance—especially of a public nature—is much more developed in Europe. This is due, in part, to Europeans' never fully accepting the Enlightenment notion of the autonomous individual responsible, in toto, for his or her fate. Europeans have continued to maintain a balance— at times uncomfortable—between individual autonomy and a collective risk-sharing responsibility. It's the legacy of Catholic doctrine, feudal arrangements, and walled cities. Even the Protestant Reformation, with its near obsession on the individual, couldn't totally pry the Europeans from an older and deeper communal affiliation.

What's changed qualitatively in the last half century since the dropping of the atomic bombs on Hiroshima and Nagasaki is that risks of all kinds are now global in scale, open-ended in duration, incalculable in their consequences, and not compensational. Their impact is universal, which means that no one can escape their potential effects. Risks have now become truly democratized, making everyone vulnerable. When everyone is vulnerable, and all can be lost, then traditional notions of calculating and pooling risks become virtually meaningless. This is what European academics call a "risk society."

Americans aren't there yet. While some academics speak to global risks and vulnerabilities and a significant minority of Americans express their concerns about global risks, from climate change to loss of biodiversity, the sense of utter vulnerability just isn't as strong on this side of the Atlantic. Europeans say we have blinders on. In reality, it's more nuanced than that. Most Americans still hold firm to the underlying pillar of the American Dream—that each person is ultimately the captain of his or her own fate. Call it delusional, but the sense of personal empowerment is so firmly embedded in the American mind that even when pitted against growing evidence of potentially overwhelming global threats, most Americans shrug such notions off as overly pessimistic and defeatist. Individuals can move mountains. Most Americans believe that. Fewer Europeans do.

Can one effectively build a dream on a sense of shared global risk and vulnerabilities? European elites think yes. Less sure is the European public, although the anecdotal evidence suggests they are more likely than any other peoples in the world to give it a try. Here in America, however, where 293 million individuals have been weaned on eternal optimism, and each socialized to believe that he or she can make his or her own way against all external odds, the possibility that a collective risk-prevention approach to scientific and technological pursuits might find a responsive audience is problematic.

The European Union has already institutionalized a litmus test that cuts to the core of the differences that separate the new European view of shared risks and vulnerabilities from the older American view of unlimited personal opportunities and individual prowess. It's called "the precautionary principle," and it has become the centerpiece of EU regulatory policy governing science and technology in a globalizing world. Most European political elites, and the public at large, favor it. Far fewer American politicians and citizens would likely countenance it.

The Precautionary Principle

In November 2002, the European Commission adopted a communication on the use of the precautionary principle in regulatory oversight of science and technology innovations and the introduction of new products into the marketplace, society, and environment. According to the commission, a proposed experiment, or technology application, or product introduction is subject to review and even suspension in "cases where scientific evidence is insufficient, inconclusive or uncertain and preliminary scientific evaluation indicates that there are reasonable grounds for concern that the potentially dangerous effects on the environment, human, animal or plant health, may be inconsistent with the high level of protection chosen by the EU."[22] The key term in the directive is "uncertain." When there is sufficient evidence to suggest a potential deleterious impact but not enough evidence to know for sure, the precautionary principle kicks in, allowing regulatory authorities to err on the side of safety by either suspending the activity altogether, modifying it, employing alternative scenarios, monitoring the activity to assess causal impacts, or creating experimental protocols to better understand its effects. The architects of the commission directive are quick to point out that the precautionary principle is to be invoked in a reasoned and nonarbitrary manner to ensure that it isn't used as a political or economic hammer to advance other objectives. The directive states,

> Where action is deemed necessary, measures should be proportionate to the chosen level of protection, non-discriminatory in their application and consistent with similar measures already taken. They should also be based on an examination of the potential benefits and costs of action or lack of action and subject to review in the light of new scientific data and should thus be maintained as long as the scientific data remain incomplete, imprecise or inconclusive and as long as the risk is considered too high to be imposed on society.[23]

The first known instance where the precautionary principle was put into effect occurred in September 1854 in the parish of St. James in central London. A London physician, John Snow, was investigating the source of a cholera outbreak that had taken five hundred lives in a ten-day period. Snow had published an earlier study comparing two water companies— one whose water was clean, the other whose water was contaminated by sewage. He theorized that the unclean water was linked to cholera. The study was already producing data to support his thesis at the time of the cholera outbreak. A quick investigation showed that all of the eighty-three people that had died in the Golden Square area between August 31 and September 5 had drank water from the contaminated Broad Street water pump rather than from the cleaner water company's pump. He recommended to authorities that the pump handle of the Broad Street Water Company be removed. The action averted a further cholera outbreak. It should be emphasized that most scientists, at the time, did not share Snow's view. They believed that cholera was carried by airborne contamination. The scientific link between polluted water and cholera wasn't discovered until thirty years later.[24]

The decision to follow Snow's advice was a classic example of the precautionary principle at work—that is, taking action in a situation where there is reason to believe that there is a causal connection between an activity and deleterious consequences without yet having sufficient scientific proof to back up the claim.

The first use of the precautionary principle in public policy came in the 1970s in Germany. German scientists and public officials were voicing increasing concern over "forest death" in Germany. They suspected that acid rain caused by air pollution was the cause but did not yet have iron-clad scientific proof. Nonetheless, the German government made the decision to cut power-plant emissions with the passage of the German Clean Air Act of 1974, citing the principle of *Vorsorge*, or "forecaring."[25] The "precautionary principle" soon became a canon of German environmental law. The precautionary principle was "to be used in situations of potentially serious or irreversible threats to health or the environment, where there is a need to act to reduce potential hazards *before* there is strong proof of harm, taking into account the likely costs and benefits of action and inaction."[26]

The precautionary principle is designed to allow government authorities to respond pre-emptively, as well as after damage is inflicted, with a lower threshold of scientific certainty than has normally been the rule of thumb in the past. "Scientific certainty" has been tempered by the notion of "reasonable grounds for concern." The precautionary principle gives authorities the maneuverability and flexibility to respond to events in real time, either before they unfold or while they are unfolding, so that potential adverse impacts can be forestalled or reduced while the suspected causes of the harm are being analyzed and evaluated.

Advocates of the precautionary principle argue that had it been invoked in the past, many of the adverse effects of new scientific and technological introductions might have been prevented, or at least mitigated, and they cite the introduction of halocarbons and the tear in the ozone hole in the Earth's upper atmosphere, the outbreak of BSE in cattle, growing antibiotic-resistant strains of bacteria caused by the over-administering of antibiotics to farm animals, and the widespread deaths caused by asbestos, benzene, and PCBs.[27]

In these and other instances, there were telltale signs of potential harmful effects, often right from the time of their introductions. The warning signals were ignored for a variety of reasons, including conflict of interests among the researchers responsible for overseeing possible threats. For example, in the United States, the Animal and Plant Health Inspection Service (APHIS), of the United States Department of Agriculture (USDA), is responsible for monitoring health problems in the nation's farm animals and plants. But the USDA is also charged with the responsibility of promoting American agricultural products. In countless instances, the department has been less than rigorous in the pursuit of potential adverse environmental and health effects caused by existing agricultural practices, if those practices might, in any way, threaten the welfare of the agricultural interests they also serve.

In the case of the BSE outbreak in the U.K., it's been pointed out subsequently in government hearings and public exposés that the reason the government regulatory body was so slow to respond to the spreading crisis is that its responsibility was to safeguard the industry it monitored and not consumers. Often, potential links went unexplored because the connections required interdisciplinary approaches that were never forthcoming. For example, veterinarians examining BSE in cattle failed to make the link with the disease and Creutzfeldt-Jakob disease (CJD), a brain-wasting illness in humans, now known to be caused by eating beef from BSE-contaminated cattle. Had medical researchers been brought in early on to work with the veterinarians to explore the possible connection between the brain-wasting diseases in cattle and in humans, action to prohibit the spread of BSE to human populations might have occurred earlier, saving many more lives.[28]

In the case of halocarbons, PCBs, and methyl tertiary butyl ether (MTBE), all artificial chemicals, their novelty itself should have raised some eyebrows. Researchers knew from the very beginning that these chemicals persist in the environment, are easily dispersible, and can become ubiquitous. So if problems do arise, it would be more difficult to get rid of them.[29]

Frequently, lay evidence of potential harm precedes clinical evidence by years, and even decades, but is ignored by the "experts" and the powers that be. Workers were aware of the harmful effects of asbestos and PCBs long before regulators turned their attention to the problems. In countless instances, local communities notice the causal association between ill health and local industrial activity well before public officials. Love Canal in the United States comes easily to mind.

The precautionary principle has been finding its way into international treaties and covenants. It was first recognized in 1982 when the UN General Assembly incorporated it into the World Charter for Nature.[30] The precautionary principle was subsequently included in the Rio Declaration on Environment and Development in 1992, the Framework Convention on Climate Change in 1992, the Treaty on European Union

(Maastricht Treaty) in 1992, the Cartagena Protocol on Biosafety in 2000, and the Stockholm Convention on Persistent Organic Pollutants (POPs) in 2001.[31]

The European Union hopes that by integrating the precautionary principle into international treaties and multilateral agreements, it will become the unchallenged standard by which governments oversee and regulate science and technology around the world. While the U.S. has integrated aspects of the precautionary principle into some of its environmental regulations, for the most part America's approach and standards are far more lax than the EU's, while still arguably better than those of many other countries.

In recent years, the U.S. government, in tandem with U.S. industry, has taken every occasion to challenge the tougher approach to the precautionary principle taken by the EU. The U.S. views Europe's tightening regulatory regime as a noose around American exports and is determined to thwart its efforts to make the principle the gold standard for the world. America's National Foreign Trade Council best expressed U.S. governmental and industry concern in a report issued in May 2003. The council warned that the EU's invocation of the precautionary principle "has effectively banned U.S. and other non-EU exports of products deemed hazardous, stifled scientific and industrial innovation, and advancement."[32]

Margot Wallstrom, the EU's outspoken environmental commissioner, made clear her belief that Europe and America were beginning to diverge in a fundamental way when it comes to the issue of sustainable development and global environmental stewardship. She noted that although environmental concerns appear last among nine issues of concern among American voters, they appear among the top-five most pressing issues for European voters.[33] Wallstrom also observed that while "the environment is essentially a local issue within the U.S. . . . in Europe . . . there is a greater understanding among the broader public of the international and global dimension of the environmental challenge."[34] The bottom line, concludes Wallstrom, is that while in America environment is only a second-tier issue, "environmental policy has been one of the foundation stones of the European Union itself."[35] Wallstrom and others see the precautionary principle as the front line in their regulatory arsenal to advance the cause of sustainable development in a globalizing world.

But the import of the precautionary principle runs even deeper. It speaks to a profound shift in the way society views its relationship to nature and its approach to scientific pursuits and technological innovations. The European Enlightenment tradition, to which America has become the most enthusiastic supporter, puts a premium on power over nature. Americans, by and large, view nature as a treasure trove of useful resources waiting to be harnessed for productive ends. While Europeans share America's utilitarian perspective, they also have another sensibility that is less prominent here in America—that is, a love for the intrinsic value of nature. One can see it in Europeans' regard for the rural countryside and their determination to maintain natural landscapes, even if it means providing government assistance in the way of special subsidies or forgoing commercial development. Nature figures prominently in Europeans' dream of a quality of life. Europeans spend far more time visiting the countryside on weekends and during their vacations than Americans. It is, for them, a valued pastime.

The balancing of urban and rural time is less of a priority for most Americans, many of whom are just as likely to spend their weekends at a shopping mall, while their European peers are hiking along country trails. Of course, there are plenty of Americans who prefer to spend their time in the great outdoors, just as there are many Europeans who prefer the comforts of urban recreation. Still, anyone who spends significant time in Europe and America knows, quite well, that there is a great affinity for rural getaways among Europeans. Almost everyone I know in Europe among the professional and business classes has some small second home in the country somewhere—a dacha usually belonging to the family for generations. While working people may not be as fortunate, on any given weekend they can be seen exiting the cities en masse, motoring their way into the nearest rural enclave or country village for a respite from urban pressures.

The strongly held values about rural life and nature is one reason why Europe has been able to support green parties across the continent, with substantial representation in national parliaments as well as in the European Parliament. By contrast, not a single legislator at the federal level in the U.S. is a member of a green party.

European determination to maintain a semblance of balance between a utilitarian and an intrinsic approach to nature makes them take more seriously their responsibility to sustainable development and global environmental stewardship. The precautionary principle is perceived, in part, as a way to balance the scales, if you will, between commercial development and preservation of the natural environment.

There is, however, another dimension to the European psyche, one we've alluded to repeatedly in earlier chapters, that makes Europeans more supportive of the precautionary principle than we might be in America—that is, their sense of the "connectedness" of everything. The precautionary principle is rooted in the idea that every scientific experiment, or technology application, or product introduction affects the environment in myriad ways that are complicated and difficult to assess. The older methods of determining risks, because they are reductionist, mechanistic, and linear in nature, don't account for the subtlety of relationships in nature that are difficult to quantify or are unpredictable.

Because we Americans place such a high premium on autonomy, we are far less likely to see the deep connectedness of things. We tend to see the world in terms of containers, each isolated from the whole and capable of standing alone. Connectedness, to us, conjures up the notion of shared dependency and vulnerability, qualities we don't much admire. Our sense of self and world makes us ideal disciples of the Enlightenment frame of mind, with its emphasis on harnessing and isolating discrete bits and pieces of nature for the purpose of transforming them into productive property. We like everything around us to be neatly bundled, autonomous, and self-contained, which is the way we think of ourselves in the world. Everything in the Enlightenment model of nature is detachable and convertible. There are no relationships, just things, either in motion or at rest, bombarding other things or inert. Enlightenment nature is eminently exploitable. Every "thing" can be grabbed and used without consequence to anything else. There is only opportunity, never responsibility, because all things exist alone and therefore have no relationship to one another.

The new view of science that is emerging in the wake of globalization is quite different. We are becoming increasingly aware of the connectedness of everything. Nature is viewed as a myriad of symbiotic relationships, all embedded in a larger whole, of which they are an integral part. In this new vision of nature, nothing is autonomous, everything is connected. Any effort to sever a part of the whole has consequences to everything else. There are no islands, no safe harbors, no self-contained eddies, only continuous interactivity, mutuality, and engagement.

Europeans, because of their dense spatial and temporal history, have a far better appreciation of the new model of nature. Their lives have been lived far more communally and with greater embeddedness than have ours in America. They understand the logic of the precautionary principle because they know that in a densely lived environment, everything one does affects everything else.

The precautionary principle calls on us to look beyond immediate activity, in isolation, and toward the whole context in which that activity unfolds. The sheer magnitude of today's scientific and technological interventions can't help but have significant and often long-lasting effects on the rest of nature—those effects can be potentially catastrophic and irreversible. The precautionary principle says, in effect, that because the stakes are so high, we have to weigh even the most dramatic benefits against the prospects of even more destructive consequences. The old Enlightenment science is too primitive and sophomoric to address a world where the bar for risk has been raised to the threshold of possible extinction itself. When the whole world is at risk because of the scale of human intervention, then a new scientific approach is required that takes the whole world into consideration. That is the logic at the heart of the precautionary principle.

Systems Thinking

Here, then, is the problem. The very success of Enlightenment science is now posing a fundamental conundrum for science. The more powerful the science and technology are becoming, the more complex and unpredictable are the impacts and consequences. Many in the scientific community worry that "the growing innovative powers of science seem to be outstripping its ability to predict the consequences of its applications, whilst the scale of human interventions in nature increases the chances that any hazardous impacts may be serious and global."[36] The old Enlightenment science seems to have run out of answers for how to deal with this new reality.

Enlightenment science is wedded to the notion that the behavior of the whole is best understood by analyzing the individual parts that make it up. The analytical method reduces all phenomena to its most fundamental building blocks and then examines the individual properties of each element in the hope of better understanding the construction of the whole. As mentioned in chapter 4, this mechanistic approach to science borrowed heavily from popular mechanical metaphors of the day. Machines can indeed be understood by taking them apart, analyzing their individual components, and then re-assembling them back into the whole. But in the real world of nature, behavior is not mechanistic and fixed, but conditional, open-ended, affected by other phenomena, and continually metamorphosing and mutating in response to the patterns of activity around it.

As long as science and technology were more narrowly engaged in questions of acceleration and location, Newton's mechanistic laws served well. Phenomena that could be isolated, timed and measured, and made subject to rigorous quantification passed muster. By the twentieth century, however, the reductionist and mechanistic idea was too limited a concept to capture the embeddedness of nature. It became more apparent to scientists that understanding society or nature required understanding the myriad relationships between phenomena and not just the properties of the component parts.

Social scientists began to ask, How do we know a man except in relationship to the world around him? Taking the measure of a man—knowing his place of birth, age, height, weight, physical and emotional characteristics, etc.—tells us little of value about who he really is. It is only by understanding his relationship to the larger environment in which he is embedded and the many relationships he shares that we get a sense of him. In the old scheme, man was the sum total of his individual properties. In the new scheme, he is a snapshot of the pattern of activities in which he is engaged.

If each human being is a pattern of interactivity, why wouldn't all of nature be so as well? Science, in the twentieth century, began to re-examine many of its most basic operating assumptions, only to see them overthrown. The old idea that phenomena could be known by analyzing the individual parts gave way to the opposite conception—that the individual parts can be understood only by first knowing something about their relationships to the whole within which they are embedded. In a word, nothing exists in isolation, as an autonomous object. Rather, everything exists in relation to "the other." The new science was called "systems theory," and it put in doubt the older thinking about the nature of nature. Systems theory also cast a shadow on the rest of the Enlightenment project, including, most important, the idea of the autonomous being functioning in a detached, self-optimizing world, populated by other autonomous beings, each maximizing his or her own individual utility.

Systems theory holds that the nature of the whole is greater than the sum of its parts. That's because it is the relationship between the parts—

the organizing principles that animate the whole—that creates something qualitatively different at the level of the whole. For example, we know from personal experience that a living being is qualitatively different from a corpse. At the moment of death, all of the relationships that made that living being a whole disappear, leaving just a body of inert matter. The great twentieth-century physicist Werner Heisenberg once remarked that "the world thus appears as a complicated tissue of events, in which connections of different kinds alternate or overlap or combine and thereby determine the texture of the whole."[37]

The new systems thinking owes much to the emerging field of ecology. Ecology comes from the Greek word *oikos*, which means "household." The German biologist Ernst Haeckel was the first to define the new branch of biology as "the science of relations between the organism and the surrounding outer world."[38] Ecology challenged the Darwinian model, with its emphasis on the competitive struggle between individual creatures for scarce resources. In the newer ecological model, nature is made up of a multitude of symbiotic and synergistic relationships, where each organism's fate is determined as much by the patterns of mutual relationships as by any competitive advantage. Where Darwin's biology concentrated more on the individual organism and species and relegated the environment to a backdrop of resources, ecology views the environment as all the relationships that make it up.

The early ecologists concentrated their efforts on local ecosystems. In 1911, however, a Russian scientist, Vladimir Vernadsky, published a paper that would expand the notion of ecological relationships to include the entire planet. He described what he called "the biosphere," which he defined "as the area of the earth's crust occupied by transformers that convert cosmic radiation into effective terrestrial energy—electrical, chemical, mechanical, thermal, etc."[39]

In a follow-up book, published in 1926, which he entitled *Biospheria*, Vernadsky broke with the scientific orthodoxy of the day, arguing that geochemical and biological processes on Earth evolved together, each aiding the other. His radical idea was at odds with orthodox Darwinian theory, which hypothesized that geochemical processes evolved separately, creating the atmospheric environment in which living organisms emerged, adapted, and evolved—to wit, the environment as a storehouse of resources. Vernadsky suggested that the cycling of inert chemicals on Earth is influenced by the quality and quantity of living matter, and the living matter, in turn, influences the quality and quantity of inert chemicals being cycled through the planet. Today, scientists define the biosphere as

> an integrated living and life-supporting system comprising the peripheral envelope of Planet Earth together with its surrounding atmosphere, so far down, and up, as any form of life exists naturally.[40]

The biosphere is very thin, extending only from the ocean depths, where the most primitive forms of life exist, to the upper stratosphere. The entire length of the biosphere envelope is less than forty miles from ocean floor to outer space. Within this narrow band, living creatures, and the Earth's geochemical processes, interact to sustain each other.

In the 1970s, an English scientist, James Lovelock, and an American biologist, Lynn Margulis, expanded on Vernadsky's theory with the publication of the Gaia hypothesis. They argued that the Earth functions like a self-regulating living organism. The flora and fauna and the geochemical composition of the atmosphere work in a synergistic relationship to maintain the Earth's climate in a relatively steady state that is conducive to life.

Lovelock and Margulis use the example of the regulation of oxygen and methane to demonstrate how the cybernetic process between life and the geochemical cycle works to maintain a homeostatic climate regime. They remind us that oxygen levels on the planet must be confined within a very narrow range or the entire planet could erupt into flames, destroying all living matter, at least on the land surface. The two scientists believe that when the oxygen in the atmosphere rises above a tolerable level, a warning signal of some kind triggers an increase in methane production by microscopic bacteria. The increased methane migrates into the atmosphere, dampening the oxygen content until a steady state is reached again. (Methane acts as a regulator, both adding and taking away oxygen from the air.)

The constant interaction and feedback between living creatures and the geochemical content and cycles act as a unified system, maintaining the Earth's climate and environment and preserving life. The planet, then, is more like a living creature, a self-regulating entity that maintains itself in a steady state conducive to the continuance of life. According to the Gaian way of thinking, the adaptation and evolution of individual creatures become part of the larger process: the adaptation and evolution of the planet itself. It is the continuous symbiotic relationships between every living creature and between living creatures and the geochemical processes that ensure the survival of both the planetary organism and the individual species that live within its biospheric envelope.

Many other scientists have since weighed in on the Gaia thesis, moderating, qualifying, and expanding on Lovelock and Margulis's work. For more than two decades, the idea that the Earth functions as a living organism has become a critical avenue of exploration for rethinking the relationship between biology, chemistry, and geology.

If, in fact, the Earth does function as a living organism, then human activity that disrupts the biochemistry of that organism can lead to grave consequences, both for human life and the biosphere as a whole. The massive burning of fossil-fuel energy is the first example of human activity, on a global scale, that now threatens a radical shift in the climate of the Earth and the undermining of the biosphere that sustains all living creatures.

Our dawning awareness that the Earth functions as an indivisible living organism requires us to rethink our notions of global risks, vulnerability, and security. If every human life, the species as a whole, and all our fellow creatures are entwined with one another and with the geochemistry of the planet in a rich and complex choreography that sustains life itself, then we are, each and all, dependent on and responsible for the health of the whole organism. Carrying out that responsibility means living out our individual lives in our neighborhoods and communities in ways that promote the general well-being of the larger biosphere within which we dwell.

This is precisely the mission that the European Union has set for its twenty-five member states. The precautionary principle represents a deep acknowledgment that human beings' first obligation is to the biosphere that sustains life, even if it means waylaying a commercial development or suspending a particular economic activity. No economic activity, regardless of how lucrative or beneficial it might be, can be allowed to compromise the integrity of the life-support systems that make up the indivisible biosphere in which we all dwell, and from which we draw our sustenance. In those instances where there is reasonable, but not conclusive, evidence that a specific scientific experiment, technological application, or product introduction could do great harm to any part of the biosphere, the precautionary principle serves as a watch guard, ensuring that society will not act precipitously but will instead act conservatively, by forbidding or halting potentially adverse activity, until either the body of scientific evidence suggests that it is all right to proceed or alternatives are found to advance the same ends.

The precautionary principle is more than just a gatekeeper. It is also a more sophisticated methodology for assessing risks than the old linear models still in force in the United States. Its guiding principles and operating assumptions are based squarely on systems thinking. It takes a holistic approach to evaluating risks, asking how a said activity might affect the totality of relationships within the biospheric envelope. It requires an interdisciplinary approach to risk assessment and evaluation that examines all the possible impacts to the Earth as a whole of an intended activity.

I suspect that for Europeans, systems thinking is not so much of a stretch as it is for us in America. Here, the very idea of being part of a system seems a bit constraining. We don't easily take to the idea that we are not only a part of but also completely dependent on a larger community of relationships.

Perhaps the most interesting aspect of the new science, with its emphasis on relationships and feedback, is how closely it mirrors the network way of thinking that is beginning to permeate the commercial realm and governance. The science of ecology and the notion of a self-regulating biosphere are all about relationships and networks. Ecologist Bernard Patten has observed that "ecology *is* networks. . . . To understand ecosystems ultimately will be to understand networks."[41] Physicist and philosopher Fritjof Capra points out:

> As the network concept became more and more prominent in ecology, systemic thinkers began to use network models at all systems levels, viewing organisms as networks of cells, organs, and organ systems, just as ecosystems are understood as networks of individual organisms.[42]

In other words, every organism is made up of smaller networks of organs and cells while it is also part of larger networks that comprise biotic communities, whole ecosystems, and the biosphere itself. Each network is nested in networks above it while also made up of networks below it, in a complex choreography—what Capra calls "the web of life." Over aeons of evolutionary history, says Capra, "many species have formed such tightly knit communities that the whole system resembles a large, multicreatured organism."[43] If this description of the web of life seems remarkably similar to the emerging "network Europe" with its layers of embedded networks—the localities, the regions, the civil society organizations, the cultural diasporas, transnational companies, the member states, the European Union, and global institutions—the analogy is apt.

A new science is emerging—a second Enlightenment—whose operating principles and assumptions are more compatible with network ways of thinking. While the old science is characterized by detachment, expropriation, dissection, and reduction, the new science is characterized by engagement, replenishment, integration, and holism. The old science views nature as objects, the new science views nature as relationships. The old science is committed to making nature productive, the new science to making nature sustainable. The old science seeks power over nature, the new science seeks partnership with nature. The old science puts a premium on autonomy from nature, the new science on reparticipation with nature.

The new science takes us from a colonial vision of nature as an enemy to pillage and enslave, to a new vision of nature as a community to nurture. The right to exploit, harness, and own nature in the form of property is tempered by the obligation to steward nature and treat it with dignity and respect. The utility value of nature is slowly giving way to the intrinsic value of nature.

The second scientific Enlightenment has been in the making for nearly a century. The new fields of thermodynamics and organismic biology at the turn of the nineteenth century and the introduction of the uncertainty principle, quantum mechanics, process philosophy, and ecology in the early twentieth century; the birth of cybernetics and systems thinking along with information theory after World War II, and more recently the emergence of complexity theory; and the theories of dissipative structures and self-organization have all contributed to the deconstruction and fall of the scientific orthodoxy of traditional Enlightenment science, while helping to chart a fundamental new path for science in the coming century.

Unfortunately, much of our thinking about commerce, governance, and society and our relationship to the environment is still bound up in the old scientific paradigm. The new science needs to be more firmly imprinted in the public mind as well as in public policy to make a real difference. Still, the European Union is the first political unit to seriously entertain the new vision of the Earth as an indivisible living community deserving of respect.

By championing a host of global environmental treaties and accords and institutionalizing the precautionary principle into its regulatory policies, the EU has shown a willingness to act on its commitment to sustainable development and global environmental stewardship. The fact that its commitments in most areas remain weak and are often vacillating is duly noted. But at least Europe has established a new agenda for conducting science and technology that, if followed, could begin to wean the world from the old ways and toward a second scientific Enlightenment, one more in accord with its dream of inclusivity, diversity, sustainability, quality of life, and harmony.

Walking the Walk

The European Union is currently engaged in a number of initiatives, some small, others more grandiose, that represent a breakthrough in the way it approaches science and technology. All of these initiatives share a common theme. They are ecologically sensitive and designed and executed with an eye toward systems thinking and sustainable development. Together, they are vanguard projects of a second Enlightenment science.

At the very top of the list is Europe's new plan to become a fully integrated renewable-based hydrogen economy by mid-century. The EU has led the world in championing the Kyoto Protocol on climate change. To ensure compliance with the terms and deadlines outlined in the Kyoto Protocol, the EU has made a commitment to produce 22 percent of its electricity and 12 percent of all of its energy using renewable sources of energy by 2010.[44] Although a number of member states are lagging behind on meeting their renewable-energy targets, much to the consternation of Brussels, the very fact that the EU has set benchmarks at all puts them far ahead of the United States in making the shift from fossil fuels to renewable energy sources. The Bush Administration has consistently fought back attempts in the U.S. Congress to establish similar benchmarks for ushering in a renewable-energy regime in America.

In June 2003, the EU announced a bold plan to become a clean hydrogen economy by mid-century.[45] Interestingly enough, when U.S. industry got wind of Europe's plan, it lobbied the White House for an American initiative, fearing that the EU might leap ahead of the U.S. in the race to a hydrogen future. President Bush announced his administration's intentions to lead the world to a hydrogen economy in his State of the Union Address in 2003. But President Bush's approach to hydrogen differs significantly from the European undertaking.

Hydrogen is the basic element of the universe, the lightest element in existence, and, when used, emits only two by-products, pure water and heat. It is not, however, free-floating in nature but, rather, has to be extracted from other sources. Hydrogen can be extracted from fossil fuels, especially natural gas and coal, but then we're still left with CO_2 emissions. Nuclear power can also be harnessed to the task, but then we're left with nuclear waste that is dangerous to transport and not yet safe to bury. The other approach is to use renewable sources of energy—solar, wind, hydro, geothermal—to create electricity, and then use some of the excess electricity to electrolyze water, separating out hydrogen for storage and later use for transport needs or for backup generation for the power grid. Hydrogen can also be extracted from renewable energy crops and garbage. In other words, there's black hydrogen and green hydrogen, depending on the source from which the hydrogen is extracted.

Here's the problem. While Europe is committed to making a green hydrogen future, the Bush White House plan is to promote a black hydrogen future, using coal and nuclear power as the favorite means to extract the hydrogen. Critics accuse the administration of using hydrogen as a Trojan horse to bolster the interests of the old-energy industries. That's not to say that Europe is not engaged in the old energies as well, but its objective is to quickly wean the continent off of fossil fuels and nuclear power and move it toward a renewable-based hydrogen economy.

In his opening speech at the EU Conference on the Hydrogen Economy in June 2003, President Prodi warned that "our current approach to energy relies overwhelmingly on fossil and nuclear fuels. And this cannot go on forever."[46] The real issue, observed Prodi, "is whether we have enough air, land, and sea to dispose of the gaseous, liquid, and solid wastes from spent fossil and nuclear fuels used to produce energy. The answer is a clear 'no.'"[47] "The rational solution," said Prodi, "would be to turn resolutely towards renewable energies . . ." with hydrogen as the means to store them.[48] Prodi acknowledged that other countries were moving toward extracting hydrogen from the old-energy sources but said that he wanted to be "clear about what makes the European hydrogen programme truly visionary. It is our declared goal of achieving a step-by-step shift towards a fully integrated hydrogen economy, based on renewable energy sources, by the middle of the century."[49]

When President Prodi announced the European hydrogen initiative, he said it would be the next critical step in integrating Europe after the introduction of the euro. He likened the effort to the American space program in the 1960s and 1970s, whose multiplier effect helped spawn the high-tech economy of the 1980s and 1990s.

The European game plan is being implemented with a sense of history in mind. Great Britain became the world's leading power in the nineteenth century because it was the first country to harness its vast coal reserves with steam power. The U.S., in turn, became the world's pre-eminent power in the twentieth century because it was the first country to harness its vast oil reserves with the internal combustion engine. The multiplier effects of both energy revolutions were extraordinary. The EU is determined to lead the world into the third great energy revolution of the modern era, with the hope that it can combine its goal of sustainable development with new commercial opportunities that fit its new superpower ambitions.

The EU's commitment to sustainable development and a systems approach to the application of science and technology is showing up in a diverse number of fields and endeavors. Not surprisingly, given its deep cultural identification with rural life and food, Europe is taking the lead in the shift to sustainable farming practices and organic food production. While the U.S. sports a growing organic food sector—it represents the fastest-growing sector of the food industry—the U.S. government has done little to encourage organic food production and sustainable agricultural practices. Although the U.S. Department of Agriculture fields a small organic food research program, it amounts to only $3 million, or less than .004 percent of its $74 billion budget, hardly a serious effort. Moreover, while American consumers are increasing their purchases of organic food, still less than 0.3 percent of total U.S. farmland is currently in organic production.[50]

By contrast, many of the member states of the European Union have made the transition to organic agriculture a critical component of their economic development plans and have even set benchmarks, just as the EU did for bringing renewable sources of energy online. Germany, which has long been the economic engine of Europe and, more often than not, the leader in setting new environmental goals for the continent, has announced its intention to bring 20 percent of German agricultural output into organic production by 2020. (Organic agricultural output is now 3.2 percent of all farm output in Germany.)[51]

The Netherlands, Sweden, the U.K., Finland, Norway, Switzerland, Denmark, France, and Austria also have national programs to promote the transition to organic food production.[52] Denmark and Sweden enjoy the highest consumption of organic vegetables in Europe, and both countries project that their domestic markets for organic food will soon reach or exceed 10 percent of domestic consumption.[53]

Sweden has set a goal of having 20 percent of its total cultivated farm area in organic production by 2005. Italy already has 7.2 percent of its farmland under organic production, while Denmark is close behind with 7 percent.[54]

The U.K. doubled its organic food production in 2002 and now boasts the second-highest sales of organic food in Europe, after Germany. According to a recent survey, nearly 80 percent of U.K. households buy organic food.[55] By comparison, only 33 percent of American consumers buy any organic food.[56]

The contrast between American and European approaches to the future of farming highlights the differences between an older Enlightenment view of science and the new biosphere perspective. As we noted earlier in the chapter, in the U.S., more than half the agricultural fields are already given over to the production of genetically modified food crops. GM food crops, say critics, represent the ultimate expression of the Baconian approach to science, with its emphasis on waging war against nature and creating greater distance between human beings and the natural world. GM food crops are like tiny warriors in the fields. Armed with genes to ward off pests and viruses and tolerate large amounts of herbicides, the goal is to keep the forces of nature away—to create, if you will, islands of artificial order that are impenetrable by the wild.

Organic agriculture is organized along an entirely different set of principles. The idea is to use an array of agricultural practices to integrate farm production back into its local environment. The goal is not autonomy but, rather, embeddedness. To make that happen, farmers take a systems approach to agriculture, based on establishing symbiotic and mutually reinforcing relationships between crops, insects, birds, microorganisms, and the soil. Organic farms rely on organic fertilizers rather than petrochemical fertilizers, and natural pest controls as opposed to toxic-producing genes, insecticides, and pesticides. Organic farms treat the soil as a "living community" and use state-of-the-art technologies to nourish microbial inhabitants that release, transform, and transfer nutrients, always with an eye toward working with nature rather than holding it at bay. Organic farmers also use cover crops and crop rotation as a way of preventing weeds, insects, and disease organisms from inflicting harm on their fields. They also use various means to attract beneficial insects and birds to keep pests checked. Organic farmers plant crop strains whose genomic makeups are compatible with local ecosystem dynamics while paying close attention to the natural rhythms of recycling. Organic agriculture takes a systems approach, bringing together plant pathologists, entomologists, microbiologists, plant geneticists, breeders, and others to reconfigure arable land into mini-ecosystems made up of networks of symbiotic relationships that function together as total communities.

The science of organic agriculture challenges everything we know about how Enlightenment science ought to function. While we have traditionally thought of science as a tool to exploit nature's resources, a new generation of researchers has in mind a different course—using science to re-establish environmental relationships and build up natural communities.

The Rights of Animals

The new science doesn't eliminate reason and utility in its approach to nature, but it makes these values partially conditional on empathy and intrinsic value. Nowhere is this more apparent than in the EU's approach to our fellow creatures. Mohandas Gandhi once remarked that "the greatness of a nation and its moral progress can be judged by the way its animals are treated."[57] His view is in sharp contrast to René Descartes's belief that animals are merely "soulless automata," resources to be put to work or consumed, with little regard for their welfare. The plight of the Earth's creatures has changed little since. Some say their fate has worsened. While hard to imagine, our scientists tell us that we are approaching the absolute end of "the wild" after millions of years of life on Earth. In less than a century, there will be no wild left, strictly speaking, only parks.

If the thought of loss of the wild is sad to entertain, the mass extinction of our fellow species is even more disquieting. According to a study conducted by an international group of scientists and published in the journal *Nature* in 2004, 15 to 37 percent of all the remaining plant and animal species on Earth might be heading toward extinction by 2050. Species are now going extinct at alarming rates—between one hundred and one thousand times as fast as in the past.[58] This time around, it is "man" himself, not meteorites from outer space or volcanic eruptions, who is responsible for the mass death. Global warming, say the researchers who carried out the study, is the primary contributing cause of the increased extinction rates.

While wild animals are seeing the shrinking of their habitats and a precipitous decline in their numbers, research animals and domestic farm animals face, perhaps, the grimmest existence of all the creatures on Earth. Subject to barbaric experiments in research laboratories and raised under horrific conditions on factory farms, these animals suffer cruel fates.

Now, the European Union and its member countries have embarked on a series of initiatives designed to create a far more humane environment for wild animals as well as for animals used in scientific experiments or raised for human consumption. The new European agenda extends the idea of universal rights—although tentatively—to our fellow creatures, in ways that would have been considered inconceivable in public policy just a decade or two ago.

The advanced industrial countries have long had statutes on the books protecting animal welfare and providing humane treatment of animals. Unfortunately, they have been cursory, at best, with little effective enforcement. That's all beginning to change in the EU. The big breakthrough in thinking came with the inclusion of two words in a protocol on animal welfare attached to the Amsterdam Treaty. The EU member states declared that "to ensure improved protection and respect for the welfare of animals as sentient beings," they agreed to "pay full regard to the welfare requirements of animals."[59] The key words are "sentient beings." Never before had any government recognized other creatures as sentient beings, with feelings and consciousness. Then, in March 2002, the German Bundestag shocked the world community by becoming the first parliament in the world to guarantee animal rights in its constitution. By an overwhelming vote of 543 to 15, lawmakers added animals to a clause that requires the government to respect and protect the dignity of humans.[60] The new German law reads: "The state takes responsibility for protecting the natural foundations of life and animals in the interest of future generations."[61] The new law will require the German government to weigh animal rights against other rights for the first time, including the rights to conduct research and practice religion. (Many religions, for example, use ritual slaughter in their ceremonies.)

The very idea of extending fundamental rights to animals would be greeted with bewilderment in American public policy circles. Have Europeans lost their minds? That's the kind of response one hears, especially from American researchers and representatives of agribusiness. Yet, strangely enough, new behavioral research studies conducted by scientists are giving credence to the idea that animals are indeed sentient beings, deserving of respect and the protection of their fundamental rights under the law. Even stranger, much of the new research on animal behavior is sponsored by companies such as McDonald's, Burger King, KFC, and other fast-food purveyors.

Pressured by animal rights activists and by growing public support for the humane treatment of animals, these companies have financed research into, among other things, the emotional, mental, and behavioral states of animals. What the researchers are finding is unsettling. It appears that many animal species are more like us than we had ever imagined. They feel pain, suffer, and experience stress, affection, excitement, and even love. Studies on pigs' social behavior at Purdue University in the United States, for example, have found that they crave affection and are easily depressed if isolated or denied playtime with one another. The lack of mental and physical stimuli can result in deterioration of health and increased incidence of various diseases. The European Union has taken such studies to heart and outlawed the use of inhumane isolating pig stalls by 2012 and mandated their replacement with open-air stalls. In Germany, the government is encouraging pig farmers to give each pig twenty seconds of human contact each day and to provide them with two or three toys to prevent them from fighting with one another.[62]

The pig study only scratches the surface of what is going on in the exploding new field of research into animal emotions and cognitive abilities. Researchers were taken back recently by the publication of an article in the journal *Science* that reported on the conceptual abilities of New Caledonian crows. In controlled experiments, scientists at Oxford University reported that two birds named Betty and Abel were given a choice between using two tools, one a straight wire, the other a hooked wire, to snag a piece of meat from inside a tube. Both chose the hooked wire. But then, unexpectedly, Abel, the more dominant male, stole Betty's hook, leaving her with only a straight wire. Unphased, Betty used her beak to wedge the wire in a crack and then bent it with her beak to produce a hook, like the one stolen from her. She then snagged the food from inside the tube. Researchers repeated the experiment ten more times, giving her just straight wires, and she fashioned a hook out of the wire nine of the times, demonstrating a sophisticated ability to create tools.

Then there is the story of Alex the African gray parrot, who was able to master tasks previously thought to be the preserve of human beings. Alex can identify more than forty objects and seven colors and can add and separate objects into categories. He is even able to learn abstract concepts like "same" or "different" and solve problems using information provided to him.[63]

Equally impressive is Koko, a 300-pound gorilla who was taught sign language and has mastered more than one thousand signs and understands more than two thousand English words. On human IQ tests, she scores between 70 and 95, putting her in the slow learner—but not retarded—category.[64]

Toolmaking and the development of sophisticated language skills are just two of the many attributes we thought were exclusive to our species. Self-awareness is another. Philosophers and animal behaviorists have long argued that other animals are not capable of self-awareness because they lack a sense of individualism. Not so, according to a spate of new studies. At the Washington National Zoo, orangutans given mirrors explore parts of their bodies they can't see otherwise, showing a sense of self. An orangutan named Chantek, who lives at the Atlanta Zoo, showed remarkable self-awareness. He used a mirror to groom his teeth and adjust his sunglasses, says his trainer.[65]

When it comes to the ultimate test of what distinguishes humans from the other creatures, scientists have long believed that mourning for the dead represents the real divide. Other animals have no sense of their mortality and are unable to comprehend the concept of their own death. Not necessarily so. Animals, it appears, experience grief. Elephants will often stand next to their dead kin for days, in silence, occasionally touching their bodies with their trunks. Kenyan biologist Joyce Poole, who has studied African elephants for twenty-five years, says that elephant behavior toward their dead "leaves me with little doubt that they experience deep emotion and have some understanding of death."[66]

We also know that virtually all animals play, especially when young.

Anyone who has ever observed the antics of puppies, cats, and bear cubs cannot help but notice the similarities in the way they and our own children play. Recent studies in the brain chemistry of rats show that when they play, their brains release large amounts of dopamine, a neurochemical associated with pleasure and excitement in human beings.

Noting the similarities in brain anatomy and chemistry between humans and other animals, Steven Siviy, a behavioral scientist at Gettysburg College in Pennsylvania, asks a question increasingly on the minds of other researchers: "If you believe in evolution by natural selection, how can you believe that feelings suddenly appeared, out of the blue, with human beings?"[67]

The new findings of researchers are a far cry from the conceptions espoused by orthodox science. Until very recently, scientists were still advancing the idea that most creatures behaved by sheer instinct and that what appeared to be learned behavior was merely genetically wired activity. Now we know that geese have to teach their goslings their migration routes. In fact, we are finding out that learning is passed on from parent to offspring far more often than not and that most animals engage in all kinds of learned experience brought on by continued experimentation and trial-and-error problem-solving.

So what does all of this portend for the way we treat our fellow creatures? What about the thousands of animals subjected each year to painful laboratory experiments? Or the millions of domestic animals raised under the most inhumane conditions and destined for slaughter and human consumption? Should we ban leghold traps and discourage the sale and purchase of fur coats? And what about killing animals for sport? Foxhunting in the English countryside, bullfighting in Spain, cockfighting in Mexico? What about entertainment? Should wild lions be caged in zoos? Should elephants be made to perform in circuses?

These questions are beginning to be raised in courtrooms and in legislation around the world. Today, Harvard and twenty-five other law schools in the United States alone have introduced law courses on animal rights, and an increasing number of cases representing the rights of animals are entering the court system.

But it's in Europe where the campaign on behalf of animals has progressed the furthest. The House of Commons of the British Parliament voted overwhelmingly in June 2003 to ban the ancient practice of foxhunting.[68] The bill still faces tough opposition in the House of Lords, whose aristocratic members have long regarded the sport as a national pastime of British royalty. Still, even Queen Elizabeth now has her doubts, according to observers. The British paper *The Mirror* reports that the queen has asked Prince Charles to give up the sport to avoid further adverse publicity in the media and negative feelings among the general public.[69]

The growing interest in the plight of animals in the European Union is the logical outcome of the commitment to sustainable development and global environmental stewardship. Protecting the biosphere means looking after all the other creatures who sojourn with us here on Earth. And, if all the networks of living communities that make up our common biosphere are indeed connected and embedded in myriad symbiotic relationships, then harm to any particular species is likely to have negative repercussions for other species, including human beings. Certainly that has been the case when it comes to the humane treatment of farm animals. For example, BSE in cattle occurred because farmers fed cattle remnants to cattle, to save costs. Feeding cattle back to cattle—a form of cattle cannibalism—precipitated the brain-wasting disease. Ultimately, human beings who ate contaminated beef died of Creutzfeldt-Jakob disease.

The best current example of the dictum that what's harmful to the other animals is harmful to us is the overuse of antibiotics. Because cattle, pigs, chickens, and other farm animals are kept in close containment facilities on factory farms, the stress weakens their immune systems, making them more prone to disease. The diseases, in turn, spread quickly among cramped herds and flocks. The result is that more antibiotics are required. The increase in antibiotics leads to the buildup of more resistant strains of bacteria, making existing antibiotics less effective in treatment. Today, our species faces what health officials call a grave health danger because our current antibiotics are less effective in stamping out deadly bacteria. There are now new bacteria strains that are resistant to virtually all of the known antibiotics on the market, raising the very real danger of spreading global pandemics.

The notion of the connectivity and embeddedness of all of life, then, is becoming powerfully clear when it comes to the spread of diseases from animals to humans. Much of the new EU animal-protection legislation is intended to create a virtuous cycle between animals and humans, with the understanding that if animals suffer from ill health at our hands, the health effects can and often do come back to haunt us as well.

Consider, for example, the case of poultry. The vast majority of the world's 4,700 million egg-laying hens are kept in tiny battery cages so small that they are unable to even flap their wings, let alone make room for a nest for their eggs.[70] The spaces are so cramped that the birds' bones become brittle and often snap with the slightest disturbance. The inhumane treatment of hens in factory farms causes periodic outbreaks of salmonella and campylobacter jejuni in eggs and poultry and outbreaks of food poisoning among humans. The European Union, which is the world's second-largest egg producer, after China, has agreed to ban battery cages by 2012.[71] The United States government has yet to pass similar legislation, and the prospects are dim that it ever will.

Perhaps no area of animal protection elicits more heated debate than animal experimentation for medical research. That is because in the minds of scientists and much of the public, the issue often becomes one of the rights of animals versus the rights of human beings. Medical researchers argue that if they are unable to test new drugs or surgical procedures on animals, it could mean that cures for serious human diseases won't be found in time and that lives will be needlessly lost. Animal-rights activists counter that far more animals are sacrificed than necessary in these experiments and that little is often gained in attempting to extrapolate from clinical studies in animals and then apply the results to humans. And even if some testing of animals does result in medical breakthroughs, it doesn't justify sacrificing, for example, the chimpanzee's life for a human life. Besides, alternatives to animal testing now exist, especially with sophisticated computer modeling—making the barbaric practices both antiquated and unnecessary.

The European Union has become the first government to issue a directive to state "that efforts must be undertaken to replace animal experiments with alternative methods."[72] Where alternative models are not available, the European Commission directs researchers to choose "between experiments, those which use the minimal number of animals, involve animals with the lowest degree of neurophysiological sensitivity, cause the least pain, suffering, distress or lasting harm and which are the most likely to provide satisfactory results."[73] The commission even suggests that a benchmark and timetable be set for replacing 50 percent of the animal experiments with alternative models.[74] While the benchmarking has not yet been accepted, its mere proposal puts the EU far ahead of public policy consciousness on the matter in the United States.

The European Union has already agreed to ban the testing of animals for cosmetic products, something American animal-rights activists have sought for years to no avail. The EU ban not only covers animal testing within member states but also prohibits the sale of cosmetic products in the EU that have been tested on animals, including those coming from outside the Union.[75]

These bold undertakings designed to advance the interests of our fellow creatures and establish a more balanced ecology between humans and animals have not come without costs. The European Union worries that its progressive policies on animals are putting it at a disadvantage with countries whose animal-protection laws are weak or virtually nonexistent. For example, the EU estimates that the cost of eliminating individual sow stalls is 0.006 to 0.02 euros per kilogram of pig carcass. In egg production, creating more space for hens is expected to increase costs by 16 percent in 2012.[76] To meet this challenge, the EU is taking its case for animal protection and animal rights to its trading partners, with the hope that bilateral efforts will help promote similar animal-welfare reforms in other countries. The EU is also actively pursuing labeling so that consumers can be informed of humane practices. Egg labeling has already been enacted.

In a communiqué issued in November 2002, the European Commission made clear that the focus of the EU agricultural policy is increasingly on "quality rather than quantity."[77] For the EU, a "quality approach" means thinking about how best to optimize the entire network of relations that comprise the food system. The commission defines the quality concept as one that "embraces a range of priorities including improved food safety, environmental protection, rural development, the preservation of the landscape and animal welfare."[78] The U.S. has no sequel in public policy to this kind of broad systems approach that looks at integrating all of these spheres in a single network of mutual interests.

The extension of human empathy to a consideration of the integrity of our fellow creatures marks a watershed event in human governance. If all beings are truly connected in an indivisible web of life, tucked inside the biospheric envelope, then recognizing and safeguarding those relationships is essential to realizing a new, more holistic scientific vision, as well as to promoting sustainable development and a truly global consciousness.

Reuniting Ecosystems

Nowhere is this new understanding of nature as an indivisible web of life more in evidence than in the promotion of "transborder peace parks," a radical new concept that is fast gaining currency around the world, but especially in Europe. The idea is to establish trans-frontier conservation areas to reconnect natural ecosystems formerly severed by nation-state borders. The logic behind these transboundary protected areas was eloquently stated by Dr. Z. Pallo Jordan, then South African minister of Environmental Affairs and Tourism, in an opening address at the meeting on Transboundary Protected Areas in Cape Town, South Africa, in 1997. Jordan observed that

> the rivers of Southern Africa are shared by more than one country. Our mountain ranges do not end abruptly because some 19th century politician drew a line on a map. The winds, the oceans, the rain and atmospheric currents do not recognize political frontiers. The earth's environment is the common property of all humanity and creation, and what takes place in one country affects not only its neighbors, but many others well beyond its borders.[79]

Transboundary protected areas are first and foremost designed to secure the integrity of regional ecosystems and preserve biodiversity and natural habitats. They also serve two other related functions: to preserve cultural resources and values, especially of transboundary people, and to promote peace among countries. Europe boasts the largest number of transborder parks, some forty-five in all, followed by Africa, with thirty-four transnational parks. There are currently one hundred and fifty-eight such parks around the world, and their numbers have grown rapidly each year.[80]

The notion of setting aside valued natural environments and establishing parks is not a new idea. Kings and lords often cordoned off areas as special game preserves to be used exclusively for hunting by members of the royal family.

The modern notion of national parks was inaugurated on March 1, 1872, when the U.S. government declared the Yellowstone area of Wyoming a "public park and pleasuring ground for the benefit and enjoyment of the people."[81] The national-park movement spread throughout the world in the ensuing century. Where formerly countries saw the environment as a force to tame and harness for productive economic value, the national-park idea introduced the concept of the intrinsic value of nature as something worth preserving, unspoiled, for the aesthetic enjoyment of people. It was only later that national parks were viewed also as a way of conserving natural ecosystems in order to enhance the proper functioning of the Earth's life-support systems. The Amazon park system is a good example of this second rationale.

The idea of transborder parks is even more radical in concept and design. Recall that the early science of the Enlightenment was dedicated to enclosing nature and transforming it into private property negotiable in the marketplace and protected inside nation-state boundaries. Nature as resource has been the dominant theme of science for the past several centuries.

Transborder peace parks are an acknowledgment by governments that nature's boundaries eclipse state boundaries—that they exist a priori over any political border and deserve to be reconnected and maintained as integral systems. Europe has taken the lead in advancing transborder parks, although African nations have made significant strides of their own. The idea that natural ecosystems are to be reunited and that governments have the responsibility to work together to create a transnational space for managing them would have been unthinkable just a few years ago. Again, as we've seen in the case of extending universal human rights, there is a growing awareness in Europe, and elsewhere, that national boundaries are no longer the endgame when it comes to managing both human affairs and our relationship to the natural world.

Transborder peace parks are managed cooperatively by the countries involved. The objectives include

> supporting long-term co-operative conservation of biodiversity, ecosystem services, and natural and cultural values across boundaries; promoting landscape-level ecosystem management through integrated bioregional land-use planning and management; building trust, understanding, reconciliation and co-operation between and among countries, communities, agencies and other stakeholders; preventing and/or resolving tension, including over access to natural resources; promoting access to, and equitable and sustainable use of natural resources, consistent with national sovereignty; and enhancing the benefits of conservation.[82]

The recognition that natural ecosystems need to be managed as integral wholes, and not severed into bits and pieces to conform to arbitrary political boundaries, is a reflection of the extent to which systems analysis has gained a foothold in scientific thinking and public policy. Only by reconnecting the deep network of relationships that allow natural ecosystems to function appropriately can natural environments be preserved in any meaningful way. For example, a large contiguous and unrestricted area is often essential in order to maintain the minimum viable population of specific species—especially large carnivores. Where flora and fauna exist across a political boundary, it is easier to manage their populations and ensure their survival if done cooperatively and jointly. Likewise, research agendas are easier to carry out if knowledge and expertise can be shared between countries. Transborder parks are often managed by a network of interested parties, including states, localities, and regions as well as scientists, CSOs, and the private sector.

Italy and France established a transborder park in 1992 to better protect the migratory range of the ibex. The wild goats use a summer range in France and spend winters in Italy. The Italians established the Grand Paradiso National Park in 1922, primarily to protect the ibex. Since the ibex was protected only in the winter in Italy, the French finally made the decision to create the Vanoise National Park to ensure a seamless protected zone for the ibex throughout its migratory range. A formal agreement between the two parks to twin came in 1972, leading to an expansion of their common boundary from six to fourteen kilometers. Now the ibex is protected year-round in a transborder park.[83]

Poland and Slovakia created a transnational park along their border. The park creates a seamless region in the Tatra Mountains, the highest point in the Carpathian mountain range. The region is rich in biodiversity and includes karst limestone and dolomite scenery, alpine meadows, and temperate forests, lakes, and rocky peaks, and is the home of many endemic or relic species such as the Tatra subspecies of the chamois deer, the marmot, and bear and lynx populations. A number of glacial relic fish also inhabit mountain lakes in the region. The park has become a major tourist destination, with more than eight million people visiting the area each year.[84]

The potential of transborder parks to play a peace role while carrying out an environmental mission is brought home in the case of two national parks that bridge the borders between Poland and Belarus. It turns out that the Bialowieza National Park in Poland and the Belovezhskaya Pushcha

National Park just across the border in Belarus together encompass the last remaining primeval forest in all of Europe. The forest dividing the two countries is also the home of the last remaining herds of rare European bison, the largest land animal on the continent. The creature once roamed all of Europe like its North American counterpart. Now, the five hundred or so remaining animals are separated from one another by an eight-foot-high metal fence. In addition, a thirty-foot-wide security road patrolled by guards cuts through the forest where the bison roam. The fence is a relic of the Soviet era and was constructed to keep Polish dissidents from entering Belarus. Today, the fence still keeps people from enjoying full access to both parks and bison from freely crossing through the forest.

Conservationists and peace activists have been actively pursuing the idea of creating a transborder peace park as a way to lessen tensions along the border between the two countries and create a common ground for cooperation in managing their shared ecosystems, with the hope that such cooperation might expand to include greater political, cultural, and commercial exchanges. Cross-border cooperation is slowly increasing between the two countries, but they are a long way from creating a formal structure that will make the park management truly seamless. Recently, when Belarus needed bison, Poland provided them, and when the Poles needed rare pines, the Belarusians gave them trees. Still, not until the fence comes down and the bison can roam freely through the primeval forest will the ecosystem be on its way to being truly reconnected.[85]

Reuniting ecosystems is a revolutionary idea, especially when it means placing nature's boundaries above national boundaries. Transborder peace parks also challenge still another fundamental assumption of the modern era—the sanctity of private property. With peace parks, "mine vs. thine" is replaced with the notion of "ours." Ownership of nature becomes less important than access to it. The utility value of nature is no longer the only measure of its worth. Rather, its intrinsic value comes to the fore and becomes of equal worth. With the reintroduction of intrinsic value, humanity gives credence to the notion that nature, too, has a right to exist and be recognized just like every human being. Transborder peace parks extend the notion of universal human rights to include the rights of the rest of nature.

IT'S TOO EARLY to say for sure whether Europe is leading the world into a second Enlightenment. Certainly its multilateral agreements, its internal treaties and directives, and its bold cutting-edge initiatives suggest a radical re-evaluation in the way science and technology are approached and executed. The increased reliance on the precautionary principle and systems thinking puts Europe out in front of the United States and other countries in re-envisioning science and technology issues in a globally connected world. Still, a word of caution is in order. The old power-driven Enlightenment science remains the dominant approach in the research, development, and market introduction of most new technologies, products, and services in Europe, America, and elsewhere in the world. Whether the EU government can effectively apply new-science thinking in its regulatory regime to old-science commercial applications in the marketplace remains to be seen. In the long run, a successful transition to a new scientific era will depend on whether industry itself can begin to internalize the precautionary principle and systems thinking into its R&D plans, creating new technologies, products, and services that are, from the get-go, ecologically sensitive and sustainable.

16

Universalizing the European Dream

E UROPE HAS BECOME the new "city upon a hill." The world is looking to this grand new experiment in transnational governance, hoping it might provide some much needed guidance on where humanity ought to be heading in a globalizing world. The European Dream, with its emphasis on inclusivity, diversity, quality of life, sustainability, deep play, universal human rights and the rights of nature, and peace is increasingly attractive to a generation anxious to be globally connected and at the same time locally embedded.

Although it's too early to tell exactly how successful the "United States" of Europe will ultimately prove to be, what I think is sure is that in an era where space and time are quickly being annihilated and identities are becoming multilayered and global in scale, no nation will be able to go it alone twenty-five years from now. European states are the first to understand and act upon the emerging realities of a globally interdependent world. Others will follow.

Exporting the EU Model

Steps are being taken in various regions of the world to establish free-trade zones and cross-border political alliances. The North American

Free Trade Agreement (NAFTA), Mercorsur in South America, and the Organization of African States (OAS) are all attempting to create the beginning of a transnational political model to harmonize their markets and gain some global advantage in developing regional economies of scale.

NAFTA is least likely among the experiments to develop into a full-fledged political union, at least along the EU lines. The United States is so much more powerful than its two trading partners, Canada and Mexico, that it would be impossible to create anything remotely resembling a partnership among relatively equal players. The U.S. GDP is nearly eight times the size of Canada's and Mexico's combined GDP.[1] The only way to imagine a regional political union even occurring would be if both Canada and Mexico were to become the fifty-first and fifty-second states, which, though far-fetched, is not entirely impossible. Even though Canadian sensibilities are far more closely aligned with Europe than with the U.S., the economic necessities of a regionalizing world may force Canada to increasingly give up its sovereignty and become an extension of the U.S. There is also the possibility that Canada might eventually join the European Union. After all, Hawaii and Alaska joined the United States of America even though they are not part of the country's contiguous geography. Mexico, although far poorer than the U.S.—it ranks as the world's tenth economic power—could potentially be absorbed into the United States as Mexican immigration over the next half century transforms a large portion of America into a Hispanic cultural diaspora, further blurring the lines between the two countries.[2]

But the absorption of Canada and Mexico into the United States, creating, in effect, a superstate, would only make the U.S. more of an oddity in a globalized world where other nations are pooling or giving up much of their sovereignty and becoming part of transnational regional political organizations. What's more likely to happen is that the three countries of North America will move closer toward a free-trade zone but fall short of creating either a superstate or a transnational political space.

China and India face even greater obstacles in a world where the nation-state model is less able to accommodate global commercial and cultural forces. The very idea that either of these two nation-states could effectively contain and manage more than a billion people, each under the aegis of a singular national identity, is hard to comprehend in a world where crosscutting identities and loyalties are pushing people into more flexible networks of convenience. Chances are that both India and China will at least partially deconstruct into more semiautonomous local regions and that these regions will establish their own trans-regional and global commercial and political networks. Both nation-states could simply disappear altogether under the weight of fractionalization, leaving their respective regions the tasks of reconstituting themselves into transnational political unions, more along the European Union lines.

The most likely candidate region to follow on the heels of the European Union is the East Asian community, with or without China's participation. The region has been flirting with the idea of an Asian version of the European Union for more than thirty-five years. In 1967, Indonesia, Malaysia, the Philippines, Singapore, and Thailand established the Association of Southeast Asian Nations (ASEAN) with the objective of furthering economic and social cooperation in the region and providing a measure of collective security from outside interference.

In 1976, the countries that make up ASEAN signed the Declaration of ASEAN Accord, which committed the member states to "the early establishment of the Zone of Peace, Freedom, and Neutrality."[3] The parties agreed to "noninterference in the internal affairs of one another" and provided for the creation of a ministerial high council to mediate disputes between member states and recommend measures to resolve conflicts.

Brunei Darussalam joined ASEAN in 1984, followed by Vietnam in 1995. Laos and Myanmar joined the association in 1997, and Cambodia in 1999, bringing all ten Southeast Asian countries under the ASEAN umbrella.[4]

In 1998, the ten member countries of ASEAN joined with the republics of Korea, Japan, and China to form the East Asian Vision Group (EAVG). In 2001, EAVG issued a report entitled "Towards an East Asian Community: Region of Peace, Prosperity and Progress." The vision group made a number of recommendations that, if carried out, would pave the way toward an Asian version of the European Union. The key proposals fall into six categories: economic cooperation; financial cooperation; political and security cooperation; environmental cooperation; social and cultural cooperation; and institutional cooperation.

The authors of the report called for establishing the East Asia Free Trade Area (EAFTA): promoting development and technological cooperation among the signatory countries; realizing a knowledge-based economy across the region; establishing and strengthening mechanisms for addressing threats to peace in the region; broadening political cooperation with respect to national governing issues; amplifying the East Asian voice in international affairs; institutionalizing multilateral environmental cooperation within the region and on a global level; establishing poverty alleviation programs; adopting programs to provide greater access to basic health-care services; implementing a comprehensive human resource development program focusing on improvement of basic education, skills training, and corporate building; promoting regional identity and consciousness; and cooperating on projects in the conservation and promotion of East Asian arts and culture.[5]

The report noted that "in the past, political rivalries, historical animosities, cultural differences and ideological confrontations posed barriers to cooperation among East Asian nations."[6] On the other hand, the report also observed that "East Asian nations share geographical proximity, many common historical experiences, and similar cultural norms and values."[7] The report's authors said they envision "the progressive integration of the East Asian economy, ultimately leading to an East Asian economic community."[8]

An East Asian economic community would be a formidable economic and political force on the world stage. The combined land area of East Asia (including China, Korea, and Japan) is 50 percent larger than the United States. Its GDP would approach the European Union's and the United States'. The volume of East Asian trade is already larger than that of the United States, but only 40 percent of the EU's.[9] With a population of two billion, it would represent one-third of the human race.

China is the wild card in any attempt to forge an Asian union. Because of its sheer size, China might simply try to dominate and intimidate its neighbors, forcing them to submit to its suzerainty as it has so frequently done in the past. The formation of an East Asian economic community with the potential inclusion of Japan and South Korea could serve as a counterweight to Chinese hegemony in the region.

How serious is the possibility that the member states of the Southeast Asian nations might forge an Asian version of the European Union, with or without the participation of Japan, South Korea, and China? The Asian Development Bank, for one, thinks that the prospect is likely enough that it prepared and published a report, in 2002, on the costs and benefits of a common currency for ASEAN. The report concluded that "although the constraints on the adoption of the common currency by ASEAN are formidable, the long-run goal of a common currency for the region may be worth considering seriously, especially because, judged by the criterion of an optimum currency area, the region is as suitable for the adoption of a common currency as Europe was prior to the Maastricht Treaty."[10]

As of late 2003, ASEAN found itself at a historic juncture. Already well along the way toward creating an East Asia Free Trade Area, the member countries have now embarked on a serious discussion around the prospect of creating an ASEAN economic community, similar to the EU, by 2020.[11] A full-fledged common market would mean a free flow of trade in the region as well as free mobility of labor and capital. Closer political cooperation and a pooling of national sovereignty interests within a larger transnational union are likely to follow suit.

No one doubts the commercial advantages of Asian countries pooling their economic interests. The question remains whether there is enough of a common bond beyond pure pecuniary interests to suggest that a more integrated political partnership is doable and viable in the long run. For all of the conflicts between nationalities and governments in Europe over the course of the past two millennia, there is at least some common philosophical, theological, and cultural bonds that Europeans share, including Greek science, Roman law, Christianity, the Renaissance and Reformation, Enlightenment science, and the first and second industrial revolutions.

In the fall of 2003, I attended a gathering in Seoul, South Korea, of government ministers and business leaders, academics, and CSOs from across Asia, on the subject of how best to create an Asian union similar to the European Union. The sponsoring organization, the East Asian Common Space, has been one of the key players in advancing the idea of a transnational governing body for Asia. I put the question of community to some of the members of the association's executive committee. Koji Kakizawa, the former minister for foreign affairs for Japan, pointed out that the historical influence of Taoism, Confucianism, and Buddhism in East Asia provided a common philosophical, theological, and cultural context for uniting Asian people and that, in many ways, Asians were even better prepared than Europeans to advance the European Dream of inclusivity, diversity, sustainability, quality of life, deep play, and peace because of their shared worldview.

Richard E. Nisbett has written an insightful book on the topic of "how Asians and Westerners think differently," entitled *The Geography of Thought*. His account of the Asian mind gives credence to the idea that Asian peoples and countries might be even better suited than Europeans to create network governance, a transnational space, and a global consciousness.

Nisbett points out that the Western mind sees the world more as objects in isolation, while the Eastern mind views the world more as relationships that exist within an overall context. The Western mind puts a premium on the individual, the Eastern mind on the group. In the East, individual identity is inseparable from the group relations of which one is a part. In Confucian thought, writes philosopher Henry Rosemount, "There can be no me in isolation, to be considered abstractly: I am the totality of roles I live in relation to specific others. . . . Taken collectively, they weave, for each of us, a unique pattern of personal identity, such that if some of my roles change, the others will of necessity change also, literally making me a different person."[12]

The Eastern mind is also conditioned to appreciate a world full of contradictions. The Western mind, and especially the American mind, is quite different. We tend to see the world more in rational terms and act to resolve or overcome contradictions, believing them to be impediments to pure knowledge and progress. The Eastern mind, notes Nisbett, takes the view that "to understand and appreciate one state of affairs requires the experience of its opposite."[13] The whole, in this schema, lies in the relationship that exists between opposite forces. Together they complete each other.

Confucianism, Taoism, and Buddhism all concentrate on the whole rather than the parts—what we in the West call a systems approach. "All three orientations," says Nisbett, share "concerns about harmony, holism, and the mutual influence of everything on almost everything else."[14] The idea that every event is related to every other event makes the Asian mind more interested in the relationships between phenomena rather than the phenomena in isolation.

The constant attention to relationships also makes Asians more sensitive to the feelings of others, according to Nisbett. American parents concentrate on objects and prepare their kids to think in terms of expropriation, acquisition, and property relations—a "mine vs. thine" mentality. Asian parents spend far more time with their kids focusing on feelings and social relations, to help children "anticipate the reactions of other people with whom they will have to coordinate their behavior."[15]

It's not surprising, given their more holistic orientation, that Asians emphasize harmony of humans and nature. While Enlightenment science is based on the idea of remaking nature to suit man's image, the Eastern way, says political scientist Mushakaji Kinhide, "rejects the idea that man can manipulate the environment and assumes instead that he adjusts himself to it."[16] In practice, Asian peoples have become as adept as Westerners at manipulating and despoiling the environment for short-term commercial ends. The difference, however, is that whereas in the West, the exploitation of nature is part and parcel of the Enlightenment worldview, in the East, current environmentally harmful policies are, at least, at odds with the traditional Asian notion of humanity's harmonious relationship to the natural world.

Given their preoccupation with relationships, Asians are understandably less interested in discovering the truth than in knowing "the way." It's knowing how to relate to "the other," not how to acquire "the other," that's ultimately important. If "the way" seems suspiciously close to Whiteheadian process philosophy, it is.

Because of their emphasis on harmonious relationships and the good of the whole, Asians are more likely to emphasize the success of the group rather than the self-interest of the individual. Indeed, in Chinese, Nisbett reminds us, "there is no word for 'individualism.' The closest one can come is the word for 'selfishness.' "[17]

Try to imagine the Asian mind grasping hold of the essentials of the American Dream, with its emphasis on individuality, self-advancement, autonomy, and exclusivity. Nisbett sums up the difference between an Asian frame of mind and a Western frame of mind this way:

> East Asians live in an interdependent world in which the self is part of a larger whole; Westerners live in a world in which the self is a unitary free agent. Easterners value success and achievement in good part because they reflect well on the groups they belong to; Westerners value these things because they are badges of personal merit.[18]

The Asian frame of mind, at first glance, seems tailor-made for a network world and a globalizing society, with its focus on relationships, inclusivity, consensus, harmony, and contextual thinking. To a good extent, this common mindset is likely to serve Asian societies well in a quest to create a transnational political space in an increasingly interconnected and interdependent world. On the other hand, and this may just be my Western bias, what's lacking from the Asian frame is sufficient individual differentiation to make each person feel a sense of deep personal responsibility for making his or her own way in the new world. The Asian way doesn't always allow the individual to flower. If the self isn't completely sacrificed for the whole, at least its full potential is often muted in the interest of advancing the welfare of the collective. If the American mindset is too individualistic and Darwinian, the Asian mindset might be equally criticized for being too oriented toward "group think." Neither mentality alone is ideally suited for a connected world. New technologies are so decentralized and democratized but at the same time so globally connective that they foster both extreme individuation and extreme integration concurrently. Creating a new vision of humanity that can bring together these two seemingly contradictory forces into a new synthetic relationship is the key to making the coming era a transformative period in human history.

My personal belief is that Europe is best positioned between the extreme individuation of America and the extreme collectivism of Asia to lead the way into the new age. European sensibility makes room for both the individual spirit and collective responsibility. To the extent that the European vision can incorporate the best qualities of the American and Asian ways of looking at the world, its dream will become an ideal for both West and East to aspire to.

Cold Evil and Universal Ethics

Creating a global consciousness presupposes an integrated persona that is capable of combining both individual free will and a collective sense of responsibility on a planetary playing field. Accepting another individual's humanity is a deeply personal act. It requires each individual to recognize "the other." While a group can help condition individual behavior and predispose its members to be empathetic, the feeling itself has to emanate from the individual, not the group. Where the collective responsibility comes in is in guaranteeing universal human rights and establishing codes of conduct and rules of enforcement to ensure compliance and punish wrongdoers.

How, then, does the European Dream become a truly universal dream? It would have to incorporate a new code of behavior that allows the individual to fully comprehend how his or her own very personal behavior and choices ripple out and affect the rest of the world. Universal human rights will succeed only if personal morality and ethics are universalized as well.

The European Dream has begun to advance the cause of universal morality, but only very tentatively. In a post-modern world where meta-narratives are treated with suspicion, any talk of universal morality is likely to be regarded with nervous dread. Post-modernism, after all, is a reaction to the Enlightenment idea that "one container fits all," whether that container be a specific theology or ideology. But aren't universal human rights a meta-narrative? The term "universal" before human rights certainly suggests so. Rights can't exist without codes of conduct to go along with them. So if rights are universal, so, too, must there be a universal code of morality to accompany them.

The problem with our current notions of morality, at least in the West, is that they are too linear and localized to condition behavior whose effects are often far removed, far-reaching, and systemic in nature. Western morality is derived from the Ten Commandments. Judaism, Christianity, and Islam all ascribe to what we might call a morality based on intimate, verifiable, causal harm. Murder, robbery, bearing false witness, and adultery are easily identifiable acts perpetrated by one person or group against another. These kinds of acts are relatively easy to attach responsibility to. They are what we might refer to as examples of "hot evil."

But, in an increasingly globalized society of ever more dense connections, where everyone's behavior affects everyone else, there is a new kind of morality, what one might call "cold evil." (The term can be used in either a religious or secular sense to convey the idea of immoral behavior.) Cold evil is actions whose effects are so far removed from the behavior that caused them that no causal relationship is suspected, no sense of guilt or wrongdoing is felt, and no collective responsibility is exercised to punish the errant behavior.

For example, millions of Americans drive sport-utility vehicles (SUVs). These vehicles, in turn, burn far more gasoline per mile driven than other cars and therefore discharge more carbon dioxide into the atmosphere, increasing the risk of global warming. While an educated elite is aware of the relationship between SUV use and global warming, the vast majority of Americans either don't know or don't care. Even though they might see a television news story attributing record rainfall, coastal flooding, and lost lives and property to the effects of global warming, it is unlikely they would associate their use of an SUV with the misfortunes unfolding somewhere else. And even if they did suspect some kind of causal relationship, it's unlikely they would feel the same level of remorse and guilt as they would if, say, they were driving their SUV recklessly in a heavy rainstorm in some coastal region and smashed into another car, killing both its driver and passengers.

Or take another example. Millions of European and American youngsters wear designer athletic shoes from brand-name companies like Nike, not suspecting that the shoes might have been manufactured in a sweatshop in Vietnam where child labor is exploited under the most draconian working conditions. If they were told about such conditions, would they likely still buy the shoes, knowing they would be contributing to the misfortune of exploited children halfway around the world?

Millions of well-to-do consumers in advanced industrial countries enjoy a diet rich in meat consumption, never suspecting a relationship between their food choices and increased poverty in the third world. Today, 36 percent of the grain grown in the world is fed to livestock. In the developing world, the share of grain grown for animal consumption has tripled since 1950 and now exceeds 21 percent of the total grain produced. In Mexico, 45 percent of the grain is livestock feed, in Egypt it's 31 percent, in Thailand 30 percent, and in China 26 percent.[19] Tragically, 80 percent of the world's hungry children live in countries with an actual food surplus, much of which is in the form of feed given to animals who, in turn, will be consumed by only the well-to-do consumers of the world. It's important to bear in mind that an acre of cereal produces two to ten times more protein than an acre devoted to meat production; legumes (beans, peas, lentils) can produce ten to twenty times more protein; and leafy vegetables, fifteen times more protein.[20]

The human consequences of the transition from food to feed grain were dramatically illustrated in 1984 in Ethiopia, when thousands of people were dying each day from famine. The public was unaware that, at the very time, Ethiopia was using some of its best agricultural land to produce linseed cake, cottonseed cake, and rapeseed meal for export to European countries to be used as feed for livestock.

The irony of the present food-production system is that millions of wealthy consumers in the first world are increasingly dying from diseases of affluence—heart attacks, strokes, diabetes, and cancer—brought on by gorging on fatty grain-fed beef and other meats, while the poor in the third world are dying of diseases of poverty brought on by being denied access to land to grow food grain for their families. More than twenty million people die each year around the world from hunger-related diseases.

Few people in Europe, America, and Japan know anything about the relationship between food, feed, and hunger in the world. But if they did, would they feel morally compelled to eat lower on the global food chain with a more vegetable-oriented diet so that more agricultural land could be freed up to raise food grain rather than feed grain?

If we were to hear about our next-door neighbors' starving their children, we would be morally outraged. Law enforcement would arrest the parents for child neglect and abuse. That's hot evil. But could we muster up the same sense of moral outrage or feel as morally culpable if we knew that our dietary choices were contributing, at least in part, to maintaining an elite global food chain at the expense of the poor, resulting in starvation and death for millions of people throughout the world? In other words, would cold evil move us to act with the same moral passion and ardor as hot evil?

Recently, a broad coalition of religious groups in the United States launched a public-education campaign decrying America's profligate use of gasoline, and targeted SUV owners. The campaign literature asked provocatively, "What Would Jesus Drive?" One of the religious sponsors accused Chevrolet and other car manufacturers of "encouraging people to buy automobiles which are poisoning God's creation."[21] Another religious spokesman asked, "How can I love my neighbor as myself if I'm filling their lungs with pollution?"[22] The campaign touched a raw nerve. Other religious leaders and political commentators rushed to the defense of the auto industry. One irate respondent even suggested that "Jesus would drive a Hummer."[23] This exercise in the ethics of cold evil drew an angry response. It's one thing to talk abstractly about the global-warming crisis. It's quite another to suggest that millions of owners of SUVs might be morally culpable.

A similar campaign waged by social activists and trade unionists to boycott the products of Nike and other shoe companies whose subcontractors in Asia were exploiting child labor drew mixed responses. While some college students in the U.S. and Europe stopped buying the Nike brand, most consumers continued to remain loyal to Nike, showing little interest in the fuss around child labor exploitation in Nike's subcontracting factories.

Campaigns waged against the fast-food hamburger chains have met with similar mixed reviews.

Still, what's important to point out is that these kinds of moral campaigns to address the systemic results of destructive human behavior are new on the world scene. It's going to take time to create a felt morality based on systems thinking. Europeans seem slightly ahead of the game in this regard. Even so, we are a long way off from the day when cold evil is treated with the same sense of personal and public moral urgency as hot evil.

For hundreds of millions, even billions, of human beings to internalize and act upon a systems approach to moral behavior, it is probably going to require more dramatic and even catastrophic events being visited upon the world. There are a number of scenarios by which I could imagine our species coming to grips with cold evil and adopting a systems-based morality. Violent weather changes induced by global warming, the spread of deadly new bacteria and viruses resulting from inhumane animal-husbandry practices and factory farming, terrorist attacks using chemical and even biological and nuclear weapons of mass destruction, more prolonged power blackouts around the world brought on by global energy shortages, massive starvation, and a global depression all could hasten a new systems approach to morality and ethics. But it's just as likely that terrible events of this magnitude could lead to retrenchment, xenophobia, a breakdown of personal and public morality, and a lashing out at scapegoats of all kinds.

The nature of the human response will depend on whether the increasingly harmful systemic effects of the activity create a sense of shared vulnerability and responsibility for one another and the Earth or whether the fear generated by catastrophic activity creates a siege mentality and a feeling that everyone better fend for him- or herself in a war of survival. The latter approach would only exacerbate the systemic evil by creating a continuous positive feedback effect, with potentially devastating consequences for humanity and the world.

These, then, are the questions: How do we create a new moral bridge between "the self" and "the other" that is expansive enough and encompassing enough to be global in scale and universal in outlook? Can we establish a systemic approach to ethics that allows us to identify cold evil in all of its various guises? Equally important, can we learn to exercise the Golden Rule on a much broader playing field that includes not only our immediate relations with our neighbors but also the totality of relationships that make up the larger planetary community in which we are all embedded? . . . A tall order, but that's why we call it global consciousness.

The Third Stage of Human Consciousness

For the European Dream to become the world's dream, it will have to create a new story about the human mission—a new meta-narrative that can unite the human race in a shared journey while allowing each person and group to take their own particular path.

Owen Barfield, the British philosopher, has offered up some thoughts on the matter. His ideas help bring the American notion of individual autonomy and volition and the Asian notion of collective consensus and contextual thinking together in a new synthesis. That synthesis could provide a proper historical context for advancing a global consciousness and the promulgation of the new European Dream to every part of the world.

Barfield views history as an unfolding of human consciousness. His insights into history dovetail with Sigmund Freud's insights into the history of each person's own mental development. We touched very briefly on the subject of the dialectical pull between individual differentiation and collective integration in chapter 5 and again, in a little more detail, in chapter 13.

Freud, recall, starts with the idea that in the earliest stage of development, an infant experiences an undifferentiated union with his mother. The self is not yet formed. The baby experiences his mother as a whole. There is not a sense of "the I" and "the other," but only of what Freud called the "oceanic" feeling of oneness. That unity breaks down when the infant realizes that his every urge and desire can't be met immediately. His mother's breast is not always available. The baby begins to distinguish between his desires and the objects of desire denied him. The feeling of omnipotence, that "he is the world," is undermined by the restraints imposed on him by the outside world. The "pleasure principle," says Freud, is challenged by the "reality principle."

The baby slowly becomes aware of his own separation from his mother and the outside world as well as his dependency on external forces, over which he has little or no control. He experiences the anxiety of separation as death and begins fashioning various mental defenses to deny the pain he is feeling. The rest of one's life, according to Freud, is spent in attempting to recapture the feeling of oceanic oneness, while denying the original loss because the pain of separation, dependence, and death is more than one can bear.

Freud refers to the original feeling of oneness as the "life instinct," or eros. The feelings of bodily contact, sexuality, and love are all a part of the life instinct. As a baby develops, he is increasingly separated from unconditional eros by toilet training, schedules, and other external restraints. The child compensates for the sense of loss, anxiety, and powerlessness he feels by sublimating his bodily feelings and substituting what Freud calls the "death instinct" for the life instinct. He denies his original separation by becoming detached and by seeking autonomy. He attempts to control events, dominate his surroundings, and assert his own individuality. Every parent is aware of the "terrible twos," when the child begins to assert himself and claim a sense of autonomy in the world.

The death instinct continues to shadow each child through adolescence and adulthood. People surround themselves with substitutes to try to regain the sense of oceanic oneness they experienced as infants. Freud believed that the Christ story served as a surrogate for the loss of the original feeling of oneness by offering God's unconditional love and the hope of eternal salvation. In the modern era, nationalist ideology became the favored substitute. Patriotic fervor gives many people a sense of being part of a larger, loving, immortal whole. Ideology often serves the same purpose. Many capitalists and socialists have found refuge in an all-embracing ideological bubble.

At the same time, our technologies and material possessions come to substitute for our own repressed sense of bodily loss. They become, in effect, surrogate extensions of our bodies, and we increasingly surround ourselves with them to fill the void left by our own sense of bodily loss with our own mothers. But in our pursuit of ever more advanced technologies and greater material success, we become ever further removed from the original participation we seek to reclaim. Psychologist Norman O. Brown notes that "the more the life of the body passes into things, the less life there is in the body, and at the same time the increasing accumulation of things represents an ever fuller articulation of the lost life of the body."[24] Virtual-reality environments and genetic-engineering technologies are the most recent attempts to create technological substitutes in hopes of recovering the human body. Unfortunately, argues Brown, the "sequestration of the life of the body into dead things" in the name of technological and material progress only draws humanity further into the realm of the death instinct.[25] It is the gnawing fear of death, which the baby first experiences upon the initial separation from his mother, that has, up to now, driven so much of human progress. The history of civilization for Freud, Brown, and other psychologists is little more than the projection of the death instinct out onto the external world.

We have created great pyramids, grand cathedrals, and majestic skyscrapers to secure a measure of immortality, hoping to cheat death and find that elusive sense of being, that oceanic oneness that remains deep in the memory trace of every person that has ever lived. Our near obsession with creating a material cornucopia in the modern era is so powerful exactly because it is a substitute for the cornucopia we experienced in infancy at our mother's breast.

The death instinct has become pervasive over the course of the modern era. We have increasingly detached ourselves from the body of nature, severed its relationships, deadened it into bits and pieces, and expropriated it in the form of property, all in an effort to inflate our individual being in the world. Enlightenment science, market relations, and nation-state governance all work in tandem to create the illusion of the autonomous individual, free of any dependency on the natural world. We increasingly live out our lives in a cocoon of technological and economic autonomy. We are no longer surrounded by living nature but, rather, by dead artifacts.

The tragedy of it all is that we long thought that by becoming increasingly autonomous and less dependent on nature, we could better assure our security and be free. Now the death instinct, the aggressive drive to master and deaden nature, has come back to plague us in the form of global threats such as climate change, nuclear proliferation, growing poverty, and social upheaval. We have sought to make ourselves more secure, only to end up more vulnerable than ever before. We have, in effect, arrived at the very brink of our own self-induced annihilation. The death instinct has prevailed.

Freud had little to say in his own day about how to turn the human predicament around. Barfield, however, has made an attempt at offering a new historical framework for addressing the human condition. For Barfield, historical consciousness seems to follow a path not too dissimilar from the path each person follows in the development of his or her own individual consciousness. Human history, like individual history, observes Barfield, is conditioned by the dialectical pull of two competing forces, one seeking unification and interdependence, or the life instinct, the other seeking separation and independence, or the death instinct. The great unfinished task before civilization is how to reconcile these two contradictory forces.

Barfield outlines three stages in the history of human consciousness. He points out that for most of history, human beings lived as hunter-gatherers. Paleolithic existence was, by its very nature, lived in close and deep participation with the natural world. Humans enjoyed a non-sublimated bodily intimacy with the life around them, as well as with their own bodies. The few remaining hunter-gatherer tribes in the Amazon rain forests, the jungles of Borneo, and the other remaining pockets of wild nature still enjoy a kind of unrepressed bond with the natural world.

While hunter-gatherers experienced some sense of self, it was not yet well developed. They lived their lives in a relatively undifferentiated way, as part of a larger social whole that, in turn, was perceived to be part of an even larger undifferentiated nature. Their day-to-day lives were lived deep inside the temporal rhythms and spatial restraints imposed by the natural world. Mother Earth was regarded less as a metaphor and more as a primordial mother, and treated with the same love, respect, and awe as they might confer on their own tribal mothers. And like their own mothers, hunter-gatherers depended on Mother Earth for their sustenance and used various ritual means to placate her in order to secure her benevolence.

The beginning of agriculture marked the onset of the second great period of human consciousness. Human beings began to domesticate wild plants and animals for productive use. With agriculture came a steady detachment of human beings from nature and even one's own bodily nature. The idea of the self began to slowly emerge out of the undifferentiated fog. As mentioned in chapter 5, the late medieval and early modern eras saw a rapid advance in "man's" detachment from nature and a steady differentiation into the kind of autonomous self we know today. The emergence of the totally detached, autonomous self brought with it an increasing self-awareness on the part of human beings. With self-awareness came the sense of personal volition, the belief in one's ability to affect the world around one's self. The gain in self-awareness and personal sense of identity has come at a very high price, however—the loss of intimate participation and communion with the natural world.

The evolutionary history of the species, argues Barfield, has recapitulated the evolutionary history of each individual's own personal development. The human race has gone from an undifferentiated oneness with Mother Nature to a detached, self-aware isolation from her. In the process, we have lost that primordial sense of oceanic indivisibility that is the life instinct and instead have settled for a new relationship with nature based on domination from a distance, with all of the deleterious systemic effects that flow from our attempts at mastery. Humanity has, indeed, passed from the life instinct to the death instinct.

So where does this leave humanity? Barfield suggests that we are on the cusp of the third great stage in human consciousness—the stage where we make a self-aware choice to re-participate with the body of nature. It's here that Barfield's ideas align with the thinking of European intellectuals, scientists, and visionaries, who increasingly view the world as an indivisible living entity deserving of respect and care.

The third stage of human consciousness shifts our notion of engagement from the geosphere to the biosphere. Geopolitics has always been based on the assumption that the environment is a giant battleground—a war of all against all—where we each fight with one another to secure resources to ensure our individual survival. Biosphere politics, by contrast, is based on the idea that the Earth is a living organism made up of interdependent relationships and that we each survive and flourish by stewarding the larger communities of which we are a part.

So how does Barfield suggest we reconcile the drive for individuality with the desire for oceanic oneness? Were it not for the death instinct, we would never have separated ourselves sufficiently from that oceanic oneness to create a sense of the self and, with it, self-awareness. And without self-awareness, we would not be able to exercise volition, make personal choices, and exercise our individual will. On the other hand, self-awareness and individuality have only made us all the more aware, and thus anxious, about our own finite existence and mortality. The anxiety, in turn, fuels our aggressive drives to master, deaden, and expropriate everything around us, in the hope of inflating our being and warding off our own inevitable demise.

The solution to our dilemma lies in integrating the life instinct and death instinct in a new unity. The early-twentieth-century poet Rainer Maria Rilke provides us with a clue. He wrote, ". . . whoever rightly understands and celebrates death, at the same time magnifies life."[26] In other words, we can't really begin to live until we first accept the fact that one day we will die. How do we come to terms with our own death and make the choice to live? By making a self-aware decision to leave the death instinct behind, to no longer seek mastery, control, or domination over nature, including human nature, as a means of fending off death. Instead, accept death as part of life and make a choice to re-participate with the body of nature. Cross over from the self to the other, and reunite in an empathetic bond with the totality of relationships that together make up the Earth's indivisible living community.

The decision to re-participate, to choose the life instinct, is quite different from the kind of original participation that marks the life of the infant or the early development of the human species. In these other instances, participation is not willed but is, rather, fated. The self is not developed sufficiently to make self-aware choices. In the case of an infant, dependency determines the relationship between the mother and baby. In the case of our Paleolithic forebears, fear of nature's wrath, as much as dependency, conditioned the relationship. To re-participate with nature willingly, by exercising free will, is what separates the third stage of human consciousness from everything that has gone before. By freely choosing to be part of nature, one retains one's unique identity, while embedding oneself in the oceanic oneness of the biosphere.

A Global Persona

In a post-modern era characterized by increasing individuation, where personal identity is fractured into a myriad of sub-identities and meta-identities, reintegration with the whole of the biosphere may be the only antidote encompassing enough to ensure that the individual does not lose all of his or her moorings and disintegrate into a nonbeing.

Some observers of the post-modern psyche are growing concerned about the loss of personal identity in an increasingly thick world. Kenneth J. Gergen, professor of psychology at Swarthmore College, notes that young people today must navigate their way in a highly dense globalizing culture with competing demands streaming into their central nervous systems from every conceivable direction. In their efforts to mediate all of the stimuli and accommodate all of the possible connections, young people continue to create new sub-selves and meta-selves—in effect, giving over bits and pieces of their persona to each new relationship just to stay engaged in all of the networks that surround them. The fear is being excluded. If being propertied and enjoying autonomy and exclusivity was the sine qua non of the American Dream, having access and being embedded is the much sought-after goal in the new era. Worried they may lose access, young people divide their attention into smaller and smaller fragments just to keep up with all the possible connections beckoning them. Gergen warns,

> This fragmentation of self-conceptions corresponds to a multiplicity of incoherent and disconnected relationships. These relationships pull us in myriad directions, inviting us to play such a variety of roles that the very concept of an "authentic self" with knowable characteristics recedes from view. The fully saturated self becomes no self at all.[27]

Where Gergen worries about the disintegration of the self, psychologist Robert J. Lifton is more hopeful. He argues that multiple personas are a coping mechanism that allows the psyche to adjust to the growing density in an increasingly globalized society. He believes that multiple personas represent a more mature state of consciousness—one that allows individuals to live with the complexities and ambiguities around them as they try to make their way in a more interconnected global environment.[28]

Both Gergen and Lifton have a point. The post-modern persona is increasingly fragmented and plastic. The question becomes, Is there a way to reintegrate the extreme individuation of the post-modern personality into a more unified global whole? Failure to do so will only exacerbate the sense of personal alienation and existential dread that so many young people already experience in a world where they are increasingly connected but in which they feel more and more isolated. According to a survey conducted by the Kaiser Family Foundation entitled *Kids and Media at the New Millennium*, American children now spend an average of five and a half hours a day, seven days a week, interacting with various electronic media for recreation. Youngsters eight and older spend even more leisure time with television, the Internet, video games, and other media, averaging six hours and forty-five minutes a day. What's more troubling, the study found that most children interact with electronic media alone. Older children spend up to 95 percent of their time watching television alone, while children between the ages of two and seven watch television alone more than 81 percent of the time.[29]

Overcoming the sense of personal isolation and alienation that can accompany an electronically mediated environment requires a new integrative mission powerful enough to be transformative in nature. What's sorely missing is an overarching reason for why billions of human beings should be increasingly connected. Toward what end? More commerce, greater political participation, increased pleasure, access to information, or just plain curiosity? All the above, while relevant, seem, nonetheless, insufficient to justify why six billion human beings should be connected and mutually embedded in a globalized society. Six billion individual connections, absent any overall unifying purpose, seems a colossal waste of human energy. More important, global connections without any real transcendent purpose risk a narrowing rather than an expanding of human consciousness.

The good news is that the increasing connectivity of the human race is advancing personal awareness of all the relationships that make up a complex and diverse world. A younger generation is beginning to view the world less as a storehouse of objects to expropriate and possess and more as a labyrinth of relationships to gain access to. While an older generation thought of itself more like property and was preoccupied with "making something out of oneself," the younger generation is more likely to think of its life as a continually changing process operating in a myriad of network relationships. In an era of global connectedness, the old idea of a fixed, self-contained, autonomous consciousness is giving way to the new notion of the self as an unfolding story whose plot lines and substance are totally dependent on the various characters and events with whom one enters into a relationship. Gergen suggests that "the final stage in this transition to the postmodern is reached when the self vanishes fully into a stage of relatedness." In a globally connected world, concludes Gergen, "one ceases to believe in a self independent of the relationships in which he or she is embedded . . . thus placing relationships in the central position occupied by the individual self for the last several hundred years of Western history."[30] The Western sense of consciousness comes to resemble the Asian one, although it arrived at its present state by taking a very different journey.

How, then, will we choose to use our newfound relational consciousness? Barfield and other thinkers suggest that human beings are maturing in their self-development to the point where they can make a personal choice to re-participate with the myriad relationships that make up the biosphere. Our growing involvement in networks, our newfound ability to multitask and operate simultaneously on parallel tracks, our increasing awareness of economic, social, and environmental interdependencies, our search for relatedness and embeddedness, our willingness to accept contradictory realities and multicultural perspectives, and our process-oriented behavior all predispose us to systems thinking. If we can harness systems thinking to a new global ethics that recognizes and acts to prevent cold evil and is dedicated to harmonizing the many relationships that make up the life-sustaining forces of the planet, we will have crossed the divide into a new third stage of human consciousness.

The key to a successful journey will depend on how deep the re-participation becomes. Re-participation with the body of nature means intimate engagement in real time, unencumbered by layers of technological barriers. When Barfield talks of re-participation, what he has in mind is a personal reaching out to "the other" in the spirit of deep communion. That kind of relationship can't be accomplished at a distance in virtual-reality environments. If we simply expand our connections but become increasingly alone and isolated in the process—a world where everyone is e-mailing everyone else but seldom touching up against one another's being—the relationships become illusory, and our sense of self becomes delusional and more at risk of dissolution. Re-participation, a true reaching out to the other, requires actually being there. One can't be detached and empathize at the same time.

The new globalizing technologies do indeed compress space and time and draw the human family together in tighter webs of interdependent relationships. We become more aware of the many connections that make up the larger systems within which we dwell. But if that awareness is not balanced with intimate, face-to-face re-participation with the body of nature, our journey into a new stage of consciousness will be stillborn. Our relational selves will be more of a technological than of a truly human nature, only prolonging the older journey with its fetishization of the death instinct. The life instinct can be rekindled only by really living life, and living life means deep participation in the life of the other that surrounds us.

As long, then, as we choose detachment from the natural world and occupy ourselves almost exclusively with deadening our environment and expropriating and consuming it in the form of wasteful indulgences and sport, our own lives remain caught up in that death culture. We are reminded of our own death in every destructive act we engage in. How do we experience life if continually surrounded by death and consumed with the thought of death? By choosing deep re-participation with nature, by stewarding the many relationships that nurture life, we surround ourselves with a life-affirming environment. We are constantly reminded of the intrinsic value of life by every empathetic experience we pursue.

The American and European Dreams

While all of this might sound a bit esoteric and airy, in the real world where people dream of and act on the kind of life they would like to live and be part of, making choices between the death instinct and life instinct has real and profound consequences for the individual, the human family, and the planet.

The American Dream is largely caught up in the death instinct. We seek autonomy at all costs. We overconsume, indulge our every appetite, and waste the Earth's largesse. We put a premium on unrestrained economic growth, reward the powerful and marginalize the vulnerable. We are consumed with protecting our self-interest and have amassed the most powerful military machine in all of history to get what we want and believe we deserve. We consider ourselves a chosen people and, therefore, entitled to more than our fair share of the Earth's bounty. Sadly, our self-interest is slowly metamorphosing into pure selfishness. We have become a death culture.

What do I mean by "death culture"? Simply this. No one, and especially no American, would deny that we are the most voracious consumers in the world. We forget, however, that consumption and death are deeply intertwined. The term "consumption" dates back to the early fourteenth century and has both English and French roots. Originally, to "consume" meant to destroy, to pillage, to subdue, to exhaust. It is a word steeped in violence and until the twentieth century had only negative connotations. Remember that as late as the early 1900s, the medical community and the public referred to tuberculosis as "consumption." Consumption only metamorphosed into a positive term at the hands of twentieth-century advertisers who began to equate consumption with choice. By the last quarter of the twentieth century, at least in America, consumer choice began to replace representative democracy as the ultimate expression of human freedom, reflecting its new hallowed status.

Today, Americans consume upwards of a third of the world's energy and vast amounts of the Earth's other resources, despite the fact that we make up less than 5 percent of the world's population. We are fast consuming the Earth's remaining endowment to feed our near insatiable individual appetites. And what lies below our obsessive, if not pathological, behavior is the frantic desire to live and prosper by killing and consuming everything else around us. Cultural historian Elias Canetti once observed, "Each of us is a King in a field of corpses."[31] If we Americans were to stop and reflect on the sheer number of creatures and Earth's resources and materials each of us has expropriated and consumed in the course of our lifetime to perpetuate our profligate lifestyles, we would likely be appalled at the carnage. It's no wonder so many people around the world look at America's wanton consumption and think of us as a death culture.

But is that all we are? Some critics of the American experience would argue that there is no more to say on the matter. This is what America has become. But they are wrong. There is another side to the American experience. We open up our country to newcomers. We believe that every human being deserves a second chance in life. We champion the underdog and glorify the person who has overcome life's adversities to make something out of him- or herself. We believe that everyone is ultimately responsible for his or her own life. We each hold ourselves accountable. It is this other side of our individualism that is still our saving grace. If our sense of personal accountability can be exorcised from the death instinct and put in service to the life instinct, America might again lead the way for the world.

The unfinished business of the human family is the adoption of a "personal ethics" of accountability to the larger communities of life that make up the living Earth. In the final analysis, a commitment to our fellow human beings, our fellow creatures, and our common biosphere must be personally felt as much as collectively legislated for any real transformation to occur. Ethics flourishes only in a world where everyone feels individually accountable. If we Americans could redirect our deeply held sense of personal responsibility from the more narrow goal of individual material aggrandizement to a more expansive commitment of advancing a global ethics, we might yet be able to remake the American Dream along lines more compatible with the emerging European Dream.

How likely is such a turnaround in the United States? To begin with, a sizable minority of Americans are already responsive to what we might call "universal ethics." They exercise personal responsibility and accountability in their consumer behavior, their workplaces, and their communities in ways that reflect the new global consciousness. They are supporters of initiatives that extend universal human rights and that protect the rights of nature and make conscious decisions not to participate in activity that might contribute to cold evil, whether it be in their choice of automobile, dietary preferences, or stock and bond purchases. They have become global citizens.

But what about the majority of Americans whose sense of personal responsibility rarely extends beyond self-interest or national interest? How do they make the breakthrough to the other side and begin to "think globally and act locally"?

Surprisingly, the best hope might be within America's religious community. A great struggle has been going on among theologians as well as in both mainline and Evangelical congregations, the Catholic Church, and Judaism on interpretation of the creation story in the Book of Genesis. At issue is the biblical passage where God says to Adam and Eve,

> Be fruitful and multiply, and replenish the earth, and subdue it; and have dominion over the fish of the sea, and over the fowl of the air, and over every living thing that moveth upon the earth.[32]

For most of Christian history, the concept of dominion has been used to justify the ruthless detachment from and exploitation of the natural world. Now, a new generation of religious scholars and a growing number of believers are beginning to redefine the meaning of "dominion." They argue that since God created the heavens and the Earth, all of his creation is imbued with intrinsic value. God also gave purpose and order to his creation. Therefore, when human beings attempt to undermine the intrinsic value of nature, or manipulate and redirect its purpose and order to suit their own self-interests, they are acting with hubris and in rebellion against God himself.

The idea of "dominion" is being redefined to mean "stewardship." Human beings are to serve as God's caretakers here on Earth, nurturing rather than exploiting and destroying his creation. In the new religious scheme of things, people are both part of nature and also separate from it. We are part of God's creation and therefore dependent on all other living things and nonliving things that make up God's earthly kingdom. At the same time, because human beings are made in God's image, we have a special responsibility to act as his custodians on Earth and to take care of his creation.

Each and every person, in the Christian eschatology, is endowed with free will. One can use that free will and choose to be redeemed by accepting Christ as Lord. If one makes that choice, however, it also requires him or her to tend God's garden. Here we have a Christian version of Barfield's third stage of consciousness—that is, each person is called upon to make a self-aware choice to accept Christ and, by so doing, to participate in deep communion with the whole of God's creation.

Although the new interpretation of Genesis has been steadily gaining support across the American religious community, it has not yet become a centerpiece of American religious life. Were that to happen, however, millions of Americans might find themselves on the cusp of a new global consciousness. One's unconditional love for a suffering Christ would include one's unconditional love for his creation—a potentially powerful new religious story that could bring those of faith to a new commitment to the Earth and all of its inhabitants. I'd caution, however, that there is still a long way to go from rhetorical reinterpretation of the Genesis story to active personal commitment on the part of millions of Americans to live their lives in a way that reflects a moral responsibility for preventing cold evil and acting on behalf of the biosphere. It's still too early to suggest that the American Dream might undergo a true metamorphosis and give rise to a universal ethics.

The European Dream, by contrast, has all the right markings to claim the moral high ground on the journey toward a third stage of human consciousness. Europeans have laid out a visionary roadmap to a new promised land, one dedicated to re-affirming the life instinct and the Earth's indivisibility. I have no doubt of European sincerity in this regard, at least among the elite, the well educated, and the young generation of middle-class standard-bearers of a united Europe. The Europeans I have come to know do have a dream. They want to live in a world where everyone is included and no one is left by the wayside. According to a Pew survey conducted in 2003, solid majorities in every European country say they "believe it is more important for government to ensure that no one is in need, than it is for individuals to be free to pursue goals without government interference."[33] Only in America, among all of the populations of the wealthy nations of the world, does a majority—58 percent—of the people say they care more about personal freedom to pursue goals without government interference, while only 34 percent say it's more important for the government "to take an activist approach to guaranteeing that no one is in need."[34] Similarly, when it comes to extending help to the poor in countries other than one's own, a Gallup poll conducted in 2002 reports that nearly 70 percent of all Europeans believe that more financial help should be given to poorer nations, while nearly half of all Americans believe rich countries are already giving too much.[35]

Europeans also want to be globally connected without losing their sense of cultural identity and locality. They find their freedom in relationships, not in autonomy. They seek to live a good quality of life in the here and now, which for them means also living in a sustainable relationship with the Earth to protect the interests of those who will come later. Eight out of ten Europeans say they are happy with their lives, and when asked what they believe to be the most important legacy of the twentieth century, 58 percent of Europeans picked their quality of life, putting it second only to freedom in a list of eleven legacies. At the same time, 69 percent of European citizens believe that environmental protection is an immediate and urgent problem. In stark contrast, only one in four Americans are anxious about the environment. Even more interesting, 56 percent of Europeans say "it is necessary to fundamentally change our way of life and development if we want to halt the deterioration of the environment,"[36] making them the most avid supporters of sustainable development of any people in the world.

Europeans work to live, rather than live to work. Although jobs are essential to their lives, they aren't sufficient to define their existence. Europeans put deep play, social capital, and social cohesion above career. When asked what values are extremely or very important to them, 95 percent of Europeans put helping others at the top of their list of priorities. Ninety-two percent said it was extremely or very important to value people for who they are, 84 percent said they put a high value on being involved in creating a better society, 79 percent valued putting more time and effort into personal development, while less than half (49 percent) said it was extremely or very important to make a lot of money, putting financial success dead last of the eight values ranked in the survey.[37]

Europeans champion universal human rights and the rights of nature and are willing to subject themselves to codes of enforcement. They want to live in a world of peace and harmony, and, for the most part, they support a foreign policy and environmental policy to advance that end.

But I'm not sure how thick the European Dream is. Is Europe's commitment to cultural diversity and peaceful coexistence substantial enough to withstand the kind of terrorist attacks that we experienced on 9/11 or that Spain experienced on 3/11? Would Europeans remain committed to the principles of inclusivity and sustainable development were the world economy to plunge into a deep and prolonged downturn, maybe even a global depression? Would Europeans have the patience to continue sporting an open, process-oriented form of multilevel governance if they were facing social upheaval and riots in the streets? These are the kinds of tough challenges that test the mettle of a people and the vitality and viability of their dream. Regardless of what others might think about America, the American Dream has stood the test, in good times and bad. We never lost hope in our dream until very recently, even in the darkest hours. Will Europeans be able to say the same about their own nascent dream?

And finally, there is the question of personal accountability, America's strength and Europe's soft spot. Europe can attempt to legislate its dream. It can issue directives, sign global agreements, set up task forces, and establish benchmarks. That's pretty much what it is already doing. And there's nothing wrong with that. It's a sign of Europe's commitment to fulfilling its new dream. But if the personal sense of accountability and responsibility is not deep enough and thick enough to weather the inevitable storms that will accompany the new journey, then, all of the legislative and executive actions and intellectual support notwithstanding, the European Dream will fail.

My biggest concern, having spent nearly twenty years of my life working in both Europe and America, is whether Europeans' sense of hope is sufficient to the task of sustaining a new vision for the future. Dreams require optimism, a sense that one's hopes can be fulfilled. Americans are flush with hope and optimism, Europeans are less so, as a people. Still, they are guardedly hopeful about their new union. And the public opinion surveys show that a younger generation is measured in its optimism. Perhaps that's all we can or should expect. The kind of unexamined optimism that has been so characteristic of the American Spirit has not always served us well. In a world of increasing global threats, tempered enthusiasm, balanced against a realistic assessment of risks, might be more appropriate. But there's also a deep pessimistic edge ingrained in the European persona—understandable, I guess, after so many misbegotten political and social experiments, and so much carnage over so many centuries of history. Failures can dash hopes. But they can also make a people stronger, more resilient, and wise. Overcoming cynicism for Europeans is going to be as difficult and challenging as we Americans overcoming our naïve optimism. Still, no dream, regardless of how attractive it might be, can succeed in an atmosphere clouded by pessimism and cynicism.

At the risk of ruffling feathers on both sides of the Atlantic, perhaps there are lessons to share. We Americans might be more willing to assume a collective sense of responsibility for our fellow human beings and the Earth we live on. Our European friends might be more willing to assume a sense of personal accountability in their individual dealings in the world. We Americans might become more circumspect and tempered in our outlook, while Europeans might become more hopeful and optimistic in theirs. By sharing the best of both dreams, we may be in better stead to make the journey together into a third stage of human consciousness.

These are tumultuous times. Much of the world is going dark, leaving many human beings without clear direction. The European Dream is a beacon of light in a troubled world. It beckons us to a new age of inclusivity, diversity, quality of life, deep play, sustainability, universal human rights, the rights of nature, and peace on Earth. We Americans used to say that the American Dream is worth dying for. The new European Dream is worth living for.

NOTES

CHAPTER 1: THE SLOW DEATH OF THE AMERICAN DREAM

1. Decker, Jeffrey Louis. *Made in America: Self-Styled Success from Horatio Alger to Oprah Winfrey.* Minneapolis: University of Minnesota Press, 1997. p. 92.
2. Ibid. pp. 154–155.
3. Ibid.
4. Miller, Perry. *Errand into the Wilderness.* Cambridge, MA: Harvard University Press, 1984. p. 11; Winthrop, John. "A Model of Christian Charity." 1630.
5. Cullen, Jim. *The American Dream.* New York: Oxford University Press, 2003. p. 24.
6. Morgan, Edmund S., ed. *The Diary of Michael Wigglesworth, 1653–1657.* New York: Harper, 1965. p. 8.
7. Melville, Herman. *White-Jacket; Or, the World in a Man-of-War.* (1850) Oxford, U.K.: Oxford Press (Oxford World's Classics), 2000. ch. 36.
8. "Americans Struggle with Religion's Role at Home and Abroad." Pew Research Center for the People and the Press. March 20, 2002. *www.people-press.org*
9. Ibid.
10. Ibid.
11. "Spirituality and Faith Undergird and Motivate Americans to a Surprising Degree: News-Release." The Gallup Organization. March 4, 2003. *www.gallup.org*
12. Gallup, George H. Jr., and Byron R. Johnson. "Religion & Values: New Index Tracks 'Spiritual State of the Union.'" The Gallup Organization. January 28, 2003. *www.gallup.org*
13. "American Values: A Survey of Americans on Values." *The Washington Post*/Kaiser/Harvard Survey Project. September 1998. *www.kff.org/content/archive/1441/values.html*
14. "Religion & Politics: The Ambivalent Majority." The Pew Research Center for the People and the Press. September 20, 2000. *www.people-press.org/reports*
15. "American Values: A Survey of Americans on Values." *The Washington Post*/Kaiser/Harvard Survey Project.

16. Robison, Jennifer. "Religion & Values: The Devil and the Demographic Details." The Gallup Organization. February 25, 2003. *www.gallup.com*
17. Ibid.
18. Ibid.
19. Ibid.
20. Brooks, Deborah Jordan. "Substantial Numbers of Americans Continue to Doubt Evolution as Explanation for Origin of Humans." The Gallup Organization. March 5, 2001. *www.gallup.com/poll/releases/pr*
21. "Public Favorable to Creationism." The Gallup Organization. February 14, 2001. *www.gallup.com/poll/releases/pr*
22. "Poll: 40 Percent of Americans Believe in Apocalyptic End." *DayWatch*. March 25, 1999.
23. Leland, John. "Afterlife for Everyone: Heaven Comes Down to Earth." *The New York Times*. December 21, 2003.
24. "Among Wealthy Nations U.S. Stands Alone in Its Embrace of Religion." The Pew Research Center for the People and the Press. December 19, 2002. *www.people-press.org*
25. Ibid.
26. Ibid.; Inglehart, Ronald. "Cultural Cleavages in the European Union." Institute for Social Research, University of Michigan. 2002.
27. Inglehart, Ronald. "Cultural Cleavages in the European Union."
28. "Among Wealthy Nations U.S. Stands Alone in Its Embrace of Religion." The Pew Research Center for the People and the Press.
29. Ferguson, Niall. "Why America Outpaces Europe (Clue: The God Factor.)" *The New York Times*. June 8, 2003.
30. Ibid.
31. Ibid.
32. Inglehart, Ronald. *1990 World Values Survey*. Table 2-2. Ann Arbor, MI: Institute for Social Research, 1990.
33. Ibid.
34. Smith, Tom W., and Lars Jarkko. "National Pride in Cross-National Perspective." National Opinion Research Center, University of Chicago. April 2001.
35. "Living with a Superpower." *The Economist*. January 4, 2003.
36. "What the World Thinks in 2002." Pew Global Attitudes Project. The Pew Research Center for the People and the Press. 2002.
37. Lipset, Seymour Martin. *American Exceptionalism: A Double-Edged Sword*. New York: Norton, 1996. p. 20.
38. "Views of a Changing World." The Pew Global Attitudes Project. The Pew Research Center for the People and the Press. June 2003.
39. Ibid.
40. Ibid.
41. "What the World Thinks in 2002." Pew Global Attitudes Project.
42. Hastings, Elizabeth Hawn, and Phillip K. *Index to International Public Opinion, 1988–1989*. New York: Greenwood Press, 1990. p. 612.
43. "*Newsweek* Poll—750 Adults Nationwide." Princeton Survey Research Associates. June 24–25, 1999.
44. Ibid.
45. Ibid.
46. Ibid.
47. Lasch, Christopher. *The Culture of Narcissism: American Life in an Age of Diminishing Expectations*. New York: Norton, 1979. pp. 30, 33.
48. "Gambling in America." The Gallup Organization. May 7, 2003. *www.gallup.com*
49. Berenson, Alex. "The States Bet Bigger on Betting." *The New York Times*. May 18, 2003.

50. Ibid.
51. Ibid.
52. Ibid.
53. "Who Wants to Be a Millionaire: Changing Conceptions of the American Dream." *American Studies Online*. February 13, 2003. p. 5. *www.americansc.org.uk*
54. Ibid.
55. Ibid.; Michael J. Sandel. "The Hard Questions: Bad Bet State Lotteries Are Shooting Craps with the Lives of the Poor." *The New Republic*. March 10, 1997. p. 27.
56. "National Gambling Impact Study Commission Final Report." National Gambling Impact Study Commission. 1999. *govinfo.library.unt.edu*. May 9, 2003.
57. Ibid.
58. "Reality Television Show Directory." *Reality TV Links*. *www.realitytvlinks.com*. December 22, 2003.
59. Adams, Michael. *Fire and Ice: The United States, Canada, and the Myth of Converging Values*. Toronto: Penguin, 2003. p. 53.
60. Ibid.
61. Ibid.
62. Ibid. p. 54.
63. Ibid.
64. Ibid.
65. Ibid.
66. Eisenberg, Pablo. "The Voluntary Sector: Problems and Challenges." In O'Connell, Brian, ed. *America's Voluntary Spirit*. Washington, DC: Foundation Center, 1983. p. 306; O'Neill, Michael. *The Third America: The Emergence of the Nonprofit Sector in the United States*. San Francisco: Jossey-Bass Publishers, 1989. p. 13.
67. Sokolowski, S. Wojciech, and Lester M. Salamon. "The United States." In Salamon, Lester M., Helmut Anheier, Regina List, Stefan Toepler, and Wojciech S. Sokolowski. "Global Civil Society: Dimensions of the Nonprofit Sector." Comparative Nonprofit Sector Project, The Johns Hopkins Center for Civil Society Studies, 1999. pp. 267–268. *www.jhu.edu/~ccss/pubs/books/gcs*
68. Ibid. p. 261.
69. Ibid. p. 268.
70. Ibid. p. 272.
71. Ibid. p. 270.
72. Putnam, Robert D. *Bowling Alone: The Collapse and Revival of American Community*. New York: Simon & Schuster, 2000. p. 283.
73. Bostrom, Meg. "Achieving the American Dream: A Meta-Analysis of Public Opinion Concerning Poverty, Upward Mobility, and Related Issues." Douglas Gould & Co. for the Ford Foundation. September 27, 2001.

CHAPTER 2: THE NEW LAND OF OPPORTUNITY

1. Lazarus, Emma. "The New Colossus." From *The New Dictionary of Cultural Literacy*, Third Edition. 2002. *www.bartleby.com*. August 13, 2003.
2. Smeeding, Timothy M. "Globalization, Inequality, and the Rich Countries of the G-20: Evidence from the Luxembourg Income Study (LIS)." July 30, 2002. p. 14.
3. Ibid.
4. Ibid. p. 11.
5. Ibid. p. 22; Jesuit, David, and Timothy Smeeding. "Poverty and Income Distribution." Luxembourg Income Study White Paper No. 293. Syracuse, NY: Syracuse University, January 2002. p. 6.
6. Mishel, Lawrence, Jared Bernstein, and Heather Boushey. *The State of Working America*

2002/2003. The Economic Policy Institute. Ithaca, NY: Cornell University Press, 2003. pp. 403–404.

7. Uchitelle, Louise. "A Recovery for Profits, But Not for Workers." *The New York Times*. December 21, 2003; Meyerson, Harold. "Un-American Recovery." *The Washington Post*. December 24, 2003.

8. Herbert, Bob. "Another Battle for Bush." *The New York Times*. December 15, 2003.

9. Uchitelle, Louise. "A Recovery for Profits, But Not for Workers."

10. Mishel, Lawrence, Jared Bernstein, and Heather Boushey. *The State of Working America 2002/2003*. p. 405–406.

11. Ibid. pp. 407, 410–411.

12. Jesuit, David, and Timothy Smeeding. "Poverty Levels in the Developed World." Maxwell School of Citizenship and Public Affairs at Syracuse University. July 23, 2002. pp. 8,9; Jesuit, David, and Timothy Smeeding. "Poverty and Income Distribution." p. 7.

13. "Views of a Changing World." The Pew Global Attitudes Project. The Pew Research Center for the People and the Press. June 2003. pp. 8, 108.

14. Ibid. p. 108.

15. Glazer, Nathan. "Why Americans Don't Care About Income Inequality." Paper presented at the Inequality and Social Policy Seminar Series. February 11, 2002. pp. 9–10.

16. Ibid. p. 10.

17. Ibid. p. 5; Inglehart, Ronald. *1990 World Values Survey*.

18. "Views of a Changing World." The Pew Global Attitudes Project. p. 8.

19. Bernstein, Robert. "Poverty, Income See Slight Changes; Child Poverty Rate Unchanged, Census Bureau Reports." United States Department of Commerce News. September 26, 2003. *www.census.gov*

20. Harrison, Paige M., and Jennifer C. Karberg. "Prison and Jail Inmates at Midyear 2002." Bureau of Justice Statistics. April 2003; "Two Million Inmates, and Counting." *The New York Times*. April 9, 2003.

21. Glazer, Nathan. "Why Americans Don't Care About Income Inequality." p. 3; "Economic Portrait of the European Union 2002." European Commission, 2002.

22. Glazer, Nathan. "Why Americans Don't Care About Income Inequality." pp. 3–4.

23. Mishel, Lawrence, Jared Bernstein, and Heather Boushey. *The State of Working America 2002/2003*. pp. 420–421.

24. Ibid. pp. 399–402; "Progress on the Lisbon Strategy." European Commission, 2003. *www.europa.eu.int*. p. 2.

25. Gordon, Robert J. "Two Centuries of Economic Growth: Europe Chasing the American Frontier." *Economic History Workshop, Northwestern University*. October 17, 2002. p. 126.

26. McGuckin, Robert H., and Bart van Ark. "Performance 2002: Productivity, Employment, and Income in the World Economies." The Conference Board. March 2003. pp. 3, 7. *www.conference-board.org/publications/describe.cfm?id=649*.

27. Ibid. pp. 4, 14.

28. Rhoades, Christopher. "U.S., EU Productivity Gap Is Widening." *The Wall Street Journal*. January 19, 2004.

29. Broad, William J. "US Is Losing Its Dominance in the Sciences." *The New York Times*. May 3, 2004.

30. Foster, Ian, and Carl Kesselman, eds. *The Grid: Blueprint for a New Computing Infrastructure*. San Francisco, CA: Morgan Kaufman Publishers, 1999. p. xix.

31. Ibid.

32. Ibid.

33. Markoff, John, and Jennifer L. Schenker. "Europe Exceeds U.S. in Refining Grid Computing." *The New York Times*. November 10, 2003.

34. Ibid.

35. Ibid.
36. McGuckin, Robert H., and Bart van Ark. "Performance 2002: Productivity, Employment, and Income in the World Economies." p. 5; "Progress on the Lisbon Strategy." European Commission, 2003. p. 2.
37. Honore, Carl. "A Time to Work, a Time to Play: France's 35-hour Week: Shorter Hours Result in a Social Revolution." *National Post.* January 31, 2002.
38. Trumbull, Gunnar. "France's 35 Hour Work Week: Flexibility Through Regulation." The Brookings Institution. January 2001.
39. "Making France Work." *The Wall Street Journal.* October 10, 2003.
40. Honore, Carl. "A Time to Work, a Time to Play: France's 35-hour Week: Shorter Hours Result in a Social Revolution."
41. Foroohar, Rana, et al. "Eat, Drink, and Go Slow: The Post-Crash Backlash Against American Taste." *Newsweek International, Atlantic Edition.* July 2, 2001.
42. "French Law: The Standard French Working Week." Triplet and Associés. March 30, 2004. *www.triplet.com*
43. Jeffries, Stuart. "The World: C'est magnifique! Le weekend Just Goes On and On for French Workers." *The Guardian.* May 27, 2001.
44. Honore, Carl. "Slowing the World: Last in a Series." *National Post.* January 31, 2002.
45. Rhoads, Christopher. "Clocking Out: Short Work Hours Undercut European Economic Drive." *The Wall Street Journal.* August 8, 2002.
46. Mishel, Lawrence, Jared Bernstein, and Heather Boushey. *The State of Working America 2002/2003.* p. 425; "Employment Outlook: Average Annual Hours Worked in the OECD, 1979–2000." Paris: OECD, 2001.
47. Mishel, Lawrence, Jared Bernstein, and Heather Boushey. *The State of Working America 2002/2003.* p. 425.
48. "Changeover from Career Breaks to Time Credits Proves Complex." European Industrial Relations Observatory. August 2001. *www.eiro.eurofound.eu.int*
49. "Inter-community Dispute on Time Credit Scheme." European Industrial Relations Observatory. February 2002. *www.eiro.eurofound.ie/2002/02/inbrief/BE0202305N.html*
50. Ibid.; "Changeover from Career Breaks to Time Credits Proves Complex." European Industrial Relations Observatory.
51. McGuckin, Robert H., and Bart van Ark. "Performance 2002: Productivity, Employment, and Income in the World Economies."
52. Scheier, Lee. "Call it a Day, America." *Chicago Tribune.* May 5, 2002.
53. Ibid.
54. "Main Economic Indicators: Purchasing Power Parities." OECD. February 2004. *www.oecd.org*
55. "Employment Outlook: Average Annual Hours Worked in the OECD, 1979–2000." Paris: OECD, 2001.
56. "Annual Average Unemployment Rate, Civilian Labor Force 16 Years and Older." March 18, 2003. Bureau of Labor Statistics. *www.bls.gov/cps/prev_yrs.htm*; "Labor Force Statistics from the Current Population Survey." Bureau of Labor Statistics. May 26, 2004. *www.bls.gov.*
57. "Labor Force Statistics from the Current Population Survey (SIC)." U.S. Department of Labor. Bureau of Labor Statistics. *http://data.bls.gov.* August 12, 2003; "Prison Statistics." Bureau of Justice Statistics Prison Statistics. December 31, 2002. *www.ojp.usdoj.gov;* "Key Facts at a Glance: Correctional Populations." U.S. Department of Justice. Bureau of Justice Statistics. July 27, 2003. *www.ojp.usdoj.gov/bjs/glance*
58. Herbert, Bob. "Despair of the Jobless." *The New York Times.* August 7, 2003; "Jobs and the Jobless." *The Washington Post.* May 5, 2003.
59. "U.S. Personal Savings Rates." Bureau of Economic Analysis. October 3, 2003.
60. "New ILO Study Highlights Labour Trends Worldwide: US Productivity Up, Europe Improves Ability to Create Jobs." International Labour Organization. September 1, 2003.

www.ilo.org; "Productivity and Costs, Second Quarter 2003, revised." Bureau of Labor Statistics. September 4, 2003. *www.bls.gov*; Berry, John M. "Efficiency of U.S. Workers Up Sharply." *Washington Post*. February 7, 2003.

61. Jones, Del, and Barbara Hansen. "Companies Do More with Less." *USA Today*. August 12, 2003.

CHAPTER 3: THE QUIET ECONOMIC MIRACLE

1. "Economic Portrait of the European Union 2002." European Commission. 2002. p. 55.
2. Ibid. p. 74; Patten, Christopher. "The European Union and the World." In Guttman, Robert J. *Europe in the New Century: Visions of an Emerging Superpower*. Boulder, CO: Lynne Rienner Publishers, 2001. p. 79.
3. "United Nations Human Development Report 2002: Deepening Democracy in a Fragmented World." *United Nations Development Program*. Oxford, U.K.: Oxford University Press, 2002. Sec. 3, p. 15.
4. "Main Economic Indicators: Gross Domestic Product." *OECD*. February 2004. *www.oecd.org*; "Current Dollar and Real Gross Domestic Product." Bureau of Economic Analysis. March 25, 2004.
5. "The World Economic Outlook (WEO) Database: Selected World Aggregates." *International Monetary Fund*. April 2003. *www.imf.org*
6. "The World Economic Outlook (WEO): GDP Current Prices." *International Monetary Fund*. April 2003.
7. "Trans-European Networks." European Commission. August 8, 2002. *www.europa.eu.int*
8. "The Europe of Knowledge." *Le Magazine: Education and Culture in Europe*. Issue 18. 2002. pp. 14–15.
9. Thomas, Daniel. "Offshore Gartner Urges Users to Consider New EU States as Potential Offshore Outsourcing Destinations." *Computer Weekly*. March 9, 2004.
10. Aoki, Naomi. "Gillette to Build a Plant in Poland, Jobs Would Be Shifted from Germany, Britain." *The Boston Globe*. March 17, 2004.
11. "Dollar Weakens, G7 Warning Dismissed." *Reuters*. February 10, 2004.
12. McCartney, Robert J. "Global Anxiety Propels Euro Above Dollar." *The Washington Post*. January 31, 2003.
13. Monbiot, George. "The Bottom Dollar." *The Guardian*. Tuesday, April 22, 2003.
14. "The Not-So Mighty Dollar." *The Economist*. December 6, 2003.
15. Becker, Elizabeth, and Edmund L. Andrews. "I.M.F. Says Rise in U.S. Debts Is Threat to World's Economy." *The New York Times*. January 8, 2004.
16. "Statement on the President's Fiscal Year 2005 Budget by Office of Management and Budget Director Joshua B. Bolten Before the Committee on the Budget United States House of Representatives." Executive Office of the President. February 3, 2004; Andrews, Edmund L. "G-7 Statement Signals Worry About Dollar." *The New York Times*. February 8, 2004.
17. Becker, Elizabeth, and Edmund L. Andrews. "I.M.F. Says Rise in U.S. Debts Is Threat to World's Economy."
18. Ibid.
19. "A Comparison of the Top 25 United States GSPs with the Top 25 European Union GDPs." U.S. Department of Commerce: Bureau of Economic Analysis. November 15, 2002. *www.bea.gov*
20. "The 2003 Global 500." *Fortune*. July 21, 2003. *www.fortune.com*
21. Durman, Paul. "Nokia Bets on a Mobile World." *The Sunday Times*. June 22, 2003; Reinhardt, Andy. "Something for Everyone." *BusinessWeek*. March 31, 2003; Verdin, Mike. "Why Nokia Is Winning the Phone War." *BBC News Online*. April 20, 2001. *http://news.bbc.co.uk*; "Global 500: Nokia." *Fortune*. July 21, 2003. *www.fortune.com*

22. Guyon, Janet. "Why Big Is Better for Vodafone." *Fortune.* February 3, 2002. *www. fortune.com;* "Profile—VodafoneGroup plc." Yahoo! Finance. April 9, 2003. *Biz.yahoo.com*

23. Barnard, Bruce. "Business and the Technologies of the Future." In Guttman, Robert J. *Europe in the New Century: Visions of an Emerging Superpower.* p. 171; Fox, Justin. "Bertelsmann: Tomas Middelhoff Wants Respect." *Fortune.* May 15, 2002. *www.fortune.com;* "Pearson." Yahoo! Finance UK & Ireland. December 31, 2002. *uk.biz.yahoo.com*

24. Rossant, John. "How to Build a Better EU Constitution." *BusinessWeek.* June 30, 2003.

25. Tomlinson, Richard. "International Fortune: AHOLD." *Fortune.* June 27, 2002; "The 2003 Global 500: Royal Ahold." *Fortune.* January 21, 2003. *www.fortune.com*

26. Brooks, Rick. "FedEx, UPS Join Forces to Stave Off Foreign Push into U.S. Market." *The Wall Street Journal.* February 1, 2001.

27. "The 2003 Global 500: Industry Snapshot: Banks: Commercial and Savings." *Fortune.* July 21, 2003. *www.fortune.com*

28. "The 2003 Global 500: Industry Snapshot: Chemicals." *Fortune.* July 21, 2003. *www. fortune.com*

29. "The 2003 Global 500: Industry Snapshot: Engineering, Construction." *Fortune.* July 21, 2003. *www.fortune.com*

30. "The 2003 Global 500: Industry Snapshot: Consumer Food Products." *Fortune.* July 21, 2003. *www.fortune.com*

31. "The 2003 Global 500: Industry Snapshot: Food & Drug Stores." *Fortune.* July 21, 2003. *www.fortune.com*

32. "Top Ten World Reinsurance Companies." Insurance Information Institute. 2001. *www. internationalinsurance.org*

33. "The 2003 Global 500: Industry Snapshot: Life, Health (stock)." *Fortune.* July 21, 2003. *www.fortune.com*

34. "The 2003 Global 500: Industry Snapshot: Insurance: P&C (stock)." *Fortune.* July 21, 2003. *www.fortune.com*

35. "The 2003 Global 500: Industry Snapshot: Telecommunications." *Fortune.* July 21, 2003. *www.fortune.com*

36. "The 2003 Global 500: Industry Snapshot: Pharmaceuticals." *Fortune.* July 21, 2003. *www.fortune.com*

37. "The 2003 Global 500: Industry Snapshot: Motor Vehicles & Parts." *Fortune.* July 21, 2003. *www.fortune.com*

38. Johnson, Mark, et al. "The World's Best Companies 2002." *Global Finance.* November 2002.

39. "SMEs in Europe, Including a First Glance at EU Candidate Countries." European Commission. 2002. p. 13. *www.europa.eu.int*

40. "SMEs in Europe: Competitiveness, Innovation, and the Knowledge Driven Society." European Commission. 2002. pp. 8–9.

41. "European Trend Chart on Innovation: 2002 European Innovation Scoreboard Technical Paper No. 1: Member States and Associate Countries." European Commission. December 4, 2002. pp. 2, 5. *www.europa.eu.int*

42. Ibid. pp. 5–6; Wagstyl, Stefan. "EU Nears US and Japan in Promoting Innovation." *Financial Times.* December 11, 2002.

43. Wagstyl, Stefan. "EU Nears US and Japan in Promoting Innovation."

44. Schroeder, Michael. "The Economy: World Economy Expected to Grow 4.75% in 2004." *The Asian Wall Street Journal.* April 5, 2004.

45. "Euro-Indicators: First Notification of Deficit and Debt Data for 2003." *Eurostat.* March 16, 2004; "Debt Outstanding by Type of Debt: The Debt to the Penny and Who Holds It." Bureau of the Public Debt, U.S. Department of the Treasury. April 5, 2004. *www.publicdebt. treas.gov;* "Main Economic Indicators: Key Short-Term Indicators for OECD Member Countries." OECD. April 2004; "BEA News: Personal Income and Outlays: February 2004." Bureau of Economic Analysis. March 26, 2004.

46. Tran, Muoi. "By the Numbers: New Money: The Very Rich, by Region." *Fortune*. June 24, 2003.

47. Foroohar, Rana, et al. "Eat, Drink, and Go Slow." *Newsweek International, Atlantic Edition*. July 2, 2001.

48. Cobb, Clifford, Ted Halstead, and Jonathan Rowe. "If the GDP Is Up, Why Is America Down?" *The Atlantic*. October 1995. *www.theatlantic.com/politics/ecbig*

49. "Measuring Progress: Annex 1—What's Wrong with the GDP?" Friends of the Earth. March 13, 2003. *www.foe.co.uk*

50. Cobb, Clifford, Ted Halstead, and Jonathan Rowe. "If the GDP Is Up, Why Is America Down?" pp. 16–17.

51. Ibid. p. 17.

52. Tomkins, Richard. "How to Be Happy." *Financial Times Weekend*. March 8–9, 2003.

53. Ibid.; "Genuine Progress Indicator: Contents of the GPI." Redefining Progress. March 13, 2003. *www.redefiningprogress.org/projects/gpi/gpi_contents*

54. "Alternatives to the GDP." McGregor Consulting Group. March 25, 2003. *www.consultmcgregor.com*

55. Osberg, Larry, and Andrew Sharpe. "Human Well-Being and Economic Well-Being: What Values Are Implicit in Current Indices?" Center for the Study of Living Standards. July 2003.

56. "The Social Situation in the European Union, 2002." European Commission. May 22, 2002. *www.europa.eu.int*

57. "World Development Indicators Database: Total GDP 2002." The World Bank. July 2003. "Fiscal Year 2004 Budget." Center for Defense Information. August 4, 2003. *www.cdi.org*

58. "Country/Region Population." Eurostat. August 8, 2003. *www.europa.eu.int*; "Energy Information Administration: State Energy Data 2000." Energy Information Administration. *www.eia.doe.gov*; "Historical National Population Estimates." Population Estimates Program, Population Division, U.S. Census Bureau. April 11, 2000. *www.census.gov*; "Regional Indicators: European Union (EU)." Energy Information Administration. October 2002. *www.eia.doe.gov*

59. "Energy Information Administration: State Energy Data 2000."

60. "Justice Expenditure and Employment in the United States, 1999." *Bureau of Justice Statistics Bulletin*. U.S. Department of Justice, Office of Justice Programs. February 2002. *www.ojp.usdoj.gov*; "U.S. Department of Justice: Summary of Budget Authority by Appropriation." Bureau of Justice Statistics, 2002.

61. Blau, Francine D., and Lawrence Kahn. "Do Cognitive Test Scores Explain Higher U.S. Wage Inequality?" National Bureau of Economic Research." September 2000. p. 13. *http://papers.nber.org*

62. "Education at a Glance: OECD Indicators 2002." Organization for Economic Co-operation and Development. 2002. p. 66.

63. Ibid. p. 69.

64. Ibid. pp. 74, 77, 161, 214, 222.

65. "United Nations Human Development Report 2002: Deepening Democracy in a Fragmented World." *United Nations Development Program*. pp. 23, 29.

66. Ibid. pp. 18, 21. "Preventing Infant Mortality." U.S. Department of Health and Human Services. April 18, 2001.

67. "Economic Portrait of the European Union 2002." p. 129; "United Nations Human Development Report 2002: Deepening Democracy in a Fragmented World." United Nations Development Program. pp. 18–19.

68. "The World Health Report 2000." The World Health Organization, 2000.

69. "The US Health Care System." Bureau of Labor Education of the University of Maine. pp. 4, 6.

70. Ayers, Stephen M., M.D. "Health Care in the United States: The Facts and the Choices." Chicago and London: American Library Association, 1996. p. xii.
71. Rhoades, Jeffrey A., Ph.D. "Statistical Brief #19: The Uninsured in America—2002." Medical Expenditure Panel Survey. Agency for Healthcare and Research Quality. July 2003.
72. "OECD Data Show Health Expenditures at an All-time High." Organization for Economic Co-operation and Development. (OECD) June 23, 2003. *www.oecd.org*
73. "The US Health Care System." Bureau of Labor Education of the University of Maine. pp. 2–3.
74. "Real Gross Domestic Product and Related Measures." U.S. Department of Commerce. Bureau of Economic Analysis. August 6, 2003. *www.bea.doc.gov*
75. "Obesity Rates Among the Adult Population." OECD Health Data, 2003. *www.oecd.org/dataoecd/10/20/2789777.pdf*; Power, Carla. "Big Trouble." *Newsweek.* August 11, 2003.
76. "Obesity in Europe: The Case for Action." International Obesity Task Force and European Association for the Study of Obesity. September 2002.
77. "Obesity Rates Among the Adult Population." OECD Health Data. 2003.
78. "Obesity and Overweight." World Health Organization: Global Strategy on Diet, Physical Activity and Health, 2003.
79. "Innocent Report Card: A League Table of Child Poverty in Rich Nations." UNICEF. No. 1. June 2000. p. 6.
80. Ibid.
81. Ibid. pp. 6–7.
82. Ibid. p. 7.
83. "Basic Facts on Poverty." Children's Defense Fund. December 2002. *www.childrens defense.org*
84. Graff, James. "Gunning for It." *Time Europe.* Vol. 159. No. 19. May 13, 2002.
85. "Rates of Homicide, Suicide, and Firearm-related Death Among Children—26 Industrialized Countries." *Morbidity and Mortality Weekly Report.* Vol. 46, No. 5. February 7, 1997. p. 102.
86. Barclay, Gordon, and Cynthia Tavares. "International Comparisons of Criminal Justice Statistics 2000." July 12, 2002; "Two Million Inmates and Counting." *The New York Times.* April 9, 2003.
87. Barclay, Gordon, and Cynthia Tavares. "International Comparisons of Criminal Justice Statistics 2000."
88. Noll, Heinz-Herbert. "Towards a European System of Social Indicators." *Social Indicators Research.* Special Issue Vol. 58. 2002.
89. Argyle, M. "Subjective Well-Being." In Offer, A. *In Pursuit of the Quality of Life.* Oxford, U.K.: Oxford University Press. January 1997. pp. 18–45.
90. Ibid.
91. "Our Common Future." World Commission on Environment and Development. Oxford, U.K.: Oxford University Press, 1987.
92. Baker, Linda. "Real Wealth: The Genuine Progress Indicator Could Provide an Environmental Measure of the Planet's Earth." *E/The Environmental Magazine.* March 13, 2003. *www.emagazine.com*

CHAPTER 4: SPACE, TIME, AND MODERNITY

1. "United Nations Human Development Report 2002." United Nations Development Program. Oxford, U.K.: Oxford University Press, 2002. p. 38.
2. "The Mobiles: Social Evolution in a Wireless Society." Context Based Research Group, 2002. p. 15.
3. Ibid. pp. 23, 25, 27.
4. Gimpel, Jean. *The Medieval Machine.* New York: Penguin, 1976. pp. 43–44.

5. White, Lynn, Jr. *Medieval Technology & Social Change*. London.: Oxford University Press, 1962. p. 78.
6. Ibid. pp. 88–89.
7. Gimpel, Jean. *The Medieval Machine*. p. 195; Pagden, Anthony. "Europe: Conceptualizing a Continent." In Pagden. *The Idea of Europe: From Antiquity to the European Union*. Cambridge, U.K.: Cambridge University Press, 2002. p. 50.
8. Johnson, Paul. *The Birth of the Modern*. New York: HarperPerennial, 1991. p. 203.
9. Wright, Lawrence. *Clockwork Man*. New York: Horizon Press, 1969. p. 154.
10. Hansen, Marcus Lee. *The Atlantic Migration*. Cambridge, MA: Harvard University Press, 1940. pp. 178ff.
11. Randall, John Herman. *The Making of the Modern Mind*. Cambridge, MA: Houghton Mifflin, 1940. p. 223.
12. Ibid. p. 224.
13. Bacon, Francis. "Novum Organum." *The Works of Francis Bacon*, vol. 4. London: W. Pickering, 1850. p. 246.
14. Ibid. p. 114.
15. Randall, John Herman. *The Making of the Modern Mind*. p. 241. Quotation by Descartes.
16. Ibid. pp. 241–242.
17. Locke, John. "Second Treatise." In Locke. *Two Treatises of Government*. Peter Laslett, ed. Cambridge, U.K.: Cambridge University Press, 1967. p. 315.
18. Locke, John. *The Second Treatise of Civil Government: Chapter V: Of Property, Section 40*. 1690.
19. Strauss, Leo. *Natural Right and History*. Chicago: University of Chicago, 1950. Quotation by John Locke. p. 315.
20. Ibid. p. 258.
21. Randall, John Herman. *The Making of the Modern Mind*. p. 259. Quotation by Descartes.
22. Quotation by Bertrand Russell, 1872–1970.
23. Newton, Isaac. *Mathematical Principles of Natural Philosophy*. Book 3. Author's Preface.
24. Randall, John Herman. *The Making of the Modern Mind*. p. 259.
25. Whitehead, Alfred North. *Science and the Modern World*. New York: Free Press, 1967.
26. Le Goff, Jacques. *Your Money or Your Life: Economy and Religion in the Middle Ages*. New York: Zone Books, 1988. p. 29. Quotation by St. Thomas Aquinas.
27. [On the question of time.] Le Goff, Jacques. *Time, Work, and Culture in the Middle Ages*. pp. 51–61; Quinones, Ricardo J. *The Renaissance Discovery of Time*. Cambridge, MA: Harvard University Press, 1972. pp. 5–8; de Grazia, Sebastian. *Of Time, Work, and Leisure*. New York: Anchor/Doubleday, 1964.
28. Chobham, Thomas. *Summa Confessorum*. F. Broomfield, ed. Paris: Louvain, 1968. p. 505, question XI, ch. 1.
29. Le Goff, Jacques. *Time, Work, and Culture in the Middle Ages*. p. 30.
30. Woodcock, George. "The Tyranny of the Clock." *Politics*. Vol. 1. 1994. pp. 265–266.
31. de Grazia, Sebastian. *Of Time, Work, and Leisure*. p. 41.
32. Ibid. p. 54.
33. McCann, Justin. *The Rule of St. Benedict*. London: Sheed & Ward, 1970. chapter 48.
34. Zerubavel, Eviatar. *Hidden Rhythms: Schedules and Calendars in Social Life*. Chicago: University of Chicago Press, 1981. p. 33.
35. Ibid. p. 32.
36. Bendix, Reinhard. *Max Weber*. Garden City, NY: Anchor-Doubleday, 1962. p. 318.
37. Wright, Lawrence. *Clockwork Man*. p. 208.
38. Boorstin, Daniel J. *The Discoverers*. New York: Random House, 1983. p. 38.
39. Wright, Lawrence. *Clockwork Man*. p. 62.
40. Ibid. p. 55.
41. Ibid.

42. Mumford, Lewis. *Technics and Civilization*. New York: Harcourt, Brace, 1934. p. 15.
43. Landes, David. *Revolution in Time*. p. 16.
44. Ibid. pp. 72–73.
45. Le Goff, Jacques. *Time, Work, and Culture in the Middle Ages*. p. 35.
46. Goody, Jack. "Time: Social Organization." *International Encyclopedia of the Social Sciences*. David Sills, ed. Vol. 16. New York: Free Press/Macmillan, 1968. pp. 38–39.
47. Mumford, Lewis. *Technics and Civilization*. New York: Harcourt, Brace and World, 1934. p. 16.
48. Frederick, Christine. "The New Housekeeping." *Ladies' Home Journal*. Vol. 29. No. 9. September 1912.
49. Frederick, Christine. "Housekeeping with Efficiency." New York: *Ladies' Home Journal*, 1913. Preface.
50. Warren, Maude Radford. *The Saturday Evening Post*. March 12, 1912. pp. 11–12, 34–35.
51. "Proceedings." National Education Association, 1912. p. 492.
52. Mencken, Henry L. *The American Language: An Inquiry into the Development of English in the United States*, 4th ed. New York: Knopf, 1936.
53. Tichi, Cecelia. *Shifting Gears: Technology, Literature, Culture in Modernist America*. Chapel Hill, NC: University of North Carolina Press, 1987. pp. 116–117.
54. Book, William F. *The Intelligence of High School Seniors*. New York: Macmillan, 1922.

CHAPTER 5: CREATING THE INDIVIDUAL

1. "Entrepreneurship." *The European Commission: Eurobarometer*. January 2004. *www.europa.eu.int*; Buck, Tobias. "Europeans Balk at Starting Their Own Business." *Financial Times*. March 3, 2004.
2. Duby, Georges. "Solitude: Eleventh to Thirteenth Century." In Duby, Georges ed. *A History of Private Life: Revelations in the Medieval World*. Vol. 2. Cambridge, MA: Harvard University Press, 1988. p. 510; Tuan, Yi-Fu. *Segmented Worlds and Self: Group Life and Individual Consciousness*. Minneapolis: University of Minnesota Press, 1982. p. 58.
3. Thomas, Keith. *Man and the Natural World: A History of the Modern Sensibility*. New York: Pantheon, 1983. p. 95.
4. Beresford, Maurice, and John G. Hurst, eds. *Deserted Medieval Villages*. New York: St. Martin's Press, 1972. p. 236.
5. Weiner, Philip P. "Man-Machine from the Greeks to the Computer." In Weiner, ed. *Dictionary of the History of Ideas*. New York: 1973–74. p. iii.
6. Thomas, Keith. *Man and the Natural World: A History of the Modern Sensibility*. p. 39.
7. Lamont, William, and Sybil Oldfield, eds. *Politics, Religion and Literature in the 17th Century*. London: Dent, Rowman & Littlefield, 1975. pp. 61–62.
8. Desiderius, Erasmus. *De civilitate morum puerilium (On the Civility of Children.)*. 1540. Robert Whittinton, trans.; Tuan, Yi-Fu. *Segmented Worlds and Self: Group Life and Individual Consciousness*. pp. 48–50; Elias, Norbert. *The Civilizing Process: The History of Manners*. New York: Urizen Books, 1978. pp. 73–74.
9. Furnivall, Frederick J. *English Meals and Manners*. Detroit, MI: Singing Tree Press, 1969. p. xvi; Tuan, Yi-Fu. *Segmented Worlds and Self: Group Life and Individual Consciousness*. p. 42.
10. Tuan, Yi-Fu. *Segmented Worlds and Self: Group Life and Individual Consciousness*. p. 42.
11. Rifkin, Jeremy. *Biosphere Politics*. New York: Crown, 1991. p. 198.
12. Tuan, Yi-Fu. *Segmented Worlds and Self: Group Life and Individual Consciousness*. p. 42.
13. Ibid. p. 44; Elias, Norbert. *The Civilizing Process: The History of Manners*. p. 118.
14. Elias, Norbert. *The Civilizing Process: The History of Manners*. p. 121.
15. Ibid. p. 126.
16. Ibid. p. 68; Tuan, Yi-Fu. *Segmented Worlds and Self: Group Life and Individual Consciousness*. p. 45; Cooper, Charles. *The English Table in History and Literature*. London: Sampson Low, Marston & Company, n.d. pp. 17, 19.

17. Elias, Norbert. *The Civilizing Process: The History of Manners.* p. 107; Tuan, Yi-Fu. *Segmented Worlds and Self: Group Life and Individual Consciousness.* p. 46.

18. Brett, Gerard. *Dinner Is Served: A History of Dining in England, 1400–1900.* London: Rupert Hart-Davis, 1968. p. 116.

19. Barley, M. W. *The House and Home: A Review of 900 Years of House Planning and Furnishing in Britain.* Greenwich, CT: New York Graphic Society, 1971. pp. 40–41; Aries, Philippe. "The Family and the City." In Rossi, Alice, ed. *The Family.* New York: Norton, 1965. pp. 227–235; Holmes, U. T. Jr. *Daily Living in the Twelfth Century: Based on the Observations of Alexander Neckham in London and Paris.* Madison: University of Wisconsin Press, 1952. p. 231.

20. Tuan, Yi-Fu. *Segmented Worlds and Self: Group Life and Individual Consciousness.* pp. 59–60; Everett, Alan. "Farm Labourers." In Thirsk, Joan, ed. *The Agrarian History of England and Wales: 1500–1640.* Cambridge, U.K.: Cambridge University Press, 1967. pp. 442–443.

21. Aries, Philippe. *Centuries of Childhood: A Social History of Private Life.* New York: Random House, 1962. p. 369.

22. Berman, Morris. *Coming to Our Senses: Body and Spirit in the Hidden History of the West.* New York: Simon & Schuster, 1989. p. 48.

23. Giedion, Siegfried. *Mechanization Takes Command: A Contribution to Anonymous History.* New York: Norton, 1969. pp. 268–269.

24. Lukacs, John. "The Bourgeois Interior." *American Scholar* 39. Fall 1970, Vol. 623; Tuan, Yi-Fu. *Segmented Worlds and Self: Group Life and Individual Consciousness.* p. 83.

25. Elias, Norbert. *The Civilizing Process: The History of Manners.* p. 177; Duby, Georges. "Solitude." In Duby, ed. *A History of Private Life: Revelations in the Medieval World.* pp. 589–590.

26. Elias, Norbert. *The Civilizing Process: The History of Manners.* pp. 178–180; Aries, Philippe. *Centuries of Childhood: A Social History of Family Life.* pp. 100–127.

27. Duby, Georges. "Solitude." In Duby, ed. *A History of Private Life: Revelations in the Medieval World.* p. 605.

28. Tuan, Yi-Fu. *Segmented Worlds and Self: Group Life and Individual Consciousness.* pp. 125–126.

29. Rifkin, Jeremy. *Biosphere Politics.* p. 212.

30. Ibid. p. 214; Corbin, Alain. *The Foul and the Fragrant: Odor and the French Social Imagination.* Cambridge, MA. Harvard University Press, 1986. pp. 143–144.

CHAPTER 6: INVENTING THE IDEOLOGY OF PROPERTY

1. Schaff, Philip. *America: A Sketch of Its Political, Social, and Religious Character.* Cambridge, MA: Harvard University Press, 1855, 1961. p. 87; Tocqueville, Alexis de. *Democracy in America.* George Lawrence, trans. New York: Harper, 1988. p. 238.

2. Schlatter, Richard. *Private Property: The History of an Idea.* New York: Russell & Russell, 1973.

3. Ibid. p. 64.

4. Randall, John Herman, Jr. *The Making of the Modern Mind.* Cambridge, MA: Riverside Press, 1940. p. 140.

5. Marty, Martin E. *A Short History of Christianity.* New York: Collins World, 1959. pp. 220, 223; Weber, Max. *The Protestant Ethic and the Spirit of Capitalism.* New York: Scribner's, 1958. pp. 104–105, 108, 116–117.

6. Tawney, R. H. *The Acquisitive Society.* New York: Harcourt, Brace, 1920. p. 13.

7. Ibid. p. 17.

8. Schlatter, Richard. *Private Property: The History of an Idea.* pp. 118–120; *Les Six Libres de la Republique.* 1576. Reference Richard Knolles's English translation of the Latin, London, England: 1606.

9. Schlatter, Richard. *Private Property: The History of an Idea.* p. 119.

10. Ibid. p. 120.

11. Tawney, R. H. *The Acquisitive Society.*

12. Ibid. p. 20.
13. Reeve, Andrew. *Property*. London: Macmillan, 1986. p. 124; Schlatter, Richard, *Private Property: The History of an Idea*. p. 154.
14. Locke, John; Schlatter, Richard. *Private Property: The History of an Idea*. p. 154.
15. Schlatter, Richard. *Private Property: The History of an Idea*. p. 242.
16. Ibid. p. 249.
17. Reeve, Andrew. *Property*. p. 137.
18. Ibid. pp. 137–138.
19. Ibid. p. 138.
20. Ibid. pp. 298–299.
21. Beaglehole, Ernest. *Property: A Study in Social Psychology*. New York: Macmillan, 1932. p. 303.
22. Ely, James W. *The Guardian of Every Other Right*. New York: Oxford University Press, 1992. p. 26.
23. Locke, John. *Second Treatise of Civil Government*. Peter Laslett, ed. Cambridge, U.K.: Cambridge University Press, 1963. #123, #124.
24. Kelley, Donald R. *Historians and the Law in Postrevolutionary France*. Princeton, NJ: Princeton University Press, 1984. p. 129.
25. Bethell, Tom. *The Noblest Triumph: Property and Prosperity Through the Ages*. p. 98. Quotation by Say.
26. De Soto, Hernando. *The Mystery of Capital*. New York: Basic Books, 2000. p. 5.
27. Ibid. p. 35.
28. Ibid. p. 6.
29. Ibid. p. 10.
30. Ibid. p. 8.
31. Kelley, Donald R. *Historians and the Law in Postrevolutionary France*. p. 131.
32. Condorcet, Marquis de. *Outlines of an Historical View of the Progress of the Human Mind*. London: J. Johnson, 1795. pp. 4–5.
33. Rousseau, Jean-Jacques. *Discourse on the Origin of Inequality*. In Rousseau, *Basic Political Writings*, Donald A. Cress, trans. and ed. Indianapolis: Hackett Publishing, 1987. p. 60.
34. Sombart, Werner. *Why Is There No Socialism in the United States?* White Plains, NY: International Arts and Sciences Press, 1976. p. 106.
35. Jameson, Anna Brownell. *Winter Studies and Summer Rambles in Canada*. Reissue edition. Toronto: New Canadian Library, 1990.
36. Johnson, Paul. *The Birth of the Modern*. New York: Harper Perennial, 1991. p. 211.
37. "The Homestead Act." The National Park Service. August 20, 2003. *www.nps.gov*
38. Skaggs, Jimmy M. *Prime Cut*. College Station: Texas A&M University Press, 1967. p. 79.
39. Turner, Frederick Jackson. *The Frontier in American History*. Tucson: University of Arizona Press, 1994. p. 1.
40. "Strategies for Housing and Social Integration in Cities." Organization for Economic Cooperation and Development. Paris: OECD, 1996. p. 40.
41. Jackson, Kenneth. *Crabgrass Frontier: The Suburbanization of the United States*. New York: Oxford University Press, 1985. p. 57.
42. Ibid. p. 58.
43. "British Homes the Smallest in Europe." Bradford & Bingley, 2003. Sources: HM Land Registry Residential Property Price Report, Oct.–Dec. 2001; "Characteristics of New Single-Family Homes (1987–2002)." National Association of Home Builders. August 21, 2003. *www.nahb.org*
44. Platt, Rutherford H. *Land Use and Society*. Washington, DC: Federal Highway Administration Office of Highway Information Management. July 1992. pp. 23–24.
45. Diamond, Henry L., and Patrick F. Noonan. *Land Use in America*. Washington, DC: Island Press, 1996. p. 85.

46. Arendt, Randall G. *Conservation Design for Subdivisions.* Washington, DC: Island Press, 1996. p. 19.
47. Schueler, Tom. *Site Planning for Urban Stream Protection.* Washington, DC: Metropolitan Council of Governments, Environmental Land Planning Series, 1995. p. 73.
48. Newman, Peter W. G., and Jeffrey R. Kenworthy. *Cities and Automobile Dependence: A Sourcebook.* Aldershot, U.K., and Brookfield, VT: Gower Publishing Co., 1989. pp. 40–44.
49. Jackson, Kenneth T. *Crabgrass Frontier: The Suburbanization of the United States.* pp. 204–209.
50. "British Have Smallest Homes in Europe." The Move Channel. May 3, 2002. *www.themovechannel.com*
51. Ibid.; "Housing Vacancy Survey—Annual 2002." The U.S. Census Bureau, 2002. *www.census.gov*; Maclennan, Duncan. "Decentralization and Residential Choices in European Cities: The Roles of State and Market." In Summers, Anita A., Paul C. Cheshire, and Lanfranco Senn, eds. *Urban Change in the United States and Western Europe: Comparative Analysis and Policy.* Washington, DC: Urban Institute, 1993, p. 517.
52. "British Have Smallest Homes in Europe"; Nivola, Pietro S. *Laws of the Landscape: How Politics Shape Cities in Europe and America.* Washington, DC: Brookings Institution Press, 1999. p. 22.
53. Jackson, Kenneth. *Crabgrass Frontier: The Suburbanization of the United States.* p. 280.
54. Stegman, Michael A., and Margery Austin Turner. "The Future of Urban America in the Global Economy." *Journal of the American Planning Association.* Vol. 62. Spring 1996. p. 157.
55. Suplee, Curt. "Slaves of Lawn." p. 20.
56. Jackson, Kenneth. *Crabgrass Frontier: The Suburbanization of the United States.* p. 50.
57. "The Social Situation in the European Union, 2002." European Commission. May 22, 2002. *www.europa.eu.int*
58. Diamond, Henry L., and Patrick F. Noonan. *Land Use in America.* Washington, DC: Island Press, 1996. p. 68; Davis, Judy S., Arthur C. Nelson, and Kenneth J. Ducker. "The New 'Burbs: The Exurbs and Their Implications for Planning Policy." *Journal of the American Planning Association.* Vol. 60, Winter 1994. pp. 45–46.
59. "Guiding Principles for Sustainable Spatial Development of the European Continent." European Conference of Ministers Responsible for Regional Planning (CEMAT). February 6, 2003. *www.coe.int*
60. Turner, Frederick Jackson. *The Frontier in American History.* p. 320.
61. Ibid.
62. Ibid.
63. Ibid. p. 312.
64. Ibid. p. 211.
65. Ibid. p. 288.
66. Adams, Charles. *For Good and Evil: The Impact of Taxes on the Course of Civilization.* New York: Madison Books, 1993. pp. 360–364.
67. Roosevelt, Theodore. *The New Nationalism.* Englewood Cliffs, NJ: Prentice-Hall, 1910. (1961 reprint). p. 33.

CHAPTER 7: FORGING CAPITALIST MARKETS AND NATION-STATES

1. Heilbroner, Robert L. *The Making of Economic Society.* Englewood Cliffs, NJ: Prentice-Hall, 1962. pp. 36–38, 50.
2. Polanyi, Karl. *The Great Transformation: The Political and Economic Origins of Our Time.* Boston: Beacon, 1944. p. 70; Jones, E. L. *The European Miracle: Environments, Economies and Geopolitics in the History of Europe and Asia.* Cambridge, U.K.: Cambridge University Press, 1981. pp. 101–102.

3. Jones, E. L. *The European Miracle: Environments, Economies and Geopolitics in the History of Europe and Asia.* pp. 98–100.

4. Dobb, Maurice M. A. *Studies in the Development of Capitalism.* New York: International Publishers, 1947. p. 123.

5. Ibid. p. 150.

6. Ibid. pp. 140–141.

7. Ibid. p. 143.

8. Heilbroner, Robert L. *The Making of Economic Society.* pp. 51–52.

9. Ibid.

10. Ibid.

11. Ibid.

12. Polanyi, Karl. *The Great Transformation: The Political and Economic Origins of Our Time.* p. 65.

13. Hobsbawm, E. J. *Nations and Nationalism since 1780: Programme, Myth, Reality.* Cambridge, U.K.: Cambridge University Press, 1990. p. 45. Said at the first meeting of the parliament of the newly united Italian kingdom (1861). (Latham, E. *Famous Sayings and Their Authors.* Detroit, 1970.) (Refers to "We have made Italy, now we have to make Italians.")

14. Brunot, Ferdinand, ed. *Histoire de la langue francaise.* 13 vols. Paris: 1927–43; de Mauro, Tullio. *Storia linguistica dell'Italia unita.* Bari. 1963, p. 41; Wehler, H. U. *Deutsche Gesellschaftgeschichte 1700–1815.* Munich, Ger: 1987. p. 305.

15. Hobsbawm, E. J. *Nations and Nationalism since 1780: Programme, Myth, Reality.* p. 54.

16. Wright, Lawrence. *Clockwork Man.* New York: Horizon Press, 1969. p. 121.

17. Flora, Peter. *Economy and Society in Western Europe 1815–1975.* Vol. 1, chap. 5. Frankfurt, London, and Chicago, 1983.

18. Mumford, Lewis. *The Culture of Cities.* New York: Harcourt, Brace, 1963. p. 79.

19. Held, David, Anthony McGrew, David Goldblatt, and Jonathan Perraton. *Global Transformations: Politics, Economics and Culture.* Stanford, CA: Stanford University Press, 1999. pp. 33–34.

20. Jones, E. L. *The European Miracle: Environments, Economies and Geopolitics in the History of Europe and Asia.* pp. 130–131.

21. Smith, Dennis. "Making Europe—Processes of Europe-Formation since 1945." In Smith, Dennis, and Sue Wright, eds. *Whose Europe? The Turn Towards Democracy.* Oxford, U.K.: Blackwell Publishers, 1999. pp. 240–241.

22. Rousseau, Jean-Jacques. *On the Social Contract.* Roger Masters, trans. New York: St. Martin's Press, 1978. p. 130.

23. Hindess, Barry. "Neo-liberalism and the National Economy." In Dean, M., and B. Hindess, eds. *Governing Australia: Studies in Contemporary Rationalities of Government.* Cambridge, U.K.: Cambridge University Press, 1988. pp. 210–226; Held, David, Anthony McGrew, David Goldblatt, and Jonathan Perraton. *Global Transformations: Politics, Economics and Culture.* p. 37.

24. Held, David, Anthony McGrew, David Goldblatt, and Jonathan Perraton. *Global Transformations: Politics, Economics and Culture.* pp. 37–38.

25. Dobb, Maurice. *Studies in the Development of Capitalism.* p. 193; "Mercantilism." *The Columbia Encyclopedia.* Sixth Edition, 2001. www.bartleby.com

26. Shapiro, Michael J., and Hayward R. Alker. *Challenging Boundaries: Global Flows, Territorial Identities.* Minneapolis: University of Minnesota Press, 1996. p. 238; "French Revolution." *The Columbia Encyclopedia.* Sixth Edition, 2001. www.bartleby.com; "Declaration of the Rights of Man and the Citizen." Article 3. Adopted by the National Assembly, August 27, 1789. www.history.binghamton.edu

27. Smith, Anthony D. *Nationalism: Theory, Ideology, History.* Cambridge, U.K.: Polity Press, 2001. p. 45. For further information, see Brubaker, Rogers. *Citizenship and Nationhood in France and Germany.* Cambridge, MA: Harvard University Press, 1992; Sluga, Glenda.

"Identity, Gender, and the History of European Nations and Nationalism." *Nations and Nationalism*. 1998. 4, 1: pp. 87–111.

28. Hobsbawm, E. J. *Nations and Nationalism Since 1780: Programme, Myth, Reality*. pp. 82–83.
29. Maier, Charles S. "Does Europe Need a Frontier?: From Territorial to Redistributive Community." In Zielonka, Jan. *Europe Unbound*. London: Routledge, 2002. p. 26.
30. Lowe, Donald M. *History of Bourgeois Perception*. Chicago: University of Chicago Press, 1982. p. 38.
31. "Spread of Railways in 19th Century." *Modern History Sourcebook*. Fordham University. September 22, 2001.
32. Russell, J. C. *Medieval Regions and Their Cities*. Newton Abbot: David and Charles, 1972. pp. 244, 246; Strayer, Joseph R. *On the Medieval Origins of the Modern State*. Princeton, NJ: Princeton University Press, 1970. p. 61; Tilly, Charles, ed. *The Formation of the National State in Western Europe*. Princeton, NJ: Princeton University Press, 1975. p. 15; Wesson, Robert. *State Systems: International Pluralism, Politics, and Culture*. New York: Free Press, 1978. p. 21.
33. "Table A-1. Reported Voting and Registration by Race, Hispanic Origin, Sex and Age Groups: November 1964–2000." U.S. Census Bureau. June 3, 2002. *www.census.gov*

CHAPTER 8: NETWORK COMMERCE IN A GLOBALIZED ECONOMY

1. Kirkham, Jan, and Timothy McGowan. "Strengthening and Supporting the Franchising System." International Franchise Association. *The Franchising Handbook*. p. 12.
2. Smith, Adam. *An Inquiry into the Nature and Causes of the Wealth of Nations*. Edwin Cannan, ed. London: Methuen & Co., 1961. Vol. I. p. 475.
3. Castells, Manuel. *The Rise of the Network Society*. Cambridge, MA: Blackwell Publishers, 1996. p. 207; Ernst, Dieter. *Inter-firms Networks and Market Structure: Driving Forces, Barriers and Patterns of Control*. Berkeley, CA: University of California, BRIE working paper 73, 1994. pp. 5–6.
4. Scharpf, Fritz W. *Games in Hierarchies and Networks*. Frankfurt am Main, Ger.: Campus Verlag, 1993. pp. 69–70.
5. Uzzi, Brian. "The Sources and Consequences of Embeddedness for the Economic Performance of Organizations: The Network Effect." *American Sociological Review*. Vol. 61. No. 4. August 1996. p. 682.
6. Ibid. pp. 682–683.
7. Ibid. p. 679.
8. Ibid. p. 678.
9. Ibid.
10. Ibid. p. 682.
11. Jones, Candace, William S. Hesterly, and Stephen P. Borgatti. "A General Theory of Network Governance: Exchange Conditions and Social Mechanisms." *The Academy of Management Review*. Vol. 22. No. 4. October 1997. p. 921.
12. Powell, Walter W. "Neither Market Nor Hierarchy: Network Forms of Organization." *Research in Organizational Behavior*. Vol. 12. 1990. p. 325.
13. Blackstone, Sir William. *Ehrlich's Blackstone*. J. W. Ehrlich, ed. San Carlos, CA: Nourse Publishing, 1959. p. 113.
14. McKenzie, Evan. "Common-Interest Housing in the Communities of Tomorrow." Housing Policy Debate: Vol. 14. Issues 1 and 2. Fannie Mae Foundation, 2003.
15. MacPherson, Crawford. *Democratic Theory: Essays in Retrieval*. Cambridge, U.K.: Oxford University Press, 1973. p. 139.
16. Ibid.
17. Ibid. p. 140.

CHAPTER 9: THE "UNITED STATES" OF EUROPE

1. "Cross-Border and Interregional Cooperation: Four Motors for Europe." *Interreg. www. baden-wuerttemberg.de*

2. Byatt, A. S. "What Is a European?" *The New York Times Magazine*. October 31, 2002.

3. Sciolino, Elaine. "Visions of a Union: Europe Gropes for an Identity." *The New York Times*. December 15, 2002.

4. "Treaty of Rome." March 25, 1957. *www.europa.eu.int*

5. Commission of the European Communities (CEC). *Treaties Establishing the European Communities*, abridged edition. Luxembourg: Official Publications of the European Communities (OOPEC), 1983.

6. Shore, Chris. *Building Europe: The Cultural Politics of European Integration*. London: Routledge, 2000. p. 15.

7. "How Europeans See Themselves." The European Commission. September 2000; Ratnesar, Romesh. "Generation Europe." *Time Europe*. April 2, 2001.

8. Emerson, Tony. "The Power of Europe." *Newsweek*. September 16–23, 2002.

9. "Treaty Establishing the European Coal and Steel Community." *The European Union On-Line*. *www.europa.eu.int/abc/obj/treaties*. November 4, 2003.

10. Ibid.

11. Ruttley, Philip. "The Long Road to Unity." In Pagden, Anthony. *The Idea of Europe: From Antiquity to the European Union*. Cambridge, U.K.: Cambridge University Press, 2002. p. 234.

12. "Treaty Establishing the European Community (Treaty of Rome)." Part 1: Principles. March 25, 1957. *www.europa.eu.int*

13. Ibid.; "The First Treaties." European Parliament Fact Sheets. June 9, 2000. *www.europarl.eu.int*

14. "The First Treaties." European Parliament Fact Sheets.

15. "Treaty Establishing the European Community (Treaty of Rome)." March 25, 1957. Articles 48–73.

16. Monnet, Jean. Quotation from his speech in Washington, DC. April 30, 1952.

17. George, Stephen. *Politics and Policy in the European Community*. Oxford, U.K.: Clarendon, 1985. p. 20.

18. Smith, Dennis. "Making Europe—Processes of Europe-formation Since 1945." In Smith, Dennis, and Sue Wright, eds. *Whose Europe? The Turn Towards Democracy*. Oxford, U.K.: Blackwell Publishers/The Sociological Review, 1999. pp. 242–243.

19. Hoffman, Paul. Speech to the Organization for European Economic Co-Operation (OEEC). October 31, 1949. Paris.

20. Ruttley, Philip. "The Long Road to Unity." pp. 243–245.

21. Ibid.; "Single European Act." June 29, 1987. *www.europa.eu.int*

22. Calleo, David P. *Rethinking Europe's Future*. Princeton, NJ: Princeton University Press, 2001. p. 185; Ruttley, Philip. "The Long Road to Unity." p. 247.

23. Ruttley, Philip. "The Long Road to Unity." p. 248.

24. "The Treaty of Accession 2003." Signed in Athens on April 16, 2003. *www.europa.eu.int*

25. "Committee of the Regions: Members and Mandate." Committee of the Regions. *www.cor.eu.int*

26. Smith, Dennis, and Sue Wright. *Whose Europe? The Turn Towards Democracy*. p. 14.

27. Ruttley, Philip. "The Long Road to Unity." pp. 246, 250.

28. "So That's All Agreed, Then." *The Economist*. December 16, 2000. pp. 25–28; Calleo, David P. *Rethinking Europe's Future*. p. 254.

29. "Eurobarometer Reveals Growing Support for EU Constitution." *EurActiv*. February 18, 2004. *www.euractive.com*

30. Healthcoat-Amory, David. "The Constitution Is a Sham." *The Wall Street Journal Europe*. June 20–22, 2003.

31. "Special Report: Europe's Constitution." *The Economist.* June 21, 2003. p. 22.
32. Mitchener, Brandon. "EU Backs Initiative on Draft Constitution." *The Wall Street Journal Europe.* June 23, 2003.
33. Greene, Robert Land. "We're Still the One." *The New York Times.* July 17, 2003.
34. "Special Report: Europe's Constitution." *The Economist.*
35. Ibid.
36. Parker, George, and Daniel Dombey. "'Not Perfect But More Than We Could Have Hoped For': Europe's Draft Constitution." *Financial Times.* June 20, 2003.
37. Fuller, Thomas. "Europe Debates Whether to Admit God to Union." *The New York Times.* February 5, 2003.
38. Ibid.
39. Woodward, Kenneth L. "An Oxymoron: Europe Without Christianity." *The New York Times.* June 14, 2003.
40. "Treaty Establishing a Constitution for Europe: Article 3: The Union's Objectives." The European Convention. Brussels. June 20, 2003.
41. Ibid.
42. Rothstein, Edward. "Europe's Constitution: All Hail the Bureaucracy." *The New York Times.* July 5, 2003.
43. "Treaty Establishing a Constitution for Europe." The European Convention.
44. Ibid.

CHAPTER 10: GOVERNMENT WITHOUT A CENTER

1. Vinocur, John. "Jospin Envisions an Alternative EU." *International Herald Tribune.* May 29, 2001.
2. Taylor, Frederick. *The Principles of Scientific Management.* New York: Norton, 1947. pp. 39, 63.
3. Wiener, Norbert. *The Human Use of Human Beings.* New York: Avon Books, 1954. pp. 26–27.
4. Ibid. p. 35.
5. Rumford, Chris. *The European Union: A Political Sociology.* Oxford, U.K.: Blackwell Publishers, 2002. pp. 71–72. Quotation by Michel Foucault.
6. Dean, Mitchell M. *Governmentality: Power and Rule in Modern Society.* London: Sage, 1999. p. 2.
7. Ibid. p. 201.
8. Axford, Barrie, and Richard Huggins. "Towards a Post-national Polity: The Emergence of the Network Society in Europe." In Smith, Dennis, and Sue Wright. *Whose Europe? The Turn Towards Democracy.* pp. 192–193.
9. Ibid. p. 194.
10. Ibid.
11. Hirst, Paul, and Grahame Thompson. *Globalization in Question: The International Economy and the Possibilities of Governance.* Cambridge, U.K.: Polity Press, 1996. p. 53.
12. Gellner, Ernest. *Nations and Nationalism.* Ithaca, NY: Cornell University Press, 1983. p. 6.
13. Latour, B. *On Actor Network Theory: A Few Clarifications.* 1993. *www.keele.cstt.latour.html*
14. Bull, Hedley. *The Anarchical Society.* New York: Columbia University Press, 1977. p. 245.
15. Ibid.
16. Ibid.
17. Ibid. pp. 245–246.
18. Ibid. p. 246.
19. Ibid.
20. Ibid.

21. Beck, Ulrich. "The Reinvention of Politics: Towards a Theory of Reflexive Modernization." In Beck, Ulrich, Anthony Giddens, and Scott Lash. *Reflexive Modernization: Politics, Tradition and Esthetics in the Modern Social Order.* Stanford, CA: Stanford University Press, 1994. p. 39.
22. Luke, Tim. "World Order or Neo-World Orders. Power, Politics, and Ideology in Informationalizing Glocalities." In Featherstone, M., S. Lash, and R. Robertson. *Global Modernities.* London: Sage, 1995.
23. Lowe, P., and S. Ward., eds. *British Environmental Policy and Europe.* London: Routledge, 1998.
24. Barry, Andrew. "The European Network." *Technoscience.* Autumn 1996. No. 29. pp. 33–34.

CHAPTER 11: ROMANCING THE CIVIL SOCIETY

1. Nectoux, François. "European Identity and the Politics of Culture in Europe." In Axford, Barrie, Daniela Berghahn, and Nick Hewlett. *Unity and Diversity in the New Europe.* Oxford, U.K.: Peter Lang, 2000. p. 149.
2. Salamon, Lester M., Helmut Anheier, Regina List, Stefan Toepler, and Wojciech S. Sokolowski. "Global Civil Society: Dimensions of the Nonprofit Sector." Comparative Nonprofit Sector Project. The Johns Hopkins Center for Civil Society Studies. 1999. *www.jhu.edu/~ccss/pubs/books/gcs*
3. Ibid.
4. Ibid. Chart: "Changes in Nonprofit Sector FTE Employment, by Country, 1990–1995."
5. Ibid. pp. 29–30.
6. "Civil Society Sector FTE Revenue, by Field, 32 Countries." The Johns Hopkins Comparative Nonprofit Sector Project. April 15, 2003. *www.jhu.edu/~cnp/pdf/comptable4.pdf*
7. Rumford, Chris. *The European Union: A Political Sociology.* Oxford, U.K.: Blackwell, 2002. p. 90.
8. Economic and Social Committee (ESC). *Opinions of the Economic and Social Committee on Organized Civil Society and European Governance: The Committee's Contribution to the Drafting of the White Paper.* Brussels: European Economic and Social Committee, 2001.
9. Prodi, Romano. "Towards a European Civil Society." Speech at the Second European Social Week. Bad Honnef. April 6, 2000.
10. Ibid.
11. Murphy, C. *International Organization and International Change: Global Governance Since 1850.* Cambridge, U.K.: Polity Press, 1994. pp. 47–48.
12. Ruberti, Antonio. "Science in European Culture." In Durant, John, and John Gregory, eds. *Science and Culture in Europe.* London: Science Museum, 1993. p. 15.
13. Krut, R. "Globalization and Civil Society: NGO Influence in International Decision-making." Paper presented at the Globalization and Citizenship Conference of the United Nations Research Institute for Social Development. Geneva. December 9–11, 1996. p. 19.
14. Edelman, Richard. "Non-Governmental Organizations, the Fifth Estate in Global Governance." Edelman Public Relations Worldwide. February 2, 2002.
15. Ibid.
16. Ibid.

CHAPTER 12: THE IMMIGRANT DILEMMA

1. "A Europe of Regions?" *The Wall Street Journal.* November 13, 2002; Nectoux, François. "European Identity and the Politics of Culture in Europe." In Axford, Barrie, Daniela Berghahn, and Nick Hewlett, eds. *Unity and Diversity in the New Europe.* Oxford, U.K.: Peter Lang, 2000. p. 146.

2. Fuller, Thomas. "Foreign Workers Face Turning Tide: Backlash in Europe." *International Herald Tribune*. December 24, 2002.

3. Ibid.

4. Ibid.

5. Ibid.

6. "Mixed Reaction to EU Asylum and Immigration Plans." Press Association Newsfile. November 22, 2000.

7. "Christian Democrats to Target Far-Right Voters." *Reuters*. December 11, 2000.

8. Gallagher, Stephen. "Towards a Common European Asylum System: Fortress Europe Redesigns the Ramparts." *International Journal*. June 2002; "Germany Opens the Door Slightly Wider." *Times*. January 26, 2001.

9. Held, David, Anthony McGrew, David Goldblatt, and Jonathan Perraton. *Global Transformations: Politics, Economics and Culture*. Stanford, CA: Stanford University Press, 1999. pp. 299, 312–313, 319–320; SOPEMI. *Continuous Reporting System on Migration*. Organization for Economic Co-Operation and Development. Paris. 1991.

10. Held, David, Anthony McGrew, David Goldblatt, and Jonathan Perraton. *Global Transformations: Politics, Economics and Culture*. p. 299.

11. SOPEMI. *Continuous Reporting System on Migration*. Organization for Economic Co-Operation and Development.

12. "The Social Situation in the European Union, 2002." European Commission. May 22, 2002. pp. 23, 26 c1. *www.europa.eu.int*

13. Beck, Ulrich. *What Is Globalization?* Cambridge, U.K.: Polity Press, 2000. p. 48.

14. Nyberg-Sorenson, Ninna, Nicholas Van Hear, and Poul Engberg-Pedersen. "The Migration-Development Nexus Evidence and Policy Options." International Organization for Migration. July 2002.

15. Fidler, Stephen, and Virginia Marsh. "Sense of Crisis as Migrants Keep Moving." *Financial Times*. July 25, 2002.

16. Vitorino, Antonio. "Migratory Flows and the European Labor Market: Towards a Community Immigration Policy." Speech. July 9, 2001.

17. "The Social Situation in the European Union, 2002." The European Commission. May 22, 2002. pp. 11 c1, 61 c1, 63 c1, c2. *www.europa.eu.int*

18. "World Population Prospects the 2002 Revision: Highlights." United Nations Population Division. February 26, 2003. p. 16.

19. Bernstein, Richard. "An Aging Europe May Find Itself on the Sidelines." *The New York Times*. June 29, 2003.

20. Wolf, Martin. "The Challenge Facing Old Europe." *Financial Times*. March 4, 2003.

21. "The Old World—Shrinking with Age." *Financial Times*. March 1–2, 2003.

22. Bruni, Frank. "Persistent Drop in Fertility Reshapes Europe's Future." *The New York Times*. December 26, 2002.

23. Ibid.

24. Bernstein, Richard. "An Aging Europe May Find Itself on the Sidelines."

25. "The Social Situation in the European Union, 2002." European Commission. p. 11 c1.

26. Wolf, Martin. "The Challenge Facing Old Europe."

27. Emerson, Tony. "The Power of Europe." *Newsweek*. September 16–23, 2002. p. 53.

28. Bruni, Frank. "Persistent Drop in Fertility Reshapes Europe's Future."

29. Theil, Stefan. "A Heavy Burden." *Newsweek*. June 30, 2003. p. 28.

30. Ibid.

31. Ibid.

32. Bernstein, Richard. "An Aging Europe May Find Itself on the Sidelines."

33. Theil, Stefan. "A Heavy Burden."

34. "Germany Faces Looming Aging Crisis." Center for Strategic and International Studies. March 5, 2003.

35. Bernstein, Richard. "An Aging Europe May Find Itself on the Sidelines."
36. Wolf, Martin. "The Challenge Facing Old Europe"; "Economic Portrait of the European Union 2002." European Commission. 2002. p. 55; "The World Economic Outlook (WEO) Database: Selected World Aggregates." International Monetary Fund. April 2003. *www.imf.org*
37. Bernstein, Richard. "An Aging Europe May Find Itself on the Sidelines." Quotation by Wolfgang Lutz; Lutz, Wolfgang, Brian C. O'Neill, and Sergei Scherbov. "Europe's Population at a Turning Point." *Science Magazine*. Vol. 299. March 28, 2003.
38. Ibid.
39. Theil, Stefan. "A Heavy Burden."
40. Bernstein, Richard. "An Aging Europe May Find Itself on the Sidelines."
41. "The Social Situation in the European Union, 2002." European Commission. p. 25 c1.
42. Ibid.
43. Bruni, Frank. "Persistent Drop in Fertility Reshapes Europe's Future."
44. Paine, Thomas. *Rights of Man*. 1795.
45. Cohen, R. *Global Diasporas*. London: University College London Press, 1997. pp. ix–x.
46. "China's Control of Media Entities Abroad." Falun Dafa Information Entities Abroad. November 21, 2003. *www.faluninfo.net*
47. Beck, Ulrich. *What Is Globalization?* p. 28; Friedman, J. "Cultural Logics of the Global System." *Theory, Culture and Society*. Vol. 5. Special Issue on Postmodernism. 1988. p. 458.
48. Pries, Ludger. *Internationale Migration*. Special Issue of *Soziale Welt*, Baden-Baden, Ger., 1997.
49. Ibid.
50. Ibid.
51. "IOM News: Inside, a Sneak Preview of World Migration." International Organization on Migration. December 2002.
52. Fleming, Charles, and John Carreyrou. "In French High Schools, Muslim Girls Depend on Headscarf Mediator." *The Wall Street Journal Europe*. June 26, 2003.
53. Ibid.
54. Ibid.
55. Sciolino, Elaine. "France Steps Closer to a Head-scarf Ban." *The New York Times*. February 12, 2004.
56. Sciolino, Elaine. "A Maze of Identities for the Muslims of France." *The New York Times*. April 9, 2003.
57. Fleming, Charles, and John Carreyrou. "In French High Schools, Muslim Girls Depend on Headscarf Mediator."
58. Ash, Timothy Garton. "How the West Can Be One." *The New York Times Magazine*. April 27, 2003.
59. Ibid.
60. Sciolino, Elaine. "Spain Will Loosen Its Alliance with U.S., Premier-Elect Says." *The New York Times*. March 16, 2004.
61. Appadurai, Arjun. *Modernity at Large: Cultural Dimension of Globalization*. Minneapolis: University of Minnesota Press, 1996. p. 166.
62. Ibid. pp. 166, 171.
63. Milbank, John. "Against the Resignations of the Age." In McHugh, F. P., and S. M. Natale, eds. *Things Old and New: Catholic Social Teaching Revisited*. New York: University of America, 1993. p. 19.
64. Ibid.
65. Foucault, Michel. "Of Other Spaces." *Diacritics*. Vol. 16. No. 1. Spring 1986. p. 22.
66. Christiansen, Thomas, and Knud Erik Jorgensen. "Transnational Governance 'Above' and 'Below' the State: The Changing Nature of Borders in the New Europe." *Regional & Federal Studies*. Vol. 10. 2000. p. 74.

67. Ruggie, John Gerard. "Territoriality and Beyond: Problematizing Modernity in International Relations." *International Organization.* Vol. 47. No. 1. Winter 1993. pp. 168–170.
68. Ibid.
69. Hassner, Pierre. "Fixed Borders or Moving Borderlands?: A New Type of Border for a New Type of Entity." In Zielonka, Jan, ed. *Europe Unbound: Enlarging and Reshaping the Boundaries of the European Union.* London: Routledge, 2002. p. 39.
70. Ibid. p. 45.
71. Ibid. p. 46.
72. Guéhenno, Jean-Marie. *The End of the Nation-State.* Minneapolis: University of Minnesota Press, 1995. p. 139.

CHAPTER 13: UNITY IN DIVERSITY

1. Beetham, David. "Human Rights as a Model for Cosmopolitan Democracy." In Archibugi, Daniele, David Held, and Martin Kohler, eds. *Re-Imagining Political Community: Studies in Cosmopolitan Democracy.* Stanford, CA: Stanford University, 1998. p. 60.
2. Beck, Ulrich. "From Industrial Society to Risk Society: Questions of Survival, Structure and Ecological Enlightenment." *Theory, Culture and Society.* Vol. 9. 1992. p. 109.
3. Turner, Bryan S. "Outline of a Theory of Human Rights." *Sociology.* Vol. 27. No. 3. August 1993. p. 503; Gehlen, A. *Man: His Nature and Place in the World.* New York: Columbia University Press. 1988.
4. Ibid.
5. Moore, Barrington. *Reflections on the Causes of Human Misery and Upon Certain Proposals to Eliminate Them.* Boston: Beacon Press, 1970. pp. 1–2.
6. Turner, Bryan S. "Outline of a Theory of Human Rights." p. 501.
7. Ibid. p. 503.
8. Ibid.
9. Ibid. p. 506.
10. Sellers, Frances Stead. "A Citizen on Paper Has No Weight." *The Washington Post.* January 19, 2003.
11. Marshall, T. H. *Citizenship and Social Class.* Cambridge, U.K.: Cambridge University Press, 1950.
12. Stevenson, N. "Globalization, National Cultures and Cultural Citizenship." *The Sociological Quarterly.* Vol. 38. 1997. pp. 41–66; Yuval-Davis, N. *National Spaces and Collective Identities: Borders, Boundaries, Citizenship and Gender Relations.* Inaugural Lecture, University of Greenwich. 1997; van Steenbergen, B. "Towards a Global Ecological Citizen." In van Steenbergen, ed. *The Condition of Citizenship.* London, U.K.: Sage, 1994; Held, David. *Democracy and the Global Order.* Cambridge, U.K.: Polity, 1991; Urry, John. *Consuming Places.* London, U.K.: Routledge, 1995; Bauman, Z. *Postmodern Ethics.* London: Routledge, 1993.
13. Urry, John. *Beyond Societies: Mobilities for the Twenty-First Century.* London: Routledge, 2000. p. 166.
14. "Charter of the United Nations: Chapter 1: Article 1:3." The United Nations, 1945. *www.un.org/aboutun/charter/chapter1.html*
15. "Ongoing Struggle for Human Rights: The Universal Declaration of Human Rights (Timeline)." Franklin and Eleanor Roosevelt Institute. November 2, 2003. *www.udhr.org/history/timeline.htm*; Beetham, David. "Human Rights as a Model for Cosmopolitan Democracy." p. 63.
16. Brownlie, I., ed. *Basic Documents on Human Rights.* 3rd ed. Oxford, U.K.: Oxford University Press, 1992. pp. 115, 172; "Ongoing Struggle for Human Rights: The Universal Declara-

tion of Human Rights (Timeline)." Franklin and Eleanor Roosevelt Institute; "Biodiversity and the Environment." The United Nations. November 24, 2003. *www.un.org*

17. Beetham, David. "Human Rights as a Model for Cosmopolitan Democracy." pp. 62–63; Rumford, Chris. *The European Union: A Political Sociology*. Oxford, U.K.: Blackwell, 2002. p. 226.

18. Closa Montero, Carlos. "The Concept of Citizenship in the Treaty on European Union." *Common Market Law Review*. Vol. 29. 1992. p. 1139.

19. Scruton, Roger. *A Dictionary of Political Thought*. London: Pan, 1982. pp. 63–64.

20. Soysal, Yasemin. "Changing Citizenship in Europe: Remarks on Postnational Membership and the National State." In Cesarini, D., and M. Fulbrook, eds. *Citizenship, Nationality, and Migration in Europe*. London: Routledge, 1997. p. 21.

21. Delanty, Gerard. *Inventing Europe: Idea, Identity, Reality*. London: Macmillan, 1995.

CHAPTER 14: WAGING PEACE

1. Hobsbawm, E. J. *The Age of Extremes: The Short Twentieth Century, 1914–1991*. London: Michael Joseph, 1994. p. 12.

2. "Protocol No. 13 to the Convention for the Protection of Human Rights and Fundamental Freedoms, Concerning the Abolition of the Death Penalty in All Circumstances." Council of Europe. May 3, 2002. *http://conventions.coe.int*

3. Hodgkinson, Peter. "Living without the Death Penalty: The Experience in Europe." *The Lawyer Journal of the Taipei Bar Association*. April 2002. p. 6.

4. "EU Memorandum on the Death Penalty." European Union in the U.S. February 5, 2003. *www.eurunion.org/legislat/DeathPenalty/eumemorandum.htm*

5. Ibid.

6. "Poll Topics and Trends: Death Penalty." The Gallup Organization. October 9, 2003. *www.gallup.com*

7. "EU Memorandum on the Death Penalty." European Union in the U.S.

8. Ibid.

9. The Holy Bible, King James Version. Matthew 5:38, 5:39.

10. Ibid. Matthew 5:43, 5:44.

11. "Poll Topics and Trends: Death Penalty." The Gallup Organization.

12. Nisbett, Richard E. *The Geography of Thought: How Asians and Westerners Think Differently . . . and Why*. New York: Free Press, 2003. p. 88.

13. "EU Memorandum on the Death Penalty." European Union in the U.S. p. 3.

14. Ibid.

15. Bonczar, Thomas P., and Tracy L. Snell. "Capital Punishment, 2002." Bureau of Justice Statistics. November 2003.

16. Chace, James. "Present at the Destruction: The Death of American Internationalism." *World Policy Journal*. Spring 2003. p. 2; Tyler, Patrick E. "U.S. Strategy Plan Calls for Insuring No Rivals Develop." *The New York Times*. March 8, 1992.

17. Ibid.

18. Chace, James. "Present at the Destruction: The Death of American Internationalism."

19. "President Bush Delivers Graduation Speech at West Point." The White House. June 1, 2002. *www.whitehouse.gov*

20. Ibid.

21. "Secretary Rumsfeld Media Availability." Speech by Donald Rumsfeld. May 22, 2002. *www.globalsecurity.org*

22. Glennon, Michael J. "Why the Security Council Failed." *Foreign Affairs*. Vol. 82. No. 3. May/June 2003. p. 20.

23. "Charter of the United Nations: Chapter 1: Purposes and Principles." The United Nations. *www.un.org*
24. Ikenberry, G. John. "America's Imperial Ambition." *Foreign Affairs*. Vol. 81. No. 5. September/October 2002. pp. 56–57.
25. Ibid.
26. Hoffman, Stanley. "The High and the Mighty." *American Prospect*. January 23, 2003.
27. Bush, George W. "Text: Bush's 2003 State of the Union Address." *The Washington Post*. January 28, 2003.
28. Gordon, Philip H. "Bridging the Atlantic Divide." *Foreign Affairs*. Vol. 81. No. 1. January/February 2003. pp. 76–77.
29. "Seventy-Two Percent of Americans Support War Against Iraq." The Gallup Organization. March 24, 2003.
30. Gordon, Philip H. "Bridging the Atlantic Divide." p. 77.
31. Ibid.
32. "Views of a Changing World." The Pew Global Attitudes Project. The Pew Research Center for the People and the Press. June 2003. p. 101.
33. Glennon, Michael J. "Why the Security Council Failed." p. 21.
34. Fischer, Joschka. Speech at Humboldt University. Berlin, Germany. May 12, 2000.
35. Daley, Suzanne. "French Minister Calls U.S. Policy 'Simplistic.'" *The New York Times*. February 7, 2002.
36. Prodi, Romano. Speech at the Institu d'Etudes Politiques. Paris. May 29, 2001.
37. Kagan, Robert. *Of Paradise and Power: America and Europe in the New World Order*. New York: Knopf, 2003. p. 60.
38. Kennedy, Craig, and Marshall M. Bouton. "The Real Trans-Atlantic Gap." *Foreign Policy*. December 2002. p. 5.
39. Ibid.
40. Kagan, Robert. *Of Paradise and Power: America and Europe in the New World Order*. pp. 3–4.
41. Kennedy, Craig, and Marshall M. Bouton. "The Real Trans-Atlantic Gap."
42. Patten, Chris, CH. "A European Foreign Policy: Ambition and Reality." Speech at Institut Francais des Relations Internationales (IFRI). Paris. June 15, 2000.
43. Ibid.
44. Patten, Chris. "From Europe with Support." *Yediot Ahronot*. October 28, 2002.
45. Nye, Joseph S. Jr. *The Paradox of American Power*. Oxford, U.K.: Oxford University Press, 2002. pp. 8–9.
46. "The Biggest Threat to Peace: You Vote." *Time Europe*. August 25, 2003. *www.time.com*
47. "Global Survey Results Give a Thumbs Down to US Foreign Policy." Gallup International. September 7, 2002.
48. Ioannides, Isabelle. "The European Rapid Reaction Force." Bonn International Center for Conversion (BICC). September 2002. p. 8.
49. Kaldor, Mary. "Reconceptualizing Organized Violence." In Archibugi, Daniele, David Held, and Martin Kohler, eds. *Re-imagining Political Community: Studies in Cosmopolitan Democracy*. Stanford, CA: Stanford University Press, 1998. p. 108.
50. Moravcsik, Andrew. "How Europe Can Win without an Army." *Financial Times*. April 2, 2003.
51. Gelb, Leslie H., and Justine Rosenthal. "The Rise of Ethics in Foreign Policy." *Foreign Affairs*. Vol. 82. No. 3. May/June 2003. pp. 2–7.
52. "European Union Factsheet: Development Assistance and Humanitarian Aid." European Commission. June 25, 2003.
53. Ibid.
54. Ibid.

55. Barber, Lionel. "The New Transatlantic Agenda." In Guttman, Robert J., ed. *Europe in the New Century: Visions of an Emerging Superpower*. Boulder, CO: Lynne Rienner Publishers, 2001. p. 97; Lennon, David. "The European Union: A Leader in Humanitarian and Development Assistance." In Guttman, Robert J., ed. *Europe in the New Century: Visions of an Emerging Superpower*. p. 131.

56. Lennon, David. "The European Union: A Leader in Humanitarian and Development Assistance." p. 127.

57. "Ranking the Rich." *Foreign Policy*. May/June 2003. pp. 57–58.

58. Ibid. pp. 60–61.

59. Clark, Wesley K. *Waging Modern War*. New York: Public Affairs, 2001. p. 426.

60. Ibid.

61. Zinsmeister, Karl. "Old and In the Way." *The American Enterprise Magazine Online*. 2002. *www.americanenterprise.org*; Hartmann, Andreas. "Europe's Military Ambitions—Myth or Reality?" European Documentation Centre, 2002. *www.edc.spb.ru*

62. Kennedy, Paul. "Time for an American Recessional?" *Newsweek—Special Edition: Issues 2003*. December 2002–February 2003. p. 86.

63. "Fiscal Year 2004 Budget." Center for Defense Information. March 19, 2003. *www.cdi.org/budget/2004/world-military-spending.cfm*; "CIA Country Fact Sheets 2003." *CIA World Factbook*. *www.cia.gov/cia/publications/factbook*

64. Walker, Martin. "Europe: Superstate or Superpower?" *World Policy Journal*. Vol. XVII. Issue 4. Winter 2000/2001. p. 9.

65. "United Nations Human Development Report 2002." United Nations Development Program. Oxford, U.K.: Oxford University Press, 2002. p. 45.

66. Heisbourg, François. "Emerging European Power Projection Capabilities." Geneva Centre for Security Policy. July 16, 1999.

67. "Defence & Foreign Affairs: Strong Popular Support for Common EU Policies." *European Report*. May 3, 2003.

68. "Europe Gets Its Guns." *European Security*. January 2001. *www.europeansecurity.net*

69. Wolf, Charles Jr., and Benjamin Zycher. *European Military Prospects, Economic Constraints and the Rapid Reaction Force*. Santa Monica, CA: RAND Publications, 2001. p. 22.

70. Moravscik, Andrew. "How Europe Can Win without an Army." *Financial Times*. April 2, 2003.

71. Ioannides, Isabelle. "The European Rapid Reaction Force."

72. Zinsmeister, Karl. "Old and In the Way."

73. Ibid. p. 8.

74. Rice, Condoleezza. "How to Pursue the National Interest: Life after the Cold War." *Foreign Affairs*. January/February 2000.

75. Ash, Timothy Garton. "How the West Can Be One." *The New York Times Magazine*. April 27, 2003. p. 14.

76. Ibid.

77. Kennedy, Craig, and Marshall M. Bouton. "The Real Trans-Atlantic Gap." p. 7.

78. Glennon, Michael J. "Why the Security Council Failed." Quotation by Jacques Chirac.

79. Walker, Martin. "Europe: Superstate or Superpower?" p. 11.

80. Hartmann, Andreas. "Europe's Military Ambitions—Myth or Reality?" pp. 1–2.

81. Ibid.

82. Ibid.

83. Ibid.

84. Ibid. p. 3.

85. Ibid. pp. 1–2; "The European Military Structures and Capabilities." Council of the European Union. 2002. *http://ue.eu.int*

86. Walker, Martin. "Europe: Superstate or Superpower?" p. 8.

87. "Presidency Conclusions." EU Council. Helsinki. December 1999.
88. Hartmann, Andreas. "Europe's Military Ambitions—Myth or Reality?" p. 4.
89. Ibid. pp. 4–5.
90. Ibid.
91. Ibid.
92. Ibid.
93. Walker, Martin. "Europe: Superstate or Superpower?" p. 8.
94. Ibid.
95. Assemblée nationale, Commission de la defense nationale et des forces armés. Rapport de réunion no. 32 (en application de l'article 46 du Réglement). 18 avril 2001. Président: M. Paul Quilés. Cited in Ioannides, Isabelle. "The European Rapid Reaction Force."
96. Ioannides, Isabelle. "The European Rapid Reaction Force"; "Public Opinion in the European Union." European Commission Eurobarometer. No. 56. April 2002.
97. Savic, Misha. "EU Peacekeepers Arrive in Macedonia." *The Washington Post*. April 1, 2003.
98. Geitner, Paul. "EU to Send Peacekeepers to Congo." *The Associated Press*. June 4, 2003.

CHAPTER 15: A SECOND ENLIGHTENMENT

1. Rees, Martin. *Our Final Hour*. New York: Basic Books, 2003. p. 8.
2. Ibid. p. 120.
3. Ibid. p. 121.
4. Ibid.
5. Ibid.
6. Davidson, Keay. "Saving the Universe by Restricting Research." *San Francisco Chronicle*. April 14, 2003.
7. Rees, Martin. *Our Final Hour*. pp. 125, 128.
8. Ibid. p. 132.
9. "American and European Public Opinion & Foreign Policy." *Worldviews*. 2002. pp. 25 c2–26 c2. *www.worldviews.org*; "Views of a Changing World." The Pew Global Attitudes Project. The Pew Research Center for the People and the Press. June 2003. pp. 90–99. *www.people-press.org*
10. "Commission and Industry Divided Over Impact Assessment of Chemicals Review." *EurActiv*. April 30, 2003. *www.eruactiv.com*
11. Becker, Elizabeth, and Jennifer Lee. "Europe Plan on Chemicals Seen as Threat to U.S. Exports." *The New York Times*. May 8, 2003.
12. Ibid. Quotation by Margot Wallstrom.
13. Loewenberg, Samuel. "Europe Gets Tougher on U.S. Companies." *The New York Times*. April 20, 2003.
14. Becker, Elizabeth, and Jennifer Lee. "Europe Plan on Chemicals Seen as Threat to U.S. Exports."
15. Ibid.
16. Ibid.; "Commission and Industry Divided Over Impact Assessment of Chemicals Review." *EurActiv*. April 30, 2003. *www.euractiv.com*
17. Becker, Elizabeth, and Jennifer Lee. "Europe Plan on Chemicals Seen as Threat to U.S. Exports."
18. "REACH on Its Way—Risk or Opportunity for Chemicals Sector?" *EurActiv*. October 29, 2003. *www.euractiv.com*
19. Ibid.
20. Loewenberg, Samuel. "Europe Gets Tougher on U.S. Companies."
21. Ibid.; "Commission and Industry Divided Over Impact Assessment of Chemicals Review."
22. "Commission Adopts Communication on Precautionary Principle." EU Online. November 26, 2002. *www.europa.eu.int*
23. Ibid.

24. Harremoes, Poul, David Gee, Malcolm MacGarvin, Andy Stirling, Jane Keys, Brian Wynne, and Sofia Guedes Vaz, eds. *The Precautionary Principle in the 20th Century: Late Lessons from Early Warnings*. European Environment Agency. London: Earthscan Publications, 2002. p. 7.

25. Pollan, Michael. "The Year in Ideas: A to Z." *The New York Times*. December 9, 2001.

26. Harremoes, Poul, David Gee, Malcolm MacGarvin, Andy Stirling, Jane Keys, Brian Wynne, and Sofia Guedes Vaz, eds. *The Precautionary Principle in the 20th Century: Late Lessons from Early Warnings*. p. 4.

27. Ibid. p. 200.

28. Ibid. pp. 191, 194.

29. Ibid. p. 189.

30. "Communication from the Commission on the Precautionary Principle." Commission of the European Communities. February 2, 2000. p. 11. *www.europa.eu.int*

31. Harremoes, Poul, David Gee, Malcolm MacGarvin, Andy Stirling, Jane Keys, Brian Wynne, and Sofia Guedes Vaz, eds. *The Precautionary Principle in the 20th Century: Late Lessons from Early Warnings*. p. 6.

32. Alden, Edward. "Cautious EU Rules Are 'Bar to Trade,' Say US Companies." *Financial Times*. May 6, 2003.

33. Wallstrom, Margot. "The EU and the US Approaches to Environment Policy: Are We Converging or Diverging?" European Institute. April 25, 2002. *www.eurunion.org*

34. Ibid.

35. Ibid.

36. Harremoes, Poul, David Gee, Malcolm MacGarvin, Andy Stirling, Jane Keys, Brian Wynne, and Sofia Guedes Vaz, eds. *The Precautionary Principle in the 20th Century: Late Lessons from Early Warnings*. p. xiii.

37. Heisenberg, Werner. *Physics and Philosophy: The Revolution in Modern Science*. New York: Harper, 1958.

38. Maren-Grisebach, Manon. *Philsophie der Brunen*. Munchen, Ger.: Olzog, 1982. p. 30. Quotation by Ernst Haeckel.

39. Lovelock, James. *The Ages of Gaia: A Biography of Our Living Earth*. New York: Norton, 1988. p. 312. Quotation by Vladimir Vernadsky.

40. Polunin, N. "Our Use of 'Biosphere,' 'Ecosystem,' and Now 'Ecobiome.'" *Environmental Conservation* 11. 1984. p. 198; Serafin, Rafal. "Noosphere, Gaia, and the Science of the Biosphere." *Environmental Ethics* 10. Summer 1988. p. 125.

41. Patten, Bernard C. "Network Ecology." In Higashi, M., and T. P. Burns, eds. *Theoretical Studies of Ecosystems: The Network Perspective*. New York: Cambridge University Press, 1991.

42. Capra, Fritjof. *The Web of Life: A New Scientific Understanding of Living Systems*. New York: Anchor Books, 1996. pp. 34–35.

43. Ibid. p. 34; Thomas, Lewis. *The Lives of a Cell*. New York: Bantam, 1975. pp. 26ff., 102ff.

44. Prodi, Romano. "The Energy Vector of the Future." Conference on the Hydrogen Economy. Brussels. June 16, 2003.

45. This author serves as an adviser to Romano Prodi, the president of the European Commission and, in that capacity, provided the strategic memorandum that led to the adoption and implementation of the EU hydrogen plan.

46. Prodi, Romano. "The Energy Vector of the Future."

47. Ibid.

48. Ibid.

49. Ibid.

50. Greene, Catherine, and Amy Kremen. "U.S. Organic Farming in 2000–2001: Adoption of Certified Systems. Table 5." Agriculture Information Bulletin. No. 55 (AIB780). April 2003. *www.ers.usda.gov/publications*; Scowcroft, Bob. "Bush's Squeeze on Organic Farmers." Organic Consumers Association. June 28, 2003. *www.organicconsumers.org*

51. "How to Facilitate the Development of Transnational Co-Operation in Research in Or-

ganic Farming by Member and Associated States." Paper presented at Seminar on Organic Farming Research in Europe (Brussels). September 24–25, 2002. p. 2.

52. Ibid. p. 6.

53. "The European Market for Fresh Organic Vegetables." M2 Presswire. December 17, 2002.

54. "How to Facilitate the Development of Transnational Co-Operation in Research in Organic Farming by Member and Associated States." pp. 3, 5.

55. Brown, Amanda. "UK Organic Food Sales the Second Highest in Europe." *The Journal (of Newcastle)*. October 15, 2002.

56. "Market Research Shows Rapid Growth of Organic Food." Organic Consumers Association. June 20, 2003. *www.organicconsumers.org*

57. Wynne-Tyson, Jon. *The Extended Circle*. Sussex, England: Centaur Press, 1985. p. 91. Quotation by Mohandas Gandhi.

58. "Feeling the Heat: Climate Change and Biodiversity Loss." *Nature*. Vol. 427. January 8, 2004. *www.nature.com*. Gorman, James. "Scientists Predict Widespread Extinction by Global Warming." *The New York Times*. January 8, 2004; Gugliotta, Guy. "Warming May Threaten 37% of Species by 2050." *The Washington Post*. January 8, 2004; Houlder, Vanessa. "Global Warming 'Will Kill Tenth of Species.'" *Financial Times*. January 7, 2004.

59. "Animal Welfare and the Treaty of Amsterdam." Eurogroup for Animal Welfare. 2000–2001. *www.eurogroupanimalwelfare.org*

60. "Germany Votes for Animal Rights." CNN. May 17, 2002. *www.cnn.com/2002/WORLD/europe/05/17/germany.animals*

61. Ibid.

62. Barboza, David. "Animal Welfare's Unexpected Allies." *The New York Times*. June 25, 2003.

63. Pepperberg, Irene M., Ph.D. "Referential Communication with an African Grey Parrot." Harvard Graduate Society Newsletter. Spring 1991.

64. "Koko's World." The Gorilla Foundation. *www.koko.org/world*

65. "Grantees in the News." The Glaser Progress Foundation. January 19, 2004. *www.progessproject.org*

66. Tangley, Laura. "Animal Emotions." *U.S. News & World Report*. October 30, 2000.

67. Ibid.

68. Noah, Sherna. "Fox Hunting Will Never End—Prince." *"PA" News*. December 12, 2003. *www.news.scotsman.com*

69. "Blair to Woo Anti-hunt MPs." BBC News. December 27, 2002. *www.news.bbc.co.uk/2/hi/uk_news*

70. Lymbery, Philip. "The Welfare of Farm Animals in Europe: Current Conditions & Measures." Paper presented at Symposium on Organic Livestock Farming & Farm Animal Welfare in Japan and the EU/U.K. November 30, 2002. p. 4.

71. Ibid.

72. "The Welfare of Non-human Primates Used in Research: Report of the Committee on Animal Health and Animal Welfare." The European Commission. December 17, 2002. p. 72.

73. Ibid.

74. Ibid.

75. "Conciliation Agreement on Animal Test Ban Does Not Go Down Well." European Report. November 9, 2002.

76. "Higher EU Standards 'Hit Farmers in the Pocket.'" European Report. November 20, 2002.

77. "Communication from the Commission to the Council and the European Parliament on Animal Welfare Legislation on Farmed Animals in Third Countries and the Implications for the EU." Commission of the European Communities. November 18, 2002. p. 4. *www.europa.eu.int*

78. Ibid.

79. Jordan, Dr. Z. Pallo. Opening Address to the 1997 Cape Town meeting on Transboundary Protected Areas.

80. Kliot, Nurit. "Transborder Protected Areas in Europe: Environmental Perspective to Cross-Border Cooperation." University of Haifa. *www.ut.ee/SOPL/english/border/nk.htm*
81. "Wonderland: Touring Yellowstone Before the Automobile." "Lying Lightly" exhibit. The National Parks Service. *www.cr.nps.gov*
82. Sandwith, Trevor, Clare Shine, Lawrence Hamilton, and David Sheppard. "Transboundary Protected Areas for Peace and Co-operation." World Commission on Protected Areas. (WCPA). The World Conservation Union, 2001.
83. Cornelius, Steve. "Transborder Conservation Areas: An Option for the Sonoran Desert?" *Borderlines*. Vol. 8. No. 6. July 2000. p. 3.
84. "A Transboundary Biosphere Reserve in the Carpathians." Global Transboundary Protected Areas Network. December 17, 2003. *www.tbpa.net*
85. Sochaczewski, Paul Spencer. "Across a Divide." *International Wildlife*. July/August 1999.

CHAPTER 16: UNIVERSALIZING THE EUROPEAN DREAM

1. "Total GDP 2002." *World Development Indicators Database*. World Bank. July 2003.
2. Ibid.
3. Chalermpalanupap, Termsak. "Towards an East Asian Community: The Journey Has Begun." East Asia Vision Group Report, 2001. p. 3.
4. Ibid.
5. "Towards an East Asian Community: Region of Peace, Prosperity and Progress." East Asia Vision Group Report, 2001. pp. 1–2.
6. Ibid. p. 6.
7. Ibid. p. 7.
8. Ibid. p. 10.
9. Chalermpalanupap, Termsak. "Towards an East Asian Community: The Journey Has Begun." p. 12.
10. Madhur, Srinivasa. "Costs and Benefits of a Common Currency for ASEAN." ERD Working Paper Series No. 12. Economics and Research Department. Asian Development Bank. May 2002. p. vii.
11. Soesastro, Hadi. "Regional Integration Initiatives in the Asia Pacific: Trade and Finance Dimensions." Centre for Strategic and International Studies. Presented at the 15th PECC General Meeting: Focus Workshop on Trade, Brunei Darussalam. September 1, 2003.
12. Nisbett, Richard E. *The Geography of Thought*. New York: Free Press, 2003. p. 5.
13. Ibid. p. 13.
14. Ibid. p. 17.
15. Ibid. p. 59.
16. Ibid. p. 76.
17. Ibid. p. 51.
18. Ibid. p. 76.
19. "United States Leads World Meat Stampede." Worldwatch Institute. July 2, 1998. *www.worldwatch.org*
20. "Meat Production Is Making the Rich Ill and the Poor Hungry." Transnational Corporations Observatory. *Global Policy Forum*. May 21, 2002. *www.globalpolicy.org*
21. Hakim, Danny. "A Heavenly Drive for Greater Fuel Efficiency." *The New York Times*. November 20, 2002.
22. Ibid.
23. Ibid.
24. Brown, Norman O. *Life Against Death: The Psychoanalytical Meaning of History*. 2d ed. Middletown, CT: Wesleyan University Press, 1985. p. 297.
25. Ibid. pp. 297–298.
26. Ibid. p. 108. Quotation by Rainer Maria Rilke.

27. Gergen, Kenneth J. *The Saturated Self: Dilemmas of Identity in Contemporary Life*. New York: Basic Books, 1991. p. 7.
28. Lifton, Robert J. *The Protean Self: Human Resilience in an Age of Fragmentation*. New York: Basic Books, 1993. p. 17.
29. Edwards, Ellen. "Plugged-In Generation." *The Washington Post*. November 18, 1999. p. A1.
30. Gergen, Kenneth J. *The Saturated Self: Dilemmas of Identity in Contemporary Life*. pp. 17, 246–247.
31. Canetti, Elias. *Crowds and Power*. Carol Stewart, trans. London: Gollancz, 1962. p. 448.
32. The Holy Bible, King James Version. Genesis 1:28.
33. "View of a Changing World." The Pew Global Attitudes Project. The Pew Research Center for the People and the Press. June 2003. p. 105.
34. Ibid.
35. "Poverty and Not Terrorism Is the Most Important Problem Facing the World." Gallup International: Voice of the People. September 29, 2002.
36. "What Do Europeans Think About the Environment?" The European Commission, 1999. p. 10; "How Europeans See Themselves." European Commission. September 2000. pp. 7, 41. *www.europa.eu.int*; Dunlap, Riley, and Lydia Saad. "Only One in Four Americans Are Anxious About the Environment." The Gallup Organization. April 16, 2001. pp. 2, 6. *www.gallup.com*
37. "How Europeans See Themselves." European Commission. September 2000. *www.europa.eu.int*

BIBLIOGRAPHY

Adams, Charles. *For Good and Evil: The Impact of Taxes on the Course of Civilization.* New York: Madison Books, 1993.

Adams, Michael. *Fire and Ice: The United States, Canada, and the Myth of Converging Values.* Toronto: Penguin, 2003.

Albrow, Martin. *The Global Age.* Stanford, CA: Stanford University Press, 1996.

Anderson, Benedict. *Imagined Communities.* London: Verso, 1983.

Appadurai, Arjun. *Modernity at Large: Cultural Dimension of Globalization.* Minneapolis: University of Minnesota Press, 1996.

Archibugi, Daniele, David Held, and Martin Kohler, eds. *Re-imagining Political Community: Studies in Cosmopolitan Democracy.* Stanford, CA: Stanford University Press, 1998.

Arendt, Randall G. *Conservative Design for Subdivisions.* Washington, DC: Island Press, 1996.

Aries, Philippe. *Centuries of Childhood: A Social History of Private Life.* New York: Random House, 1962.

Axford, Barrie, Daniela Berghahn, and Nick Hewlett, eds. *Unity and Diversity in the New Europe.* Oxford, U.K.: Peter Lang, 2000.

Babe, Robert E. *Communication and the Transformation of Economics.* Boulder, CO: Westview Press, 1995.

Bacon, Francis. *Novum Organum.* 1620. *The Works of Francis Bacon.* Vol. 4. London: W. Pickering, 1850.

Barley, M. W. *The House and Home: A Review of 900 Years of House Planning and Furnishing in Britain.* Greenwich, CT: New York Graphic Society, 1971.

Beaglehole, Ernest. *Property: A Study in Social Psychology.* New York: Macmillan, 1932.

Beck, Ulrich. *What Is Globalization?* Cambridge, U.K.: Polity Press, 2000.

Beck, Ulrich, Anthony Giddens, and Scott Lash. *Reflexive Modernization: Politics, Tradition and Aesthetics in the Modern Social Order.* Stanford, CA: Stanford University Press, 1994.

Becker, Ernest. *Escape from Evil.* New York: Free Press, 1975.

Bendix, Reinhard. *Max Weber.* Garden City, NY: Doubleday/Anchor, 1962.

Benfield, F. Kaid, Matthew D. Raimi, and Donald D. T. Chen. *Once There Were Greenfields*. New York: Natural Resources Defense Council, 1999.

Beniger, James R. *The Control Revolution: Technological and Economic Orgins of the Information Society*. Cambridge, MA: Harvard University Press, 1986.

Beresford, Maurice, and John G. Hurst, eds. *Deserted Medieval Villages*. New York: St. Martin's Press, 1972.

Berman, Morris. *Coming to Our Senses: Body and Spirit in the Hidden History of the West*. New York: Simon & Schuster, 1989.

Bethell, Tom. *The Noblest Triumph*. New York: St. Martin's Press/Griffin, 1998.

Birdsall, Nancy, and Carol Graham. *New Markets: New Opportunities?* Washington, DC: Brookings Institution Press, 2000.

Boorstin, Daniel J. *The Discoverers*. New York: Random House, 1983.

Braudel, Fernand. *The Perspective of the World: Civilization & Capitalism 15th–18th Century*. Vol. 3. New York: Harper & Row, 1979.

Brett, Gerard. *Dinner Is Served: A History of Dining in England, 1400–1900*. London: Rupert Hard-Davis, 1968.

Brown, Norman O. *Life Against Death: The Psychoanalytic Meaning of History*. Middletown, CT: Wesleyan University Press, 1959.

Brownlie, I., ed. *Basic Documents on Human Rights*. 3rd ed. Oxford, U.K.: Oxford University Press, 1992.

Brunot, Ferdinand, ed. *Histoire de la langue francaise: des origines à nos jours*. 13 vols. Paris: n.p., 1900.

Bull, Hedley. *The Anarchical Society*. New York: Columbia University Press, 1977.

Calleo, David P. *Rethinking Europe's Future*. Princeton, NJ: Princeton University Press, 2001.

Canetti, Elias. *Crowds and Power*. Trans. Carol Stewart. London: Gollancz, 1962.

Capra, Fritjof. *The Web of Life: A New Scientific Understanding of Living Systems*. New York: Doubleday, 1996.

Casey, Edward S. *The Fate of Place: A Philosophical History*. Berkeley: University of California Press, 1997.

Castells, Manuel. *The Information Age: Economy, Society and Culture*. Vol. 3, *End of Millennium*. Cambridge, MA, and Oxford, U.K.: Blackwell, 1996, 1998.

Cesarini, D., and M. Fulbrook, eds. *Citizenship, Nationality, and Migration in Europe*. London: Routledge, 1997.

Chandler, Alfred D. *The Visible Hand: The Managerial Revolution in American Business*. Cambridge, MA: Harvard University Press, 1977.

Ciaramicoli, Arthur P., and Katherine Ketcham. *The Power of Empathy*. New York: Dutton, 2000.

Clark, Wesley K. *Waging Modern War*. New York: Public Affairs, 2001.

Condorcet, Marquis de. *Outlines of an Historical View of the Progress of the Human Mind*. London: J. Johnson, 1795.

Cooper, Charles. *The English Table in History and Literature*. London: Sampson, Low, Marston & Company, n.d.

Cooper, Robert. *The Post-Modern State and the World Order*. London: Demos, 1996.

Cullen, Jim. *The American Dream*. New York: Oxford University Press, 2003.

Dean, M., and B. Hindess, eds. *Governing Australia: Studies in Contemporary Rationalities of Government*. Cambridge, U.K.: Cambridge University Press, 1988.

Dean, Mitchell. *Governmentality: Power and Rule in Modern Society*. London: Sage, 1999.

Decker, Jeffrey Louis. *Made in America: Self-Styled Success from Horatio Alger to Oprah Winfrey*. Minneapolis: University of Minnesota Press, 1997.

de Grazia, Sebastian. *Of Time, Work, and Leisure*. New York.: Doubleday, 1964.

Delanty, Gerard. *Inventing Europe: Idea, Identity, Reality*. New York: St. Martin's Press, 1995.

Delbanco, Andrew. *The Real American Dream*. Cambridge, MA: Harvard University Press, 1999.

de Mauro, Tullio. *Storia linguistica dell'Italia unita*. Bari, Italy: n.p., 1963.

Desiderius, Erasmus. Trans. Robert Whittinton. *De civilitate morum puerilium* (*On the Civility of Children*). 1530.

de Soto, Hernando. *The Mystery of Capital.* New York: Basic Books, 2000.

Diamond, Henry L., and Patrick F. Noonan. *Land Use in America.* Washington, DC: Island Press, 1996.

Dobb, Maurice M. A. *Studies in the Development of Capitalism.* New York: International Publishers, 1947.

Downes, Larry, and Chunka Mui. *Unleashing the Killer App: Digital Strategies for Market Dominance.* Boston: Harvard Business School Press, 1998.

Duby, Georges, ed. *A History of Private Life: Revelations in the Medieval World.* Vol. 2. Cambridge, MA: Harvard University Press, 1988.

Durant, John, and John Gregory, eds. *Science and Culture in Europe.* London: Science Museum, 1993.

Ehrlich, J. W., ed. *Ehrlich's Blackstone.* San Carlos, CA: Nourse Publishing, 1959.

Elias, Norbert. *The Civilizing Process.* Oxford, U.K.: Blackwell, 1994.

Ely, James W. *The Guardian of Every Other Right.* New York: Oxford University Press, 1992.

Featherstone, M., S. Lash, and R. Robertson. *Global Modernities.* London: Sage, 1995.

Flora, Peter. *State, Economy and Society in Western Europe, 1815–1975.* Vol. 1. London: St. James Press, 1983.

Foster, Ian, and Carl Kesselman, eds. *The Grid: Blueprint for a New Computing Infrastructure.* San Francisco, CA: Morgan Kaufmann, 1999.

Frederick, Christine. "Housekeeping with Efficiency." New York: *Ladies' Home Journal,* n.p., 1913.

Freud, Sigmund. Trans. James Strachey. *Civilization and Its Discontents.* New York: Norton, 1961.

Furnivall, Frederick J. *English Meals and Manners.* Detroit, MI: Singing Tree Press, 1969.

Gehlen, A. *Man: His Nature and Place in the World.* New York: Columbia University Press, 1988.

Gellner, Ernest. *Nations and Nationalism.* Ithaca, NY: Cornell University Press, 1983.

Gergen, Kenneth J. *The Saturated Self.* New York: Basic Books, 1991.

Giedion, Siegfried. *Mechanization Takes Command.* New York: Norton, 1948.

Gimpel, Jean. *The Medieval Machine.* New York: Penguin, 1976.

Ginsberg, Roy H. *The European Union in International Politics.* Lanham, MD: Rowman & Littlefield, 2001.

Guéhenno, Jean-Marie. *The End of the Nation-State.* Minneapolis: University of Minnesota Press, 1995.

Guttman, Robert J., ed. *Europe in the New Century: Visions of an Emerging Superpower.* Boulder, CO: Lynne Rienner Publishers, 2001.

Hansen, Marcus Lee. *The Atlantic Migration, 1607–1860: A History of the Continuing Settlement of the United States.* Cambridge, MA: Harvard University Press, 1940.

Harremoes, Poul, David Gee, Malcolm MacGarvin, Andy Stirling, Jane Keys, Brian Wynne, and Sofia Guedes Vaz, eds. *The Precautionary Principle in the 20th Century: Late Lessons from Early Warnings.* London: Earthscan Publications, 2002.

Hastings, Adrian. *The Construction of Nationhood.* Cambridge, U.K.: Cambridge University Press, 1997.

Hastings, Elizabeth Hawn, and Phillip K. Hastings. *Index to International Public Opinion, 1988–1989.* New York: Greenwood Press, 1990.

Heilbroner, Robert L. *The Making of Economic Society.* Englewood Cliffs, NJ: Prentice-Hall, 1962.

Heisenberg, Werner. *Physics and Philosophy: The Revolution in Modern Science.* New York: Harper & Row, 1958.

Held, David, Anthony McGrew, David Goldblatt, and Jonathan Perraton. *Global Transformations: Politics, Economics and Culture.* Stanford, CA: Stanford University Press, 1999.

Hirst, P., and G. Thompson. *Globalization in Question: The International Economy and the Possibilities of Governance.* Cambridge, U.K.: Polity Press, 1996.

Hobsbawm, E. J. *The Age of Extremes: The Short Twentieth Century, 1914–1991*. London: Michael Joseph, 1994.

——— *Nations and Nationalism Since 1780: Programme, Myth, Reality*. Cambridge, U.K.: Cambridge University Press, 1990.

Holmes, U. T., Jr. *Daily Living in the Twelfth Century: Based on the Observations of Alexander Neckham in London and Paris*. Madison: University of Wisconsin Press, 1952.

Jackson, Kenneth. *Crabgrass Frontier: The Suburbanization of the United States*. New York: Oxford University Press, 1985.

Jacoby, Russell. *The End of Utopia*. New York: Basic Books, 1999.

Jameson, Anna Brownell. *Winter Shades and Summer Rambles*. London: n.p., 1838.

Johnson, Paul. *The Birth of the Modern*. New York: HarperPerennial, 1991.

Jones, E. L. *The European Miracle: Environments, Economies and Geopolitics in the History of Europe and Asia*. Cambridge, U.K.: Cambridge University Press, 1981.

Kagan, Robert. *Of Paradise and Power: America and Europe in the New World Order*. New York: Knopf, 2003.

Karabell, Zachary. *A Visionary Nation*. New York: HarperCollins, 2001.

Kelley, Donald R. *Historians and the Law in Postrevolutionary France*. Princeton, NJ: Princeton University Press, 1984.

Kern, Stephen. *The Culture of Time and Space, 1880–1918*. Cambridge, MA: Harvard University Press, 1983.

Kickert, Walter J. M., Erik-Hans Klijn, and Joop F. M. Koppenjan. *Managing Complex Networks: Strategies for the Public Sector*. London: Sage, 1997.

Kupchan, Charles A. *The End of the American Era*. New York: Knopf, 2002.

Lamont, William, and Sybil Oldfield, eds. *Politics, Religion, and Literature in the 17th Century*. London: Dent, Rowman & Littlefield, 1975.

Landes, David. *Revolution in Time: Clocks and the Making of the Modern World*. Cambridge, MA: Harvard University Press, 1985.

Lasch, Christopher. *The Culture of Narcissism: American Life in an Age of Diminishing Expectations*. New York: Norton, 1979.

Le Goff, Jacques. *Your Money or Your Life: Economy and Religion in the Middle Ages*. New York: Zone Books, 1988.

Lifton, Robert Jay. *The Protean Self*. New York: Basic Books, 1993.

Lipset, Seymour Martin. *American Exceptionalism: A Double-Edged Sword*. New York: Norton, 1996.

Locke, John. *Second Treatise of Civil Government*. Chap. 5, "Of Property." Ed. Thomas P. Peardon. NY: Liberal Arts Press, 1952.

——— *Two Treatises of Government*. Ed. Peter Laslett. Cambridge, U.K.: Cambridge University Press, 1967.

Lovelock, James. *The Ages of Gaia: A Biography of Our Living Earth*. New York: Norton, 1988.

Lowe, Donald M. *History of Bourgeois Perception*. Chicago: University of Chicago Press, 1982.

Lowe, P., and S. Ward, eds. *British Environmental Policy and Europe*. London: Routledge, 1998.

Lukacs, John. *Historical Consciousness: The Remembered Past*. New Brunswick, NJ: Transaction Publishers, 1994.

Macfarlane, Alan. *The Origins of English Individualism*. New York: Cambridge University Press, 1978.

MacPherson, Crawford. *Democratic Theory: Essays in Retrieval*. Cambridge, U.K.: Oxford University Press, 1973.

Manuel, Frank E., and Fritzie P. Manuel. *Utopian Thought in the Western World*. Cambridge, MA: Belknap Press of Harvard University Press, 1979.

Marcuse, Herbert. *Eros and Civilization*. Boston: Beacon Press, 1955.

Maren-Grisebach, Manon. *Philosophie der Grünen*. Munich, Ger.: Olzog, 1982.

Marshall, T. H. *Citizenship and Social Class*. Cambridge, U.K.: Cambridge University Press, 1950.

Marty, Martin E. *A Short History of Christianity*. New York: Collins World, 1959.

Marvin, Carolyn. *When Old Technologies Were New*. New York: Oxford University Press, 1988.

Marx, Leo. *The Machine in the Garden*. New York: Oxford University Press, 1964.

McCann, Justin. *The Rule of St. Benedict*. London: Sheed & Ward, 1970.

McHugh, F. P., and S. M. Natale, eds. *Things Old and New: Catholic Social Teaching Revisited*. New York: University of America, 1993.

McKenzie, Evan. *Privatopia: Homeowner Associations and the Rise of Residential Private Government*. New Haven, CT: Yale University Press, 1996.

McLuhan, Marshall. *Understanding Media: The Extensions of Man*. New York: McGraw-Hill, 1964.

Melville, Herman. *White-Jacket; or, The World in a Man-of-War*. 1850. Oxford, U.K.: Oxford World's Classics, 2000.

Meyrowitz, Joshua. *No Sense of Place: The Impact of Electronic Media on Social Behavior*. New York: Oxford University Press, 1985.

Milberg, William, and Robert Heilbroner. *The Making of Economic Society*. Inglewood Cliffs, NJ: Prentice-Hall, 1980.

Miller, Perry. *Errand into the Wilderness*. Cambridge, MA: Harvard University Press, 1984.

Miringoff, Marc, and Marque-Luisa Miringoff. *The Social Health of the Nation: How America Is Really Doing*. New York: Oxford University Press, 1999.

Misgeld, Dieter, and Graeme Nicholson. *Hans-Georg Gadamer on Education, Poetry, and History: Applied Hermeneutics*. Albany: State University of New York Press, 1992.

Mishel, Lawrence, Jared Bernstein, and Heather Boushey. *The State of Working American 2002/ 2003*. Ithaca, NY: Cornell University Press, 2003.

Moore, Barrington. *Reflections on the Causes of Human Misery and Upon Certain Proposals to Eliminate Them*. Boston: Beacon Press, 1970.

Morgan, Edmund S., ed. *The Diary of Michael Wigglesworth, 1653–1657*. New York: Harper & Row, 1965.

Morris, Colin. *The Discovery of the Individual, 1050–1200*. New York: Harper Torchbooks, 1972.

Mumford, Lewis. *The Culture of Cities*. New York: Harcourt, Brace, 1963.

———. *The Pentagon of Power*. New York: Harcourt Brace Jovanovich/Harvest Book, 1964.

———. *Technics and Civilization*. New York: Harcourt, Brace, 1934.

———. *Technics and Human Development*. New York: Harcourt Brace Jovanovich/Harvest Book, 1966.

Murphy, C. *International Organization and Industrial Change: Global Governance since 1850*. Cambridge, U.K.: Polity Press, 1994.

Newman, Peter W. G., and Jeffrey R. Kenworthy. *Cities and Automobile Dependence: A Sourcebook*. Aldershot, U.K., and Brookfield, VT: Gower Publishing, 1989.

Newton, Isaac. *Mathematical Principles of Natural Philosophy*. Book 3. NY: Philosophical Library. 1964.

Nisbett, Richard E. *The Geography of Thought: How Asians and Westerners Think Differently . . . and Why*. New York: Free Press, 2003.

Nivola, Pietro S. *Laws of the Landscape*. Washington, DC: Brookings Institution Press, 1999.

Nye, Joseph S., Jr. *The Paradox of American Power*. Oxford, U.K.: Oxford University Press, 2002.

Ong, Walter J. *Orality and Literacy*. London: Methuen, 1982.

Pagden, Anthony. *The Idea of Europe: From Antiquity to the European Union*. Cambridge, U.K.: Cambridge University Press, 2002.

Polanyi, Karl. *The Great Transformation: The Political and Economic Origins of Our Time*. Boston: Beacon Press, 1944.

Putnam, Robert D. *Bowling Alone: The Collapse and Revival of American Community*. New York: Simon & Schuster, 2000.

Quinn, James Brian. *Intelligent Enterprise: A Knowledge and Service Board Paradigm for Industry*. New York: Free Press, 1992.

Quinones, Ricardo J. *The Renaissance Discovery of Time*. Cambridge, MA: Harvard University Press, 1972.

Randall, John Herman, Jr. *The Making of the Modern Mind: A Survey of the Intellectual Background of the Present Age.* Cambridge, MA: Houghton Mifflin, 1940.

Rank, Otto. *Beyond Psychology.* New York: Dover, 1941.

Rees, Martin. *Our Final Hour.* New York: Basic Books, 2003.

Reeve, Andrew. *Property.* London: Macmillan, 1986.

Rhodes, Martin, Paul Heywood, and Vincent Wright. *Developments in West European Politics.* New York: St. Martin's Press, 1997.

Rieff, Philip. *The Triumph of the Therapeutic.* Chicago: University of Chicago Press, 1966.

Rifkin, Jeremy. *The Age of Access.* New York: Tarcher/Putnam, 2000.

———. *Algeny.* New York: Viking, 1983.

———. *Beyond Beef.* New York: Penguin, 1992.

———. *Biosphere Politics.* New York: Crown, 1991.

———. *The Biotech Century: Harnessing the Gene and Remaking the World.* New York: Tarcher/Putnam, 1998.

———. *The Emerging Order.* New York: Ballantine, 1979.

———. *The End of Work.* New York: Tarcher/Putnam, 1995.

———. *Entropy.* New York: Bantam, 1981.

———. *The Hydrogen Economy.* New York: Tarcher/Putnam, 2002.

———. *Time Wars.* New York: Holt, 1987.

Roosevelt, Theodore. *The New Nationalism.* 1910. Englewood Cliffs, NJ: Prentice-Hall, 1961.

Rose, Nikolas. *Powers of Freedom: Reframing Political Thought.* Cambridge, U.K.: Cambridge University Press, 1999.

Rossi, Alice, ed. *The Family.* New York: Norton, 1965.

Rousseau, Jean-Jacques. *Basic Political Writings.* Trans. and ed. Donald A. Cress. Indianapolis: Hackett Publishing, 1987.

———. *On the Social Contract.* Trans. Roger Masters. New York: St. Martin's Press, 1978.

Rumford, Chris. *The European Union: A Political Sociology.* Oxford, U.K.: Blackwell, 2002.

Russell, J. C. *Medieval Regions and Their Cities.* Newton Abbot, U.K.: David and Charles, 1972.

Salamon, Lester, et al. *Global Civil Society: Dimensions of the Nonprofit Sector.* Baltimore, MD: Johns Hopkins Center for Civil Society Studies, 1999.

Schaff, Philip. *America: A Sketch of Its Political, Social, and Religious Character.* Cambridge, MA: Harvard University Press, 1855, 1961.

Scharpf, Fritz W. *Games in Hierarchies and Networks.* Frankfurt, Ger.: Campus Verlag, 1993.

Schlatter, Richard. *Private Property: The History of an Idea.* New York: Russell & Russell, 1973.

Scruton, Roger. *A Dictionary of Political Thought.* London: Pan, 1982.

Shafer, Byron E. *Is America Different?* Oxford, U.K.: Clarendon Press, 1991.

Shapiro, Michael J., and Hayward R. Alker. *Challenging Boundaries: Global Flows, Territorial Identities.* Minneapolis: University of Minnesota Press, 1996.

Shore, Cris. *Building Europe: The Cultural Politics of European Integration.* London: Routledge, 2000.

Siedentop, Larry. *Democracy in Europe.* New York: Columbia University Press, 2001.

Skaggs, Jimmy M. *Prime Cut.* College Station: Texas A&M University Press, 1967.

Smith, Adam. *An Inquiry into the Nature and Causes of the Wealth of Nations.* 1776. Ed. Edwin Cannan. London: Methuen, 1961.

Smith, Anthony D. *Nationalism: Theory, Ideology, History.* Cambridge, U.K.: Polity Press, 2001.

Smith, Dennis, and Sue Wright, eds. *Whose Europe? The Turn Towards Democracy.* Oxford, U.K.: Blackwell, 1999.

Soja, Edward W. *Postmodern Geographies.* London: Verso, 1989.

Sombart, Werner. *Why Is There No Socialism in the United States?* White Plains, NY: International Arts and Sciences Press, 1976.

Strauss, Leo. *Natural Right and History.* Chicago: University of Chicago Press, 1950.

Strayer, Joseph R. *On the Medieval Origins of the Modern State.* Princeton, NJ: Princeton University Press, 1970.

Tawney, R. H. *The Acquisitive Society.* New York: Harcourt, Brace, 1920.

Taylor, Charles. *Sources of the Self.* Cambridge, MA: Harvard University Press, 1989.

Taylor, Frederick. *The Principles of Scientific Management.* New York: Norton, 1947.

Thomas, Keith. *Man and the Natural World: A History of the Modern Sensibility.* New York: Pantheon, 1983.

Thomas, Lewis. *The Lives of a Cell.* New York: Bantam, 1975.

Thompson, Grahame, Jennifer Frances, Rosalind Levacic, and Jeremy Mitchell. *Markets, Hierarchies & Networks.* London: Sage, 1991.

Tichi, Cecelia. *Shifting Gears.* Chapel Hill: University of North Carolina Press, 1987.

Tilly, Charles, ed. *The Formation of the National State in Western Europe.* Princeton, NJ: Princeton University Press, 1975.

Tocqueville, Alexis de. *Democracy in America.* 1835, 1840. Trans. George Lawrence. New York: HarperCollins, 1988.

Tuan, Yi-Fu. *Segmented Worlds and Self: Group Life and Individual Consciousness.* Minneapolis: University of Minnesota Press, 1982.

Turner, Frederick Jackson. *The Significance of the Frontier in American History.* 1893. Tucson: University of Arizona Press, 1994.

Urry, John. *Sociology Beyond Societies: Mobilities for the Twenty-First Century.* London: Routledge, 2000.

Vernadsky, Vladimir. *The Biosphere.* Trans. David Langmuir. Ed. Mark McMenamin. New York: Copernicus Books, 1998.

Vibert, Frank. *Europe Simple Europe Strong: The Future of European Governance.* Cambridge, U.K.: Polity Press, 2001.

Wallach, Lori, and Michelle Sforza. *An Assessment of the World Trade Organization.* Washington, DC: Public Citizen, 1999.

Weber, Max. *The Protestant Ethic and the Spirit of Capitalism.* New York: Scribner, 1958.

Weber, Steven. *Globalization and the European Political Economy.* New York: Columbia University Press, 2001.

Wehler, Hans-Ulrich. *Deutsche Gesellschaftsgeschichte, 1700–1815.* Munich, Ger.: n.p., 1987.

Weiner, Antje. *"European" Citizenship Practice.* Boulder, CO: Westview Press, 1998.

Wesson, Robert. *State Systems: International Pluralism, Politics, and Culture.* New York: Free Press, 1978.

White, Lynn, Jr. *Medieval Technology & Social Change.* London: Oxford University Press, 1962.

Whitehead, Alfred North. *Science and the Modern World.* New York: Free Press, 1967.

Wiener, Norbert. *The Human Use of Human Beings: Cybernetics and Society.* New York: Da Capo, 1950.

Windolf, Paul. *Corporate Networks in Europe and the United States.* New York: Oxford University Press, 2002.

Wolf, Charles, Jr., and Benjamin Zycher. *European Military Prospects, Economic Constraints, and the Rapid Reaction Force.* Santa Monica, CA: RAND Publications, 2001.

Wolf, Edward N. *Top Heavy.* New York: New Press, 2002.

Wright, Lawrence. *Clockwork Man.* New York: Horizon Press, 1969.

Wynne-Tyson, Jon. *The Extended Circle.* Sussex, U.K.: Centaur Press, 1985.

Zerubavel, Eviatar. *Hidden Rhythms: Schedules and Calendars in Social Life.* Chicago: University of Chicago Press, 1981.

Zielonka, Jan, ed. *Europe Unbound: Enlarging and Reshaping the Boundaries of the European Union.* London: Routledge, 2002.

INDEX